# Political Islam in the Age of Democratization

**Middle East Today**

Series editors:

Mohammed Ayoob
University Distinguished Professor
of International Relations
Michigan State University

Fawaz A. Gerges
Professor and Chair of Middle Eastern
Politics and International Relations
Director of the Middle East Centre
London School of Economics

The Iranian Revolution of 1979 and the subsequent Gulf Wars, along with the overthrow of the Iraqi President Saddam Hussein, have dramatically altered the geopolitical landscape of the contemporary Middle East. This series puts forward a critical body of first-rate scholarship that reflects the current political and social realities of the region, focusing on original research about the Israeli–Palestine conflict; social movements, institutions, and the role played by nongovernmental organizations such as Hamas, Hezbollah, the Taliban, and the Muslim Brotherhood; Iran and Turkey as emerging preeminent powers in the region—the former an Islamic republic and the latter a democracy currently governed by a party with Islamic roots; the oil-producing countries in the Persian Gulf and their petrol economies; potential problems of nuclear proliferation in the region; and the challenges confronting the United States, Europe, and the United Nations in the greater Middle East. The focus of the series is on general topics such as social turmoil, war and revolution, occupation, radicalism, democracy, and Islam as a political force in the context of modern Middle East history.

# Political Islam in the Age of Democratization

Kamran Bokhari and Farid Senzai

POLITICAL ISLAM IN THE AGE OF DEMOCRATIZATION
Copyright © Kamran Bokhari and Farid Senzai, 2013.

First published in 2013 by
PALGRAVE MACMILLAN®
in the United States—a division of St. Martin's Press LLC,
175 Fifth Avenue, New York, NY 10010.

Where this book is distributed in the UK, Europe and the rest of the World,
this is by Palgrave Macmillan, a division of Macmillan Publishers Limited,
registered in England, company number 785998, of Houndmills, Basingstoke,
Hampshire RG21 6XS.

Palgrave Macmillan is the global academic imprint of the above companies
and has companies and representatives throughout the world.

Palgrave® and Macmillan® are registered trademarks in the United States, the
United Kingdom, Europe and other countries.

ISBN: 978–1–137–00848–0 (HC)
ISBN: 978–1–137–00804–6 (PBK)

Library of Congress Cataloging-in-Publication Data is available from the
Library of Congress.

A catalogue record of the book is available from the British Library.

Design by Integra Software Services

First edition: December 2013

10 9 8 7 6 5 4 3 2 1

Dedicated to:
Naheed and Chandni and our children Zakaria, Eesa and Enaya

# Contents

# List of Tables and Figure

**Tables**

**Figure**

# Acknowledgments

There are many people who have helped us in writing this book and whose contributions we wish to acknowledge. We have been fortunate to enjoy the kindness, insight and support of many scholars. In particular, we would like to thank Fawaz Gerges and Mohammad Ayoob for their initial suggestion that we write a book on this subject. Their thoughts and insights into this complex topic has always been a valuable resource for us to bounce ideas and shape the contours of our argument. We would like to especially thank our mentors and friends James Piscatori and Abdelwahab El-Affendi. We always appreciated the high standards they set and grateful for the numerous conversations, which helped shape our own understanding of the topic. Over the years we have also benefited greatly from comments by and discussions with numerous scholars on the topic of political Islam and democratization. We would like to especially thank Graham Fuller, Yahya Sadowski, John Esposito, Gilles Kepel, Olivier Roy, Peter Mandaville, Muqtedar Khan, Nader Hashemi, Moataz Fattah, Marina Ottaway, Amr Hamzawy, Nathan Brown, Emad El-Din Shahin, Asef Bayat, Carrie Wickham, Jillian Schwedler, Humeira Iqtidar, Larbi Sadiki, Alfred Stepan, Larry Diamond, and Laurence Whitehead. The arguments in the book are stronger due to their invaluable contributions on the subject.

As is often the case in a project of this sort, some of the most helpful comments we have received have come from numerous conferences, presentations and private discussions in the United States, Canada, in Europe and throughout the Middle East and South Asia. While we cannot hope to thank everyone who has influenced our work, we are grateful to the many people that shaped our thinking through countless discussions. We would also like to express our gratitude to the many individuals, scholars, religious leaders and activists that provided personal thoughts, analyses, and access to valuable resources both here and abroad. These include Tony Sullivan, Charles Butterworth, Louay Safi, Jamal Barzinji, Hisham al-Talib, Ahmed Totonji, Omer Totonji, Fathi Malkawi, Radwan Masmoudi, Laith Kubba, Abdulwahab Alkebsi, Abdulaziz Sachedina, Asma Afsaruddin, Husain Haqqani, Hassan Abbas, Vali Nasr, Tariq Ramadan, Ibrahim Kalin, Saad Eddin Ibrahim, Ahmet Davutoglu, Anwar Ibrahim, Rachid al-Ghannouchi, Essam El-Erian, Yusuf al-Qaradawi, Abul Ela al-Madi, Abdul Latif Arabiat, Ibrahim al-Houdaiby, Kemal Helbawy, Jamal Khashoggi, Ali al-Ahmed, Hisham Hellyer, Shadi Hamid, Omar Ashour, Khalil al-Anani, Yasir Kazi, Abdelrehman Ayyash, Ali Mohammad, Michael Georgy, Mehrdad Haghayeghi, Ahmed Ibrahim, Kamran Aghaie, Sulayman Nyang, Beth Baron,

Maria Holt, Roland Dannreuther, Daniel Greenwood, Dibyesh Anand, Simon Joss, Heba Raouf, Merve Kavakci, Shaheen Malik, Fahim Senzai, Tauqeer Ansari, Arshad Khawaja, Ali Swaby, Nasir Mahmood, Shafaqat Ali, Ayaz Parvez and Nisar Ahmed Mirza and many others who are too many to count. Their generosity, good-natured humor, and continued desire for positive change in their respective countries gives us hope for a brighter future in many Muslim societies.

Writing a book is never an easy endeavor but there were many friends and colleagues that provided support throughout the process. We would especially thank several individuals that helped us with the editing of the final manuscript, including Hena Khan and Jay Willoughby, for reading every single chapter and providing their valuable editorial assistance. They both invested considerable time and energy to get the book done by the deadline including Hena's feedback sent to us while on vacation in Spain. They provided immense help in bringing the project to fruition and in achieving greater consistency in the text. We also wanted to thank the superb editorial staff at Palgrave including Farideh Koohi-Kamali, Sara Doskow, Sara Nathan, Flora Kenson, Tara Knapp, and the rest of the production team. We also wanted to thank our research assistants Morgen Munoz, Danielle Giacchetti, Allie Barr, Brooke Latham, Ashley Loetscher and Samra Ahmed for their help at various stages of this project. We would like to especially thank our colleagues at the Institute for Social Policy and Understanding including Iltefat Hamzavi, Shireen Zaman, Siwar Bizri, Farhan Latif, Hamada Hamid and Zareena Grewal. A special thanks is due to our colleagues at Stratfor, in particular George and Meredith Friedman, Rodger Baker, Fred Burton, Scott Stewart, Robert Kaplan, Nate Hughes, Reva Bhalla, Karen Hooper, Lauren Goodrich, Mark Schroeder, and David Judson; the numerous conversations with them and many others helped us. We also wish to thank our many colleagues at Santa Clara University including Janet Flammang, Terri Peretti, Jane Curry, Bill Stover, Dennis Gordon, Peter Minowitz, Elsa Chen, Greg Corning, Eric Hanson, Timothy Lukes, James Lai, Jim Cottrill, Kenneth Faulve-Montojo, Naomi Levy, Diana Morlang, Yahia Mahamdi, and Philip "Boo" Riley as well as the countless students at Santa Clara University who continue to provide encouragement and an incentive to finish the book. In many ways it is for their continued curiosity and ongoing questions about the topic of political Islam and democratization that encouraged us to put our thoughts on paper and write this book.

We are grateful to our parents Asghar and Salim Bokhari and Daud and Hamida Senzai for all they have done for us. Finally, we would like to thank Naheed and Chandni and our kids who watched us spend month after month working on the book. They patiently waited outside our office door countless times to ask if the book was done so that we could go outside and play. Without their support and sacrifice we are convinced that we would never have made it through. Now we can finally go outside and play.

# Acronyms

| | |
|---|---|
| AKP | Justice and Development Party |
| FIS | Front Islamique de Salut |
| FJP | Freedom and Justice Party |
| FLN | Front de Libération Nationale |
| GAI | Gamaah al-Islamiyah |
| HAMAS | Harakat al-Muqawamah al-Islamiyah |
| HT | Hizb al-Tahrir |
| ISA | Islamic Salafi Alliance |
| ISCI | Islamic Supreme Council of Iraq |
| JI | Jamaat-e-Islami |
| MB | Muslim Brotherhood |
| MMA | Mutahiddah Majlis-i-Amal in Pakistan |
| NDP | National Democratic Party |
| NGO | Nongovernmental Organizations |
| PIJ | Palestinian Islamic Jihad |
| PLO | Palestinian Liberation Organization |
| PMB | Palestinian Muslim Brotherhood |
| JMB | Jordanian Muslim Brotherhood |
| TAJ | Tandheem al-Jihad |
| MENA | Middle East & North Africa |
| IDF | Israeli Defense Forces |
| STL | Special Tribunal for Lebanon |
| PSP | Progressive Socialist Party |
| ICG | Iraqi Governing Council |
| CPA | Coalition Provisional Authority |
| UIA | United Iraqi Alliance |
| IIP | Iraqi Islamic Party |
| SCIRI | Supreme Council of the Islamic Revolution in Iraq |
| UNSC | United Nations Security Council |
| CHP | Republican People's Party |
| NATO | North Atlantic Treaty Organization |
| IRGC | Islamic Revolutionary Guards Corps |
| IRGC-QF | Islamic revolutionary Guards Corps – Qods Force |
| INA | Iraq National Alliance |
| NA | National Alliance |
| SoL | State of Law |

| | |
|---|---|
| TSK | Turkish Armed Forces |
| EU | European Union |
| NATO | North Atlantic Treaty Organization |
| IMF | International Monetary Fund |
| GCC | Gulf Cooperation Council |
| FPM | Free Patriotic Movement (Lebanon) |
| TTP | Tehrik-i-Taliban Pakistan |
| PJD | Justice & Development Party (Morocco) |
| NSF | National Salvation Front |
| CA | Constituent Assembly |
| SCC | Supreme Constitutional Court |
| SCAF | Supreme Council of the Armed Forces |
| IAF | Islamic Action Front |
| PNA | Palestinian National Authority |
| RCD | Constitutional Democratic Rally |
| PDPA | People's Democratic Party of Afghanistan |

# Foreword

*Fawaz A. Gerges*

By the end of 2012, Islamist-led governments of varying colors and shades were ruling more than half of the population of the Middle East, including Egypt, Tunisia, and Morocco, and playing an important governmental role in Lebanon, Palestine, and Yemen. Iran is also a crucial case, and Islamist groups in the Gulf play an influential political role, although they have yet to gain access to the executive offices. After the large-scale Arab popular uprisings of 2011, the Middle East is witnessing a watershed in its modern history, one that may not have reached its peak yet.

For scholars interested in social movements, particularly religious-based ones, these ongoing events are historic—an "Islamist moment" par excellence. Islamism is not only a social movement, but also a powerful political force that is now in power in several countries. This unforeseen scenario has injected a great deal of uncertainty into the region and into the foreign ministries of key great powers. The implications of the Islamists' rise to power directly affect the daily life and future of the region's peoples and will have serious implications for global politics.

After decades of persecution, what is unfolding today clearly shows the relevance of the Islamists, most of whom are centrist and modernist and accept the rules and procedures of the democratic game in shaping their societies' future political trajectories. In contrast, the majority of Salafis and ultraconservatives in general, who believe that Islam controls all social spheres and regulate the whole of human life, are in the minority.[1]

Over the last four decades, centrist and reformist Islamists skillfully positioned themselves as a credible alternative to the failed secular authoritarian order, an order that unwittingly facilitated the Islamist movements' rise and expansion. They invested considerable resources in building national and local social networks, including nongovernment professional civil society associations, welfare organizations, and family ties. In contrast to their secular-minded opponents, Islamists mastered the art of local politics and built a formidable political machine that delivered the vote. Their recent parliamentary victories were not surprising, because they had paid their dues and earned popular credibility and the voters' trust. Now they are cashing in on their longstanding social investments.

Although the Islamists did not trigger the large-scale popular uprisings, their decades-long resistance to autocratic rulers had turned them into shadow governments in peoples' eyes. A vote for them implied a clean break with the failed past and a belief (still to be tested) that they can deliver the goods—jobs, economic stability, and transparency. Thus their political fortunes will ultimately depend upon whether they live up to their promises and meet the rising expectations of the Arab publics.

Scholars have examined the many manifestations of political Islam and utilized various theories (e.g., social movement, constructivism and communitarianism, parliamentarization, and historical sociology) to make sense of the Islamists' conduct. *Political Islam in the Age of Democratization* makes an important contribution to the growing critical literature on Islamists by using democratization as a conceptual framework to assess their record in this arena, as well as applying it to seven distinct case studies. Kamran Bokhari and Farid Senzai's analysis of Islamism over the last three decades offers a systematic way of making sense of the existing discourse while connecting it with the broader scholarship. One of their major findings is that the vast majority of Islamists are "participatory" actors as opposed to hardcore ideologues. Not only have the Islamists shaped the political landscape, but they have also been shaped by it.

For the last four decades, religious-based activists have struggled to participate in their societies' political space and, on the whole, have accepted the rules of politics. Despite the alarming statements made by some Islamists, particularly the Muslim Brothers, on balance, ideology now takes a back seat to the movements' interests and political wellbeing. More than ever, their message targets specific constituencies and interest groups—a sign of an ideological shift and socialization. Islamists are travelling a similar path as did the Christian Democrats and Euro-communists of Western Europe who, in the twentieth century, subordinated ideology to economic interests and political constituencies.

Stathis Kalyvas, who analyzed the Christian Democratic parties' evolution, reminds readers that these parties emerged from the illiberal and often intolerant Catholic movement, a counter-revolutionary reaction against liberalism. The Catholic movement was built on an ideology of opposition to the liberal state, a project that was "fundamentalist" and "openly theocratic."[2] Today, however, these parties retain no traces of illiberalism, intolerance, or subservience to the Church; rather, they have become anchored in democratic political discourse and practice. According to Kalyvas, this transformation occurred because voters became the "paramount source of support and legitimacy," and not necessarily because of secularization, integration, or acceptance of democracy: it was the result of "the choices made by the new parties in response to endogenous constraints that were built in the process of their formation."[3] Like these religious- and ideological-oriented parties, their Islamist counterparts will likely be transformed by means of political engagement and governance. Their members' desire for reelection will exercise a moderating influence upon the parties as a whole, regardless of where they are located within the region.[4]

This gradual transformation is consistent with what scholars have been saying about the more gradual, inexorable, and perhaps structural trends that come with "parliamentarization." According to the "moderation thesis" discussed by Jillian

Schwedler in her book on Jordan and Yemen, as well as the longer theoretical lineage of argument covered previously by Kalyvas and others, history shows that the shift from movement activism to parliamentary seat-holding leads to compromise, moderation, and corruption. Schwedler's moderation thesis contrasts the evolution of Yemen's Islah Party with Jordan's Islamic Action Front (IAF). She shows that the former's fragmented and hierarchical structure left it somewhat paralyzed and therefore unable to cooperate and engage with Leftist and liberal groups, whereas the latter's unified and democratic internal structure allowed it to engage in "sustained cooperative bodies with Leftists and liberals." Her arguments suggest that those Islamist parties that were able to engage openly with other social groups dramatically changed and moved away from their formerly "closed" and "rigid" worldviews and toward a more "moderate" discourse and practice.[5]

For too long, democratization theorists have insisted that democracy can take root only if religion is extracted from the political arena. Bokhari and Senzai challenge this premise by proposing that democratic theory needs to be revisited and expanded in order to take religion into consideration. Building on the theoretical and empirical research of scholars like Alfred Stepan and Nader Hashemi, they argue that contrary to conventional wisdom, religion can play a role in shaping democratic politics. What makes Bokhari and Senzai's examination critical, however, is their use of democratization as a theoretical framework to assess the behavior of Islamist groups and their insistence that religion will, to varying degrees, play a role in public affairs as democratization moves forward in Muslim nation-states. *Political Islam in the Age of Democratization* raises pertinent questions about the place and role of religion in the political arena and expands the debate on a highly important topic facing those Arab societies in transition: Does religion impede or facilitate the transition from authoritarianism to democracy?

Going to great lengths to maintain their objectivity on a contentious and oft-politicized topic, Bokhari and Senzai do not subjectively project what ought to happen to the various Islamist actors; rather, they focus on what is likely to happen. Whether readers agree or disagree with their conclusions, this book could not have been written at a more important moment for the region in particular, and a global audience at large.

Fawaz A. Gerges
Director of the Middle East Centre and a professor of
International Relations at the London School of
Economics and Political Science.
Author of *The New Middle East: Social Protest and
Revolution in the Arab World* (Cambridge University Press).

# 1

# Introduction: The Role of Religion in Politics

The winds of change blowing across the Middle East and North Africa have replaced autocratic leaders with popularly elected officials. But within a span of two years these democratically elected leaders too succumbed to the upheaval that continues throughout the region. The 2011 "Arab Spring" that toppled several military dictators and the ensuing democratization process raised fears among policymakers that Islamists were likely to consolidate power through the ballot box. In several countries, Islamist groups took advantage of popular demands for political reform and won elections, only to find themselves very quickly under pressure from the old civil-military establishment and many of their political opponents. It did not take long for a critical mass to develop, one that led to the July 3, 2013, coup that toppled Egypt's newly elected Islamist government. The tug of war between the Muslim Brotherhood and its Islamist allies and their opponents has led to a major crackdown and continued violence.

As this manuscript goes to press, the country remains unstable and Brotherhood-type Islamists in other countries remain on the defensive. Regardless of the exact outcome of the unfolding turmoil, what is certain is that the status quo is untenable and that political transformation will continue. What is less certain is whether this transition will lead to liberalization and the eventual consolidation of democracy. The unraveling of entrenched authoritarian regimes, the general lack of coherent secular opposition forces, and a complex array of Islamists have left many wondering who is most likely to fill the void. What type of governments will emerge in the coming years and decades? What role will Islamists play in the future of Muslim-majority countries? More importantly, will religion be incorporated into politics?

Most Western scholars insist that modern Muslim-majority countries must separate religion from the political arena and that the state must be secular to be considered a democracy.[1] The possibility that religion might play a role in the political arena is difficult for most Western scholars of democracy to accept. Since the 1980s, the Western public consciousness has perceived Islam as synonymous with violence,[2] and the idea that Islamists might have something meaningful to contribute to the political discourse is unfathomable.[3] The most recent transformations across the region are fueling these fears as Westerners watch, with growing concern, the increasing presence of Islam in their own countries, as well as the Islamists' expanding presence in Muslim societies.[4] For many it comes as a disappointment that the 2011 Arab uprising did not result in liberal secular democrats—but rather Islamists from the Muslim Brotherhood or, even worse, from the ultraconservative Salafis—dominating the ballot-box.

What most outside observers miss is the complex relationship between religion and politics within Muslim societies.[5] The common tendency to misunderstand Islamist views on the subject, which vary greatly, is often based on the false assertion that Islam makes no distinction between the religious and the political realms.[6] Commentators share a common exaggeration about the importance or absence of religion in political life. The view of many—ironically in both Western and Muslim countries—is that Muslim thought, in contrast to Western thought, sees the indivisibility of the whole *din wa dawla* (religion and state).[7] This is in sharp contrast to the West's demarcation between God and Caesar, which separates church and state. However, in reality there is little consensus on the exact relationship between religion and politics even in Western societies.[8] As Nader Hashemi correctly points out, "[H]istorically, the development of liberal democracy in the West (especially in the Anglo-American tradition) emerged not in strict opposition to religious politics but often in concert with it."[9] Furthermore, it is often assumed—mistakenly—that the development of democracy in the West was a smooth process. Religious values were fundamental to the founding of its states and remain firmly rooted in the very fabric of modern Western democratic societies.[10] It should therefore come as no surprise that many Americans insist that religion must have a role to play in politics, such as in official policies on abortion, same-sex marriage, or teaching the theory of evolution in public schools.[11] Political development was not a smooth process in Western history, so why should it be expected to be so in other regional or cultural contexts?[12]

The tension evident in these public debates on political transition has entered the scholarly writing of political scientists.[13] The longstanding underlying assumption in comparative politics is that religion is structurally incompatible with democratization.[14] Comparativists writing on democracies often highlight the American or British model, or even the French concept of *laïcité*, as a secular democratic model for others to emulate.[15] Consequently, those writing on the process of democratic transition in Muslim-majority countries tend to superimpose these Western secular democratic systems of government and the implementation of democratic reform on the Muslim states in question.[16]

Similarly, modernization theorists have asserted since the 1950s that religion diminishes in importance as a country's citizens become wealthier and better educated.[17] Contemporary modernization theorists such as Ronald Inglehart argue that in modern economies urbanization and higher levels of education leading to job opportunities set in motion changes that produce a more secular society.[18] Their studies downplay the importance of leaders who base their power on claims to religious legitimacy.

Some scholars of Muslim societies view religion as the major obstacle to development. Bernard Lewis, the renowned Orientalist scholar, argues that Islam is to blame for the Arab/Muslim world's lack of modernization.[19] While Islamism has been gaining ground there since at least the 1940s, most social scientists did not acknowledge it until the 1979 Iranian Revolution, which toppled a pro-Western monarchy and brought to power a cleric-led hybrid political order. Only after this astonishing event did the academic community start to undertake a concerted study of religion's revival in the public affairs of Muslim societies. The ensuing deluge of studies of Islam and Islamism led the epistemic community away from searching for signs of secularism as a way to measure development and toward focusing on Islam as the main factor shaping Muslim countries. The key, as Robert D. Lee points out, is to move one's view away from the deterministic modernism of social scientists of the 1950s and 1960s, which downplayed religion's importance generally, and the reactive overemphasis, within the Muslim context, on Islam that has been characteristic since the 1980s.[20]

The prominence of religion in politics—particularly in the public sphere—is an important part of history in general and the struggle for democracy in particular. But this has been underappreciated by Western democratic theorists, particularly when commenting on the politics of the Muslim world after September 11, 2001.[21] At least four inferences can be drawn from this view:

(1)  Muslims in general and Islamists in particular will continue to insist on some role for religion within the political landscape of their respective states. The lack of consensus on this subject is the key factor shaping this trend.

(2)  Islamists may not have initiated the uprisings in most Arab countries and currently may seem to be in retreat, but they will continue to be key players in post-autocratic rule.

(3)  A variety of competing Islamist tendencies exist within any given state.

(4)  The institutional context in each country will likely force Islamists to adjust their position toward democracy as they insist that certain aspects of Islam be integrated into the political arena.

## Islamists

Islamists remain key players in the ongoing transformation even as they have seen the reversal of their initial electoral success. The Muslim Brotherhood's loss of power in Egypt threatens the credibility of Islamists and their ability to govern elsewhere in the region. While the weakening of the region's autocratic regimes initially created opportunities for Islamists, their ensuing squandering of it will force them to reassess their political strategy, internal decision-making, and ideology. There are two likely scenarios in regards to their ideological outlook: Many will push for a more inclusive worldview, whereas others will be tempted to shun electoral politics altogether and feel that violence is the only option. But just as the ongoing social turmoil has manifested itself in different ways in the region, future Islamist behavior will also differ according to the context. Even after the recent Islamist fall in Egypt, international perceptions continue to treat them as a myopic whole while disregarding the acceleration of intra-Islamist fragmentation.

The diversity within Islamism goes back nearly a century. But even now, despite the deluge of ink spilled in newspapers and books, it remains misunderstood. This continuing lack of nuanced examination has only been exacerbated since the 9/11 attacks. Given that this diversity has been around since the early decades of the twentieth century, this exacerbation is rather surprising. For over seventy years Islamism functioned as the political opposition, during which time it underwent considerable fragmentation—primarily along ideological lines and competing strategies on how to realize the shared aim of changing the secular geopolitical status quo. In the 1970s, these differences and the autocratic postcolonial regimes' suppression further complicated the landscape when a significant number of Islamists adopted armed struggle. This led to the rise of *jihadism,* a subsidiary form of Islamism that was initially confined to the boundaries of a given nation-state.

The current Arab uprising is based on the demand for social, political, and economic reform.[22] With few exceptions, Islamists have engaged with secular civil society actors through nonviolent means and have exerted pressure on the state in an attempt to achieve their political goals through democratic means. The more violent Islamists were almost totally irrelevant throughout this process, although they are now trying to exploit the vacuum created by the meltdown of autocratic orders. A number of former radical and militant Islamists have also been able to play a role in mainstream politics. But even they contain different flavors and diverse currents. In the case of Egypt, the largest Arab state, such historically apolitical forces as the Salafis and even former militant forces such as Tandheem al-Jihad and Gamaah al-Islamiyah are adopting the democratic route in order to compete with the main Islamist movement: the Muslim Brotherhood.

Much has been written about the Islamists' metamorphosis during these early decades—a critical formative period for individuals seeking to understand the revival of political Islam. This work, however, is about unpacking the increasing complexity of political Islam during a time of democratization in the Arab world. But even more important is how these two trends will interact over time to produce Muslim democracies in which religion is likely to play a role in public affairs.[23] In order to understand how democratization will evolve in a Muslim context featuring politically powerful Islamists, one must examine both Islamism and democratization. As authoritarian regimes began to lose their grip on power, Islamists evolved and ultimately became key drivers of democratization. The 1991 Gulf War proved to be a watershed event that brought Salafis into the Islamist fold and led to transnational jihadism with the founding of al-Qaeda. Observers of Islamism are still trying to make sense of the growing post–9/11 Islamist convolution. Al-Qaeda's terrorist attacks and Washington's response in the form of a global war against militant Islamists have further complicated the picture.

Both the intended and unintended consequences of Washington's nearly decade-long campaign against Islamist militancy have altered Islamism from within. The United States needed to isolate extremists from the wider Muslim landscape, which created opportunities for mainstream Islamists. Although some Islamists continue to engage in violence, many others opted for mainstream democratic politics even after the ouster of President Mohamed Morsi. The democratic openings accelerated this shift for some previously violent groups such as Tandheem al-Jihad and Gamaah al-Islamiyah. Many radical and even militant Islamists embraced electoral politics, either because of specific circumstances within the country or because the Arab Spring brought new-found reason to moderate their position and abandon violence. This latest wave of moderation differs greatly from previous ones, because Islamists have transformed themselves from purely societal forces to forces that work within the state. In other words, the issue is no longer simply about Islamism's complexity as a non-state ideological phenomenon, but rather about the messy process of democratization and how the latter shapes Islamists as key stakeholders in the emerging post-autocratic (dis)order.

## Democratization

The popular unrest that toppled autocratic rulers in Tunisia, Egypt, Libya, and Yemen is the most profound sociopolitical development that the Middle East and North Africa region has experienced in nearly a century.[24] Not since the collapse of the Ottoman Empire in 1920 has it witnessed such a massive upheaval and unraveling. Authoritarian rule is gradually being replaced by a mixed system located somewhere between authoritarianism and democracy.[25] Some have referred to these as "hybrid regimes" (Karl 1995, Diamond 2002)[26] or as "illiberal democracies" (Zakaria 2003).[27] Others view them as "semi-authoritarianism" (Ottaway 2003)[28] or "liberalized autocracies" (Brumberg 2002).[29] Each of these terms refers to mixed regimes situated in the messy "gray zone" (Carothers 2002),[30] located somewhere between the poles of authoritarian dictatorship and liberal democracy.

The literature on democratization, although still unable to define these mixed systems clearly,[31] nevertheless provides an important theoretical framework for assessing regimes in Muslim-majority countries during this transitional period. It also offers an important vantage point for reviewing the role of Islamists engaging with the political system, as well as a unique opportunity to make sense of the political landscape as we evaluate the fluid and dynamic relationship between religion and politics in those countries. The most important questions are as follows: What type of governments will emerge as a consequence of the ongoing momentous changes? Will the transition lead to stable, consolidated democracies? If so, will these democracies be secular or religious? What role will Islamists play, and should there be a role for them to play, in shaping modern Muslim societies?

In order to better understand the nature of the political systems that will emerge in the Arab and (by extension) the wider Muslim world, we need to dispassionately take stock of what has taken place so far and where the region is headed. The popular agitation that began in Tunisia in December 2010 has led to the ouster of three dictators in North Africa and one in the Arabian Peninsula. That same culture of protest also led to the toppling of Egypt's first democratically elected president in July 2013. All eyes at the time of writing this book are on the Levant, where the next major fall of an autocratic regime is expected to take place in Syria. This will have far-reaching consequences for the entire region. Autocratic governments in Tunisia and Egypt were thrown out, and their counterpart in Libya collapsed. Meanwhile, in Yemen former president Ali Abdullah Saleh (r. 1978–2012) negotiated an exit; however, his regime remains in place under the leadership of his former vice-president Abd Rabbuh Mansur Hadi, who succeeded him. In Jordan, Morocco, and Kuwait, monarchs were forced to make notable concessions in 2011 that enabled them, to varying degrees, to control the process of democratization.

But in other countries, among them Saudi Arabia, Bahrain, and Syria, the rulers continue to try to crush indigenous uprisings. In the case of Syria and Bahrain force has been used, while in Saudi Arabia a combination of coercion and financial incentive has been the primary means for stifling unrest.[32] Thus far, largely military-run autocratic republics are experiencing the most dramatic changes, whereas the region's monarchies (especially in the Gulf) continue to hold on to power with less upheaval. The one exception is the tiny Persian Gulf island monarchy of Bahrain that, with considerable assistance from regional powerhouse Saudi Arabia, managed to quell the agitation in large part by exploiting the growing geosectarianism—another major trend that could arrest democratization.

The commonality among these upheavals is that they were all launched by largely young, educated, liberal, and often secular societal forces. In ideological terms, this revolutionary vanguard was of a liberal mindset in that its *raison d'être* was to pursue the secular goals of democracy, justice, and the rule of law. While this movement's mobilization achieved the unthinkable—forcing out long-standing dictators—it was quickly overtaken by the struggle between the far better organized religiously oriented political forces and the military-dominated secular establishments. As a result, revolution gave way to evolution, which explains why the democratic process has been disrupted by the July 3, 2013, coup in Egypt and the problems faced by the elected governments in Tunisia, Libya, and Morocco. The electoral constitutional processes now underway have allowed the secularists within the establishment to retard the pace of change so as to prevent the complete and sudden loss of their traditional authority. After emerging as the biggest beneficiaries of the electoral process, Islamists are now struggling against a realignment of their secular opponents and the military, economic, bureaucratic, and judicial establishments.

This new reality has come about due to several factors, all of which will help us understand the pivotal role that Islamists will play in shaping the region's newly emerging polities.[33] Undoubtedly Egypt's Muslim Brotherhood has suffered a major blow, but it has by no means been knocked out. Likewise, its counterparts in other countries are facing reversals. But these mainstream Islamist forces are not about to wither away given their deep roots. The Egyptian regime knows this and realizes that the Brotherhood cannot be stamped out through force. Thus the goal of the current suppression tactics is to force the movement to accept the coup and compromise. The Brotherhood knows this strategy and is therefore driving a hard bargain. What this shows is that while it has weakened considerably and, in the process, damaged the Islamist brand in the region, it will remain a force to be reckoned with. Therefore, Islamists will attempt to use this to their advantage with the hope of regaining public support by playing the victim card in an effort to benefit in future elections. Being more effective as an opposition force than as a governing party, the Brotherhood and its Islamist allies will be taking advantage of the country's dire political economic circumstances to try and stage a comeback.

The decline of Islamist fortunes since Morsi's ouster has not automatically resulted in the secularists gaining ground for a number of reasons. First and foremost is the fact that there is no unified secular organization that can fill this void. Second, the lens of the Islamist vs. secularist struggle fails to explain the ground reality of why the region's largest Salafist political party has decided to support the military regime. Third, many conservative Muslims do not support the Islamists. Recent decades have seen a tremendous growth in personal (both public and private) Islamic practice and social conservatism. This region-wide trend was distinct from Islamism in that it was not necessarily aligned with Islamist groups. Although many observant voters came out against Islamists, they can be expected to switch sides if they see that their religio-political ideals are not being catered to in the post-coup era. Fourth, to a great extent the public still identifies secularism with the old authoritarian regime (*feloul*). Thus, the genuine secular opposition forces pushing for democracy are still having a hard time translating anti-Islamist sentiment into support for their political program. While the Islamists' commitment to democracy has been lacking at times, the secular camp suffers from a similar predicament in that the democratic forces are far weaker than those who favor autocracy. For these reasons, secularists alone cannot put the region back on the democratic path. Progress toward democratization will take place only when democratic-minded secularists join forces with those Islamists who are more adept organizationally and share a common desire for a genuine transition toward democracy.

For these reasons, secularists in the region will struggle to compete electorally with Islamists even though the latter have been weakened; however, they will still serve as critical arresters in the path of Islamist forces. One of the reasons why the Brotherhood lost power within a year of taking office is because it won by a slim margin. The anti-Islamist candidate in the second round of Egypt's 2012 presidential race, former prime minister Ahmad Shafik, garnered just under half of the ballots cast. In addition, non-Islamist forces outperformed their Islamist counterparts in Libya's 2012 elections. Increasingly, since 2012 the Tunisian Islamists who formed a coalition government with secularist parties have faced a growing secular opposition. Even though secularists are clearly on the offensive, they remain a reactive force against the Islamists, whose early electoral victories gave them the potential to shape the transition toward democracy. Different types of Islamists are trying to steer this process. The largest grouping consists of those who have traditionally sought to establish an Islamic state via democratic politics. Furthermore, a growing number of Islamists who had traditionally rejected democracy as un-Islamic have now embraced democratic politics (some albeit with reservations).

All of these Islamist forces desire to dominate the democratization process, even though they know they cannot sideline their secular opponents. Not only will

Islamists of various stripes need to arrive at a modus vivendi at the intra-Islamist level, they will also need to reach an accommodation with secularists in order to establish democratic polities. Muslim democracies will allow for religion to have a role in politics, but one that will be defined by the ensuing and mutually acceptable compromise.

Muslim and non-Muslim scholars have ruminated about the shape of these future states and on the relationship between Islam and democracy. In recent decades, a great deal of theoretical research has been conducted on Islamists and democracy, given that scholars were largely dealing with undemocratic political orders. Our book will not only advance a theoretical framework for assessing the Islamists' views on democracy, but also provide case studies to ascertain their behavior and attitude toward the process of democratization.

## Religion and Politics

As noted above, Western thinkers have long considered secularism a precondition for democracy.[34] Indeed, many have cited the Arab/Muslim resistance to secularism as a key reason for the Islamic world's democratic deficit.[35] One problem with this theory is the fact that the post-colonial regimes that ruled Muslim nation-states founded in the second half of the twentieth century were, for the most part, both secular and undemocratic polities. Many Westerners might find it rather ironic that now the Islamist forces are instrumental in the unfolding democratic transition. However, this is no more than a logical outcome of how tradition and modernity have blended in the Arab/Muslim world. The role of the Islamists does not represent a victory over the secularists, because Islamism itself is in a state of evolution—now more than ever before, given that its proponents' ideology is no longer simply an opposition phenomenon. In fact, once Islamists assume power— to varying degrees—they are likely to temper their original ideological positions, as these took root while they were in opposition. Governance in general, and particularly governance of a democratic type, necessitates compromise. As a result, Islamism as an ideology will undergo some form of dilution.[36]

Recent scholarship views this development as Islamists undergoing a process of secularization.[37] But this is only partially true, and a great deal of nuance is missed in such renditions. Removed from their siege mentality, Islamists will gradually accept the secular space in both state and society. At the same time, and far more significantly, they will most likely not abandon the idea that religion has a certain role to play in public affairs. Consensus over its precise role in matters of state and society, however, will take time to develop.[38] In fact, even when a baseline agreement is reached it will need to be modified constantly due to spatial and temporal considerations.

Despite this evolution, Islamists are unlikely to accept the Western notion that religion must be confined to the personal sphere or dilute their worldview so much that they cease to believe that Islam has a certain role to play in public affairs—even though the nature of this role is not exactly clear and thus likely to remain a point of contention.

The public in Muslim-majority countries generally supports a type of democracy that includes Islam. Recent polls on attitudes toward religion and politics suggest that the majority of Muslims in these countries want religious authorities to have a greater role in politics. A 2010 Pew study reported that more than nine out of ten Indonesians favored religion's increased influence in politics; in Egypt, Nigeria, and Jordan, more than three out of four supported this view; and in Pakistan more than two-thirds did so.[39] A majority in Lebanon and a plurality in Turkey supported more influence for the religious leadership in the political arena. According to a 2006 Gallup study, the majority of Muslims in eight out of nine countries agreed that *shari'a* should be *a* source of legislation in their country, and the majority in four countries said that it should be *the only* source.[40] Support for both democracy and Islam was evident in a March/April 2011 Pew poll of Egyptians. More than 70 percent of respondents stated that democracy is always preferable to any other kind of government; however, almost nine out of ten said they preferred laws based on Islamic principles, with 62 percent stating that laws should adhere to the Qur'an's commandments.[41]

A key feature of the region's former authoritarian political systems was that they induced reactionary tendencies in both Islamist and secularist camps. Islamists who rejected Western secularism (to varying degrees) remain opposed to ideas emanating from extra-religious sources. Conversely, many secularists went to the other extreme: rejecting religion in the public sphere. The resulting polarization engendered a charged atmosphere, a worldview of binary categories perpetuated among the people by despotic regimes. Democratization, however, is serving as a crucible in which both sides can organically reexamine their ideas.

Islamists are increasingly realizing that the term *secular* does not necessarily connote an ideology that calls for abandoning religion. Likewise, secularists concede that core Islamic principles can be allowed to guide public affairs. Through this process, Islamists and Muslim secularists could find a middle ground that would allow their shared religious values—the common denominator—to shape the democratic republics being constructed. One hypothesis put forth well before the Arab uprising is that democratization tends to moderate Islamist forces. In the post-Arab uprising environment, this theory has become all the more pertinent and is a focus for both researchers and policymakers.[42] One of the key shifts in the attitude of Islamists and religiously oriented conservative Muslims will be how they approach secularism. As an ideology rooted in the Western experience, it never really took root in Muslim milieu and is unlikely to do so in the future—as is apparent in the decline of the secular ideologies of nationalism and Marxism and, much more recently, with secular polities in retreat. Islamists will likely recognize the existence of a secular space, given that Muslims have long accepted secularism as a process, especially in the natural and applied sciences. The problem has always been how to apply secularism in the social realm. To a great extent, this is the result of the relative lack of emphasis on the study of social sciences in comparison with the physical sciences. Islam has been treated as something separate from all non-religious curriculums, especially those of the social sciences.

A key upshot of democracy's growth will be the freedom to generate new discourses based on a synthesis of various bodies of knowledge. As this happens, there will be a greater acceptance of the idea of a secular social space in which extra-religious ideas will be seen as very much in keeping with the classical Islamic concept of *mubah*. Classical jurists came up with taxonomies of the different types of human behavior in keeping with Islamic principles. *Mubah* refers to those actions that are permissible or optional. In other words, human reason is the sole judge in matters of choice and, as more liberal Muslim thinkers would argue, even in many theological matters. Put differently, this is where extra-religious ideas come into play and where Islamic principles acknowledge a secular space. A key characteristic of *mubah* actions is that they constitute the largest body of human enterprise, as opposed to the far fewer actions deemed *fardh* (obligatory) or *haram* (forbidden) as per the teachings of Qur'an and the Sunnah. While Islamic scholarship has declined over the centuries, modernization has caused the realm of potential *mubah* actions to expand greatly. Over time, and with the Muslim world's intellectual revival, there might be opportunities to assert that a secular social space is something natural and not merely an invention of the West.

Democratization is about grassroots sentiments channeled as inputs into the political process. Thus far, despotic leaders and their authoritarian states have prevented Islamists from participating in the political sphere and playing any role in governing their country. Moving forward, however, polities will likely be shaped by the demands of the common citizens, for whom religion has great meaning, one that is beyond rituals and is often a central part of their identity. Unlike in the contemporary Judeo-Christian tradition, religion has a very different social role in Muslim societies. Confining Islam to the private sphere is not likely to happen in most Muslim-majority countries. Consequently, democracies there will look very different from those of the West. As in the West, there will be a plurality of democracies in the Muslim world. Just as there are differences in American, British, French, and other Western democracies, democracies in the Muslim world will also likely differ from one another. In fact, given their unique experiences, Egyptian democracy will differ from the Turkish and Pakistani versions as well as from those emerging in countries with monarchies (e.g., Morocco and Jordan). Furthermore, it is important to note that not all Arab/Muslim countries will necessarily undergo democratization. Those riven by factionalism and unable to agree upon a new social contract will most likely remain in the "gray zone" for years, if not decades. But these will tend to be the exception rather than the rule, and Muslim democracies will likely emerge over time.

## Purpose of the Book

There is no shortage of academic literature on contemporary political Islam. Yet the novice as well as the informed reader continues to struggle to understand the topic, since so much of the literature confuses (rather than clarifies) the issue. The result is a vast collection of disparate pieces of information that has no overarching framework to help one make sense of Islamism. Much of this literature is, in fact, polemic in nature. Not only is there an entire genre of literature that examines either one form or multiple forms of Islamism, but also most studies on political Islam are single-country case studies of a particular issue. While the latter are invaluable contributions to a detailed understanding of political Islam in a particular country,[43] their theoretical implications rarely move beyond the borders of the case studies being examined.[44]

This book will build a theoretical framework that situates each Islamist group within the political spectrum in three distinct time periods: the decade following the 1991 Gulf war, the post-9/11 period, and the ongoing post-Arab Spring unrest that began in January 2011. As it maps out the various trends thematically and locates them geopolitically, it will also clarify the concepts and terminology associated with political Islam. We will try to minimize normative discussions on the subject in order to concentrate on unpacking the shades across the Islamist spectrum.

This book will use democratization as a theoretical framework to examine and analyze the landscape in which Islamism is evolving. This approach is especially useful in helping tie together the many strands of Islamism as the Arab world adjusts to the meltdown of authoritarian structures.[45] Given the region's current transformative climate, we believe that democratization (as opposed to other conceptual lenses such as religion and politics, civil society, political violence, social movement theory, etc.) offers the greatest theoretical purchase in the current context to understanding Islamism. With moderate as well as radical Islamist forces seeking to make use of the atmosphere of collapsing autocratic structures, we desire to contribute to the literature on democratic transition as well as to explain the ongoing metamorphosis of Islamism itself. A considerable amount of intellectual work has focused on democratization in Europe, Latin America, and Africa.[46] Far less has been written about democratization as it applies to Arab countries, the wider Muslim world, and (to a lesser extent) the Islamist context. We hope to provide a much-needed update on the relationship between democratization and Islamism.

Scholars are often "accustomed to writing to one another" rather than to the general public. In contrast to this, our book is designed to contribute to the scholarly debate on political Islam and to be relevant to both policymakers and the general public. It is, therefore, directed toward three separate audiences: (1) our academic peers, with whom we wish to engage in a fruitful discussion (the primary audience); (2) policymakers and government officials, in the hope that the information and analysis provided will help them make more informed decisions when dealing with Islamists; and (3) the general public, which both needs and deserves a far more nuanced and accurate discussion of this increasingly misinterpreted topic. Therefore, we hope that our work will be welcomed by multiple audiences: graduate and undergraduate students, faculty, analysts, researchers, policymakers, journalists, and general readers. The book will also appeal to those who are looking for a wide-ranging, informed analysis of Islamism, a social force that is generally smothered by the scholarly and media focus on radical, violent, and jihadist Islamists. Many will be interested in a detailed examination of the individuals and groups advocating democracy, social development, and nonviolence within the Islamic tradition.

## Outline of the Book

In this introduction we have presented a wide-ranging examination of the relationship between religion and politics, democratization, and the complex nature of political Islam. These reasons alone underscore the need for a new, comprehensive, and rigorous treatment of the issue. And now, with the heart of the Islamic world experiencing historic developments that will reshape not just the Arab states but the region itself, a "nuanced, granular, and rigorous"[47] understanding of the phenomenon has become even more crucial.

Chapter 2 examines the terms *political Islam* and *Islamism* and places them in their proper contexts. Perhaps the major shortcoming of the existing body of literature is its lack of clarity in regards to the terminology surrounding Islamism. The chapter seeks to clarify these terms and the existing body of knowledge so that the diversity within Islamism can be untangled and analyzed.

Chapter 3 examines democratization as a theoretical framework for understanding Islamism. In particular, this chapter will examine the following questions: What does democratization theory say? How does the relevant literature apply to political Islam? How has democratization been applied by Islamists in the Arab/Muslim context? Furthermore, this theoretical framework guides the discussion in each subsequent chapter. We conclude by presenting a three-tiered typology that categorizes Islamist groups based on their attitudes toward democracy. Cognizant that reality cannot be boxed into neat analytical classifications, we will also expound upon the exceptions to the rule.

Chapter 4 will be a substantive case study of the Muslim Brotherhood (MB) with particular emphasis on its branches in Egypt, Jordan, Syria, Yemen, Morocco, Algeria, and Tunisia. The world's first Islamist group, the Muslim Brotherhood is the name of Egypt's single largest and most well-organized opposition movement as well as the largest trend within Islamism. This chapter will trace the MB from its origins to the present time, when it is faced with opportunities and threats from within, especially the efforts of the younger generation's leaders to reform it in light of the post-Morsi period. The chapter will also look at Hamas and democratization in the absence of a state. The victory of Hamas—an otherwise militant entity fighting Israel's occupation of the Palestinian Territories—in the 2006 Palestinian legislative election represents a unique case study of a radical Islamist movement embracing democratic politics despite the lack of a state. This chapter will expound on the parallel dynamics involved in Hamas being an armed resistance movement, a participant in democratic politics, and even a subnational ruling entity.

Chapter 5 tackles Salafism in Saudi Arabia and the Gulf states and how it has emerged in Egypt and elsewhere. This includes examining its origins, discussing it as a late entrant into the Islamist universe, and focusing on its factionalization, particularly as the Salafis are being democratized in Egypt and other parts of the Middle East. The embrace of Islamism and democratization by some Salafis is pushing this category of Muslim religio-political actors toward increasing fragmentation, which we examine in greater detail.

Chapter 6 looks at al-Qaeda and the notion of transnational jihadism, which only became a reality within the last two decades with al-Qaeda acting as the vanguard of those Islamists who seek to establish their envisioned "Islamic" state via armed conflict. The weakening of al-Qaeda prime—the organization founded by Osama bin Laden—in the war on terror has led to its devolution. The chapter will illustrate jihadism's evolution and its future trajectory as the above-mentioned war continues and the drive toward democratization in the Islamic world gains speed, especially given that the Arab/Muslim world has been democratizing for the past decade while the West has focused on jihadism.

Chapter 7 assesses the national jihadist Taliban phenomenon in Afghanistan. The chapter will discuss its rise and spread from Afghanistan to Pakistan, as well as the challenges its members pose to the neighboring countries. It will also delve deeply into how the term *Taliban* is no longer just the name of an organization, but is now a moniker for all sorts of competing nationalist Pashtun jihadist groups. We will pay special attention to the possibility that even the Taliban may embrace certain aspects of democratization, given the talks underway between the United States and the Afghan jihadist movement.

Chapter 8 examines Shia Islamism in the context of Iran, where it has assumed a unique form. The merger of *veleyat-e-faqih* and Western parliamentary democracy has produced a theo-democratic polity that has inspired Islamists elsewhere even as it continues to evolve, given the struggle between clerical and non-clerical stakeholders. We will explore this evolution within the context of Iran's geopolitical rise, which is the major unintended consequence of the American war on terror.

Chapter 9 will switch gears to look at Shia Islamism within the Arab context, which differs markedly from the form it has assumed in Iran. The rise of the Islamic Republic of Iran, and especially since the fall of the Baathist regime in Iraq, has led to the rise of Shia Islamists in the Arab world, where they have used democratic procedures in Lebanon, Iraq, and Bahrain to gain a sectarian advantage. The chapter will examine this phenomenon as a unique manifestation of Islamist actors and their engagement with democratic politics.

Chapter 10 focuses on the more recently coined concept of "post-Islamism." This will be examined in the context of Turkey. Its ruling Justice and Development Party (AKP) has become the ideal for many Islamists across the Arab/Muslim world who seek to move away from ideological/identity politics and toward pragmatism, and who wish to embrace democratization as a political norm. But many Islamists resist the party's path and its subsequent post-Islamism. The chapter will discuss the most significant development in Islamism's history—the trend toward post-Islamism—by defining what it is and highlighting it as the next stage in Islamism's evolution. It will focus on the AKP's experiences and then lay out the prospects for its incarnation in various milieus around the world.

In Chapter 11, we conclude the book by stepping back and examining the topic of democratization and Islamism. Having taken the readers on a journey through the complex geopolitics of political Islam, we will tie the various threads together into a coherent narrative of how they all originate from the concept of Islam's role in an age of nation-states. In addition to recapping the various forms of Islamism and tying them to the democratization framework laid out in chapter 2, the conclusion will leave readers with a sense of political Islam's future trajectory in the post-modern world and our final thoughts on Muslim democracies that could emerge in the coming decades.

# 2

# Understanding the Complexity of Political Islam

The contemporary phenomenon popularly referred to as *political Islam* or *Islamism* has existed for well over a century, and yet much of the scholarly literature on it only appeared after the 1960s. This was due largely to regional developments that overshadowed the Islamists' visibility, including the British and French occupation of Middle Eastern lands after the Ottoman Empire's collapse shortly after World War I, the region's subsequent decolonization after World War II, and the indigenous struggle for independence. But more importantly, during this tumultuous period Islamists were no more than marginal players in a region ideologically dominated by secular nationalist forces. Consequently, the scholarly literature of that time reflected this reality and was therefore dominated by books and articles on Arab nationalism.

Several major political developments sparked a surge in interest in a resurgent political Islam. The first one was the 1979 Iranian revolution, which toppled the Shah and established the world's first Islamist (albeit Shia) polity on February 11 of that fateful year.[1] This watershed event represented the Islamists' first overthrow of a sitting pro-Western regime in the heart of the Muslim world and culminated in the establishment of an Islamic republic, which raised fears in the West that other Middle Eastern regimes would go through a similar experience. Furthermore, Tehran's new clerical regime sought to export its revolution to the wider Arab/Muslim world, which stoked Western fears even more.[2] A second key event was the rise of Pakistan's military leader General Muhammad Zia-ul-Haq to power on July 5, 1977. In his first address to the nation, he declared that Islamic law would be enforced and that a concerted effort would be made to establish the Islamic society for which Pakistan had been created. He immediately launched a major effort to Islamize the country's legal system in the hope of aligning its legal, social, economic, and political institutions with Islamic principles. A Federal Shariah Court was established to decide cases according to Islamic law, while a Majlis-i-Shura (Consultative Council) was founded in 1980 to act in place of the National Assembly.

The third major event was the seizure of Makka's Grand Mosque on November 20, 1979. This two-week armed attack and seizure was led by Juhaiman ibn Muhammad ibn Saif al-Utaybi and over 500 dissident militant Salafis from the Najd region of Saudi Arabia. Utaybi's justification was that the Al Saud royal family was corrupt, ostentatious, and blindly following the West—in other words, it had lost its legitimacy.[3] The group demanded that the monarchy terminate crude oil exports to the United States and throw out all foreign civilian and military officials. The final and far more consequential event of that year was the December 1979 Soviet intervention in Afghanistan, which triggered a multinational move to send Islamist insurgents from across the Muslim world to participate in what would come to be a global cause to support the Islamists. The bulk of the financial, military, and intelligence assistance came from the United States, Saudi Arabia, and Pakistan. The Reagan administration provided hundreds of millions of dollars of financial, military, and logistical assistance to tens of thousands of Afghan Islamist insurgents (commonly referred to as mujahideen) and to Islamist fighters from throughout the Arab/Muslim world to counter Soviet advances and strategic aims to consolidate a Marxist regime in Kabul. The resulting decade-long war proved to be a crucible in which Islamists of different national and ideological backgrounds created pan-Islamist linkages.

The 1980s witnessed several additional developments that further escalated Islamism's momentum. In the Persian Gulf, the United States and its regional oil-rich allies supported the war launched by Iraq in the fall of 1980 against an expansionist Islamist regime in Iran. In Egypt, President Anwar Sadat's assassination during October 1981 by junior military officers affiliated with a militant Islamist group (Tandheem al-Jihad) resulted in a major nationwide crackdown against all indigenous Islamist forces. In early 1982, the Syrian regime brutally suppressed an insurrection led by the local branch of the Muslim Brotherhood; as many as 50,000 people died in its epicenter: the flash-point city of Hama. The following year saw the emergence of Hezbollah, the radical Shia Lebanese Islamist movement that has engaged in suicide attacks against American, French, and Israeli forces as well as embassies. Rapidly emerging as a major political force, it enjoyed critical support from Iran and Syria.

Five years later, in 1987, the Palestinian Islamist movement Hamas was founded and eventually became a major competitor of the secular nationalist Fatah by leading the first Palestinian intifada (uprising). During the 1990s and 2000s, it waged a campaign of suicide terrorist attacks against Israel. In June 1989, Islamists in Muslim-majority Sudan assumed power after a coup engineered by the military and the country's main Islamist movement. In November of the same year, Jordan's Muslim Brotherhood movement won 22 out of the 80 seats in the parliamentary elections—marking the first time an Islamist movement had made major gains at the ballot box. This flurry of events played an instrumental role in bringing Islamists to the world's center stage.

The preceding series of events led to an upsurge of interest in political Islam and a subsequent proliferation of journalistic reporting, academic books, and journal articles on the subject.[4] Political Islam had not only gained ground within national political contexts, but had also become relevant to international geopolitical interests. This occurred largely within the framework of the Cold War alliance among the United States, Saudi Arabia, and other Islamist forces against leftist regimes to counter Soviet influence in the region.

By the 1990s, political Islam had become a major international phenomenon. A diverse array of Islamists appeared on the global stage, thereby refuting early perceptions that they represented a monolithic threat. The end of the Cold War enabled Islamists in various countries to gain widespread momentum. The Soviet collapse in 1991 significantly weakened leftist forces worldwide and gave Islamists further momentum and openings to exert their influence and demand change. In fact, they were often the only organized force that posed a serious challenge to the largely secular autocratic regimes. The Islamist insurgents who had forced the Soviets to withdraw from Afghanistan were emboldened and came to believe that they had played a decisive role in this victory. For some Arab Islamists, this victory represented a "triumph against an atheist superpower" and ultimately caused the USSR's collapse. They now focused on trying to effect political change in their native lands against American-supported— and therefore illegitimate in their eyes—despotic regimes. The 1991 Gulf War proved to be an extremely influential event, for it caused new types of Islamists to emerge and thus further complicated the evolving landscape of political Islam.

Over the next two decades, two parallel trends took shape within Islamism: (1) the vast majority of Islamists, like the MB and the Salafi Islamists, sought change largely through peaceful political means, and (2) a small minority of violent Islamists, like al-Qaeda and others, pursued armed struggle against the existing autocratic regimes.

The September 11, 2001, terrorist attacks on American soil catapulted Islamism from being a political issue in the Arab/Muslim world to one of immense global geopolitical and strategic significance, particularly in the West. The attacks also had a tremendous impact on the Islamist groups, for it brought about a greater polarization between the two main trends listed above. Many remained somewhere in between, as they were nonviolent but pursued radical agendas. During this decade, the American-led global war on radical and militant Islamism, including the military campaigns designed to effect regime change in Iraq and Afghanistan, became the driving issue shaping Islamist perceptions and behavior. The political landscape changed drastically as Islamists worldwide adjusted to the reality of a post-9/11 world. Both mainstream Islamists (e.g., the MB and its counterparts) and the far more austere Islamist manifestation (viz., the Salafis) moved aggressively to distinguish themselves from al-Qaeda and jihadism. The American-led pressure on the Arab/Muslim world drove many to further radicalization and acts of violence, and persuaded many others to moderate their views and practices. Put differently, an already confusing landscape became increasingly more complex.

A key analytical problem has been that while Islamism itself became increasingly difficult to map, the global public domain (which by now had increased exponentially given the advances in communication technology and 9/11's global impact) was bombarded with competing renditions about the phenomenon. The resulting vast accumulation of information, as well as the overemphasis on radical and militant actors as *the* key players in the Arab/Muslim world, further contributed to the popular confusion on this issue.

For three decades, with the exception of a handful of scholars, analysts, and journalists, most in the West saw the political options as a choice between the existing autocratic secular regimes and radical Islamists. Many preferred the secular autocratic leaders because they were seen as moderates. This dichotomous perspective prevented many policymakers from seeing the democratic trajectory of the Middle Eastern Islamists until the outbreak of the Arab Spring. In fact, even weeks after Tunisians began protesting in December 2010 most Western scholars failed to comprehend the magnitude of the unrest. The public demonstrations seemed anomalous, and many assumed that the well-entrenched regime would soon quell the agitation. But the following month saw the incumbent dictatorial president, Zine El-Abidene Ben-Ali (r. 1987-2011), flee the country. Only after this unexpected development did the West begin to focus on something other than Islamist extremism and terrorism.

When the public unrest spread from Tunis to other Arab capitals, particularly Cairo, policymakers finally realized that a regional trend toward democratization was underway. This became glaringly apparent when Egypt's president, Hosni Mubarak (r. 1981-2011), stepped down on February 11, 2011. A key reason why the Arab Spring took the global community by surprise was that the world had spent the preceding decade obsessively focused on al-Qaeda, thereby blinding itself to any alternative and non-jihadist Islamist agenda.[5] Western policymakers and even Western scholars of democracy still feel a great deal of trepidation toward Islamists, given their electoral rise in the wake of the Arab uprisings. Given the recent terrorist events in Syria, Egypt, Iraq, Libya, Algeria, Mali, Yemen, and Afghanistan/Pakistan, al-Qaeda and its militant Islamist allies still shape the narrative for many of those who continue to view Islamists through the prism of violence. Some scholars still insist that al-Qaeda remains a threat and make a compelling case that transnational jihadists can exploit the post–Arab Spring vacuum left by deposed regimes.[6] However, from a strategic point of view and when placed in the wider Islamist milieu, jihadists remain the fringe, especially after the MB and even the Salafis became legal political actors.[7] The Arab Spring has managed to lift the veil on the far more prevalent and rising tide of potential Islamist democrats.

## Defining Islamism

What does the term *Islamism*, often used interchangeably with *political Islam*, really mean? While the earliest usage of the term can be traced as far back as mid-eighteenth-century France, French scholars only adopted it to denote the twentieth-century ideology in the 1970s.[8] Specifically, it refers to the rise of movements drawing on Islamic referents—terms, symbols, and events taken from the Muslim religious tradition—in order to articulate a distinctly political agenda (hence the expression *political Islam*).[9] At a very general level, one might use Graham Fuller's proposed definition: The adherents of political Islam believe that "Islam as a body of faith has something important to say about how politics and society should be ordered in the contemporary Muslim world and implemented in some fashion."[10] But as Mohammad Ayoob correctly points out, this definition is too nebulous to act as an analytical guide that can explain either the nature of Islamist ideology or the scope of those political activities undertaken in the name of Islam.[11]

Guilain Denoeux provides a more precise and analytically useful definition, namely, that political Islam is "a form of instrumentalization of Islam by individuals, groups and organizations that pursue political objectives. It provides political responses to today's societal challenges by imagining a future, the foundations for which rest on re-appropriated, reinvented concepts borrowed from the Islamic tradition."[12] This highly diverse array of individuals believes that Islam is not just a religion in the Western sense of the word; rather, it has a role to play in politics, which they see as the central part of realizing Islam as a way of life. Thus they share a common goal of establishing an "Islamic" polity having a legal system that would be based, to varying degrees, on shari'a.

While *political Islam* and *Islamism* are often used interchangeably, we wish to point out that the former refers to all political manifestations of Islam from the Prophet's time until today as well as to all those that will emerge in the future, whereas the latter is an ideology—a twentieth-century response to the Western-led secular nation-state-based international system. This ideology originated in the calls for reviving an Islamic political order during the Ottoman Empire's implosion. Prior to its collapse there was, more or less, a continuity of the Islamic geopolitical order established by the Prophet in 622 in Madina that had evolved greatly over a millennium under various regimes. Thus, all of the many caliphates, emirates, and sultanates were manifestations of a pre-modern political Islam. In contrast, Islamism is a specific ideology adhered to by a distinct collection of non-state actors seeking the geopolitical revival of Islam in the post-imperial age.

Several problems arise when scholars use these terms interchangeably. On the one hand, they ignore the differences between the nation-state era and the dynastic, imperial, and classical eras. In addition, they implicitly—but mistakenly—assume that political Islam did not exist before the modern age. Linguistically, *political Islam* refers to Islam's political aspects. Clearly, Islam's political dimension is not something conjured up by twentieth-century Muslim non-state actors. On the contrary, Islamists of all shades base their ideology and political objectives on their respective understandings of Islam's political history.

What, then, is Islamism? Islamism is an early twentieth-century construct, a specific Muslim religio-political response to an otherwise secular modernity. A principal Islamist goal is the founding of an "Islamic" state—one that will implement the shari'a, which again is a very modern notion. Whether they seek to *establish* "Islamic" states within the structural and functional contexts of the secular nation-states in which they operate, or wish to *reestablish* transnational caliphates or emirates, these actors clearly emphasize that they wish to restore what they perceive to be the status quo ante. In other words, political Islam is not a new phenomenon. What is new is Islamism, for this particular ideology resonates with a subset of Muslims who are responding to a Western secular-dominated modernity.

In sum, *political Islam* and *Islamism* correlate in the sense that the latter is a sub-set of the wider phenomenon of the former. Moreover, political Islam has largely manifested itself in the form of state actors, whereas Islamism is mostly about non-state actors. Unfortunately, the confusion over these two terms is increased even further by the epistemic community's application of often contradictory and at times outright erroneous adjectives to political Islam and Islamism.[13] For example, using *fundamentalist* in reference to Islamists makes it difficult for both lay public and policymakers to understand the phenomenon of Islamism and to distinguish among its numerous manifestations. Such a practice ignores the fact that literalist individuals and groups comprise a small subset of Islamism. Similarly, identifying an individual as *Islamic* rather than *Muslim* is equally problematic. *Islamic* accords legitimacy to Islamists by portraying their ideology and activism as representative of Islam and over 1.5 billion Muslims worldwide.

Treating *Islamic* and *Islamist* as synonyms creates another conceptual problem: the underlying assumption that only Islamist ideas are truly in keeping with the religion of Islam. In other words, this involves the assumption that the majority of Muslims—secular and religious to varying degrees—who do not agree with the Islamist political agenda are somehow deviating from religious principles. Islamism is just one (albeit the most pronounced) Muslim political response to the rise of Western secular political thought. Non-Islamist forces offer alternative political paradigms that, according to them, do not compromise their religious values.

As mentioned earlier, Islamism is "a form of instrumentalization of Islam by individuals, groups and organizations that pursue political objectives. It provides specific political responses to today's societal challenges by imagining a future, the foundations for which rest on re-appropriated, re-invented concepts borrowed from the Islamic tradition."[14] The following four points are also relevant here. Islamism is diverse, a modern phenomenon, an instrument of political change, and a work in progress.

First, given Islamism's many shades it might be more appropriate to speak of *Islamisms*. While Islamism is not monolithic, at a generic level all Islamists do share a common dedication to implementing the shari'a. The diversity is man-ifested in the various tactics used to bring about their desired change and in the contested nature of the imagined Islamic state based on competing inter-pretations of the religious texts. The public discourse invariably treats Islamists as a monolithic category with very little appreciation for the internal differ-ences within Islamism. Very few people realize that Islamists agree on very little other than the need to establish an Islamic state, which they simplisti-cally define as a polity that implements shari'a. Their disagreements revolve around fundamental aspects of implementing their stated goal. For instance there is little agreement on what constitutes shari'a, how shari'a should be opera-tionalized, whether a republic or an alternative is preferred, whether to embrace the nation-state or a transnational entity, and how to establish the desired polity.

The diversity of views on the above issues is what often distinguishes mod-erate Islamism from more radical notions of the ideology. As Jillian Schwedler correctly points out, "moderates seek gradual reform within the existing system, while radicals seek revolutionary change often through the use of violence."[15] In addition to being an ideology, Islamism provides an identity by which its adherents can express themselves more fully in the public sphere. Islamists believe that "Islam as a body of faith has something important to say about how politics and society should be ordered in the contemporary Muslim world."[16] Just as communists, democrats, and nationalists seek to address the grievances of their own specific audiences, Islamists seek to address the grievances of a specific community: Muslims. This is important, because many scholars tend to focus on the Islamists' religious prescriptions for the state rather than on Islam's political role as a vehicle that articulates what a significant group of Muslims wants in a state. The former represents a more rigid interpretation of Islamism, one that sees it as confined to Qur'anic tenets, rather than what the latter sees as a flexible narrative that tries to relocate the experiences of Muslims within the limits imposed upon them by their respective regimes. Furthermore, Islamism transcends any group's political representation by providing political, social, and economic concerns with a moral framework. The incorporation of morals is a vital part of its appeal, as well as a point of departure from other worldviews that seek to organize society. While some groups do seek to Islamize society from the top-down, most Islamist groups seek to do so from the bottom-up; therefore, the very essence of this agenda depends on the support of the masses.

Second, Islamism is a modern phenomenon. While its origins can be traced back to the writings of Jamal al-Deen al-Afghani (d. 1897), Muhammad Abduh (d. 1905), and Rashid Rida (d. 1935) at the turn of the twentieth century, as well as to Hassan al-Banna's (assassinated 1949) Muslim Brotherhood founded during the 1920s in Egypt, it only gained prominence during the last four decades. Out of the crisis-ridden MB of the 1960s sprouted a proliferation of Islamist groups that sought political change through what they perceived as Islamic tenets. When the Muslim world's dominant narrative was one of nationalism during decolonization, Islamists sought to incorporate Islam into the process of state-building. When the policies of despotic nationalist regimes failed to provide thriving economies or viable social institutions, they moved in to fill the vacuum of social spaces left open by these ineffective regimes. Many social mobilization theorists, among them Carrie Wickham and Quintan Wiktorowicz, have written on the types of institution-building that Islamists engaged in to resolve this situation. For example, Wickham discusses Egypt's "parallel Islamic sector" during the late 1970s and 1980s, a sort of microstate that tried to fill the institutional vacuum left open by Cairo. This ground-level activism, which was independent of and competitive with the regime,[17] threatened the regime's stability.

When a wave of political liberalization swept the Muslim world during the 1980s and early 1990s, the Islamists were ready. This phenomenon sparked a frenzy of controversial literature on the compatibility of Islam and democracy in the 1990s. As regimes realized that containing Islamist voices would be harder than they had imagined, many resorted to the traditional repressive tools. An increasing number of Islamist groups either incorporated democratization into their agendas or made it a pillar of their ever-changing platforms. Democracy has been a key tool through which they can exploit the contradictory stance of most authoritarian regimes. But despite their continued rhetorical commitment to democratization, the autocratic regimes used undemocratic policies to maintain the status quo by stifling all oppositional voices. We will return to this process of liberalization later in this chapter, because we see those political openings as key to the evolution of the twenty-first century's mainstream Islamist parties, especially in the new post–Arab Spring climate.

Third, Islamism is an instrument of political mobilization, one that, as our above definition suggests, can be seen as "a form of instrumentalization of Islam by individuals, groups and organizations" so that they may "pursue political objectives." Furthermore, "it provides political responses to today's challenges by imagining a future, the foundations for which rest on reappropriated, reinvented, concepts borrowed from the Islamic tradition."[18] Islamists employ such conceptual pillars as shari'a and an Islamic state to provide symbolic reference to a project that focuses on reclaiming a common heritage in an effort to implement meaningful reforms in society. Such an approach enables them to frame platforms that suggest reform through an already deeply ingrained vocabulary. Ultimately, Islamists are modern actors seeking to reconstruct modern nation-states along the lines of the past by constructing reverse historical continuums.

Finally, given that Islamism continues to evolve according to circumstances and events, it would be incorrect "to think of Islamism as a fixed ideology to be accepted or rejected as a whole."[19] The continued existence of Islamist groups hinges on their ability to adapt and remain relevant. This means that although their ideological frameworks may appear to be identity markers, their implementation must be pragmatic in terms of operationalization due to differences between pure ideological principles and policies that can actually be put into practice, as well as constraints from the system at large and opponents that force compromise. Consequently, Islamists have moved beyond mere rhetoric in an effort to implement policies they can sell to the public and allow them to achieve their political objectives.

More recent literature (particularly over the last fifteen years) has focused on the trend of Islamist groups to behave pragmatically by placing day-to-day politics over such long-term goals as implementing shari'a and achieving an Islamic state. Many consider this a trend toward post-Islamism (e.g., Giles, Roy, Bayat, Yilmaz) to be the next phase in the evolving Islamist project. While democratic notions of freedom and pluralism may appear contrary to selective scriptural readings, an increasing number of Islamists (albeit to varying degrees) view democratization as a means to improve society through much-needed reforms—of course in keeping with their respective views toward democracy. It should therefore come as no surprise that both Islamization and democratization play a dominant role in the political agendas of Islamists and non-Islamists alike, and that how the two groups interact to produce political realities will greatly shape the Muslim's world political future.

## The Terminology of Islamism

Terms such as *fundamentalist, militant, radical, rebel, extremist*, and *terrorist* are used interchangeably for a host of different actors. This complicates the discourse even further. Equally problematic is the casual referencing of the ideology as *Islamic, Islamist, Wahhabi*, or *jihadist*.[20]

The ad hoc employment of such supposedly interchangeable terms has led to both conflation and hyperconfusion not only in political, but also, and more importantly, in security contexts. The ensuing confusion creates significant challenges for counterterrorism efforts, for intelligence and security agencies invest a great deal of time and resources in tracking down those who are identified as Islamists more broadly rather than the minority of terrorists who target civilians. The ensuing waste of precious resources is rather large. Even the term *al-Qaeda* has become a generic label, for it now refers to all types of militant groups and individuals and thus supports the tendency to identify all violent groups as belonging to it. Some efforts have been undertaken to rectify this by introducing various nuances into the discourse (e.g., "al-Qaeda-linked," "al-Qaeda-inspired," or "affiliated with the al-Qaeda network"); however, this is not sufficient.

*Islamist* cannot be used in a general sense to denote all types of militant Muslim political groups for two reasons. First, many of them are secular in orientation: for example, such Palestinian nationalist groups as the al-Aqsa Martyrs Brigade, the Popular Front for the Liberation of Palestine, and the Democratic Front for the Liberation of Palestine. This is also true of the Iraqi and Syrian Sunni nationalist insurgent groups, especially those comprised of former Baathists. Second, the bulk of these groups are *moderate* in that they pursue their political aims through democratic and constitutional means within existing nation-states (e.g., the MB and its Arab offshoots, the Jamaat-i-Islami in South Asia, and their counterparts in Central and Southeast Asia). More importantly, many Islamists work with the United States, such as the three main Iraqi Shia groups that dominate post-Saddam Iraq, namely, the Hizb al-Dawah (the Islamic Call Party), the al-Sadrite movement, and the Islamic Supreme Council of Iraq (ISCI). Even Grand Ayatollah Ali al-Sistani, the top Iraqi cleric, has cooperated with Washington—albeit indirectly. Most recently, and far more prominent, is the case of Egypt's Muslim Brotherhood-led and Tunisia's Ennahdah-led governments, both of which worked with the Obama administration.

Sectarian and ethnic issues further obscure Islamism. Most Islamists are Sunni; however, there are significant Shia Islamist groups as well. Despite being a small minority, these latter groups have been more successful in gaining power than their Sunni counterparts, given the 1979 revolution in Iran, the emergence of Hezbollah in Lebanon and its political influence in Beirut, and the rise of Islamist Shia in Iraq. While there is a great deal of Arab influence in almost all Islamist militant groups, ethnicity is a cross-cutting cleavage as well. In fact, there have been reports of infighting between Arab and Central Asian militants associated with al-Qaeda operating out of northwestern Pakistan.

Apart from mainstream Islamists, namely, those who seek their objectives through constitutional/democratic means, we have two other subtypes: *radical* and *militant*. Much of the existing literature on Islamism does not distinguish between them—an absolutely critical oversight on their authors' part. For our purposes, therefore, we define *radical Islamist groups* as those that do not necessarily employ violence as their modus operandi to achieve their goals, even though they may have a radical agenda. In contemporary political usage, *radical* refers to the political views of the Far Left or the Far Right. One might view such groups in the same way as they might view European radical Right-wing groups.[21] Consequently, *radical* is used as a general term for those favoring or seeking dramatic change to the existing political order. The transnational Hizb al-Tahrir (Party of Liberation), which seeks to reestablish the caliphate in the form of a supranational state, is the classic example of a radical Islamist group. Many radical but nonviolent Salafi groups and individuals have the same agenda and, like Hizb al-Tahrir, pursue this goal through *da'wah* (religious propagation). Hizb al-Tahrir seeks revolutionary change in government through a popular uprising followed by a military coup against the established political order, which its members deem as *kufr* (un-Islamic).[22] The key point is that while these groups may espouse radical ideas and seek dramatic change, they are not likely to pursue them through violence.

On the other hand, militant Islamists do resort to violence. The presumed *militant*, a term related to *military*, is more likely to engage in violence. In general usage, *militant* often refers to an individual or group that displays an aggressive confrontational behavior or attitude. Domestic American militant groups might include ultraconservative hate groups motivated by various ideals and/or racism, ecoterrorists who use violence to campaign for greater environmental responsibility, and socialist groups that oppose the World Trade Organization. More common militant groups, such as the Earth Liberation Front and the Animal Liberation Front, target facilities and materials that they perceive as harming the environment or animals.[23]

Similarly, militant Islamists seek to erect their "Islamic state" via armed insurrection against the incumbent regimes in the lands where they operate and/or striking at the United States and its Western allies. This suggests that militants differ from their radical counterparts who do not engage in armed struggle. Al-Qaeda, the Taliban in Afghanistan, the Jemaah Islamiyah in Indonesia, al-Shabab in Somalia, Boko Haram in Nigeria, the Ansar Dine in Mali, Jabhat al-Nusrah in Syria, and many Central Asian and Eastern Turkestani outfits constitute the more prominent organizations that typify militant Islamism. It should be noted, however, that militants, despite their high-profile attacks and the attention generated by the global media, are no more than a tiny minority within the wider Islamist universe.

Militant Islamists may further be divided into subgroups composed of organizations with significant theological, ideological, and political variations. While most of them are jihadists, in that they seek to establish their envisioned "Islamic" polities through jihad in its military sense, others are militants but not jihadists. For instance, although Hamas and Hezbollah are Islamists in ideological orientation and have armed wings that fight what they view as Israel's occupation of their lands, they seek political power largely through the legal avenues of electoral politics. Both of them also face international pressure to disarm if they want to be recognized as legitimate political entities. While both are similar to jihadist groups in that they employ the discourse of jihad and stage attacks, unlike the jihadists they view jihad as a means to free land from foreign occupation or external aggression as opposed to fighting the established political order. Another difference among such groups as al-Qaeda and Hamas or Hezbollah is that the former are transnational while the latter are nationalists. In essence, all jihadists can be referred to as *militant Islamists*, but the reverse does not hold true.

Even within the jihadist spectrum, some groups operate within a given state while others do not. For example, the Taliban are active in Afghanistan and Pakistan, the Jamaat al Mujahideen in Bangladesh, and the Jemaah Islamiyah in Indonesia, whereas the Chechen-led Caucuses Emirate group run by the successors of warlord Shamil Basayev (d. 2006), the Algerian-led groups operating in the North African and Sahel states, and the Somali-led al-Shabaab in East Africa do not recognize existing political boundaries. These three latter groups are also fighting to establish region-wide geographic- and ethnic-based imagined "Islamic states."

Lastly, the transnational jihadist al-Qaeda movement, which now has operations across several continents, is composed of branches, affiliated groups, and connections to independent Islamist militant operators. All entities that fall under its umbrella are fighting the foreign (predominantly Western) presence in the Arab/Muslim world and working to establish a global Islamic polity. What further complicates this distinction between establishing an Islamic polity and fighting perceived occupation is the situation in the North Caucasus, where Chechen Islamist militants continue their insurgency to expel Russia from the area and those who envision a regional Islamic state encompassing the Chechen Republic of Ichkeria, Karachai-Cherkessia, Kabardino-Balkaria, North Ossetia, Ingushetia, and Dagestan. Militant groups in Kashmir also exhibit these dual tendencies—they are secessionists who want to establish "Islamic" rule in the region.

Salafis in the Middle East and the Tablighi Jamaat in South Asia have often been described as Islamists. Historically both were apolitical social movements, whereas Islamist groups are by definition political entities trying to establish an "Islamic" government. More recently, Salafis have entered the political arena. As we will see in chapter 5, they have an ultraconservative and literal interpretation of religious texts but have only recently started to engage in political activity or militancy. All of this changed in 1990, when Saudi Arabia agreed to allow the stationing of American military forces in the kingdom to evict Iraqi troops, which had invaded neighboring Kuwait. This decision radicalized many Salafis, who then turned to jihadism to pursue political objectives. The most prominent example of this is Osama bin Laden, who founded al-Qaeda in the mid-1990s.

Although all Salafis are not jihadist, it would be safe to say that most jihadists tend to be Salafi to varying degrees: The Chechen militant successors of Shamil Basayev and Arab (mostly Saudi) jihadist commanders all subscribe to extreme versions of Salafism. Yet the very first jihadist groups (e.g., Tandheem al-Jihad, Gamaa al-Islamiyah, Munazzamat al-Tahrir al-Islami, and Takfir wa al-Hijrah) all started out as militant competitors of Egypt's moderate MB in the wake of the

Arab defeat in the 1967 Arab-Israeli war. The rise of Salafism has profoundly impacted jihadist ideology, which is now heavily steeped in extreme versions of Salafi thought. There are certain exceptions, such as the Taliban movement, which follows the Maturidi school of Islamic theology in terms of creed and is Deobandi-Hanafi in jurisprudence; Salafis are Hanbali in terms of their school of law.[24]

In addition, most Islamists want to establish their envisioned "Islamic" state within the confines of the nation-state in which they operate, whereas radical and militant Islamists view the Muslim world (the *ummah*), as a single political entity. They therefore reject the very notion of a nation-state in favor of a transnational "Islamic" political entity. There is really no reason to consider groups such as Hamas and Hezbollah as jihadist", for even though they use violence to fight occupation, they pursue their other political objectives within the context of a given nation-state and largely through electoral politics. There is also a tendency among many observers to mistake religiosity for Islamism. Being a practicing Muslim does not render one an Islamist, for even though a sizeable majority of the world's 1.5 billion Muslims tend to place high emphasis on religious observance, this does not automatically mean that they support the Islamist agenda. The recent uprising against the MB government in Egypt highlights this dynamic, where those who demanded the ouster of former President Mohamed Morsi included many devout Egyptians. Moreover, the fact that al-Azhar's ulema (religious scholars) have always opposed the Brotherhood's agenda underscores this point further. Traditionally, Islamists and the ulema have been in competition largely because the former viewed the latter as being incapable of providing religious leadership and of being too close to the ruling elite. Thus not only is it important to recognize the diversity within Islamism, but also to understand the central point that the term *Islamist* cannot be conflated with the average observant Muslim.

## An Islamist Nomenclature

Global developments and attempts to make sense of emerging actors have given rise to terms that, unfortunately, have obscured and blurred the distinctions rather than provide accurate portrayals of the groups that span the Islamist spectrum. The problems associated with the current terminology need to be clarified and require a language that can help scholars, policymakers, and others make distinctions among these various actors and add nuance to their analyses.

We now offer a typology for Islamist groups, one derived from how they view the current political system in which they are embedded. In our view, a taxonomy based on their competing ideologies tends to confuse more than enlighten. On the other hand, analyzing their actual behavior offers maximum clarity. More specifically, the classification below is constructed in keeping with their view of state and society. According to this criterion, Islamist groups can be placed into one of the following three categories:

- *Acceptors:* The majority of Islamist groups are *acceptors* in that they accept the reality of the nation-state(s) in which they operate. In other words, they embrace both society and the state and work within legal limits to establish an

Islamic state. We consider acceptor groups to be moderate because they play by the rules of the game and seek a democratic polity through non-violent means... Based on our definition the best exemplar of this category is the MB, which will be discussed in more detail in chapter four.

- *Propagandists:* This type of Islamist group engages with society but rejects the state. The method of change called for is radical, because propagandists reject both the concept of the nation-state as well as democracy. Instead, they work among the masses to shape public opinion by propagandizing against the status quo, and seek support from select elements within the state's security apparatus. Their ultimate goal is to foment a revolution that will trigger a military coup to replace the current polity with a new one that will then form the nucleus of a transnational caliphate. Hizb al-Tahrir and its various off-shoots are the quintessential examples within this category.[25]
- *Insurrectionists:* These militant Islamists reject both society and the state. Operating clandestinely, they call for armed insurrection against the established order. More specifically, they view jihad as the means to dismantle what they deem to be un-Islamic political systems in order to replace them with their envisioned transnational emirates or caliphate. Their goal of violent political change is based on a top-down approach that targets the state, which they expect will cause the desired changes in society. Unlike acceptors and propagandists, insurrectionists devote far fewer resources to mass outreach because they see little value in this effort. Al-Qaeda, in its many manifestations, and local jihadist groups are the prime examples of insurrectionist Islamists.

Acceptors can be found throughout the Muslim world (table 2.1)—in Egypt, Tunisia, Algeria, Libya, Jordan, Yemen, Morocco, and Iraq. While acceptors constitute the vast majority of Islamists, during the 1990s insurrectionists were able to capture the global spotlight. A significant cross-section of jihadists (al-Qaeda and its allies) adopted a transnational approach and began fighting the United States in the belief that they could force Washington to abandon its support for existing authoritarian regimes.[26]

Between these two polar positions lie several groups that espouse a radical agenda but remain largely nonviolent. Stated differently, based on their modus operandi *acceptors* can be referred to as moderates, *propagandists* as radicals, and *insurrectionists* as militants (table 2.1). Table 2.1 provides a typology of the three types of Islamists based on their attitudes toward society and state. We now turn

**Table 2.1**   Islamist views of state and society

| Type | Description | State | Society |
|------|-------------|-------|---------|
| Acceptors | Moderate (Muslim democracy) | Accept the state | Engage society |
| Propagandists | Radical (Nonviolent revolution) | Reject the state | Preach to society |
| Insurrectionists | Militant (Armed insurrection) | Fight the state | Fight society |

our attention to the extent to which Muslims emphasize religion in matters of public affairs. The range will run from those Muslims who are secular and insist that religion has no role to play in the political sphere to those Muslims at the other end of the spectrum who insist that religion alone must inform all aspects of life.

As shown in Figure 2, the *militant secularists* who occupy the left end of the political spectrum have zero tolerance for religion and are willing to confront it violently. To the immediate right are the *radical secularists* who are equally intolerant of religion in public affairs but do not resort to violence, such as those who subscribe to the French-style of "assertive" secularism (laicism) and seek to prevent religion in public life by using state coercion. A prime example of such actors are Turkey's Kemalists (viz., the military establishment and the bureaucracy) and its main opposition group, the Republican People's Party (CHP). For decades, these forces have actively prevented the practice of religion in public space.

Next in line are the *liberal secularists* who seek an American-style "passive" secularism in which religion has a limited presence in the public sphere. Liberal secularists remain strong advocates of the separation of church and state but oppose outlawing religious practices in the public realm. The problem for these people is not religion per se, but that the state must remain neutral in all religious matters. Among those who subscribe to this view are the main Iraqi opposition coalition al-Iraqiyah (led by former premier Iyad Allawi) and the Congress for the Republic, Tunisia's second largest party that is led by President Moncef Marzouki.[27]

Further along the spectrum are the *moderate secularists* who are flexible enough to allow religious values to inform public affairs; however, they do stress that the state must remain secular. Moderate secularists not only accept the public observance of religion, but are sympathetic to Islamist perspectives. Turkey's AKP is the best example here, for it holds firmly to secularism while accommodating religious values. The *centrists* occupy the middle ground as regards how much of a role religion should play in politics. These hybrids, located in the center of our spectrum, adopt some aspects that characterize moderate secularists and moderate Islamists. Centrists accept some notions of secularism, such as the civil state, but their Islamist values also inform their political point of reference. Centrist groups like Tunisia's Ennahda and Egypt's Hizb al-Wasat want to see a democracy in which Islamism and secularism can be reconciled and integrated.

The majority of Islamists of the MB-type form the next category: *moderate Islamists*. They want Islamic law to be given a specific space within their envisioned democracy. Unlike centrists who are Islamists and gradually became comfortable with secularism, moderate Islamists continue to be generally uncomfortable with the notion due to their greater rigidity and reluctance to accept views that venture outside the traditional understandings of Islamism. They disagree with the flexibility of centrists and are less receptive to ideas emanating from the secularists. Moving further along to the right on the spectrum are *conservative Islamists* who categorically reject secularism but have shown a willingness to accept procedural democracy as a political mechanism. These newcomers to democratic politics thus retain major reservations toward democracy. They accept its procedural form to the degree that they will participate in elections, but hesitate to adopt its substantive attributes, particularly its legislative function. Egypt's Salafi al-Nour

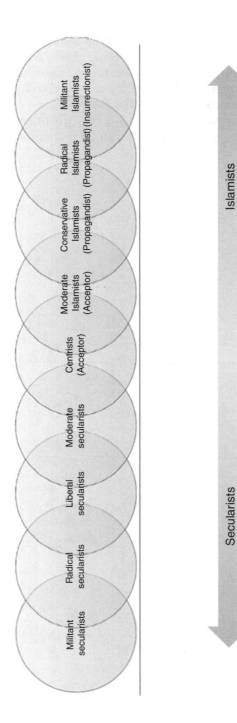

**Figure 2.1** The Islamist-secularist spectrum

Party and the country's former jihadist group, Gamaa al-Islamiyah, are the most prominent examples of conservative Islamists. The remaining two categories on the far right side of the spectrum include radical and militant Islamists. Radical Islamists share the conservative Islamists' views of secularism and categorically reject democracy as un-Islamic. Hizb al-Tahrir is the most renowned example of a radical Islamist group. Finally, *militant Islamists* go beyond the simple rejection of secularism and democracy to confronting these two ideas militarily. They seek an exclusive religiously based polity such as a caliphate or an emirate. The most prominent manifestations of militant Islamism are al-Qaeda and the Taliban.

# 3

# Theoretical Framework: Democratization and Islamism

Considering the transformation of political systems globally, it is not surprising that scholars have attempted to explicate and predict the causes, processes, and consequences of the global democratization trend. Experts have produced an impressive amount of scholarly work on various aspects of democratic transition and consolidation, ranging from elite strategies, socioeconomic structure, institutional design, and political culture to constitutional arrangements, presidential and parliamentary systems, electoral and party systems, civil–military relations, ethnic and regional cleavages, and international factors.[1]

Democracy is commonly defined as rule by the people, whereas democratization refers to the actual process of a country transitioning from an autocratic governing system to one that is more democratic. Yet such simple definitions say little about the actual relationship between the ruler and the ruled. According to Guillermo O'Donnell, democracy remains a "quintessentially contested concept" with no universally agreed upon definition.[2] Laurence Whitehead adds "if the 'what' (democracy) is contested, the 'how' (democratization) has to be equally contested."[3] Today many agree that democracy is much more than Schumpeter's notion of competitive elections[4] or what Sadiki refers to as "election fetishism." Western scholars of democracy have gravitated toward Robert Dahl's "procedural minimum," which includes the following features: (1) regular free, fair, and competitive elections; (2) full adult suffrage; (3) protection of civil liberties, including freedom of speech, press, and associational autonomy; and (4) the absence of non-elected "tutelary" authorities (e.g., militaries, monarchies, or religious bodies) that limit elected officials' effective power to govern.[5] In addition to these pillars, they add what Steven Levitsky and Lucan Way refer to as explicit criteria—such as civil liberties and minority rights—that are implicitly understood to be part of this term's overall meaning and are viewed as necessary for competitive elections to take place.[6] Furthermore, while not always explicitly stated, most Western scholars insist that democracy remain a secular endeavor. As Hashemi points out, "liberal democracy requires secularism to sustain itself."[7] Consequently, many Western social scientists frown upon the notion that democracy might include a religious element as an integral part of its definition. Certainly, Islamists' insistence that

Islamic law be part of any future government does not sit well with Western theoreticians. But as we will see in the context of Muslim societies, the most likely scenario will integrate Islam into the definition and allow religion a role in the public domain.

## Democratization Theory

The academic community's conceptual debate on the nature of democracy and democratization has largely been shaped by the "third wave" of global democratization,[8] which officially began with Portugal's 1974 revolution and led to a remarkable number of authoritarian countries transitioning to democracy. Authoritarian regimes and totalitarian states unraveled one after the other as the "democratic revolution"[9] transformed parts of Latin America, southern Europe, Asia, Africa, and in less than a generation engulfed large parts of the former Soviet bloc.[10] By the end of the 1980s, Latin America completed its journey toward electoral democracy, and democracy was further boosted in the early 1990s as the Soviet Union collapsed relatively peacefully and countries in sub-Saharan Africa engaged in a series of multiparty elections.

Despite significant differences in terms of timing, pace, and degree, transitions from authoritarian systems over the past three decades have roughly doubled the number of democratic regimes.[11] In 1974, Freedom House identified 42 "free" countries in terms of political rights and civil liberties; in 2004, it judged 89 countries to be free (out of a total of 118 "electoral democracies").

Francis Fukuyama famously predicted around the time of the Soviet Union's collapse that we had reached the "end of history" and that secular liberal democracy would triumph over all other systems of government.[12] Some scholars echoed this optimism, suggesting that these large "waves" might even reach the Muslim world, in particular the autocratic Arab Middle East. Others were more skeptical, as entrenched authoritarian rulers in Muslim-majority countries stubbornly held onto power.[13] The reality is that democracy is never a guaranteed outcome and thus even if the world were headed in that direction, it would happen slowly, with ups and downs and many painful reversals.[14] In fact, the very idea of democratic "waves" has never been smooth, since even in the European and Latin American contexts they were usually accompanied by setbacks, "halted transitions," and "reverse waves" of authoritarian regression.[15]

Comparative political scientists writing on this topic suggest that some nations may never reach consolidation; rather, they may find themselves stuck in the murky middle between democracy and authoritarianism. The literature teems with explanations and terms for such nations, including "hybrid regimes" (Diamond 2002), "the gray zone" (Carothers 2002),[16] "semidemocracy" (Smith 2005), "electoral authoritarianism" (Schedler 2006), and "competitive authoritarian" (Levitsky and Way 2010). In the context of Arab and Muslim-majority countries, Daniel Brumberg cites "liberalized autocracies" (Brumberg 2002),[17] while others have preferred "illiberal democracies" (Zakaria 2003),[18] "semi-authoritarianism" (Ottaway 2003), "semidictatorship" (Brooker

2000), and "stalled democratic transitions" (Sadiki 2009). Each term refers to mixed regimes situated in the messy middle ground between dictatorship and democracy.[19]

Many Muslim-majority countries, especially the Arab states of the Middle East, had until recently shown an extraordinary resilience to change. For decades they remained what Andreas Schedler refers to as "electoral authoritarianism," meaning regimes that engage in electoral politics and yet remain authoritarian. Some contemporary examples can be found in the Former Soviet Union (e.g., Armenia, Azerbaijan, Kazakhstan, Kyrgyzstan, Russia, and Tajikistan); sub-Saharan Africa (e.g., Burkina Faso, Cameroon, Chad, Ethiopia, Gabon, Gambia, Guinea, Mauritania, Tanzania, Togo, and Zambia); and Southeast Asia (e.g., Cambodia, Malaysia, and Singapore).[20] For our purposes, such regimes include the Arab states of Morocco, Algeria, Egypt, and Yemen.[21]

Many of these regimes have remained authoritarian even after establishing some electoral procedures. The elements of authoritarianism suggested by Schedler serve to distinguish them from electoral democracies, and the emphasis on elections sets them apart from "closed" autocracies. But while electoral democracies lack some attributes of liberal democracy (e.g., checks and balances, bureaucratic integrity, and an impartial judiciary), they do conduct relatively free and fair elections, which electoral authoritarian regimes do not.[22] According to Schedler, these latter regimes hold regular multiparty elections yet violate the liberal democratic principles of freedom and fairness.

> [E]lections are broadly inclusive (they are held under universal suffrage) as well as minimally pluralistic (opposition parties are allowed to run), minimally competitive (opposition parties, while denied victory, are allowed to win votes and seats), and minimally open (opposition parties are not subject to massive repression, although they may experience repressive treatment in selective and intermittent ways).[23]

The former single-party electoral system in Egypt (Mubarak), Iraq (Saddam), and Tunisia (Ben Ali) allowed the rulers to systematically manipulate elections. The dominant governing party used discriminatory electoral rules to exclude opposition candidates and parties, restricted media access, coerced or corrupted supporters into deserting the opposition, or simply redistributed votes and seats through electoral fraud.[24] This was not only the case in Arab republics; the monarchies of Morocco, Jordan, and, to some extent, Kuwait and Bahrain have used similar tactics. By most accounts, Schedler's "electoral authoritarianism," Brumberg's "liberalized autocracy,"[25] or what Sadiki refers to as "election fetishism," are just other names for "electoralism." This "election façade" allowed authoritarian Arab regimes to claim a high turnout—over 90 percent—while using divide-and-rule tactics and monopolizing resources so that no real alternative could arise.[26]

Some of these "liberalized autocracies," such as Egypt, Morocco, and Jordan, partially liberalized in the 1980s and 1990s but remained durable autocracies. For decades they held regular elections, tended to allow some semblance of multiparty pluralism, professed support for global human rights, and enthusiastically embraced foreign-funded anticorruption and democracy capacity-building programs.[27] All the while, however, the process was carefully stage-managed in a "theater of democratization" to give the impression of far more power-sharing and pluralism than actually existed.[28] The single-party states of Egypt and Tunisia allowed a highly restricted space for other parties. Jordan initially had no party per se, but used pro-palace tribal forces to balance the power of the Muslim Brotherhood (MB). Yemen worked out a complex arrangement between Ali Abdallah Saleh's General People's Congress and its main opponent, al-Islah (the Yemeni branch of the MB), because of the tribal and religious connections between the president and the Islamist movement. While opposition parties may occasionally gain a few seats in the state-controlled legislative body, the regime ensures that they never become meaningful political threats.[29]

Muslim-majority Malaysia and Pakistan slowly transitioned toward competitive elections while maintaining their authoritarian infrastructures, which Levitsky and Way refer to as "competitive authoritarianism." They posit that these regimes differ in their precise mixture of authoritarian and democratic politics, but nevertheless share two core characteristics[30]: (1) their elections are regular and competitive, but occur on an uneven playing field that favors authoritarian incumbents over opposition parties and candidates, and (2) they are far more likely than either democracies or the entrenched Arab authoritarian states to be located in weak states and to change regime types from one year to the next.[31] In short, they are not stable.[32] Levitsky and Way suggest that,

> competitive authoritarian regimes are civilian regimes in which formal democratic institutions are widely viewed as the primary means of gaining power, but in which fraud, civil liberties violations, and abuse of state and media resources so skew the playing field that the regime cannot be labeled democratic. Such regimes are competitive, in that democratic institutions are not a façade: opposition forces can use legal channels to seriously contest for (and occasionally win) power; but they are authoritarian in that opposition forces are handicapped by a highly uneven—and even dangerous—playing field. Competition is thus real but unfair.[33]

They point out this type of system's central reality: unfair competition. While authoritarian regimes prohibit legal competition (and, hence, of uncertainty) and democracy allows for fair competition, competitive authoritarianism is characterized by real (and often intense), but unfair, competition.[34] For decades, the armed forces of Turkey and Pakistan manipulated the multiparty system to their advantage. From 1988 to 1999, the opposition Pakistan People's Party twice won the elections (in 1988 and 1993), as did the Pakistan Muslim League–Nawaz (in 1990 and 1997); yet the military used the office of the presidency to send three governments and parliaments packing before directly taking power in 1999 with the Musharraf coup. In other words, the regime used democratic mechanisms and procedures to sustain autocratic regimes. Similarly, in Bahrain after 2006 the democratic mechanisms were very real and allowed the opposition Shia parties to win just under half the seats; yet the monarchy remained firmly entrenched.

Schedler suggests that the contradictory mix of democratic procedures and authoritarian practices have forced scholars to consider three alternative conceptual lenses: defective democracies, hybrid regimes, and new forms of authoritarianism.[35]

1. *Defective democracies.* These are defined as political regimes that fulfill the minimum conditions of electoral democracy but lack essential attributes of a liberal democracy. Scholars have devised distinctive adjectives to describe them,[36] such as "delegative" (no checks and balances) (O'Donnell 1994), "illiberal" (no rule of law) (Zakaria 2003), and "clientelist" (weak party politics) (Kitschelt 2000).[37]
2. *Hybrid regimes.* Located at the conceptual midpoint between democracy and authoritarianism/dictatorship, they are categorized as, among other terms, genuinely "hybrid regimes" (Diamond 2002), "semidemocracy" (Smith 2005), "semi-authoritarianism" (Ottaway 2000), "semidictatorship" (Brooker 2000: 252), and "the gray zone" (Carothers 2002).[38]
3. *New authoritarianism.* These regimes maintain such central authoritarian tenets as "pseudodemocracy" (Diamond, Linz and Lipset 1995: 8), "disguised dictatorship" (Brooker 2000: 228), and "competitive authoritarianism" (Levitsky and Way 2002). Scholars describe them as examples of nondemocratic rule that display "the trappings but not the substance of effective democratic participation" (Marshall and Jaggers 2002: 12). In addition, scholars have classified them as regimes that practice "democracy as deception" (Joseph 1993: 59), as they set up, to quote from John Stuart Mill, "representative institutions without representative government" (1991: 89).[39]

### Islam and Democracy

The relationship between Islam and democracy is complex, and a detailed analysis is beyond the scope of this chapter. Muslim and Western scholarly publications on this topic range from the normative to the theological to the empirical.[40] The compatibility of Islam and democracy has often pitted scholars against one another. It is, however, useful to say a few words about this ongoing debate, especially since the intellectual discourse within the academic community has had ramifications that affect democracy advocates, including many in policy circles.[41]

Beyond sharing some common basic beliefs, the world's 1.5 billion Muslims represent ideological diversity and subscribe to numerous perspectives on this compatibility.[42] Most ordinary Muslims consider Islam compatible with democracy. As proven by the changed attitudes even among Salafis and jihadists, very few Muslims insist upon the traditional assertion of incompatibility. Instead, most now are focused on how they can democratize in keeping with their religio-cultural ethos.[43] Historically, many Orientalist writers and even some Muslim intellectuals saw an Islamic exceptionalism and contended that Islam was unique and antithetical to democracy. Today, however, the majority of scholars believe that Islam and democracy *are* compatible as long as certain adjustments are made to "modernize Islam" and "secularize Muslim societies."[44] Some of these same scholars go even further by positing that under the conditions of the contemporary world, democracy can be considered a requirement of Islam.[45] These competing conceptual views range from "complete incompatibility" to "fully compatible."

The first view is articulated by many prominent scholars, among them Bernard Lewis (1988, 1990, 1993, 1996, 2002, 2003), Ernest Gellner (1994), Samuel Huntington (1993), Elie Kedourie (1994), Myron Weiner (1987), and Martin Kramer (1993).[46] Lewis, the most prominent of these scholars on the Muslim world, suggests that Islam rejects democracy and is intrinsically hostile to it (2002). Differentiating between three aspects of Islam—namely, religion, civilization, and politics—he argues that the last one is surely hostile to democracy (1996: 54)[47] and that the first two are incompatible, for "in Islam ... there is from the beginning [an] interpenetration of ... religion and the state" (1996: 61; also see Lewis 2002).[48] Gellner offered a more sophisticated articulation: Islam was not likely to democratize because "no secularization has taken place in the world of Islam: that the hold of Islam over its believers is as strong, and in some ways stronger now than it was a 100 years ago. Somehow or other Islam is secularization resistant (1991: 2)."[49] For him, Islam presents a "dramatic ... exception" to the patterns of secularization because "a church/state dualism never emerged in it [Islam]." In his view "It [Islam] was the state from the very start" (Gellner 1992: 5, 9; also see Gellner 1981: chapter 1).[50]

This first view is also espoused by some radical Islamist theoreticians who hold that *hakimiyyah* (sovereignty) rests with God alone and thus is antithetical to democracy. This opposition can be traced to the Egyptian ideologue Sayyid Qutb (1906–1966) in his *Ma'alim fi'l Tariq* ("Milestones along the Way").[51] Qutb, who was imprisoned (1954–1964) and then executed in 1966, became the leading ideologue of Egypt's Muslim Brotherhood in the mid-1950s. In *Milestones,* one of the most influential Arabic-language books of the second half of the twentieth century, he lays out a plan and a call to action to re-create the Muslim world on strictly Qur'anic grounds by casting off *jahiliyya* (ignorance, barbarity, or idolatry) that, in his words, is based on rebellion against God's sovereignty.[52] In his view, "it [democracy] transfers to man one of the greatest attributes of God, namely *hakimiyya,* and makes some men lords over others."[53]

Among the second view's strongest proponents are Bayat (2007), Esposito and Voll (1996), Esposito (2000), Filali-Ansary (1996), El Fadl (2004), and Tamimi (2000). John Esposito and John Voll both argue that there is nothing inherently undemocratic about Islamic ideas. Some predict that mosques and Muslim groups could be at the forefront of democratic change in the future, just as churches and many Catholic groups became motors of democracy in Latin America.[54] Some of these scholars posit that the barrier to democracy lies in the internal institutional structures, including the failed states and authoritarian regimes that have tainted the project in many Muslim countries.[55] Others suggest that the democracy deficit may have less to do with Islam and more to do with oil and the nature of "rentier states."[56] As Michael Ross (2001, 2008) argues, "Islam has little negative effect of its own on democracy, once one controls for oil exports."[57] This places revenues in the hands of rulers without requiring the population's consent. Since these leaders do not rely on taxation, they feel no need to give their people democratic representation. While this argument is suggestive, it is more applicable to the oil-rich Gulf countries.

As noted at the beginning of this chapter, much of the academic literature describes democracy in a positive normative connotation and continues to assume that it has universal applicability. Yet ironically, as Humeira Iqtidar points out, many of the same scholars contradict this notion by suggesting that the West was somehow more receptive to democracy, partially because it had "civic culture" as a prerequisite. In fact, many academics have argued that Muslim societies and Islam in particular are antithetical to democracy because their "culture" and higher-than-usual "religious tendencies" are obstacles to democratization.[58] In their view, "Islamic culture" poses insurmountable hurdles. Subsequently, a stream of scholarly writing focuses on this perceived clash. Moreover, a cursory review of popular media sources shows that many people in general continue to believe that Islam is not only a serious challenge to democracy, but that it is very likely *the most potent* threat.[59] More importantly, most of the scholars who speak of democracy's universal applicability insist that for countries to be democratic they have to adopt Western-style secularism.

Azzam Tamimi suggests that many Islamists have attempted to show that Islam is not inherently "undemocratic." He points out that Tunisian Islamist and theoretician Rachid Ghannouchi has been at the forefront in realigning the understanding of democracy and Islam as analytical categories.[60] Ghannouchi's unique contribution is to suggest that democracy in the Muslim context cannot be understood outside an understanding of Islam, or vice versa. He has gone beyond the criticism of Eurocentric notions of democratization and democracy raised by many others.[61] It is not just our notions regarding democratization that derives essentially from a Western experience that was universalized via colonial and postcolonial policies. Ghannoushi's argument is that there cannot be a universal definition of democracy, not only because its constituent elements and relationships are historically specific, but because that definition is itself the historical product of discursive processes.[62]

Moreover, democracy consists not just of particular minimum requirements, as Dahl might suggest, but also needs to take into account the views of its adherents. Discovering how these adherents understand the concept and incorporate their values is a key step in our understanding of how a Muslim country might democratize at a particular time and in a specific place.[63] Other Muslim scholars, such as Iranian intellectual Abdolkarim Soroush, go even further by suggesting that Islam *requires* a democratic system.[64] Others who do not fit into either group ask a different question. Saba Mahmood (2004), for instance, asks: Should Muslims take "their own resources of the Islamic tradition" to imagine a future different from the one offered by liberal democracy?[65] This proposal springs from an assumed authenticity of an Islamic tradition that is radically different from Western democracy.

The above discussion is not merely an intellectual exercise, for it has implications for academics, policymakers, and democracy practitioners.[66] After all, if Islamists did not believe that Islam and democracy were compatible, they would have been less likely to accept the views of democracy advocates. As the intellectual arguments against democracy in a Muslim context receded, democracy advocates became enthusiastic supporters of the belief that democracy and civil society were likely to flourish eventually, even within such an inhospitable terrain like the Middle East. Since the Arab Spring, many within the advocacy community are optimistic that the latest democratization wave sweeping the globe has finally hit the shores of the largely Muslim Middle East.

## Muslims and Democracy

Democratization is not inevitable in Muslim-majority countries, as it is only in the very early stages of the process and because so many factors are shaping it. Even the West's history with democratization shows that the road is bumpy and the process incremental, incomplete, and reversible even when it has been claimed to have been achieved.[67] The exact nature of democracy in Muslim-majority countries, both in substance and in form, is difficult to predict because the ongoing transitions are likely to take decades to reach maturity. In our view, the most significant factor informing this dynamic is the still-contested role of religion within these envisioned democratic polities. If the ongoing struggle in Egypt between the military and the MB is any indication, the final outcome will remain unknown for a long time. Thus it is hard to predict exactly what a Muslim democracy will look like. What can be done, however, is to examine democratization and the Islamists' pivotal role in shaping it so as to gain a general sense of its developing nature.[68]

In the Muslim context, democracy will undoubtedly differ considerably from a liberal secular democracy for it will allow religion to have a role in public affairs. As Hashemi points out, democratization and liberalization cannot be disconnected from the historical context of the society being studied: "[I]n societies where religion is a marker of identity, the road to liberal democracy, whatever other twists and turns it makes, cannot avoid passing through the gates of religious politics."[69] Obviously, this goes against the basic tenet of secular democracy. Indeed, the dominant argument made by many Western scholars is that as long as Islamists play the lead role, the outcome will likely be an Islamist form of authoritarianism (i.e., Schedler's electoral authoritarian regime) or a theocratic state as opposed to a liberal democracy. Yet democratization does not necessarily require a rejection or privatization of religion. All indications are that the current Islamist-led transitions (or those in which they play a key role) will likely produce democracies that differ from their Western counterparts due to the relatively important role that religion is likely to play in their public affairs. Many hard-line secularists will find this hard to accept, since the very notion of allowing religion any role is seen as antithetical to democracy. This view is partially based on the assumption that Western-style liberal democracy is the only genuine democracy. In fact, most of the democratic transitions discussed above are being evaluated according to a secular Western template. There is a greater tendency to dismiss Muslim democratic experiments because they do not adhere to the Western notion of separation of church and state.

A Muslim form of this separation might emerge in the future. In the classical period, for example, caliphates, sultanates, and emirates were ruled by dynastic leaderships that largely removed religious figures from matters of state.[70] For the foreseeable future, however, this separation is not clear (to say the least) because during this turbulent period both Islamists and many Muslims view it as Western imposition. It is likely that as Muslim countries democratize, they will eventually become more receptive to Western ideas while adjusting to Muslim sensitivities.

To be fair, Alfred Stepan and other prominent democracy scholars have tried to offer a more nuanced assessment of the religion-democracy relationship. For example, his "Twin Toleration" theory suggests such a balance.[71] Being an experiential process, democratization has to deal with each society's specific social, political, and economic context as well as its unique path and trajectory. As a result, newly democratic states usually differ from their Western-style counterparts.

Most theorists have expounded on democratization based on the Western experience and therefore fail to factor in the non-Western cultural aspects. The modern Turkish republic—given its suppression of religion as per the ideals of its founder Mustafa Kemal—was cited as the rare exception of Muslim democracy because it adhered to Western standard of secularism and thus was more receptive to liberal notions of democracy. Those who accept the idea that all democracies must adhere to the Western archetype cast those that do not as "defective" in nature or "illiberal."[72] But this is a very narrow definition. While there has to be a minimum criterion on what constitutes a democracy, the threshold should be wide enough to recognize that not all societies will operationalize democracy in the same way, for at a fundamental level all of them will be culturally bound. We thus agree with Sadiki that any democratic transition must be "historically situated, flexible, contingent, fragmented, nuanced, non-linear, and variable."[73] In our analysis, the particularities of Islamists and their views on democracy matter when it comes to understanding democratic transitions.

Traditionally, many moderate Islamists and conservative Muslims stressed establishing *shari'a* rather than a constitutional democracy based on the rule of law—a dynamic that blocked efforts at democratization. Secular authoritarian regimes used this scenario to their advantage and consolidated their autocratic rule, which the United States and many other Western powers supported out of fear that those Islamists who came to power would automatically oppose the United States' national interests.

This led some to see an Islamic exceptionalism, a Muslim world hostile to democracy because it rejected the church–state separation and therefore could not democratize. Yet since the Arab Spring, strong evidence supports the assertion that Muslims are not opposed to democratic political participation. Whitehead reminds us that "[l]ongstanding assumptions about a supposed Arab or Middle Eastern regional 'exceptionalism', or entrenched resistance to democratization impulses, have proved as unfounded here as they turned out to be in Latin America (its supposed Catholic anti-democratic culture) in the 1970s."[74] It is not the Muslim world that is exceptional as regards democratization, but rather the Western model and its experience that is the exception. Democracy is a universal value, but the Western form is based on its unique historical evolution through the Renaissance–Reformation–Enlightenment sequence and therefore cannot be reproduced elsewhere. All societies will follow their own courses.

The Gallup World Poll surveys conducted between 2001 and 2007 in thirty-five Muslim-majority countries confirmed that the majority of Muslims support democracy and consider it a legitimate form of government; more importantly, they wish it could be implemented in their own country (Esposito and Mogahed 2007; Fattah 2006; Hassan 2002; Norris and Inglehart 2004: 133–56).[75] In most countries, Muslims "value a number of democratic principles" and "see no contradiction between democratic values and religious principles." Yet as Esposito and Mogahed note, "along with indicating strong support for Islam and democracy, poll responses also revealed widespread support for Shari'a."[76] The authors state that most respondents do not want a theocracy, for they prefer that religious leaders have no role in drafting a constitution. At the same time, most "favor religious law as a source of legislation" (Esposito and Mogahed 2007: xiii). These and other studies confirm that Muslims "want neither a theocracy nor a secular democracy and would opt for a third model in which religious principles and democratic values coexist" (Esposito and Mogahed 2007: 35, 63).[77]

## Islamists and Democracy

Any discussion of democracy in the Muslim world must involve Islamist thought and practice. Islamist discourse greatly complicates the preexisting issues between Islamic tradition and Western modernity. Well before Islamists emerged as a major political force, Muslims were already negotiating between the two, as seen in the behavior of those members of the elites who were concerned about catching up with the West and the masses who sought to ensure that their own culture would not be discarded in the process. Key examples would be the Ottoman Empire's Rifa Tahtawi (d. 1873) and British India's Sayyid Ahmad Khan (d. 1898).

Over the past two centuries, Muslims have sought to reconcile their religious traditions with secular modernity. This was largely due to the fact that modernity was ushered in by the West in keeping with its Judeo-Christian heritage and the Renaissance–Reformation–Enlightenment experience. While the West was ascending, the Arab-Muslim world was declining in both intellectual and material terms.

However, Muslims were in contact with Western political thought and reacted to it long before European colonialism. They responded to Western modernity with a great degree of nuance and synthesis via two broad trends: (1) embracing Western secularism in order to emerge from their existing social, political, and economic stagnation, and (2) trying to protect their heritage from outside influence or change. These trends marked the beginning of what in the past three to four decades has been called the "Islamist vs. secularist divide." The secularists, who rose first and had Western encouragement, established themselves intellectually and as the political elites in the new postcolonial nation-states. In reaction, Islamists struggled both among themselves and with the secularist-dominated society.

Importantly, both of these are Muslim prescriptions for political development. Secularists see no contradiction between their Islamic faith and their push for a religiously neutral polity that allows religion a great degree of social space. In contrast, Islamists opine that religion has not been given its appropriate role in matters of state due to the adoption of the Western principle of separation of church and state. Fearing that their worldview would not resonate among the masses and that Islamists would seek a return to the "dark ages," secularists resorted to autocratic governing systems. This is a key reason why democracy has struggled to take root in the Arab/Muslim world. Further aggravating this was the Islamists' call for implementing the religious penal code.

During the ensuing decades-long status quo, the masses were caught between the secular autocratic state and Islamist-dominated opposition. They identified with both, but in different ways. On the ideational level the Islamist agenda made a lot of sense, but from a practical viewpoint the state was necessary.

The lack of democracy meant that governance was largely an elite-driven enterprise. As a result, Islamist ideology underwent no significant evolution beyond basic ideals and its principles faced no major real-life tests. The resulting more or less conflated theory of religio-political ideas went unchallenged until the 1970s, when Islamists began opposing the secular (and in many cases Left-leaning) nationalist orders by demanding adherence to religious principles. For those Islamist societal players reacting to the Western-dominated geopolitical order, implementing shari'a took precedence over ensuring constitutional governance. Likewise, secularist state actors were more interested in seeing their countries embrace Western secularism even if they had to impose it through autocratic means.

In other words, both sides lacked any serious commitment to democracy. The majority Islamist (and vehemently anti-secular) voices quickly became indistinguishable from the minority ones that categorically rejected democracy. This situation allowed the secular states to argue that their countries were not ready for democracy, which masked their own non-democratic nature and served their political interests.

In recent decades, scholars have amply addressed the state's autocratic nature by disproportionately linking the Arab/Muslim world's democratic deficit to the goals of Islamist non-state actors. Now that Islamists are the most significant political force in the wake of secular autocratic meltdown, they ought to be examined closely. Do they believe in democracy and want to participate in the democratic process?[78] How do they plan to attain their desired objectives? The difference in the various groups' approaches both to democracy and democratization is a function of how they perceive the status quo and the state.

Some scholars have suggested that the more important issue is whether the Islamists' worldview is compatibility with democracy. In their view, Islamism is a reaction against Western-style modernity and therefore Islamists cannot accommodate secular notions of democracy, a key element of modernity (Sivan 1985; Tibi 1988, 1998; Ayubi 1991).[79] Iqtidar points out that many of these writers follow Weber in terms of defining Islam via its innate absences, such as his claim that Islam could not give rise to capitalism (Turner 1974).[80] Others, like Irfan

Ahmad, suggest that Islamism is slowly becoming more receptive to secularism and democracy because it is constantly changing and now might actually support secularism.[81] The problem is that much of the relevant literature often conflates Islam and Islamism. Islamism must be seen not only as distinct from Islam but also with a great degree of nuance, for it is not monolithic. As we will see below, it contains both a great deal of resistance to and support for democracy.

While these scholars have made many contributions, in particular regarding the lack of a theological opposition within Islam toward democracy, most of their analyses revolve around whether democracy can be reconciled with Islam and/or Islamism. Very few have assessed what democracy might mean or whether Islamism can be used as a foothold to deepen our understanding of the relationship between democracy and democratization.[82] Such research has neither engaged with how democratization may actually unfold in a Muslim society, nor analyzed the actual processes that may have resulted from the lack of theological barriers to democracy in Muslim societies.[83]

Internal tensions between the new and the old guards in many Islamist parties have led to breakaway parties that are following new trajectories. Turkey's AKP has done this successfully, whereas Egypt's al-Wasat has not gathered enough of a support base to legitimize itself. These parties are offshoots of more conservative predecessors, and in both cases the leadership played an important role in their trajectory away from the parent organization. The AKP's founders were trying to avoid another shutdown, whereas their al-Wasat counterparts were seeking a license to operate in a robust one-party state that prevented competitors from making much headway. While al-Wasat's parent party, the MB, was on much firmer ground than the AKP, one could argue that al-Wasat, given the regime's resistance and its post–Arab Spring performance, is a failed experiment.

Schwedler's examination of Islamist participation in elections in Jordan and Yemen, as well as the performance of their counterparts in Algeria, Egypt, Kuwait, and Lebanon, suggest that Islamists have played by the democratic rules of the game. In dominant-power countries, they fare well when the state allows their groups to participate. In fact, they often win significant, if not majority, blocs in Parliament that, in her estimate, usually add up to about 20–40 percent of the seats.[84] Islamists have found new strategies to take advantage of such openings, including full or partial participation. In Egypt, for instance, the MB and most opposition parties boycotted the 1990 elections because of, as they claimed, gerrymandering and insufficient guarantees of fairness at the polls. Officially, only Hizb al-Tajammu' (the Tajammu' Party) and Hizb al-Umma (the Umma Party) participated. However, numerous members of Hizb al-Wafd (the Wafd Party), Hizb al-'Amal (the Labor Party), Hizb al-Ahrar (the Liberals' Party), and MB members as independent candidates.[85]

Unlike many secular groups, Islamists benefited more from the openings because they had deep roots in society due to their decades-long vast array of social and charitable services and built their organizations from the ground up. Unsurprisingly, this investment paid off at the polls. As Ayoob points out, "paradoxically, these very regimes, by successfully eliminating secular opposition movements and parties and banishing 'normal' politics, have created the political and intellectual space into which the Islamists have moved. This is because not even the most efficient repressive state can fully suppress opposition expressed through the religious idiom."[86] Members of Egypt's MB ran in alliance with other groups in 1984 and 1987, garnering 15 and 17 percent of the vote, respectively, which gave them a considerable presence in Parliament. By 2000, running as independents, MB members retained 17 seats. In the 2005 presidential election, MB members garnered 20 percent of the vote, winning 88 of the 160 seats they contested (out of a total of 444),[87] over five times the 17 they had won in 2000. Throughout these elections and in Parliament, the MB emphasized its moderate credentials. Immediately after its stunning 2005 victory, its members launched a public relations offensive to reassure both Egyptians and foreigners that they were a moderate reformist force committed to the democratic process. Muhammad Habib, its deputy general guide at that time, he told the International Crisis Group during a 2008 interview that

> Two decades ago we embraced democracy, partisanship and rotation of power. We consider the people to be the center of power. We are not vying for power, or trying to become the ruling party. The power of public opinion is what we strive for, because it is what made the Muslim Brothers rise. Nobody can claim we are against democracy or that we intend to burn the ladder once we've reached the top—otherwise we would be running with more candidates.[88]

During the Mubarak era, there was no way to gauge the MB's ability to govern democratically. Only during the group's short stint in power did it become clear that the group privileged a procedural notion of democracy. Rather than opting for consensus-building, the MB focused on its narrow electoral victory to justify its majoritarian rule, which ultimately drove its opponents into the streets. While the MB was working with the generals, it alienated the non-Islamist forces as well as its main Islamist rival. By not opting for the politics of consensus, the MB triggered a major public uprising against its rule that eventually forced the military to side with its opponents. As a result, the group quickly lost power in a popularly backed coup. It now faces two major challenges: empowered secular opponents and the al-Nour Party, the country's largest Salafi group that is trying to replace it as Egypt's major Islamist force. Not only has the Brotherhood severely damaged its reputation, it has also contributed to undermining the country's democratic transition.

This chapter began with a conceptual overview of the broad literature on democratization. We then examined the relationship between Islam and democracy and discussed how it has impacted the Muslim world. Next we focused on Islamists and the democratization process. We are now in a position to offer a typology that helps illustrate the wider Islamist landscape with respect to democratization. In chapter 2 we discussed how Islamists disagree on almost everything except the need to establish an "Islamic state." We identified three types of groups (viz., acceptors, propagandists, and insurrectionists) based on their method of achieving their desired polity. We will now categorize Islamists into three types based on their attitude toward democracy. It is important to note that these differences are not just the logical outcome of disagreements over how to establish

**Table 3.1**   Islamist attitudes toward democracy

| Type | Democracy | Groups |
| --- | --- | --- |
| Participators | Islam and democracy are compatible. Integration is both desirable and possible. | The Muslim Brotherhood, Ennahda, and the Jamaat-e-Islami |
| Conditionalists | Can be accepted, but with certain conditions. | Egypt's al-Nour party, Gamaa al-Islamiyah (GaI), Tanzeem al-Jihad (TaJ), and certain Iranian clerics |
| Rejecters | Antithetical to Islam | al-Qaeda, Saudi Salafis, and Hizb al-Tahrir |

a desired Islamic state, but rather a function of how competing interpretations of the Qur'an, Sunnah (prophetic traditions), *ijma* (consensus), *qiyas* (analogical reasoning), the historic debates over *usul al-fiqh* (the principles of Islamic jurisprudence), and *fiqh* (juristic rulings) have produced, over the decades, a range of views on democracy. This spectrum can be classified into three broad categories: Islamists who participate in, reject, and conditionally engage with democracy. Therefore, our typology comprises *participators* (Islam and democracy are compatible and must be integrated), *rejecters* (democracy is antithetical to Islam), and *conditionalists* (some reservations and limited compatibility) (table 3.1).

*Participators*

This category comprises Islamists who have embraced the political mainstream and seek to establish their envisaged Islamic state through democratic means. Having adapted to Western-style political systems, their stance should not be seen as a compromise but as one based on the understanding that democracy is not inherently un-Islamic. This compatibility is most clearly articulated in the writings of Rachid Ghannouchi, a prominent Tunisian Islamist intellectual and leader of the ruling Ennahda Party. In a 1992 interview in the *Observer*, he stated: "If by democracy is meant the liberal model of government prevailing in the West, a system under which the people freely choose their representatives and leaders, in which there is an alternation of power, as well as all freedoms and human rights for the public, then Muslims will find nothing in their religion to oppose democracy, and it is not in their interests to do so."[89]

The Egyptian MB and its counterparts around the Arab/Muslim world are prime examples of participatory Islamists. Political participation, especially in elections, became a priority for them over the last few decades. For example, Pakistani parties like the Jamaat-e-Islami (JI), the Jamiat Ulema-i-Islam (JUI), and the Jamiat Ulema-i-Pakistan (JUP) entered electoral politics in the 1950s. In countries that allowed Islamic parties (e.g., Morocco and Jordan),[90] they established a strong parliamentary presence. In many countries with a long history of banning such participation (e.g., Egypt) or forcing them into exile (e.g., Tunisia and Syria),

Islamist opposition movements have emerged as strong advocates of democracy and political participation.[91]

*Participatory Islamists* can be traced back to the late eighteenth-century Ottoman era, when efforts were initiated to bridge the growing gap between an intellectually ascendant Europe and a stagnant Muslim world. Ottoman officials, including such public intellectuals as Rifa'a Tahtawi (d. 1873), traveled to Europe, studied at Western universities, and brought back new ideas on how to conduct social, political, economic, and military affairs.[92] But by then Islamic scholarship had already been fossilized for over five centuries. The effects on Muslim political thought were clear: the Islamic world was trapped in medieval notions of politics and governance rooted in the dynastic-imperial system.

Intellectual development in Muslim societies had long since fallen behind social evolution, which facilitated its mid-nineteenth-century revival and gave way to Islamism, particularly to its participator form in the late 1920s. For these forerunners of Islamism, Islam's primary texts offered general principles that, if operationalized in keeping with spatial-temporal realities, would have produced an Islamic order. Participators viewed democracy as the latest stage of human political evolution and compatible with Islam; hence the idea of Islamic (as opposed to Western secular) democracy.

### Rejecters

Within a generation of their rise, participators began facing theoretical and practical challenges from competing Islamist forces. In terms of the latter, the participator model ran into problems given that its success was predicated upon democratizing the postcolonial Arab/Muslim nation-states that had fallen under the strong grip of secular authoritarianism.[93] It was the former group's ideological challenge that provided the foundation for rejecter Islamism. The rejecters' core issue with democracy is that it assigns sovereignty to humanity as opposed to God. Elections themselves are not the issue; rather, the issue is that elected officials would have to legislate according to the majority vote. As legislation is seen as the right of the Almighty, such a reality was clearly unacceptable. As a result of this group's radical reaction to the growth and spread of Western political thought, they felt that the MB had fallen victim to the Western intellectual onslaught, as had the secularists before them. The only difference was that participators were trying to Islamize alien concepts that rejecters deemed un-Islamic, whereas secularists did not bother with issues of compatibility.

Rejecters interpreted the idea that Islam was a complete way of life in a very austere manner. For them it offered systems to govern all facets of collective life, and so all they needed to do was to return to the original teachings of the divine texts. Furthermore, since the West's ways were based on its Christian heritage and subsequent secularization, they denounced it as *kufr* (un-Islamic) and its emulation as *haram* (forbidden). Key examples are the nonviolent but radical transnational Islamist party Hizb al-Tahrir (HT), which calls for reestablishing a global caliphate; the jihadists who began to emerge during the late 1960s who also rejected democracy as un-Islamic; and the Salafis, who largely steered clear of Islamism until the 1990s and decided to participate in elections only after the Arab Spring.

## Conditionalists

The intense debate between these two above-mentioned polar groups gave birth to a third Islamist school of thought. Initially seeing democracy as an idea emanating from outside the religious tradition, this middle-of-the-road trend evolved into a category of *conditionalist Islamists*, many of whom were not fully on board with the MB's wholesale embrace of democracy as being very much an Islamic concept.

Very soon, this camp also included those who accepted it as a procedural mechanism by which to order the political realm, even though they remained quite uncomfortable with its associated cultural ethos. The Islamic Republic of Iran—a polity based on the amalgamation of a Shia theocracy with Western parliamentary democracy—is a key manifestation of this duality. Indeed, post-revolution Iran has been a democratic polity, albeit a unique anti-Western type.

Sunni religio-political thought has historically been far more conservative, and therefore the unease with extra-religious ideas was bound to be more profound. Since the 1990s, as many Salafis moved away from being largely apolitical and entered Islamism, there has been a reexamination of democratic politics. In more recent years, transnational jihadism's strategic weakening has caused many radical and militant Islamists hitherto uncomfortable with democracy to take another look at it. This would explain why, in the post–Arab Spring political climate, Egyptian Salafis rushed to form political parties (e.g., al-Nour) to participate in the democratic process. Former jihadist groups, such as the Gamaah al-Islamiyah and the Tandheem al-Jihad, also got onboard. As a result, the MB's Freedom and Justice Party dominated with 37 percent and the Salafi's al-Nour-led Islamist bloc won some 25 percent of the 444 parliamentary seats in the 2011-12 elections. While these groups have embraced electoral politics, their commitment to democracy remains questionable, for they consider democracy as no more than a means to an end: the imposition of what they view as Islamic law. Over time, some of these *conditionalist Islamists* might join the *participators* because their current political philosophy is a rushed affair for the sake of expediency and thus suffers from a poverty of thought.

There has been a learning process even within the MB and its genre of Islamist groups that embraced democracy very early on, given that they were byproducts of the modernist trend stretching from Tahtawi through al-Afghani to al-Banna. From their beginnings until the 1950s, such Islamist groups viewed democracy as a way to establish an Islamic state, namely, by implementing *shari'a*. Complicating this utilitarian view was the MB's gradual bottom-up approach, based on its members' belief that Islamizing society would culminate in an Islamic state.

Another factor was the autocratic Arab regimes that suppressed it. Nasser forced the MB to articulate its goals in democratic terms. Starting in the 1970s under Sadat, it began to embrace democracy as a value. Under Mubarak, especially in the post-9/11 era, the process matured. Thus by the time the Arab Spring erupted, the MB had moved from emphasizing an Islamic state and democracy as a means to achieve it to advocating democratic governance as a goal in itself. The group has now evolved to where democratic governance is slowly becoming synonymous with the envisioned Islamic state.

A key element that aided the MB's evolution was the emergence of militant Islamist groups as a response to regime repression. The militants turned to internal and (much later) external terrorism. For the longest time the focus was on *al-adou al-qareeb* (the near enemy). The MB resisted the trend toward violence and continued to focus on creating grassroots networks. Democracy and human rights, which radical Islamists considered to be Western ideas and thus inapplicable to Arab/Muslim societies, found their way into the rhetoric of mainstream Islamist organizations and, most importantly, their political strategies.[94] This development took place early on for groups like the MB and even before the jihadists appeared. This is why al-Zawahiri's *Al-Hasad al-Murr: Al-Ikhawn al-Muslimum fi Sittin 'Aman* (The Bitter Harvest: The Muslim Brotherhood in Sixty Years) represents an attack on the MB's approach. Just as participators gradually moved toward greater engagement with democracy, conditionalists will have their own evolutionary trajectory. While some might become participators, others could cross over into the rejectionist category because of their inability to reconcile democracy with their religious interpretations. Still others may remain conditionalists.

Now that we have laid out a conceptual framework for understanding Islamists and democratization, the remaining chapters will apply this model to all the major manifestations of contemporary political Islam.

# 4

# Participatory Islamists: The Case of the Muslim Brotherhood

The Muslim Brotherhood (MB), the world's oldest and most significant Islamist movement, was founded in 1928 by Egyptian-born Hassan al-Banna (1906–1949), the "father of Islamism."[1] His thinking and the organization were rooted in the ideas propagated by such Ottoman-era Arab-Islamic thinkers as Rifa'a Tahtawi (1801–1873), Khairuddin al-Tunisi (1810–1899), and Abdurrahman al-Kawakibi (1849–1903).[2] These three men, who held senior positions in the Ottoman bureaucracy, played a key role in trying to effect an intellectual revival in the long-stagnant Arab-Muslim world. Faced with the rise of European modernization and Western political thought, they sought to balance modernity with Islamic traditions.

Their work was built upon by a second generation of thinkers led by the Persian Shia Jamal al-Deen al-Afghani (1838–1897) and his two prominent followers: Muhammad Abduh (1849–1905), the former Mufti of Egypt, and Rashid Rida (1865–1935).[3] Hassan al-Banna, a disciple of Rida, laid the foundation for the MB, which we now identify with the current concept of Islamism.[4] In sharp contrast with the existing religious currents, this new trend was about Islamic reformism (*Salafiyyah,* not to be confused with Salafism, which we will discuss in chapter 5) and Islam's role in public affairs (*mu'amalaat*) as opposed to personal ritualistic practices (*'ibadat*). The MB has gone far beyond Banna's original vision. In fact, its ideology has spread throughout the Muslim world and into Western Europe and the United States.[5]

This chapter traces the MB's activism within the context of hybrid authoritarian Arab regimes with limited democratic openings. As these regimes give way to more democratic systems, the MB and like-minded forces in Tunisia, Morocco, and Libya emerged as the leading electoral forces. The MB in Egypt has been the most important player in the midst of this dynamic evolution. As this book goes to print, Egypt's military regime has once again outlawed this organization. A more detailed discussion of the implications for the MB and its brand of participatory Islamism will be dealt with later in this chapter. The MB's historic decline will undoubtedly reverberate throughout the region and will likely impact its sister organizations.

In order to understand the direction in which the wider MB movement is headed, we need to evaluate the historical evolution of this particular trend. These include groups (that refer to themselves as MB) in Jordan, Syria, and Libya, as well as those that espouse the same ideology and approach (e.g., Tunisia's Ennahda, Morocco's Justice and Development Party, Yemen's al-Islah, Iraq's Hizb-i-Islami, Kuwait's HADAS, Algeria's Movement of Society for Peace, the Palestinian Territories' HAMAS, and Pakistan's Jamaat-i-Islami). Considering its origins in the 1920s and the country's geographic proximity to Jordan and Syria, the MB's principal manifestations developed in these neighboring countries. Each one faces its own unique geopolitical circumstances and trajectories, despite the common goal of achieving their political objectives via electoral means. As each of them had to deal with different types of autocratic states, this is hardly surprising.

Despite decades of suppression, Egypt's MB never abandoned its approach to transforming the state via a gradual bottom-up strategy.[6] Thus each country's MB organization continues to operate in a pragmatic manner by following tactics and strategies appropriate for its specific circumstances and according to its leaders' preferences.[7] Even though it proved short-lived, the 2012 election of MB leader Mohamed Morsi as Egypt's first-ever elected president was a culmination of this decades-long strategy. In Syria, the MB opted for confrontation in large part due to the state's use of military force against the opposition-similar to what is currently happening. Staging an armed uprising during the late 1970s, it experienced a harsh crackdown by the Assad regime in 1982 and an ensuing organizational collapse from which it never fully recovered. In sharp contrast, the MB branch in Jordan has enjoyed a relatively cordial working relationship with the monarchy ever since its inception in the late 1940s.

This chapter examines the MB as an organization, an ideology in terms of the wider movement, and an approach (participatory Islamism) to bringing about political change in an increasingly volatile democratization process. In particular, we assess the organization in three different decades and then analyze its behavior since the 2011 Arab Spring. Each MB organization is independent, shuns violence as a tactic, and seeks to establish a democratic political system within an Islamic framework. We examine each branch's behavior while keeping the focus on the parent organization.

## The 1990s

Several key international and domestic developments during the 1990s shaped Egypt's strategy for managing the MB, its largest—officially outlawed but in practice tolerated to varying degrees—opposition movement and the country's wider Islamist landscape.[8] The Soviets were forced out of Afghanistan in 1989, and the Cold War ended with the Soviet Union' collapse in 1991 and the beginning of democratization in Eastern Europe. Many Arab war veterans, emboldened by the Soviets' defeat and subsequent crumbling of their empire, chose to ignore the fact that the United States-led international campaign was instrumental in their victory. Many of these battle-hardened and radicalized Islamists returned home believing that they could initiate similar transformative changes and overthrow their own autocratic leaders. For others, the Soviets' collapse and the democratic transformations in some of the communist bloc countries provided an example of democratic reform that could be emulated. This bifurcated Islamists into a minority camp that opted for confrontation with their own regimes, against those who chose to use democratic means for political change. These competing responses further sharpened the contours of the divide between rejector and participatory Islamists.

Two additional major regional developments took place in the early 1990s: (1) the 1991 Gulf War, in which major Arab countries joined the United States to reverse Iraq's occupation and subsequent annexation of Kuwait and (2) in Algeria, the military establishment's early 1992 annulment of national elections to keep the Islamist movement, the Front Islamique de Salut (FIS), from enjoying its imminent landslide victory. The intervention of the Algerian military derailed the electoral process and led to the subsequent bloody civil war. The 1991 American-led war against Iraq shook up the Middle East and the wider Muslim world, as well as divided the Muslims between those who were concerned that Saddam had occupied a fellow Muslim country versus those who resented their governments for supporting the American attack.[9] This proved to be a watershed moment, in that it led to a major radicalization of Islamists and brought Saudi Salafis into the Islamist orbit. Furthermore, the Saudi government's decision to allow its soil to serve as a staging ground for the war against Iraq played a major role in strengthening rejector Islamists, most notably al-Qaeda, that emerged soon after the war. We will elaborate on this genre of Islamists in greater detail in chapter six.

As participatory Islamists were losing ground to rejecters, the nearly simultaneous derailment of the Algerian democratic process further discredited participators. The Islamist insurgency, which broke out in response to the imposition of martial law, was an additional blow to them, for Arab states used those events to justify their resistance to political reform. This dashed the hopes of MB-minded participatory Islamists who were hoping to benefit from potential political openings in the 1990s. For the more extreme rejectors, this negative experience with elections reinforced their view that elections organized by autocratic regimes would not be honored. In addition to this, the Algerian experience provided a logical argument to buttress their ideological basis for rejecting democracy.

*Egypt*

The preceding events, which occurred a mere decade after insurrectionist Islamists affiliated with Tandheem al-Jihad (TaJ) assassinated President Anwar El-Sadat, led to a major crackdown on all Islamists, including the much larger Gamaah al-Islamiyah (GaI).[10] Hosni Mubarak, Sadat's successor, fought both groups while seeking to broaden his base of support by cautiously reaching out to the MB to help it combat jihadists, who were a clear threat to the state. This gave the mainstream Islamist group some room in which to expand. Despite this cooperation, however, the regime constantly manipulated the formal and informal rules of the political game[11] to keep the MB off-balance. Blaydes suggests that this was no more than the "old colonial device of dividing the opposition" between militants and moderates.[12] Similarly, Sadowski points out that "Mubarak sought to temper the demands of the Islamist 'legalists' by offering them a measure of power in exchange for the renunciation of revolutionary tactics."[13] By the 1990s, the regime was suppressing both participatory and rejecter Islamists indiscriminately. Blaydes opines that this conflation of moderates and radicals limited the MB's electoral opportunities in the 1990s, but that after the radical GaI announced its nonviolence initiative in 1997 and subsequent ideological reorientation, the MB was given more space to participate in the 2000 and 2005 elections.[14]

Although prohibited from operating as a legal political entity, the Mubarak regime nevertheless allowed the MB to spread throughout civil society in the form of student groups, professional syndicates, and social service-oriented nongovernmental organizations (NGOs). During the semi-competitive parliamentary elections, the MB enhanced its public presence by articulating its vision, promoting its agenda, creating a political space for itself, and signaling its willingness to play by the rules.[15] In the 1984 elections, it won 58 out of 454 seats in a coalition with the Wafd Party. In the 1987 polls, an MB alliance with the Labor and Liberal parties won 60 seats: 30, 27, and 3, respectively.

The rise of these opposition forces, especially the MB, in the polls during the 1980s caused the regime to institute new electoral laws in 1990. However, the Supreme Constitutional Court (SCC) ruled the resulting mixed voting system unconstitutional because it did not allow people to run as independents. On the surface, this judgment looked like it would free the opposition from being bound by the traditional lists and thresholds needed to secure its candidates' election. The ruling National Democratic Party (NDP), however, implemented the new system in such a way that it benefited from the subsequent redistricting by reducing the presence of opposition parties in the legislature, surely a key aim for any state that uses elections to fortify its autocratic nature.

Between the MB's rise and the Algerian democratic experiment, the Mubarak government grew extremely apprehensive about allowing multiparty polls. Furthermore, GaI had begun a fierce bombing and assassination campaign.[16] As Mubarak could no longer afford to use the MB as a significant lever against GaI and other militant forces,[17] the opportunities for the MB shrunk. While the GaI insurgency gave Cairo an opportunity to maintain its autocratic hold, the crisis in Algeria reinforced the international mood against Islamists in general. "One Man, One Vote, One Time" became the mantra of those who felt no Islamist could be trusted with an electoral victory.[18] Democratization suffered, and the international mood toward the Islamists soured to such an extent that very few people saw any distinction among the various groups. Many scholars and practitioners of democracy began to reiterate that the Arab/Muslim world was not ready for democratization because it rejected secularism. Furthermore, the rise of transnational jihadism in the form of al-Qaeda by the mid-1990s, as well as the suicide attacks staged by Hamas and Palestinian Islamic Jihad, convoluted the picture even further. The popular view in the West was that the differences among all such movements were negligible.

The MB thus found itself facing several struggles: (1) seeking to work within the system to the extent permitted and gradually expand that space, (2) trying to prove that it was not a radical force and thus was very different from the jihadists, and (3) dealing with its own internal group of reform-minded and younger leaders and activists who wanted it to assume a more liberal and centrist position. But given that the MB was a major organization with decades of history and discipline, these more liberal voices found minimal reception. According to the MB's leaders, they could not just abandon the principles upon which the movement had been built, especially given the growing competition from rival and more conservative Islamist forces.

This struggle led to al-Wasat (Centrist), a smaller and more liberal offshoot of the MB. Promoting itself as a far more pragmatic and moderate force,[19] it sought to advance itself by conforming to the state's strict criteria for legal political status in order to take advantage of the limited opportunity for political participation. Its members hoped that the party would be allowed to operate legally, which would help the drive toward democratization (then at a stand-still) as well as the mainstreaming of Islamism. The move failed, for Cairo never approved its application to operate as a political party.

### Jordan

The Jordanian branch of the Muslim Brotherhood (JMB) has long been integrated into the political mainstream, largely because it has always accepted the monarchy as legitimate.[20] Since the JMB's inception in the late 1940s, it has forged a strong working relationship with the Hashemite kingdom. The Islamist group and the royal family aligned in the 1950s and 1960s to contain the Nasserite and leftist forces, and the JMB remained loyal to the monarchy during the 1970–1971 civil war between the national armed forces and Palestine Liberation Organization (PLO) militiamen. Political parties were banned throughout much of the 1970s and 1980s, but the JMB was allowed to operate as a registered charity. In 1992, it officially established the Islamic Action Front (IAF) as a legally recognized political party under a new law that allowed political parties to be represented at the national level.[21] Since that date the IAF, initially recognized as a charitable organization and later on as a political party, has openly fielded candidates in parliamentary elections.[22]

The turning point was the 1989 parliamentary elections—the first one held after 1967 and as part of a major political liberalization initiative—in which JMB members running as independents won 22 of the Lower House's 80 seats and thereby became the largest bloc in Parliament with almost 40 percent of the seats. Emboldened by this electoral success, it announced that Parliament should be given greater authority. But as the JMB spoke out strongly against several foreign policy issues, especially Jordan's 1994 peace treaty with Israel, its relationship with the monarchy began to deteriorate.

To contain the JMB, the monarchy began restricting the IAF's activities to mosques and professional syndicates. More importantly, it altered the electoral law via redistricting so that the urban-based Islamist movement would find it harder to sustain its presence in Parliament. As Clark points out, Jordan used several institutional maneuvers to change its electoral system from a "multiple/transferable vote system in which voters could cast as many ballots as there were seats in their constituency, to a one-person, one vote system which led most voters to choose candidates from their extended families or tribes over ideological parties such as the IAF."[23] As a result, the JMB won just 16 seats in the 1993 election. The JMB and IAF, along with liberal and leftist groups, boycotted the 1997 elections after the monarchy refused to revise the electoral law—a classic case of altering the rules of the game to prevent further political openings.

Another key factor that worked well for the state was that setting up the IAF as a separate political party further complicated internal JMB politics,[24] for it took a while for the party to institutionalize and work in harmony with the parent body. Thus in addition to the state's electoral engineering and the JMB's historical relationship with the monarchy, the JMB's evolution from a movement to a party allowed Amman to contain it while it cautiously moved toward allowing electoral politics after an interregnum of over two decades and during the final years of King Hussein (d. 1999).

## The Palestinian Territories

Hamas is a unique MB manifestation with historic roots in the Palestinian Muslim Brotherhood (PMB), which have shaped its political and ideological outlook. In fact, this organization remains very much in the MB tradition despite its ongoing armed struggle against the Israeli occupation. In general, Hamas has tried to keep those two universes separate: militancy toward the occupation and electoral politics to achieve political power. With few exceptions, this bifurcation has largely been the rule. The overlap is driven by the ambiguity inherent in Palestine being a sub-state entity. Furthermore, since 2006–2007 Hamas has been in a gray area of being a militant non-state actor and a governing authority in Gaza.

Here, it would be helpful to provide a brief overview of the PMB, for since the mid-1940s the group has stressed its original formation as a nonviolent social, political, and religious entity. Yet it was also shaped by the Arab-Israeli wars that changed both historic Palestine's geography and the group's structure and outlook. When the West Bank and Gaza were under Jordanian and Egyptian control, respectively, the PMB influenced and was deeply influenced by both the MB and the JMB, as well as by the domestic politics in which they operated. Palestinians first became aware of the MB when Hassan al-Banna sent his younger brother Abd al-Rahman al-Banna there in 1935.[25] The first Palestinian branches were established in Jerusalem (1945) and Gaza (1946).

During the 1936–1939 Great Arab Revolt, the parent organization offered to send volunteers. However, the MB only joined the armed struggle during the first Arab-Israeli war in 1948, after which Israel was established as an independent nation-state. At that time, the PMB relied on its Egyptian counterpart fighting alongside the Egyptian forces. The existence of disagreements between the MB irregular militias and the Egyptian army on how to conduct the war, when coupled with the MB's campaign against King Farouk I and other Arab regimes for what it perceived as their betrayal of the anti-Zionist struggle, increased the pre-existing tensions with Cairo. The MB's anti-British struggle put it in conflict with Cairo; it was outlawed in December of that year.

In February 1949, as per the United Nations-brokered armistice agreement, Gaza came under Egyptian control. The PMB, which had been banned along with its parent organization, now came under formal Egyptian control and was forced to reconstitute itself under the banner of the Jam'iyyat al-Tawhid, a nonpolitical socio-religious movement.[26] As part of the 1949 armistice, the United Kingdom and the United States wanted Jordan (then Transjordan) to assume control of the West Bank; it formally annexed the region in 1950. The PMB located there thus became part of the Jordanian MB.

King Hussein needed the JMB's support to counter Nasserite and other leftist forces to ensure his kingdom's domestic stability. But perhaps more important was the strategic imperative of preventing Palestinian nationalist forces from using Jordan as a base of operations against Israel. When Nasser's Free Officer toppled the Egyptian monarchy in 1952 and received the MB's parent body initial approval, the new junta appointed a founding PMB member as mayor of the Gaza municipality. In return, the MB agreed to end the anti-Israel cross-border raids being made by its members within the Gaza security forces. A group of younger MB militants led by Khalil al-Wazir (Abu Jihad) and Salah Khalaf (Abu Iyad) opposed this decision, formed dissident factions, and later became top associates of Fatah founder Yasser Arafat.

These internal schisms took a back seat when the MB faced the regime's wrath over the attempted assassination of Nasser in 1954. In the ensuing systematic suppression of the Islamist movement, the PMB lost the mayoralty of Gaza. In addition to tensions with the new Egyptian regime in 1955, it also had to contend with cross-border Israeli raids. While Nasser initially wanted to avoid reprisals, mounting criticism that the military regime, just like the monarchy that it had overthrown, was unwilling to confront Israel eventually caused him to allow irregular Palestinian fighters to strike Israel. In October 1956, the second Arab-Israeli war erupted when Israel, the United Kingdom, and France attacked Egypt for nationalizing the Suez Canal. Israel seized control of Gaza the following month, and the brief occupation caused many of the more hardline elements to flee while the MB's core continued to avoid resistance or political activities. When Gaza was returned in March 1957, Cairo acted to prevent any Palestinian militant cross-border infiltration into Israel.

Hardcore members such as Abu Jihad relocated to Kuwait but continued to press the MB to carry on with the armed struggle. The MB in Gaza was neither willing nor able to do so, since Nasser had banned the Jam'iyyat al-Tawhid in 1958. By the time that Arafat, Abu Jihad, and Abu Iyad founded Fatah in Kuwait in 1959, Gaza's PMB branch had limited itself to cultural promotion activities in society. Members saw this as a way to counter the rising secular left-wing Arab nationalism that was becoming quite popular due to the Nasserite dynamic's increasing traction in the region. In contrast with the situation now, when Hamas and other

Palestinian Islamist groups are spearheading the armed struggle while Fatah/PLO pursue a non-confrontational path toward statehood, the Islamists at that time (who would later found Hamas) were avoiding confrontation while the secularists dominated the armed resistance scene. Hamas founder Sheikh Ahmed Yasin was emerging as a leader of Gaza's PMB, for those who had founded it in the 1940s had either died, defected to Fatah, or were keeping a low profile because of Cairo's crackdown. Seeing how the parent organization had been brutally suppressed, Yasin and his associates decided to stick to religious activities, which they saw as a critical prerequisite to any attempted physical liberation of Palestine.

Another key factor informing its passivity was that Fatah was at odds with Egypt, for Cairo was trying to control the Palestinian nationalist movement via the PLO (established in 1964). Fatah, which opposed this domination, was pushing for a more aggressive posture toward Israel, whereas the Yasin-led Gaza MB sought to avoid all controversial moves. Cairo's suppression of the MB reached its peak with Qutb's incarceration and execution. The PMB abandoned all resistance for nearly two decades, Fatah was still a few years away from taking over the PLO, and the Palestinian nationalist resistance in Gaza was controlled by George Habash's Arab Nationalist Movement. This latter group was aligned with the Palestinian Liberation Army, the military wing of the Egyptian-backed PLO.

The Arab defeat in 1967 played a key role in shifting Gaza's balance of power in favor of the MB. Israel, which now reoccupied Gaza for the long haul, spent the next few years clearing it of secular nationalist fighters—all except the MB network. After it seized the West Bank in the 1967 war, the indigenous MB branch became independent of the JMB (they had been a single organization for seventeen years, and cultivated relations with its West Bank counterparts because they were now under a common jurisdiction. In 1973 Gaza's MB operated under the Mujamma al-Islamiyah and soon began to develop its own institutions and embed itself in Gazan society. On its initiative, in 1978 the Gazan, West Bank, and JMB branches became a single organization and operated as such for the next two decades. Mujamma continued to follow the MB's gradualist bottom-up approach, whereas Yasin and the seven-member leadership committee firmly adhered to the idea that fighting the occupation without the people's support would not bring about a Palestinian Islamic state.

Israel found Mujamma to be a very useful Islamist group that it could cultivate to weaken the radical secular forces. That Gaza's Israeli military governor attended the inauguration ceremony of its key facility, the Jawrat al-Shams, shows the extent of convergence of Israeli and MB interests. The secular nationalist forces would point to Israeli toleration of this proto-Hamas organization as evidence that the Islamist movement was collaborating with Israel and thus betraying the nationalist cause. A popular claim among Hamas' Palestinian/Arab/Muslim opponents is that Israel created it to undermine the Palestinian nationalist struggle. Similarly, some Israelis depict Hamas as a *golem* (a Jewish folklore creature who, fashioned from mud and brought to life, ultimately escapes his master).

Hamas and its supporters, on the other hand, claim that the group is the successor to the resistance movement initiated by Syrian cleric Izz al-Deen al-Qassam, who was killed in 1935 while fighting British forces in Mandatory Palestine. But as

Jean-Pierre Filiu argues, the reality is somewhere in between.[27] The level of contact between the Mujamma and Tel Aviv was strong enough that Mahmoud Zahar, the most radical member of Hamas' current senior leadership and its deputy leader in Gaza, once met with then Defense Minister Yitzhak Rabin.[28] What was betrayal for the radical secularists was expediency for the pragmatic Islamists and something that did not violate religious principles. After all, al-Banna had maintained channels with British occupation authorities in Egypt during the MB's early years. Such reasoning was justifiable for Mujamma but not for its secular opponents, which led to friction.

The budding Yasin-led Islamist group's non-hostile attitude toward the occupation authorities yielded great dividends; less than a generation after the occupation, the number of mosques in Gaza had doubled. While the Islamists had gained ground since the 1967 war, the secularists, despite their decisively dominant position in the Palestinian landscape, were being weakened by major setbacks, among them Fatah and PLO's expulsion from Jordan and then Lebanon, respectively, as well as the loss of Egypt as a main backer after it signed the 1978 Camp David Accords.

As the secularists were moving away from armed struggle, Islamists began gravitating toward it. While Hamas' predecessor still firmly opposed armed resistance, the 1979 Iranian revolution inspired a number of its younger members who would disagree with its strategy of first creating an Islamic state and then liberating Palestine. Led by Abdel-Qadir al-Awdah and Fathi Shiqaqi, in the early 1980s these people established the Palestinian Islamic Jihad (PIJ), the second largest Palestinian Islamist movement. According to Azzam Tamimi, the prominent London-based Palestinian Islamist intellectual who has been affiliated with both the JMB and Hamas, Awdah and Shiqaqi were expelled from the MB in the 1970s for indiscipline.[29] The PIJ's rise and attacks against Israel placed considerable pressure on Hamas' predecessor, which continued to insist on a non-confrontational approach.

After the outbreak of the First Intifada (December 1987) Mujamma's leadership moved to adopt armed resistance. But even then it initially sought to remain aloof from the protests sparked during the funerals held for four Palestinians killed when an Israeli tank transporter collided with their vehicles in northern Gaza. Such was the magnitude of the unrest, which came at a time of increased resentment of the occupation forces, that that same evening the group's seven top leaders (viz., Sheikh Ahmad Yassin, Abd al-Aziz al-Rantissi, Salah Shihadah, Abd al-Fattah Dukhan, Muhammad Shamah, Ibrahim al-Yazuri, and Isa Al-Nashar), met and established the Harakat al-Muqawamah al-Islamiyah (The Islamic Resistance Movement), which came to be known by its acronym Hamas.[30] Thus, after avoiding armed resistance for most of the Israeli-Palestinian conflict and confining itself to propagating Islam, the MB's Palestinian counterpart embraced armed struggle. In Hamas' first attack in 1989, it abducted and killed two Israeli soldiers. In retaliation, Israel arrested Yasin and sentenced him to 15 years in prison. Ironically, in 1988 Fatah/PLO, which had fought with Israel for most of its existence, renounced violence, recognized Israel, and opened negotiations. Around the same time Hamas, whose leaders for nearly two generations had done their best to avoid conflict with Israel and even cooperated with the occupation for the latter half of that period, denounced the peace process.

Hamas founded its military wing, the Izz al-Deen al-Qassam Brigades, in 1991 and began a long campaign of terrorist attacks against Israel. Meanwhile, the First Gulf War and the PLO's alignment with Saddam Hussein led Kuwait to expel several hundred thousand Palestinian workers. A number of Hamas leaders, including its current chief Khaled Meshaal, moved to Jordan (where they held citizenship) and opened Hamas' political bureau with the government's consent. This created many problems for both sides, as the movement was pursuing armed conflict even though Fatah/the PLO had signed the Oslo Accords (1993) and Jordan had concluded its own peace treaty with Israel (1994). These divergent trajectories led to tension between Hamas and Amman. Furthermore, the fact that the two Palestinian MB branches and the Jordanian branch had merged in 1978 became a major headache when Hamas was founded as the PMB's de facto successor. This fractured the JMB between the "hawks" who prioritized the Palestinian struggle and the "doves" who wanted the Jordanian branch to focus on national issues. Amman saw both of these developments as threats to its national security.

Within the Occupied Territories, the Oslo Accords led to the Palestinian National Authority (PNA), which was set up in 1994. Hamas boycotted the first elections to the Palestinian Legislative Council (PLC) in 1996 because it opposed the peace process. Here it is important to note that Hamas' non-participation does not mean that it is a rejecter group, for it was rejecting the electoral process not on religious grounds, but because it rejected any political structures and processes created under occupation. Hamas thus faced opposition on three fronts: Israel, the PNA, and Jordan. In the case of Jordan, King Hussein was able to keep the situation in check. In fact, when the Israeli intelligence service tried to assassinate Meshaal in a 1997 poisoning incident, the king intervened and was able to get the Israelis to provide the antidote and even secure the release of Hamas's founder Yasin. After the king's death in 1999, his son and successor Abdullah II moved to get rid of the Hamas politburo and thus expelled Meshaal and his colleagues. They relocated to Syria, where they would spend the next decade.

The detailed discussion presented above underscores that the Palestinian movement, at its core, is an MB-style Islamist entity. Similar to the Egyptian MB, Hamas has no ideological qualms with democracy and even embraces electoral politics, as was evident in its decision to participate in the 2006 elections (particularly after boycotting the first Palestinian legislative polls a decade earlier). Thus it is clearly a participatory Islamist organization. Yet it is distinct from all other MB-type Islamist movements because of the political context in which it operates. First, unlike all other MB type groups, Hamas operates in a non-state context. Second, it must contend with its secular rival, Fatah, which controls the West Bank and is internationally recognized as synonymous with the PNA. This struggle shapes the geopolitical divide between the two Palestinian territories. Third Hamas, as the governing party in Gaza, exists in a grey zone somewhere between a non-state actor engaged in terrorism against Israel and the ruling body of Gaza defending its dominion from Israeli military action. Fourth, and complicating the situation further, Hamas refuses to recognize Israel and tries to balance armed struggle against occupation with behaving as a participatory Islamist movement within the Palestinian context.

## Post-9/11

The 9/11 attacks, which put all Islamist movements under the most intense spotlight, created a sense of global urgency to understand the Islamist universe—both in terms of mapping out a threat matrix and to distinguish "moderate" from "radical" and "militant" Islamists. This event also shook up the Islamist landscape. For example it forced MB-type Islamists, who were already trying to distinguish themselves from al-Qaeda and jihadists, to highlight their moderation.[31] As a result, the preexisting intra-Islamist contention assumed a whole new dimension.

In addition, 9/11 posed both a threat and an opportunity for the MB. It was a threat because of the fear that the United States would conflate al-Qaeda with all other Islamist groups. But it was also an opportunity for the MB to clearly distinguish itself from its radical and militant rivals. This would help its leadership refute the dominant viewpoint among Western policymakers that more or less considered even those Islamists engaged in electoral politics as untrustworthy. The Islamists sought to take advantage of the George W. Bush administration's democracy promotion efforts, which they saw as a lever to ingratiate themselves with Washington. During this time, the traditional Washington view that only secularism could counter Islamism was slowly being replaced by the idea that jihadism and radical Islamism could be contained by working with moderate Islamists. This policy shift gave credence to the MB movement against the autocratic regimes claims.

However, as the MB also had to manage threats from within, it did not want to immediately present itself as the sought-for moderate Islamist force because that could undermine its status among its own constituency. Many Islamists and even ordinary Muslims believed, to varying degrees, that the Washington-led "war on terror" was actually a global campaign against Islam designed to make Muslims conform to Western culture. The MB and its associates were also concerned that the growing Islam–West polarization, due to the wars in Afghanistan and Iraq as well as global counterterrorism efforts, could enable others to view their mantra of "moderation" as an attempt to satisfy Western expectations of "acceptable" Islam.[32] They worried that this dynamic, along with the rise of radicalism, could undermine the MB's position as the mainstream Islamist movement. It therefore criticized the "war on terror" while hoping to benefit from the growing calls in Washington for political reform and regime change in Afghanistan and Iraq. Along with other participatory Islamist forces, it was also engaged in a balancing act with the United States, for its members did not want their criticism to be seen as support for al-Qaeda and its jihadist allies.[33]

Moreover, participatory Islamists were anxious not to provide any ammunition to the still-dominant group within the American policy community who saw all Islamists calling for democracy as concealing their radicalism under the garb of political reform.[34] Thus these mainstream Islamists were largely unable to convince Washington that they were the best partners for countering radicalism and militancy. However, they did benefit indirectly by the Bush administration's overthrow of the Taliban and Saddam and the subsequent series of elections that empowered Islamists.[35]

In the fall of 2002, Islamists made significant political gains in several Muslim-majority lands. This began in September in Morocco, where the Islamist Justice and Development Party (JDP) won 42 seats and came in a close third, which made it part of the coalition government. The most significant development, however, was the landslide victory of Turkey's post-Islamist Justice and Development Party (AKP: Adalet va Kalkilma Partisi) at the November 2002 polls. Its winning of 363 out of 550 seats enabled it to form the country's first single-party government in 15 years. The success of this pragmatic conservative successor to a series of banned Islamist parties transformed it into a template for the MB and other like-minded parties. Turkey thus became notable for having a government run by an Islamist-rooted party that governed successfully at home and maintained balanced relations between the Muslim world and the West. In June 2003, Jordan's IAF gained 22 percent of the seats in the parliamentary elections by winning 18 seats and six additional sympathizers. By 2007, it hoped to gain further seats in the municipal and national elections. Despite the regime's continued effort to weaken the JMB's political arm, the IAF continues to work within the system.[36]

The 2005 election in Egypt catapulted the MB to the political forefront, for given its major electoral success and the immense pressure from the Bush administration, the Mubarak regime was forced to allow freer elections. The legislative polls enabled the MB to secure a six-fold increase in its strength in Parliament by winning 88 seats. Parliamentary elections in Afghanistan and Iraq saw the rise of Sunni and Shia Islamists who had earlier worked with the United States to effect regime change in both countries. Although marred by many problems, at a bare minimum the Afghan and Iraqi political processes at least showed that Washington was prepared to tactically align itself with participatory Islamists to combat rejector and insurrectionist Islamists. Washington's cooperation with Iraq's Islamists was all the more evident, given that the latter dominated the Shia and Sunni vote banks in the December 2005 election. The Shia United Iraqi Alliance won 128 out of the 275 seats in the unicameral chamber; the Tawafoq Iraq Front, dominated by the Sunni-Islamist Iraqi Islamic Party (the Iraqi MB wing), won 44 seats.

A month later in January 2006, Hamas' first-ever foray into electoral participation netted it 74 of the 132 seats in the PLC. This was the first time that an MB organization had won an election. What was even more problematic is that a group still at war with Israel now dominated the PNA.[37] In November of the same year, the Bahraini monarchy in league with the al-Menbar (the local MB group) and al-Asalah (Salafis) parties gained a combined 13 seats in the 40-seat legislature; al-Wefaq, the main Shia Islamist group, won 17 seats. Manama, along with its Saudi allies, sought to limit the Shia's electoral rise by facilitating a Sunni Islamist victory.[38] While the country's Parliament has no real power, the electoral results did translate into Islamist gains at the ballot box.

Clearly, Islamism and democratization were in play well before the Arab Spring. Much of this political space was facilitated by the rise of an increasingly open discourse in the form of satellite television channels, particularly al-Jazeera, that became even more widespread after the 9/11 attacks. Furthermore, the proliferation of the Internet, email, and social media (e.g., Facebook and Twitter) began eroding the barriers erected by autocratic states. As a result of their organizational prowess participatory Islamists could exploit these limited democratic openings, whereas secular forces could not distinguish themselves from the secular autocratic ruling elites. These few democratic openings and the Islamists' subsequent electoral gains were an unintended—and certainly an undesirable—consequence of Washington's post-9/11 imperatives. The United States was completely unprepared to deal with the newly empowered Islamists, fearing that they would destabilize the incumbent autocratic regimes that were helping it counter al-Qaeda. The Bush administration therefore scaled back its earlier push for democratization, focused on the jihadist threat, and remained unaware of regional realities until the Arab Spring erupted.

*The Palestinian Territories*

The 9/11 attacks, along with the militancy launched by PIJ and the Fatah-allied al-Aqsa Martyrs Brigades, complicated Hamas' militancy campaign at a time when it was already facing political problems because of its suicide attacks targeting Israeli civilians. Such operations undermined its claim that it was resisting the occupation. After 9/11, Hamas' challenges grew exponentially because it was being seen as no different from al-Qaeda. Meanwhile, Israel responded with targeted assassinations of Hamas leaders. The outbreak of the Second Intifada in 2000 had already intensified the violence in the territories. Under pressure in early 2004, Yasin and the group's deputy leader Abdel-Aziz Rantissi announced that Hamas would end its armed resistance if Israel withdrew to the 1967 borders and a Palestinian state was established in the West Bank and Gaza. They also offered a ten-year ceasefire, thereby acknowledging that all of mandatory Palestine could not be liberated at once. Israel, which saw the offer as a Hamas attempt to buy time to enhance its military capabilities and become a state actor, opted instead for a military response. Yasin and Rantissi were killed in separate airstrikes in the spring of 2004, which represented a significant setback for Hamas both in terms of a loss of leadership and, more importantly, the ability to continue the suicide bombing campaign.

The following year, Israel unilaterally withdrew from Gaza and thus ended the occupation of Hamas' core turf. In the same year, Hamas participated in the local municipal elections and won more than one-third of the municipal council seats. More significantly, it began moving toward a participatory role by taking part in the January 2006 legislative elections; it won 74 out of the 132 seats. But despite this shift and omitting the destruction of Israel as an objective from its election manifesto, Hamas did not renounce armed struggle or recognize Israel. It therefore faced a serious problem: It could not form the next PNA government, as this would involve compromising on both points, and yet it wanted to reap the benefits of its electoral success. Thus it tried to form a coalition government with Fatah. When Fatah refused to be part of the Hamas-led cabinet, the movement unveiled a new government in which its members held all key ministerial portfolios. This new government quickly ran into problems with the Fatah-dominated PNA establishment, especially given that the PNA was controlled by Fatah's chief: President Mahmoud Abbas.

Hamas' control of the government and its retention of an armed wing created more problems and led to clashes with Fatah-dominated Palestinian security organs. A coalition government was finally formed in March 2007 after both sides agreed to a Saudi-brokered power-sharing deal. But tensions continued because Hamas suspected that Fatah, the United States, and Israel were collaborating to oust the Hamas-led government and neutralize the movement itself. Already weakened in the West Bank by the Israeli forces' arrest of its lawmakers and ministers based there (in retaliation for the June 2006 cross-border raid in which Hamas militants had abducted Israeli soldier Gilad Shalit), Hamas sought to preempt its own ouster by forcibly seizing control of Gaza in June 2007. This essentially divided the two geographically separated Palestinian Territories into two competing governing entities.

Hamas has found it extremely difficult to govern Gaza because of the Israeli blockade and Egypt's going along with it. It also had to balance being an armed resistance movement and a government. The December 2008 war showed that its ongoing resistance efforts were undermining local support, for Gazans kept on losing their lives and property. As it became even more consumed with the affairs of governance, Hamas obviously had to compromise on the resistance front. This resulted in competition from rival Islamist groups (e.g., the PIJ) but, and more importantly, also from the Salafi and jihadist groups that had gained ground over the years. These jihadist groups criticized Hamas for not implementing shari'a and began to take aggressive actions, such as firing rockets into Israel against the wishes of the Hamas-run administration.

The major incident, however, occurred during August 2009 when a Salafi preacher was leading a jihadist group announced from his mosque the establishment of an "Islamic emirate" in Gaza. Hamas sent in its security forces, and the renegade jihadist leader and many others died in the ensuing gun battle.[39] By the end of the 2000s, Hamas had evolved from being purely a militant Islamist group fighting against Israel to a governing entity. All of its efforts to reconcile with Fatah and resume the political process that had been disrupted shortly after the 2006 elections have failed. For all intents and purposes, Hamas had taken power by force and thus evolved into an authoritarian ruling entity.

## The Arab Spring and Beyond

The protests in Tunisia in mid-December 2010 began as a minor event but quickly mushroomed into the most significant geopolitical transformation that the region had witnessed since the founding of the modern Arab nation-states. Autocratic regimes that had successfully suppressed dissent for decades were now faced with an unprecedented scale of social mobilization—in great part made possible by advances in communication technology. Social media allowed people to organize demonstrations that highlighted a new social norm that had been in the making for years. At a time when the regional landscape had shifted dramatically, the United States remained preoccupied with the post-9/11 paradigm that focused its energies on the jihadist war. For this reason, even after weeks of protests in Tunisia, Washington, along with most of the world, did not realize that the region's regimes could no longer maintain power through coercive means. Only after Tunisia's long-time dictator fled on January 14, 2012, did the United States realize that it was no longer dealing with business as usual. When the unrest spread to Egypt and then to Libya, Yemen, and Bahrain, Washington finally understood that the demand for democracy (as opposed to jihadism) was the real threat to stability in the greater Middle East.

Ben-Ali's fall was unprecedented for the Arab world; however, Tunisia's geopolitical obscurity meant that it was of limited consequence. When Mubarak resigned on February 11, the regional implications became clearer. Well aware that Islamists were the best placed to benefit from the resulting political vacuum, the United States quickly tried to manage the transition. But its misunderstanding of the MB and its counterparts' nature raised the fear that the ongoing instability might undermine its regional geostrategic interests. Parallels were drawn with the 1989 democratic revolutions in Eastern Europe that toppled despotic communist regimes. The major difference between the rise of eastern European liberal democratic movements and Arab Islamist forces, however, could not be ignored. The most critical question was whether the MB and/or more hardline Islamists would hijack the "revolutions," as the Ayatollah Khomeini-led Iranian clerical movement had done with their liberal and leftist collaborators after overthrowing the Shah in 1979. Although a small number of experts rejected any such comparison as erroneous, the popular view among Western governments and the general public was at best agnostic. Most observers were between excitement about the prospects of the Arab world embracing liberal democracy and trepidations about the Islamists' commitment to democracy.

Such concerns was driven by a misreading of the scale of change underway. Further convoluting their collective viewfinder was the monolithic view of a regional fast-paced singular dynamic that ignored the significant variances within specific national contexts. The Eastern European experience and the rather quick fall of Ben-Ali and Mubarak led many to believe that a domino effect had been set in motion, and that sooner rather than later regime change would be repeated in Libya, Yemen, Bahrain, and Syria. But what most observers did not realize that the protestors were not seeking the overthrow of the entire regime. Rather they were focused on the removal of the president along with his family and friends. Towards this end the public relied on the military establishments (the real regime) to help them oust the government. For this reason, the end result was not regime-change; rather the removal of its public faces (the president and the ruling party). The regime sought to preserve itself by allowing the incumbent leader to fall, after which—and more importantly—it sought to lead the transition in order to control its scope and movement toward a multiparty system as well as to limit the political parties' empowerment.

Contrary to popular perceptions, driving the Arab rulers from power did not constitute revolutions as in most cases the *regimes* survived. This worked to the advantage of those concerned with how democratization would benefit the Islamists. Around this time, the ongoing process that came to be known as the Arab Spring began to show its true evolutionary nature. As the pace of change slowed, it gradually became clear that the security establishments, although weakened by recent events, were nevertheless far more organized and coherent than the protesters. Empowering the regimes even further was the dependency of those seeking political reform upon the military to effect the desired change, not to mention the reality of pro-democracy forces divided along ideological lines instead of just the generic Islamist–secularist divide. Thus both camps suffered from significant partisan rivalries (e.g., MB vs. Salafis, liberals vs. leftists). The security establishments exploited these differences to ensure that change would be a slow-motion, non-threatening process.

As the popular uprising spread, it adapted itself to each country's unique geopolitical underpinnings and thus produced different results. Meanwhile the MB-type Islamists, given their own specific national contexts and evolutionary paths, embraced this new era and sought to work within the space allowed by the regime. The key point was that the autocratic systems had opened just enough to allow *participatory Islamists* to try and become stakeholders in the state.

## Tunisia

This tiny North African country continues to lead the transition. It represents the most successful case in which participatory Islamists still play a critical role in the democratization process, despite major challenges from rejector Islamists and radical secularists. Much of the success has to do with Ennahda's relatively liberal form of Islamism, particularly under the leadership of Rachid al-Ghannouchi, its principal ideologue.[40] Although founded on the Egyptian MB model in the 1980s, over the past two decades Ennahda has become quite comfortable with secularism, a civil state, and pluralism and thus now has more in common with the AKP than with the MB. While this heavily proscribed party neither instigated nor led the uprising against Ben-Ali, it quickly emerged as a major national force largely due to Ghannouchi's return from exile in London. His return was facilitated by the military establishment's guarantee of the new atmosphere that had arisen. This new political environment also enjoyed the firm support of the judiciary and large parts of the civilian bureaucracy for a genuine (albeit cautious) transition. Thus within weeks of Ben-Ali's ouster the interim government purged (under continuing public pressure) all vestiges of the former dictator's ruling Constitutional Democratic Rally (RCD) party, outlawed the RCD itself, and disbanded Ben-Ali's internal security apparatus.

Most importantly, it allowed Ennahda to lead a coalition government with two secular parties (Congress for a Republic and Etakattol) after it won the October 2011 parliamentary elections. Such a cooperative attitude cannot simply be explained as a result of acting under public pressure. Far more important was Ennahda's emphasis on achieving the rule of law instead of pursuing an ideological agenda. Categorically stating that it would not impose religion in matters of public affairs helped create a democratic space in which Islamists and secularists could negotiate and begin formulating a new consensus-based constitution. The various stakeholders also agreed that the Constituent Assembly (CA) would have a year to create a new charter, for during this time the government had to find a way to stabilize the country and address the underlying economic issues that had triggered the uprising.

The coalition government has simultaneously come under tremendous pressure from Salafists and jihadists, as well as from secular opponents within the state and the broader society. This complex political struggle is the main reason why the CA, dominated by Ennahda and its two secular partners, has failed to produce a new charter well beyond the original deadline of fall 2012. The ongoing instability has prevented the interim government from addressing the economic woes and worsening security environment (especially due to Salafist vigilantism and jihadism). The assassination of two prominent secular politicians within a six-month period in early 2013 brought matters to a head: The Islamist-led provisional authority was forced to step down in favor of a neutral caretaker government. Ennahda remains in talks with the country's powerful national trade union, the Union Generale Tunisienne du Travail (UGTT), to secure a negotiated settlement to avoid a breakdown in the transition that began after the October 2011 elections. It is unclear if Ennahda will achieve its goal. What is certain, though, is that Tunisia's Islamist movement, learning from the MB's experience in Egypt, is trying to reach an accommodation with its secularist opponents. By agreeing to a technocratic caretaker administration, it is hoping that its secularist opponents (e.g., Nidaa Tounes) will cooperate in jointly completing the constitution-writing process.

These problems notwithstanding, Tunisia remains the region's leader both in terms of democratization and in strengthening participatory Islamism. The North African state has shown early signs of a maturity on three levels: (1) The mass uprising that toppled a decades-old autocratic polity was relatively peaceful, (2) The country has avoided ideological polarization between Islamists and secularists, and (3) its indigenous Islamists are integral to the ongoing democratization process. If what has happened since the toppling of Ben-Ali is any indication, Tunisia will likely continue to make gradual progress toward democracy despite future almost certain disruptions.

## Egypt

Egypt, the most Arab populous state, is the region's intellectual leader and birthplace of its two rival ideologies: Arab nationalism and Islamism. Nearly three years after Mubarak's fall, the country remains in flux with its future uncertain largely due to the autocratic nature of the secular modern republic and its struggle with the Islamist MB organization. Given that the republic was founded in 1952 via a military coup, the state continues to be heavily dominated by the military. In 1967 the armed forces decided to rule from behind the scenes, with the result that the civilian single-party state remained largely under its control.[41] Throughout its 60-year history, the MB has challenged this military-dominated polity. In addition to their ideological differences, accommodation was impossible because the Islamist movement sought a political system that would subordinate the military to civilian authorities. Therefore, during its 15 years of direct military rule followed by 44 years of a single-party state, the military contained the MB by denying it legal status and conducting periodic crackdowns. When Mubarak's fall rendered the whole system obsolete, the military quickly realized that the Supreme Council of the Armed Forces (SCAF) could not rule as a junta for too long. Therefore, it had to find a way to control the transition's scope, direction, and pace so that it could, even after handing power over to an elected government, manage the multiparty system.

Allowing multiparty politics (albeit begrudgingly) meant that the MB had to be accommodated. As a result, SCAF made it easy for the MB's newly formed Freedom and Justice Party (FJP) to obtain an official license. But SCAF also engaged in private as well as public negotiations with the MB to exploit the latter's desire for early elections to counter the demands of secular youth groups who wanted the military to cede power before any polls were held. The generals also used the Islamist–secularist divide and intra-Islamist rivalries to keep the MB in check. Most importantly, it used the judiciary and its own power to reverse gains made by the MB and the Salafis in the parliamentary polls and to undermine Islamist efforts to draft a new constitution. In June 2012, the Supreme Constitutional Court (SCC) declared the parliamentary election won by the Islamists to be unconstitutional on the grounds that the electoral process was invalid. A week later SCAF limited the president's powers. The military regime realized that Morsi would most likely win the presidential election, and the MB was already the most powerful bloc in the legislative branch. In addition to preventing the MB from dominating both the legislative and executive branches, the military limited the powers of the presidency.[42]

Despite these constraints Morsi attempted to reverse Parliament's dissolution, an act that set the stage for a battle of wills between himself and the judges. Morsi and the MB were concerned that unelected judges would try to block the elected officials' power to shape the new constitution. As Sadiki points out, the judges' position smacked of "dictatorship," especially considering that the existing courts and many of the judges were unelected and mainly relics of the Mubarak regime.[43] Before Morsi was elected, the ruling military council assumed legislative powers after the court dissolved the Lower House of Parliament. In an effort to circumvent all of these obstacles, Morsi tried to temporarily revive the dissolved Islamist-dominated Parliament to support the MB's goal of crafting a new constitution, one that would have electoral legitimacy. The SCC blocked this move, and the MB turned to the CA to push ahead with drafting the constitution.

While he was struggling with the judges, Morsi tried to re-shape the military into a slightly more cooperative institution by, among other moves, dismissing SCAF's top generals in a calculated fashion and working with the second-tier commanders. This move did not mean that he was powerful enough to subordinate the armed forces; in fact, it was not possible for him to do so within a couple of months of assuming office. Rather, to a large extent the military allowed him to make this reshuffle so it could move ahead with its long overdue and planned leadership transition. As a result, Col.-Gen. Abdel-Fattah El-Sisi emerged as military chief and defense minister, and a new set of top generals took over the leadership of Egypt's most powerful institution. The MB pursued an extremely cooperative policy with SCAF's new leadership, thinking that its non-challenging attitude would allow it to gradually consolidate its hold on power.

Meanwhile, Morsi and the MB pursued a policy informed by a majoritarian view of democracy and tried to dominate the constitutional process at the expense of the secularist political forces. The CA's composition became a controversial subject, for it was dominated by Islamists that formed the majority in Parliament. Secular opponents of the MB and the Salafis objected vehemently to their minority presence and the judiciary kept delaying a ruling on the CA legality, which allowed Islamists to make considerable headway in drafting the new charter. Fearful that the judiciary would strike down the body and derail the constitution-writing process, in late November 2012 Morsi bestowed upon himself extraordinary powers and declared the CA outside the purview of the courts. Secularist political groups, already upset at their marginal role in the constitution-writing process, took to the streets proclaiming that the MB was usurping power. Separately, most of the secular parties banded together to form the National Salvation Front (NSF) two days after this decree, a development that underscored the growing polarization between Islamists and secularists.

Morsi portrayed the decree as a temporary move designed to overcome the deadlock stalling the country's transition. To the NSF, which failed to address the secular parties' incoherence and subsequent weakness, the move represented a power grab by the MB. The decree proved to be the last straw for the secular opposition parties and the beginning of the end for the Morsi administration. Even though Morsi was forced to backtrack on the decree, the damage had been done. The MB passed the constitution via a national referendum in December 2012, despite the fact that it was rapidly losing public support. This success reinforced the secularists' fears of the MB's domination of the post-Mubarak political system. With the constitution finalized, they were all the more concerned that the Islamists were poised to win a fresh round of parliamentary polls. In the final days of 2012, Morsi appointed 90 members to the Upper House (Shura Council) of Parliament, thereby filling the last third of the vacant seats. This occurred three days before the election commission announced that the new charter had been approved by slightly under 64 percent of the voters. A few days after its passage, Morsi handed over the legislative power he had given himself a month earlier to the Upper House and called upon it to speed up work on legislation dealing with the elections to the Lower House.

In the first quarter of 2013, Morsi expanded his cabinet with additional MB members despite demands for a more inclusive government. Attempts to negotiate with the NSF proved futile because his administration refused to form a national unity government and amend controversial clauses within the charter. Nation-wide protests soon broke out, which only worsened the country's political and security situation. The Salafist al-Nour Party tried to mediate between the MB and the NSF, but unsuccessfully. In fact, al-Nour also parted ways with the MB over concerns with how the Morsi government was handling what was rapidly brewing into a major crisis. When the government announced in late February that fresh elections to the Lower House of Parliament would be held in April, the judiciary lodged a strong protest. In early March the AC overruled Morsi's attempts to hold legislative elections. In April, when he was trying to mend fences with the judiciary, it was too late; in fact, many of his own advisers had already abandoned him by then. May proved to be a pivotal month, given that the Tamarrod (Rebel) movement was founded and began trying to mobilize national protests through a signature campaign aiming to force Morsi to resign.

The economic woes making life increasingly difficult for the average Egyptian worked to Tamarrod's advantage. Improving the economy within a year may not have been realistic for any new leader; however, the deteriorating economic conditions only added to the political grievances against the Morsi government. The new president further antagonized his opponents by appointing 16 governors in June— mostly MB members and one from Gamaah al-Islamiyah who was appointed to the province of Luxor, where members of the ex-jihadist group had staged a major terrorist attack on a Pharaonic temple complex in 1997; nearly 60 foreign tourists had been killed. The MB actually accelerated the gathering anti-Morsi momentum by mobilizing its own supporters to counter Tamarrod's call for protests. The military's strong response to the growing threat of street violence consisted of El-Sisi warning Morsi that the military would be forced to intervene if he could not defuse the increasing tension. The military had hoped that the MB would be able to replace the disbanded NDP as its civilian partner. Even though the MB went to great lengths to accommodate the military's wishes, the Islamist government lost its public support, especially in the wake of the Tamarrod-led protest. The millions of Egyptians who flooded the streets on June 30 convinced the military that it was time to switch sides; hence, it mounted the July 3 coup. Since that event, the military has continued to consolidate power and crack down on the MB and its allies, thereby arresting the country's transition toward democratic rule. Thus, the authoritarian state demonstrated its hold over the political system despite the transition to multiparty politics.

*Morocco*

Morocco has held multiparty elections since obtaining its independence in 1956. In recent decades it has allowed Islamist political participation, which facilitated the Parti Justice et Developpement's (PJD; aka the Justice and Development Party) rise. The prominence of the PJD precedes the Arab Spring by nearly a decade. The PJD, along with al-Adl wa al-Ihsan (Justice and Spirtuality), are the country's two major Islamist organizations. Since its inception in 1987, the latter has refused to recognize the monarchy's legitimacy and thus has remained officially proscribed but tolerated. In contrast the PJD, whose roots date back to the 1960s, has always been a participatory Islamist group. Like Egypt's MB, its strong grassroots connection has given it a vast support base mainly among lower- and middle-class

Moroccans. Thus it is more popular than many of the older and more established political parties.[44] The palace, however, held a great deal of power—including the critical right to appoint the prime minister—which meant that Parliament's powers were highly curtailed. In the wake of the Arab Spring, King Muhammad VI quickly sought to preempt any serious spillover by initiating a unilateral process of reform.

The PJD has never questioned the nation-state's legitimacy and has always recognized its political framework as the only legitimate arena for its members' actions.[45] Thus it has continued to operate pragmatically and remains an ally of the monarchy. This was evident when the king sought to revise the 2004 family code, which some hardline Islamists considered a contravention of Islamic law.[46] The PJD, on the other hand, argued that its members should support the revisions because they were enacted democratically and because the party is committed to both Islamic principles and democracy.[47]

By early fall 2011 the country had a new constitution, and in November of that year held relatively free and fair elections. The PJD won 107 seats and the Istiqlal Party, its closest secular competitor, gained 60 out of the 305 seats up for grabs. The most notable change in the new constitution was the king's transferal of many of his powers, including the nomination of the prime minister, to Parliament. As a result, PJD leader Abdelilah Benkirane became prime minister. The palace was well aware that an election that was freer and fairer than previous ones would result in a PJD victory. Yet it was also confident that the Islamist party would not turn against it and would also be constrained by a coalition government composed of the various secular groups that had won the remaining 288 seats. The new constitution and a PJD-led government allowed the monarchy to avoid the problems facing other Arab states. By embracing limited but key reforms, the regime has managed to maintain power.

The PJD now operates within the competitive nature of politics and its pluralist imperative. As Hamzawy points out, it has adopted this attitude both in substance and in rhetoric, which has led to a decline in its former exclusionary religious rhetoric directed toward the ruling establishment and/or liberal and leftist opposition actors. It has also caused MB-type Islamists to gradually move away from ideological diatribes and categorical judgments and toward formulating practical political platforms and devising constructive plans to influence public policy.[48] The year 2013 proved to be a very rocky one for the PJD-led government. The ruling Islamist party has for months been at odds with its former main secular coalition partner, the Istiqlal Party, over power-sharing disagreements and economic policies. Morsi's ouster energized the PJD's secular rivals both inside and outside Parliament to try to weaken the Islamist government. This was especially the case when the king quickly congratulated Morsi's replacement, President Adly Mansour, and the pro-palace Authenticity and Modernity Party supported the coup as being in the interest of Egyptian democracy.

Morsi's ouster clearly had ramifications for the entire region. The PJD was forced to make some calculated adjustments based on what had happened in Egypt. But its years of experience in political pragmatism and accommodation enabled it to avoid a similar fate. Within days of the coup in Egypt, the PJD reached out to both King Muhammad VI and secular parties to resolve the crisis brought about by Istiqlal's departure from the ruling coalition. For several months it seemed that the end was near for Prime Minister Abdelilah Benkirane; however, in early September the Islamist party forged a deal with the National Rally of Independents, the third largest secular bloc in Parliament, to maintain its coalition government. For the time being, the PJD has averted the collapse of its government. But its need to pursue unpopular economic measures may still lead to early elections. That said, Morocco's participatory Islamists have been far more successful than even their Tunisian counterparts in working with their secularist competitors. The less contentious Islamist-secularist divide, especially when compared to Egypt, bodes well for the country's democratization experiment.

### Jordan

Although the Jordanian regime is glad that it is not facing any growing Arab Spring-related unrest—at least not yet—the king cannot ignore the persistence and increasing resentment of the monarchy. Unlike the Alaouites in Morocco, who have divided their internal Islamist movement between the PJD and the more radical al-Adl wa al-Ihsan, the Hashemite palace has to contend with the fact that the JMB is the only major Islamist movement. Consequently, the regime had to ensure that the JMB's influence in society did not translate into power within the state. This would explain why, after parliamentary elections were revived in 1989 and the JMB made a strong showing, the monarchy has concentrated on preventing the movement from enhancing its position in the legislature. While that strategy remains in place, the palace has had to deal with an unprecedented threat to its very foundation: the significantly declining support of the East Bankers, its traditional power base. These largely rural-based people, who make up roughly 40 percent of Jordan's population, have long dominated the country's public sector, security forces, civilian bureaucracy, and other areas of public life. Over the years, though, their situation has worsened due to losses in the agricultural sector, reduced public spending, privatization of state-owned enterprises, and corruption. Their continued domination of the legislature, given the regime's need to counter the JMB, has not offset their concerns about a loss of position due to what they see as the Palestinian majority gaining new privileges at their expense. Over the decades, these Palestinian-Jordanian citizens have embedded themselves in mainstream life, focusing on settling in urban areas (especially Amman) and eventually taking over a large portion of the private sector.

In many ways, this tribal discontent converges with the JMB's grievances against the state. Both groups oppose their disenfranchisement, albeit for different reasons. Further, although a sizeable portion of the JMB leadership is from the tribes, most of its core is concentrated in the urban areas. As a result, the two camps have adopted divergent approaches to the problems of governance: The JMB wants a level playing field in terms of electoral laws, which would mean scaling back tribal strength in the Lower House, whereas the tribes see the monarchy's alignment with the urban-dwelling Palestinian-Jordanians as a major problem. King Abdullah II needs to balance the East Bankers and Palestinian-Jordanian citizens, especially given the unrest among the former. The JMB's membership and constituency contains a large component of the latter group. In a rare television interview on July 1, 2012, the king called upon the JMB to participate in the January 2013 elections. "Our doors and hearts are open to everyone, including the Muslim Brotherhood and their party," he said. "We call on all groups to take part in this reform process and participate in the legislative elections."[49] He also enlisted the mediation of Khaled Meshaal, Hamas's central leader, in the monarchy's efforts to persuade the JMB to end its boycott of the electoral process.

As part of his recent reform initiative, the king has amended 42 articles—about one-third of the kingdom's 60-year-old constitution. Key among these are (1) the creation of an independent election commission to organize elections, which thus far has been carried out by the Interior Ministry, and (2) authorizing the legislature to appoint the cabinet. He has promised that, at some point in the future, Parliament will have the authority to appoint the prime minister, which the Moroccan king allowed as part of his 2011 constitutional reforms.

Yet the JMB boycotted the polls, demanding that the government reverse the redistricting that prevented its members from securing seats in Parliament commensurate with its social capital. The regime claims that the new electoral law grants concessions to the opposition by allowing each citizen two separate ballots, one for local candidates and one for a 17-seat national list. This approach, it claims, provides national movements like the JMB a better chance to compete with regional and local candidates. The JMB and the IAF maintain that the law still favors the regime's allies, for it enables their dominance of Parliament to continue. Thus Jordan represents a case in which the regime has undertaken some limited reforms in order to preempt a potential crisis. The state hopes these reforms will placate the two main non-state centers of power, the JMB and the East Bankers, while preserving the palace's sovereignty. The JMB's resistance means that the state will have to come up with some additional concessions coupled with threats, thereby employing the classic carrot and stick approach.

The JMB's unique relationship with the monarchy has historically limited its operating capacity. Until King Hussein's decision to resume parliamentary elections in 1989, the group enjoyed a cordial working relationship with the palace. The regime's electoral engineering in the 1990s, which was designed to limit the number of seats the movement could win in Parliament, led to a new phase in the relationship, one marked by the JMB's boycott of elections. This strategy has not helped the JMB enhance its position; however, it has so far refrained from engaging in more aggressive tactics. In addition to these domestic circumstances, the three recent changes in the wider geopolitical environment (viz., Arab spring, Morsi becoming president, and the anti-MB coup) have had little impact on the group's standing. While the Arab Spring did rattle the Jordanian regime, the JMB was unable to improve its position and could not capitalize domestically on Morsi's victory.

Finally, the post-coup decline of its parent organization in Egypt has not adversely impacted the JMB. This can partially be explained by the buffer created by Israel and the Palestinian Territories that insulates the kingdom from the geopolitics radiating out of Egypt. In contrast, developments in Syria are likely to have a far more direct impact. But the Syrian MB has been dormant since the 1980s, and even after the Arab Spring it was sidelined by insurrectionist Islamist groups fighting the Alawite regime. With little hope for democratization in Syria the JMB is unlikely to benefit from the crisis in the Levant. While the aforementioned external factors are unlikely to shape the JMB's behavior, various internal factors could force it to alter its current course. The success of the centrist Islamist Hizb al-Wasat Party, which garnered three seats in the January 2013 legislative polls, is likely influencing the JMB's internal dove-hawk debate. The decision to boycott polls has proven futile and is likely to force the group to reconsider its position and again participate in future elections.

## The Palestinian Territories

The Arab Spring and the MB's subsequent rise in the region, especially in Egypt, had profound implications for Hamas, for it created opportunities for Hamas to return to its MB roots. In fact, the group reportedly considered the idea of reviving the PMB.[50] The Palestinian Islamist group also gained immense regional recognition given Qatar's support and the restoration of ties with Jordan after the Palestinian Islamist group broke relations with Syria and distanced itself from Iran. This realignment also garnered the group greater support from Turkey. There was even hope that Hamas, in an effort to end its isolation in Gaza and revive itself in the West Bank, would make considerable strides toward entering the mainstream. Most significantly, Morsi's election meant that the most important Arab state might support the Palestinian Islamist movement.

But Hamas understood that the MB would need years to consolidate itself in Cairo. It should also be noted that under Mubarak, Hamas had close working relations with Cairo while the Egyptian state even while it was suppressing the MB. Furthermore, there was also the issue of diverging interests, which became clear during the November 2012 Israel–Gaza War, as the MB government had to balance its support for Hamas with its need to do business with Israel and the United States.[51] Hamas thus knew that the MB's empowerment in Egypt would pay limited dividends, but the Palestinian Islamist movement nevertheless sought to make the most of the existing situation. In addition to realizing the limited benefits that it could hope for, it knew that its overall favorable position in the region would only go so far in terms of entering the mainstream. Then there was the matter of working out an accommodation with Fatah, which had proven to be highly elusive over the years. And now in the post-Arab Spring period, the exacerbation of the secular movement's decline has made such a rapprochement even harder.

Even assuming that a patch-up was achievable, Hamas was not prepared to make concessions to Israel, which placed severe limits on how far it could enter the mainstream. While the group was grappling with these issues, the question of whether Hamas would follow the MB's lead in becoming an internationally recognized Islamist movement quickly became moot, as Morsi's ouster reversed whatever little gains it had managed to make during his one-year term in office.

In fact, the crackdown on the MB since the July 3 coup has gone beyond returning Hamas to status quo ante, for the military regime is behaving in an unprecedentedly hostile attitude toward it. Meanwhile, the rise of insurrectionist Islamist forces in the Sinai and Gaza has further complicated matters for Hamas. Taking advantage of Hamas' reversals, Fatah has reengaged in the American-sponsored peace talks with Israel and appears to be working with Cairo to support a Tamarrod uprising in Gaza. However, Tamarrod may not be successful in this effort due to Gaza's default leaning toward Islamist groups.

The focus on Islamism in the Palestinian Territories has long been seen in the context of militancy and terrorism because the indigenous Islamism there, especially in Gaza, has developed largely in the context of occupation. This is especially true of the armed resistance movements of Hamas, Palestinian Islamic Jihad, and, more recently, smaller Salafi and jihadist factions. The suicide bombings and subsequent rocket attacks have led to conflating Hamas with jihadist groups like al-Qaeda. Notwithstanding its terrorist activities since the 1990s, the organization's historic trajectory indicates that Hamas actually is part of the MB genre of Islamism. That said, it represents a significant exception to the MB's participatory Islamist model because its complex historical evolution means that it cannot be placed neatly into our framework. Originally conceived as an MB entity, it adopted armed struggle within three years of its founding. Following a brief period of active armed struggle in the context of the 1948 Arab-Israeli war, it became a religious organization that confined itself to peaceful societal activities and avoided both Egypt and Israel. Four decades later, the group returned to armed struggle in the form of terrorism. In the aftermath of the 2006 elections, Hamas assumed a dual role of a participator Islamist entity (in the context of Palestinian politics) that also pursued armed struggle against Israel. Soon after returning to participatory politics, Hamas' inability to reach a power-sharing agreements with its secular rival Fatah caused it to seize control of Gaza, an action that rendered it simultaneously a de facto governing body as well as a non-state actor.

Unlike most MB-style groups that are participatory Islamists, Hamas' position is undergirded not by ideological factors, but by the need to adjust to geopolitical circumstances arising out of the occupation and lack of a real state. Despite the sub-national state of Palestinian affairs and its conflict with Israel, on the domestic front Hamas has largely behaved as a sociopolitical movement. While its militant wing, the Izz al-Deen al-Qassam Brigades, was ordered to focus on terrorist attacks against Israeli targets, the movement's core was engaged in civic activism in the West Bank and Gaza. The latter was a means toward eventual political empowerment, in keeping with the MB's signature bottom-up approach. Its seizure of the Gaza transformed it into an even more complex political entity, for it effectively ended the distinction that its military wing was limited to fighting Israel and that, at least in the Palestinian context, it was a participatory group when it came to seeking power.

As the November 2012 conflict showed, Hamas now occupies a gray area because its rocket attacks on Israel can be described as a militant non-state actor attacking a state or the efforts of a ruling entity seeking to defend its citizens and territory. Additionally, because there is no sovereign Palestinian state, neither democratization nor the role of religion in public affairs is high on its list of priorities. Much of this renders Hamas an exception to our three-category schema.

## The Muslim Brotherhood and Democratization

This chapter has assessed the Muslim Brotherhood in three different time periods (1990s, post-9/11, and post-Arab Spring). Within these three time frames, we examined the MB in terms of the original organization, the wider movement represented by its sister organizations, and the political approach of participatory Islamism. Our Islamist–secularist spectrum is a useful construct that allows us to delve deeper into the participatory category and tease out the nuances within it. As we have seen in these three different periods, the MB represents the most significant example of "democrats within Islamism."[52]. What we have been able to glean from the empirical evidence is that while the wider MB movement has stayed true to the democratic rules of the game, it has displayed mixed results in terms of its ability to govern. Our overview of these periods shows that the Egyptian MB, along with its counterparts, remained committed to achieving their objectives via democratic means. In every case, MB-style organizations participated in elections, eschewed extra-constitutional means, and operated within the constraints dictated by the authoritarian states. In time they were able to use legal mechanisms to expand their operating space.

Prior to the Arab Spring, the MB phenomenon was relatively successful in expanding the boundaries for participation. The performance of the many MB-type groups in the post-Arab Spring period, during which they have been major stakeholders in government, has been marred by significant shortcomings. Morocco's PJD, followed by Tunisia's Ennahda, have generally managed to navigate the post-Arab spring political bayou. The Egyptian MB, on the other hand, is the prime example of a failure once in office. Unlike the other two groups' efforts to reach out to secular groups in order to build an inclusive coalition, it pursued an exclusionary government dominated by its own cohorts. This tactic highlighted the different ways in which participatory Islamist groups have chosen to deal with political challenges.

The nearly 25-year period we have examined also highlighted how participatory Islamists have sought to integrate religion into the political arena as part of their push for democratization. The evidence suggests that these Islamists have continued to insist on a role for Islam in public affairs, which in the post-Arab Spring period can be seen in the intense debates in Egypt and Tunisia over the constitutional-writing process. The most contentious debates revolved around the articles pertaining to the republic's ideological character in terms of the shari'a's exact in legislative matters. Tunisia's Islamists pushed forward the notion of a civil state, which allowed them to avoid a breakdown with their secularist competitors. However, their Egyptian counterparts did not have to deal with secular opponents and thus were less susceptible to compromise. There were three reasons for this. First, the MB did not have any serious secularist competition in Parliament, for more than 70 percent of the seats went to Islamists. Second, the country's political system confers considerable power upon the presidency. Third, the military, in coordination with the judiciary, dissolved Parliament and further concentrated power in the presidency as the sole governing body. With the MB in control of the presidency, the ruling Islamist movement had less of an incentive to reach out to the secularists.

As we have seen, the MB's historic approach to political power has consisted of embracing the existing political system and reforming it gradually from within. Furthermore, it is the prime example of Islamists who have embraced democracy and consider it compatible with Islam. In their view, Muslim societies naturally desire leaders who will uphold religion in politics and are likely to support them at the ballot box.[53] The MB also repeatedly justifies democracy on religious grounds by proclaiming that "the umma [the Muslim community] is the source of sulta [political authority]." In pursuit of popular authority, its leadership had formed electoral alliances with secularists, nationalists, and liberals.[54] Judging from the MB's behavior as chronicled in this chapter, both as an organization and as a broader movement, it remains committed to establishing an "Islamic state" via electoral politics. Schwedler points out that the theoretical debate on the compatibility of Islam and democracy among scholars of political Islam in recent years has largely given way to empirical research on the practices and commitment of Islamist movements.[55]

One of the existing literature's many shortcomings is that it often discounts or completely disregards the MB's fairly consistent participation in electoral politics and general support for the democratic rules of the game.[56] We believe that such practices can be traced back to its founding, since the MB has never opposed the electoral process. Rutherford, for instance, suggests that it has always considered elections the only legitimate method for selecting a leader, as the Islamic idea of consultation (*shura*) indicates.[57] The problem was that the democratic process was not always available, and thus the issue was its absence rather than the MB's opposition to it. The MB understood long ago the consequences of pushing for political change through non-democratic means, and thus did not emulate its insurrectionist counterparts.[58]

*Participatory Islamists* have consistently supported participation in parliamentary elections as well as mobilizing the public and viewing each party's electoral success as the basis for forming a legitimate government.[59] Various ideological and pragmatic factors explain why the MB has always seen its effort as a multi-generational, as opposed to a mere election-cycle, effort. It is clear that these MB-style Islamists would not gain access to power unless the state opened its political process and loosened its autocratic grip. During the year of its rule, the MB sought to cooperate with the military establishment.[60] As Blaydes and others have argued, it has always viewed elections as a chance to establish itself as the most viable opposition group without posing a direct challenge to Mubarak's authoritarian rule and as a ruling party during the subsequent SCAF-dominated regime.[61] The group has a reputation for running highly organized election campaigns based on an extensive network of grassroots political apparatus.[62]

Schwedler points out that the MB's decision to participate in elections has been based on a cost–benefit analysis in each country. According to her, the question at that time was whether participation would bring about the necessary gains to justify the costs—symbolic as well as material—of working through formal political channels and within a pluralist context.[63] Thus she points out that some of Jordan's Islamists questioned if a minority presence in Parliament would be worth it, since they would be unable to implement Islamic law.[64] Other participatory Islamists have claimed that such participation has benefits beyond the political outcome. For example, electoral campaigning gives MB members a platform to promote their vision and proselytize the masses. It is, as Abed-Kotob remarks, an "ideal apparatus for promulgating its message."[65] Furthermore, resorting to political violence would give the state a pretext for doing more (perhaps even irreparable) damage to the MB's body politic. This is one of the major reasons why the Egyptian MB has continued to shun violence despite the military's ongoing violent crackdown.

In assessing the MB's commitment to the electoral path, the case of Egypt's organization is generally indicative of what is happening elsewhere. Schwedler's assessment of Jordan's IAF concludes that incorporating Islamists into the political process has led to their embrace of democratic principles and the internalization of democratic values.[66]

> This does not necessarily mean that the group had evolved to such an extent that it could no longer be considered Islamist, or that Islam was no longer central to the group's diagnosis of the problems faced by contemporary Jordanian society and the group's prognosis for solutions. But gradually . . . . The Muslim Brother and later the IAF came to explore and accept practices that seemed unthinkable just a few years earlier. Strategies that once triggered considerable debate no longer required any justification at all . . . [T]he continued participation of the party illustrated more than an accommodation of democratic practices for strategic reasons. Rather, the internal party debates and particularly its practices illustrate that the group had seriously incorporated elements of a democracy narrative that effectively redrew the boundaries of what practices and strategies the group could justify.[67]

While we generally agree with her assessment, in our view the MB was committed to the democratic process even before it was allowed to participate. Put differently, the MB did not move from radicalism to moderation, because it was sufficiently moderate enough to begin with given that it chose the democratic process. Of course, moderation is relative and the MB's decision to partake in electoral politics did push it further along the moderation path in terms of its goals. Groups moderate their aims as an outcome of participating in an ongoing process. But when it comes to the organization's modus operandi, since its earliest days the MB has steered clear of radical approaches. Furthermore, it kept working within legal bounds and even sought to expand them. This also explains why the organization neither launched the 2011 uprising nor sought the leadership role after joining it, for it was not a propagandist movement seeking revolutionary change. As the quintessential participatory Islamist group, it sought a gradual and orderly transition to a more democratic system as opposed to seeking to bring down the entire military regime in one fell swoop, which would be inherently destabilizing. As a result it used the uprising to try and force the military to open up the political system to the extent possible.

But these considerations alone do not prove that the MB has embraced the concept of democracy, only that it adopted it (in the procedural sense) at a time of regime weakness and for practical purposes.[68] The MB's conduct while in power, particularly its inability and/or unwillingness to avoid gridlock, underscores that despite its decades-long experience as a group seeking democratization, it has still not internalized democratic norms.

Neither the coup nor the subsequent wave of suppression is likely to cause it to abandon the participatory Islamist approach. The MB's structure precludes both insurrectionist and propagandist means of empowerment, as is evident in its response to the July 3 coup: Despite suppression and prosecution, as well the arrest of its leaders and killing hundreds of its members, the MB has maintained its desire for peaceful political change. It should be noted that its activists have launched several attacks, none of which were authorized by the leadership; in fact, the leadership has condemned them. Similarly, although attacks against churches in the months after the coup have been widespread, there is no indication that such acts were initiated or supported by MB officials.

The MB's gradual assent to power across the Arab world via democratic means since the Arab Spring underscores the rise of two parallel trends—Islamism and democratization—that are bound to impact each other. One would expect that participation in electoral politics will most likely mainstream Islamist groups, based on the underlying assumption that their ideology will gradually be secularized. The MB in Morocco and Ennahda in Tunisia continue to slowly temper their ideology and embrace pragmatism, accommodation, and compromise. Such a loosening of ideological rigidity is bound to happen when Islamists learn to get along with non-Islamists in a democratic framework.

This was not the case for the Egyptian MB and led to its downfall. The sparring between Islamists and non-Islamists will continue unabated for the foreseeable future, as both sides continue to accuse the other of being inflexible. The secular opposition forces were justified in protesting some of Morsi's self-bestowed powers, such as his attempt to dominate the Constitutional Assembly via MB members and other Islamists. Yet while he may be have resorted to some of Mubarak's authoritarian tactics, as Sadiki states, serious questions arise when liberal leftists, secular protestors, and even judges from the old regime stage protests and call for the new president's downfall, as if a legitimately elected president is on par with an autocratic one. The real issue is that opposition leaders and protestors have not yet accepted the reality of an Islamist president or an Islamist-led Parliament.[69]

Most observers tend to look at the MB's behavior during its year in power as an attempt by the movement to impose its ideology on the country. At one level that is the case; however, such explanations at best offer only partial account of its intent. On a parallel level, its ideological imperatives notwithstanding, the MB is like any other political group in that it pursues its own power-related interests. With regards to the latter motivation, it is willing to compromise on some of its ideological positions but can realistically only go so far. In other words, it can be expected to constantly renegotiate religion's place in affairs of state but cannot completely drop the idea altogether. Thus this issue has remained central to the ongoing debate among participatory Islamists during the tumultuous post-Arab Spring years.

Participatory Islamists like the MB naturally seek to take advantage of the views of the majority of Arabs. Polls taken in 2013 highlighted the fact that Muslims overwhelmingly support democracy and also underscored the vast majority's (86 percent according to Pew) insistence that the laws should strictly follow the Qur'an (58 percent) or at least follow its values and Islam's principles (28 percent). The view that the legal system should follow the Qur'an is especially common among al-Nour Party members (84 percent) and the FJP (74 percent). What is perhaps most surprising is that of those Egyptians who supported the secular umbrella group (viz., the NSF), 46 percent felt that the legal system should follow the Qur'an.[70] This evidence supports our thesis that the vast majority of Egyptians, regardless of ideological leaning, feel strongly about allowing religion a role in politics.

As Islamists have taken on the responsibilities associated with governing, they have come under increasing pressure to adjust their religiously oriented ideological perspective. Groups like the Moroccan branch of the MB and Ennahda have moved away from the original Islamist goal of an Islamic state ruled by shari'a due to their rather recent realization that even the shari'a is subject to temporal and spatial interpretations as well as the necessities of governance. There is a growing awareness that reason and pragmatism are necessary to applying the revelation. The Islamists in Morocco and Tunisia are not compromising their values, but rather are adjusting how they are to be identified, defined, and applied. In many ways this is the latest stage of the Muslim world's attempted balance between tradition and modernity.

Egypt's MB had a similar opportunity to engage in a more inclusive process of interpreting the role of religion in politics, for the polls revealed that the majority of Egyptians want religion to be involved in the political sphere. This view surely plays into the movement's ideological perspective. But even despite this overwhelming public support, the MB ruined its chances by refusing to establish an inclusive constitutional committee that more fully reflected the society's makeup as well as more consensus-based cabinet. The group has paid a heavy price for its miscalculation and set back its members' hopes of playing a central role in the future of Egyptian politics.

The latest ban is significant because it comes after the decline of the group's popularity following its poor performance while in power. Unlike its decades-long historical status as a banned organization that gained strength through public sympathy, this time around the proscription will likely further weaken the group. Although it is hard to predict what will happen next the idea that it represents—participatory Islamism—will continue to endure and even be refined for the foreseeable future. The most likely scenario is that the MB will revive itself and that some of its rank and file members will establish alternative vehicles to take participatory Islamism to the next level. But more importantly, we have the Salafist al-Nour party trying to assume the mantle of participatory Islamism, even though it currently faces challenges that will prevent it from moving much beyond the conditionalist camp. We will discuss in detail in the next chapter.

# 5

# Conditionalist Islamists: The Case of the Salafis

The Salafis represent a diverse community with core constituents in Saudi Arabia and additional millions of adherents across the Muslim world and the West. Unlike the Muslim Brotherhood (MB), which is a distinct organization with easily identifiable branches, "salafi" refers to a trend or, as the Salafis prefer to describe themselves, a methodology (*manhaj*). Consequently, their universe has come to encompass a highly varied set of actors who share a common religious doctrine but exhibit quite divergent political views.[1] Thus they are comprised of multiple and often competing neighborhood preachers, societal groups, tele-vangelists, and, largely after the Arab Spring, political parties. The vast majority, however, continue to shun politics. In fact, some of its most senior scholars insist that those who engage in politics are outside the Salafi tradition. We will only touch on Salafi religious views to explain their location in the wider Islamist milieu, for our focus in this chapter is the movement's recent political manifestations and, in particular, on those groups that have moved toward political participation. But before we analyze Salafism as a political subgroup within Islamism, a definition of the phenomenon and a brief discussion of its origins are in order.

At its core, Salafism is based on an austere interpretation of Islam, one that focuses on a common religious creed (*aqeedah*) that outlines the articles of faith, which constitute its worldview's core precepts.[2] In a widely cited *hadith* (sayings and traditions of Prophet Muhammad), the Prophet told Muslims that, "[T]his *ummah* [Muslim community] will divide into seventy-three sects, all of which except one will go to Hell and they are those who are upon what I and my Companions are upon."[3] Salafis believe that they are this one sect (*firqa al-najiyya*) and thus will attain salvation on the Day of Judgment.[4] Stressing the importance of Arabic and emphasizing the study and referencing of the Qur'an and the Sunnah (Muhammad's words, deeds, and tacit approvals), they call on Muslims to return to the original teachings as outlined therein and as understood by the Sahabah (his Companions), the Tabi'een (their students), and the Tabi' Tabi'een (the students' students).

These first three generations constitute the *salaf al-saliheen* (pious predecessors, namely, the Prophet's original Companions) during whose time "true Islam" was upheld. Salafis base this view on a statement attributed to Muhammad:

> The best of mankind is my generation, then those that follow them and then those that follow them. Then there shall come a people after them who will become avaricious, who will love gluttony, and who will give witness before they are asked for it.[5]

Citing this hadith to justify their assertion that authentic interpretations of Islam persisted until the end of the third generation, they argue that each subsequent generation's ideas and practices were increasingly contaminated by philosophical, juristic, and mystical thought as well as the influence of less legitimate sources. They wish to jettison this "excess" material so that Muslims can return to the "authentic" Islamic way of life and restore Islam's past glory. Such a call, they insist, has been ongoing throughout Islam's history, for revivalists have emerged from time to time to renew the faith. They share this notion with most other Sunni Muslims; however, like almost all other factions they tend to privilege those scholars who ground their analysis directly in the Qur'an and the Sunnah and shun those who turn to other sources.

The most recent ideological heavyweight in this religious tradition is the eighteenth-century Arabian Peninsula scholar Muhammad bin Abd al-Wahhab (1703–92) and his progeny, namely, those who are members of the al-Alshaykh lineage. Western scholars often refer to him as the founder of Wahhabism;[6] its adherents consider this term a misnomer, since they self-identify as monotheists (*Ahl al-Tawhid*: Advocates of God's Oneness), *muwahidun* (monotheists), and then *salafiyyun* (*salafi*s, derived from *al-salaf al-salih*, the pious predecessors whom they claim to emulate).[7] Contemporary supporters view Ibn Abd al-Wahab simply as a *salafi*.[8] His fundamental precepts, particularly those found in his *The Book of the Oneness of God and the Removal of Doubts*, were designed to return Muslims to "orthodox" Islam, defined as the Islam practiced by the Prophet and his Companions.[9]

Ibn Abd al-Wahhab asserted that the Muslims of his day had regressed to an age of religious ignorance (*jahiliyya*) that was similar to the one preceding Islam.[10] He based his religious and political ideas on those of various scholars dating back to the Prophet, especially the controversial but renowned Levantine scholar Ahmad Taqi al-Din ibn Taymiyya (1263–1328) and his student Ibn Qayyim al-Jawziyya (1292–1350).[11] Ibn Taymiyaa was a major follower of the teachings of Imam Ahmad ibn Hanbal (d. 241), the jurist who founded the Hanbali school of Sunni legal thought.[12] This school is the intellectual heir of the Ahl al-Hadith school of thought, which took shape during Islam's second generation and placed significant limits on the use of reason when trying to understand the revelation.

Therefore, while Salafis lay claim to this very specific intellectual heritage, the notion of "salafi," an adjective applied to one who harkens back to the pious predecessors, was ironically used by their archrivals, among them such reformists as Jamal al-Deen al-Afghani (d. 1897), Muhammad Abduh (d. 1905), and Rashid

Rida (d. 1935).[13] These Islamic modernists called for a return to the original teachings of *salaf al-salih* in the sense of principles, which they then sought to use as a tool that could free them from the traditional view of religion upheld by the bulk of the ulema of their time, whom they considered an obstacle to a Muslim intellectual revival. Ibn Abd al-Wahhab's followers ultimately appropriated this notion of "return" for themselves and pushed forward with a more puritanical understanding of what it means to follow the "founding fathers" of Islamic orthodoxy. As a result of this intellectual trajectory, Salafis rejected the MB's ideology on the grounds that it had severely compromised itself in the areas of creedal tenets and interpretations of the Qur'an's doctrinal principles.

Despite the fact that they have created many waves in recent decades, Salafis remain a minority within the global Muslim population as well as a small subset within the Islamist context when compared with the MB. Most Salafis are neither political actors in the strict or formal sense of politics, nor exclusively intent on capturing the state and its levers of power.[14] In fact, for the longest time they objected to what they considered the MB's focus on politics and call for establishing an "Islamic" state, for such a state could not arise if the masses did not have an Islamic "state of mind." As a result, for most of their history Salafis have focused primarily on personal morality and individual piety by urging Muslims to embrace the pious predecessors' creed and practices. Above everything else, they are religious and social reformers who seek to create and reproduce particular forms of personal and communal authority and identity.[15] But as Bernard Haykel points out, even though the movement has historically been apolitical, "Salafis are determined to create a distinct Muslim subjectivity, one with profound social and political implications."[16]

Until fairly recently, Salafism was an apolitical tendency and thus separate from Islamism. In many ways this led to the rise of jihadists, who not only vehemently denounced the MB but also broke with the vast majority of Salafis and sought to impose their envisioned order by force. The near-absence of any political dimension to Salafi thought created another dilemma: how to transform a pious society (assuming one can be attained) into a state. Jihadists tried to resolve this by reinterpreting the classical view of jihad (in its military sense) from being a state prerogative to the modus operandi of non-state actors seeking to reestablish an "Islamic" polity. Due to the historical alliance between Ibn Abd al-Wahhab and Muhammad ibn Saud (d. 1765), the patriarch of the al-Saud family, in 1744, the Salafis gained power early on and thus had no need to develop a detailed political philosophy. The al-Saud took care of politics, and Ibn Abd al-Wahhab's descendants took care of religion. While the first two incarnations of the Saudi dynasty collapsed in 1818 and 1891, respectively, the third incarnation managed to erect a kingdom during the late 1920s and early 1930s that, empowered by massive oil revenues, still plays the critical role in supporting Salafism worldwide even today.

Saudi Arabia was officially established in 1932, when the MB was four years old. The MB emerged as a major movement in Egypt during the late 1940s and, in both organizational and intellectual terms, was soon expanding abroad. At that time the Saudis were worried that the kingdom would be affected by its ideas,[17] but considered the concurrent rise of secular left-wing Arab nationalism to be the more serious emerging threat. This became a major concern after Gamal Abdul Nasser founded the Egyptian republic and began exporting his ideas to the Levant, Iraq, and the Arabian Peninsula. The Saudis responded by using the MB as a tool to counter Nasserism. Many MB members, including Muhammad Qutb, the brother of executed radical MB figure Sayyid Qutb and an intellectual in his own right, moved to Saudi Arabia and were given fora from which they could lecture. In those days the Saudis did not consider the movement a threat, for it was rather weak— it was suppressed everywhere in the Arab world except Jordan—and the Saudi polity was firmly entrenched in its own Salafi foundations. The Saudis also hoped to influence it via financial and ideological support.

But despite the considerable bidirectional flow of ideas, the MB largely retained its distinct character. The reverse was far more significant: Salafism was seen as having been "contaminated" by MB ideas, especially since the former focused solely on personal worship and practices. MB expats steered clear of any political activity in the kingdom because they did not want to endanger their sanctuary from persecution back home. However, the natural cross-pollination of ideas had a lasting effect on some of the younger Saudi ulema and students. This intellectual interaction, which lasted from the 1950s until the late 1970s, saw many MB members embrace Salafi ideas in terms of personal religious practice. This was fine with the MB's leadership, because it did not seek to impose any particular sectarian view of Islam; rather, wanted to focus purely on political goals. Thus its leaders did not care if the members adopted Salafi practices in matters of personal faith, as long as they adhered to the movement's overall political program.[18]

The reverse, however, was a far more critical metamorphosis. Salafis drawn to MB ideas did not have to give up their religious views; however, they were exposed to political ideas that did not conform with the ideas of the Saudi rulers or of those in charge of the religious establishment. Since this was a gradual transformation and did not change their behavior, it remained below the radar for quite some time. Furthermore by the end of the 1970s, various events (e.g., Egypt's 1978 peace treaty with Israel and the 1979 Soviet intervention in Afghanistan) kept the focus elsewhere, far beyond the kingdom's borders.

The 1979 takeover of the Ka'bah by a fanatical Salafi group was dealt with rather quickly and treated as the work of tiny deviant fringe. Earlier that same year, however, the revolution that toppled the Shah and inaugurated the Islamic Republic of Iran emerged as a major challenge, given that many Sunni Islamists, including those in the MB's orbit, saw this as a positive development. Moreover, the Iranian republican model of an Islamic state was in direct competition with the Saudi dynastic model and more in keeping with MB ideals. The revolution's ethno-sectarian character, along with the ensuing Iran–Iraq war, allowed Riyadh to contain the situation for quite some time. But all during this time Salafis were drifting slowly toward Islamism, a trend that would only come to the fore a decade later.

Within the academic literature, several scholars have proffered classifications of the various Salafi groups. Quintan Wiktorowicz's conceptual framework divides them into purists, politicos, and jihadists.[19] Amel Boubekeur's study of Salafism in Algeria offers a similar typology with a slightly different nomenclature: political

Salafism (*salafiyya harakiyya*), jihadi Salafism (*salafiyya jihadiyya*), and da'wa Salafism (*ad-da'wa al-salafiyya*, aka *salafiyya 'ilmiyya* [scholarship]).[20] A more recent categorization, one developed after the outbreak of the Arab Spring, is Hassan Mneimneh's activist (*da'waiyyah*), scholastic (*'ilmiyyah*), loyalist (*ahl al-wala*), and jihadi (*jihadiyyah*).[21]

Boubekeur's pre-9/11 taxonomy is applicable only to Algeria, although the *harakiyya* category listed by both scholars could be extended to include the Kuwaiti and Bahraini Salafi parties that emerged during the 1990s and 2000s, respectively, as well as Egypt's post–Arab Spring Salafi parties. Wiktorowicz's *politicos* refers to a younger generation of Saudi ulema who broke with the establishment and engaged in political discourse and critiques of the monarchy.[22] This term does not, however, take into account the more recent manifestation of Salafis who have decided to engage in electoral politics. Mneimneh's framework does a better job in that it captures the nuance between the scholars and activists within the Saudi Salafi landscape and those who reject political dissent. That said, there is a considerable degree of overlap between the loyalist and the scholastic types. Furthermore, his system (like Wiktorowicz's) does not mention those Salafis who have entered electoral politics.

In our view, a more systematic yet inclusive categorization would entail the following four categories:

1. Apolitical Salafis (both scholarship Salafis [*salafiyya 'ilmiyya*], and proselytizing Salafis [*ad-da'wa al-salafiyya*]): Those who shun politics and focus on scholarship and proselytization—both are organically linked since those studying often preach as well. These include the majority of Salafis globally, with the bulk of them being located in the Gulf states.
2. Political Salafis (*salafiyya harakiyya*): Those who feel they need to engage in political discourse to fulfill their duty of advising and holding the rulers accountable. While this initiative has not had much success, primarily because of the lack of opportunities in monarchies like Saudi Arabia, Salafis in the post–Arab Spring republican Arab countries have embraced political participation. Currently, forming parties and competing in elections is their main activity. This group will be the primary focus of this chapter.
3. Vigilante Salafis (*salafiyya iqtisasiyya*): Those who reject mainstream politics and refrain from armed struggle in order to focus on preaching and vigilantism to make the masses comply with their understanding of Islamic norms. They insist on enjoining the good and forbidding the evil without being overtly political.[23]
4. Jihadist Salafis (*salafiyya jihadiyya*): Those who have taken up armed struggle to establish an "Islamic" polity. In our schema we refer to them as insurrectionist Islamists, which we will discuss further in Chapter 6 and 7.

This chapter will focus primarily on political Salafis and avoid any discussion of apolitical and vigilante Salafis, for these non-Islamists fall outside the scope of this book. We will also largely ignore jihadist Salafis as well, because even though jihadists constituted the Salafis' first real political or Islamist manifestation, they warrant a separate and substantive treatment on their own. As such, they will be analyzed in chapter six with the transnational al-Qaeda jihadist and the Taliban's nationalist form of jihadism will be discussed in chapter seven. Even though jihadists have increasingly captured the headlines since the 1970s and especially after the rise of al-Qaeda-led transnational jihadism in the 1990s, most Salafis avoid them. Many Salafis simultaneously eschew MB-style political activism,[24] mainly because they already have their Islamic state: Saudi Arabia. Even if many of them disagree with some of Riyadh's policies, the kingdom's historical roles as both the birthplace of and global patron of Salafism keep the movement within the Saudi orbit.

## The 1990s

During the 1990s the greater Middle East underwent several geopolitical shifts, each of which enabled various Salafi groups to enter the Islamist fold. Each event not only paved the way for their gradual politicization and membership in the larger Islamist universe, but also ensured that Salafism would become one of the most prominent subsets of the wider Islamist spectrum—second only to the MB. The single most critical development was the 1991 Persian Gulf War, which profoundly impacted the movement's global headquarters: Saudi Arabia.

### Saudi Arabia

In late 1990, Saudi Arabia allowed approximately 500,000 American troops to be based on its soil (considered by many to be holy ground) to protect the kingdom from Baathist Iraq after it had invaded and subsequently annexed Kuwait. The Saudis went to great lengths to obtain an official fatwa from Sheikh Abdulaziz bin Baz, the kingdom's top religious scholar, to religiously legitimize their decision. His support proved to be a watershed event for the Saudi religious establishment and the global Salafi landscape, for not only did it trigger an uproar over its asserted legitimacy, but it also led to a wider debate about the kingdom's internal political state of affairs. Several prominent Saudi ulema began calling for reform, what later was called the *sahwa* (awakening) movement, and many ulema responded via political activism.[25] The ensuing public criticism of the ruling al-Saud family by mainstream scholars had an impact beyond the kingdom. In fact, it led Salafis to participate in political discourse—their formal entry into Islamism.[26]

A large number of Saudi ulema, academics, and professionals who had embraced MB ideas over the years criticized the royal family's conduct during the war and demanded reform. Now on the defensive, in 1992 King Fahd (r. 1982–2005) decreed the Basic Law, the kingdom's first-ever constitution-type document; however, this reaction further emboldened those calling for reform. The dissonance from within the religious establishment was a critical development, and soon a group of prominent ulema, among them Safar al-Hawali, Salman al-Audah, Ayidh al-Qarni, and Nasser-al-Omar, were leading the calls for reform.[27] This younger generation of ulema had been influenced by Muhammad Surour, a Syrian scholar who had moved to Saudi Arabia, taught in a seminary in Burayda, and started to blend MB ideology with Salafism.[28] Riyadh tolerated them for a while and, via the senior ulema, tried to reason with them. But in 1994, backed by its allies within the religious establishment, Riyadh adopted an aggressive stance and arrested many of them.[29] But the dissenters had already created a major stir within the community of religious scholars.

Intra-Salafi conflicts broke out with those loyal to al-Saud and adherents of classic Salafi ideas accusing those who criticized the monarchy as being Ikhwanis and Qutbis (references to the MB and Sayyid Qutb, respectively) and having deviated from pure Salafism. The dissenting ulema were imprisoned for five years, a tactic that undermined this nascent dissent. By 1995, the *sahwa* was over. In the meantime, transnational jihadism was taking shape under Osama bin Laden, the founder of al-Qaeda, who had earlier broken with the al-Saud over the stationing of American troops on Saudi territory. According to the Saudis, the politicized Salafis and jihadists deviated from Salafism after being infected with "Ikhwani" (MB) ideas. Riyadh and its allies among the senior ulema managed to contain both trends and thus retain the loyalty of most of the religious establishment.

*Kuwait*

While the Saudis prevented the kingdom and its Salafis from being politicized, neighboring (and at that time newly liberated) Kuwait saw a major drive toward parliamentary life. Salafis have been key figures in this drive for a generation. In 1992, the emirate's urban-based Salafis formed the Islamic Salafi Alliance (ISA), which has been—and remains—a player in Parliament.[30] In addition to the alliance, a number of independent Salafi MPs in the legislature have represented tribes in the rural areas. According to Steve Monroe, independent Salafi lawmakers are far more serious than the ISA in demanding that the ruling al-Sabah family share power with the National Assembly and be made accountable to the unicameral legislature.

Monroe explains that both types of Salafis, while not abandoning their austere views on religion's role in public affairs, have upheld democratic norms to varying degrees. The Kuwaiti Salafis' drive toward democratic politics, states William McCants, is the result of Egyptian Salafi scholar Abd al-Rahman Abd al-Khaliq, a long-time resident in the emirate.[31] His organization, the Revival of the Islamic Heritage Society, has been highly instrumental in creating a Salafi presence in Parliament on the grounds that doing so will ensure that the party has a voice in the government. While these politicized Salafis have been involved in parliamentary politics for over 20 years, many other local Salafis oppose the idea on doctrinal grounds.

This debate between political and apolitical Salafis reinforces the conditionalist nature of those seeking to participate in elections. Apolitical Salafis criticize their politically active counterparts for participating in a legislative process that contravenes religious principles and their view that only God has sovereignty. In response, political Salafis stress that they do not subscribe fully to democracy, but rather seek to use the electoral process to prevent secularists from dominating the state. In addition, they argue that political participation is a far more effective means of propagating their ideas than the methods used by their apolitical counterparts. This dynamic reinforces the conditionalist Islamist attitude toward democracy—the democratic process ia a means to an end. This internally divided Salafi landscape, along with the fact that the ruling al-Sabah family has successfully curtailed Parliament's power, bodes ill for Salafi democratization there.

## Algeria

In 1987, a quarter of a century after obtaining independence from France, Algeria's stability under the single-party socialist government led by the Front de Libération Nationale (FLN), began to erode. Declining oil prices and rising unemployment and inflation throughout the late 1980s engendered civil unrest and calls for political reform. President Chadli Benjedid's government buckled under public pressure and instituted democratic reforms by means of a new constitution in 1988. This rushed democratization rapidly pushed the oil-rich country from mass unrest to armed insurrection. Several political parties were formed and recognized by the government, including the country's largest Islamist movement: the Front Islamique du Salut (FIS). Founded only three months after the institution of a multiparty political system in February 1989, it brought Islamists who were committed to democratic politics and others who wanted to use the electoral process to achieve power and establish an authoritarian Islamic state.

Given that its founding was a rushed affair and served as a "large tent" designed to bring its different viewpoints on Islam and democracy, the FIS had no coherent agenda beyond winning elections. Whereas its chief Abbas Madani exhibited rather moderate views in terms of the party's goals to establish an Islamic state, his deputy Ali Belhadj had a far more radical view of the envisioned "Islamic" polity. As a result, many feared that the FIS's emphasis was on Islamism rather than democratization. When the ruling FLN won only 15 seats and the FIS took 188 of the 231 seats up for grabs in the first round of voting on December 26, 1991, the army and civilian secular forces became very worried about this latter group. Weeks later, the army ousted the government and annulled the parliamentary elections in which the FIS was poised to win a two-thirds majority. After imposing direct military rule, the Islamist movement was banned and its leaders, along with thousands of its members, were arrested. Deprived of its leadership and facing a severe crackdown by the army, many FIS members who remained free joined forces with insurrectionist Islamist groups and began a guerilla insurgency. Over the next decade (1992–2002), between 150,000 and 200,000 Algerians would die.

This tragic episode is often cited as the earliest case study of democratization and Islamism. What is less talked about is the fact that this was also the first-ever case of Salafi experimentation with democratic politics.[32] In a 2008 policy brief for the Carnegie Endowment for International Peace, Amel Boubekeur goes into great detail to show how Algerian Islamism was very different from all other

Arab/Islamic Islamist groups, for Salafis (as opposed to the MB) dominated the country's landscape. Algeria had three strands of Salafism: apolitical, political, and jihadist. The state clearly torpedoed this early Salafi attempt to engage with the mainstream political process, thereby cutting short this experiment and paving the way for the rise of a host of Salafi jihadist factions that would eventually launch a brutal decade-long insurgency.

Algeria represents a lone—and brief—case in which a Salafi movement, nearly 20 years before the Arab Spring, participated in democratic politics and won the first round with an overwhelming majority. Given the FIS's reaction to the military's assuming control, it is safe to assume that had it been allowed to take power, it would eventually have replaced the secular authoritarian state with an Islamist autocracy. Although FIS represented conditionalist Islamism, after the 1992 coup many of its members became rejector Islamists. They not only rejected democracy, but also adopted the insurrectionist Islamist method of political change.

## Yemen

Several factors during the 1990s allowed Salafis in Yemen to be both politicized and to acquire a significant presence in the state,[33] among them the growing Saudi influence on Yemeni tribal and religious figures, the fragmentation of its main Islamist movement (al-Islah), and the May–July 1994 civil war. Proximity to and financial dependency upon Saudi Arabia have long been hardwired into Yemeni geopolitics. As a result, Riyadh maintained ties with Sanaa and even Aden (when the latter was the capital of the People's Democratic Republic of Yemen [aka South Yemen]) as well as various societal elements. Through these mediums, Salafism (as a religious creed) permeated the country, which has historically had a sizeable Zaydi[34] community. Great numbers of Zaydis eventually embraced Sunni Islam and, in many cases, these new converts eventually attached themselves to various strands of Salafism.

Meanwhile, by the 1990s the Yemeni branch of the MB, the al-Islah Party, had fractured along several lines. In addition, Abdel-Majeed al-Zindani, a prominent religious scholar affiliated with the group, played a key role in developing a Salafi wing within al-Islah. This internal Salafi strain differed considerably from the apolitical Salafi currents led by Muqbil bin Hadi al-Waadi, Rabi al-Madkhali, and similar preachers. Al-Islah was not a vehicle through which Salafis could gain a great deal of mainstream political exposure, for it achieved no significant electoral success. As the country was still dominated by former president Ali Abdallah Saleh's General People's Congress, this was only to be expected.

These Salafis had a rather unique opportunity: Their disproportionate representation in the security and intelligence services gave them entry to the government. The Saleh regime relied heavily on Salafi tribal fighters from the North, who played a pivotal role in subduing the rebellious forces of the South. Four years after North and South Yemem's 1990 reunification, these latter rebels sought to regain their previous status as an independent polity.

After the North prevailed over the South, these fighters were inducted into the state security organs where they gathered experience in governance, but not in politics.

Saudi Arabia's *sahwa*,[35] Algeria's brief and ill-fated experiment with democratic politics,[36] participation in Kuwait's highly circumscribed Parliament, and Yemen's atypical political experiences—all of these allowed Salafis to make several initial forays into Islamism.[37] These were obviously a small number of cases brought about by unique developments in the region. Barring these, most Salafis clung to their traditional apolitical status. By the end of the 1990s, political Salafists had started to reconstitute themselves and quickly recovered their former central position. But the environment in which these new Islamists now operated had been considerably modified.[38] In the next section we highlight how the most serious challenge to Salafism's core came not from mainstream Islamists, but from the militant Islamists who had emerged after rejecting their apolitical nature: al-Qaeda and its transnational jihadism.

## Post–September 11

When the September 11 attacks occurred, there was not much nuance in the general global awareness about Islamism, and certainly much less as regards its radical and militant forms. The attacks triggered an effort in the United States and the West in general to better understand the nature of Islamism in its various forms. Given Osama bin Laden's own Saudi origins and the fact that 15 of the 19 hijackers were Saudi citizens, the terms "Saudi Wahhabism" and subsequently "Salafism" became buzzwords.

Most Salafis, even though they held highly austere views about the role of religion in public affairs and were very bitter about American foreign policy toward the Muslim world, rejected al-Qaeda and jihadism. Faced with the global onslaught against their religious ideology, as well as being pressured by jihadists and participatory Islamists, Salafis were forced to prove their ideological difference. In turn, participatory Islamists were trying to distinguish themselves from both jihadists and Salafis.

More importantly, Salafis were under durress to reform. But how could they do so without compromising their core religious doctrines? The Saudis in particular were dealing with internal pressures (they needed to isolate jihadists from the rest of their body politic) and Washington's demands to reform kingdom's entire Salafi project both at home and abroad The Bush administration's pointed calls for Arab countries to adopt democratic reforms were a major concern for Riyadh, for how could the royals embark upon such a course of action and still maintain power at a time when they were already struggling to reform the kingdom's religious discourse?

A limited effort unfolded in 2003 when King Abdullah, in the wake of the jihadist insurgency, embarked on social and religious reforms. Despite its cautious approach and limited scope, the initiative still carried two distinct risks: (1) its reform policy might trigger a backlash from the ulema, and the Saudis were well aware that conservative social segments would vehemently oppose any changes to religious norms, and (2) the government's efforts to distance Salafis from jihadists could inadvertently push them closer to the MB's ideology. Any moderation of their religious views could make Salafis more receptive to political participation, whereas the monarchy benefited from its adherents' traditionally apolitical world-view by being granted, by default, exclusive control of the political domain. Thus the MB's political engagement represented a critical threat. The 9/11 attacks had enabled MB-style Islamists to finally assert that they represented the Islamist main-stream and that al-Qaeda, the Salafis, and others were on the fringe. Consequently, the Saudis and their Salafi allies were simultaneously trying to counter the jihadists and the MB.

The MB also posed a major challenge, especially in light of the electoral gains made by participatory Islamist parties across the Arab world. The year 2002 was particularly important, since the AKP (Turkey), the PJD (Morocco), and the Mutahiddah Majlis-i-Amal (MMA) (Pakistan) had all fared extremely well at the polls. Three years later, Egypt's MB secured a six-fold increase in Parliament by winning 88 seats. The American invasion of Iraq in 2003 and subsequent "democ-ratization," which culminated in the January and December elections, posed a further difficulty: a general regional trend might create additional pressure on Riyadh to open up the country's political system. Hamas's 2006 electoral victory in the Palestinian Legislative Council (PLC) polls made matters even worse, as this was the first time that an MB-oriented organization won an election outright. That same year, the outcome of neighboring Bahrain's election was seen as not only advancing democratic politics, but also as boosting the influence of Iran and its Arab Shia allies. The Saudis needed to ensure that the Bahraini Shia's demo-graphic edge did not translate into domination of Parliament. As a result, Riyadh and its allies in the Bahraini monarchy backed the island nation's MB (al-Menbar) and Salafi (al-Asalah) parties, which had a combined strength of 13 seats in the 40-seat legislature; al-Wefaq, the main Shia group, won 17 seats. This was one of the unique and isolated cases in which the Saudis backed an MB–Salafi alliance in a democratic process; however, Riyadh did this only to counter the geo-sectarian threat from Iran.

On the issue of the rise of Iran and its Arab allies, the Saudis and Salafis were on the same page. However, dealing with Tehran and the Shia was far less of a prob-lem for the Saudis than the democratic experiments empowering participatory Sunni Islamists. Riyadh and the Salafis also shared the desire to prevent the MB from making advances, but for very different reasons. The Saudi regime opposed participatory Islamists because the latter threatened their political legitimacy. But the Salafis, who were more concerned with remaining relevant at a time when insurrectionist Islamists had captured the global spotlight and the MB was pre-senting itself as the moderate alternative, had to find an effective way to counter the MB's domination of politics. To achieve this, they knew that they could no longer be simply religious actor. The Saudi position, however, was that the only way to keep the MB was to deny its members any operating space.

This solution worked for the Salafis within the kingdom, but could not possibly affect those Salafis living in republics that allowed limited political activity. These latter Salafis, aware that they had to go beyond religious activities in order to compete with the MB, focused on enhancing their civil society presence. This underscored a divergence between the two Salafi groups. By the end of the decade Salafism had spread across the Arab world, most notably to North Africa, thereby expanding both the number of its adherents and its institutional scope, which included social organizations engaged in charity, relief, and community work. What they stopped short of was forming formal political groups, largely because of the autocratic regimes under which they lived and because they had reservations about direct political participation. Nevertheless, they quietly developed the infrastructure that would later allow them to form political parties.

### The Arab Spring and Beyond

The post-September 11 period forced many Salafis to reassess their position on politics. They knew they needed to move beyond their apolitical status, but were unsure of how to enter the political arena. Their long-held core principle, that politics should be shunned until Muslims had sufficiently adopted correct beliefs and practices, was increasingly untenable. Salafis were still quietly grappling with this issue when popular agitation, largely led by liberal youth groups, broke out in Tunisia and been spreading. The case of Egypt is clearly the most telling. While the MB was caught unprepared and had to scramble to take advantage of this historic opening, the debate among Egyptian Salafis on politics became moot. Though initially the main Salafi group (al-Dawah al-Salafiyah) opposed the uprising, it joined the protests when it became clear that Mubarak was unlikely to survive. This was the first time that the major Salafi group outside Saudi Arabia had formally entered politics. But the movement lacked a political machine, whereas the MB had been developing its own for some 84 years. And so a conglomeration of Salafi forces haphazardly trying to assert themselves in a post-authoritarian age arose.

Soon after Mubarak's ouster, al-Dawah al-Salafiyah established a political wing, Hizb al-Nour, which was granted official status in June 2011. Several other Salafi groups applied for licenses to form political parties, the most prominent among them being al-Asalah. In addition, a few prominent Salafi individuals emerged as independent political actors—most notably Hazem Salah Abu Ismail, a former MB member. Al-Nour and al-Asalah banded together with the newly founded Construction and Development Party, the political arm of the former jihadist group Gamaah al-Islamiyah, to form the Islamist Alliance. Al-Nour was originally a member of the MB-led coalition known as the Democratic Alliance, but left it in September 2011 to lead its own Salafi-dominated coalition: the Islamist Alliance.[39]

The Salafis' decision to enter politics after decades of denouncing democracy represented a major shift in their ideological thinking. Not only did they become a bona fide Islamist movement, but they also joined the acceptor category because they now engaged the state as well as society. As a result, they gravitated increasingly toward the MB's participatory approach but did not fully adopt its methodology. Hizb al-Nour-type Salafis made a strategic decision to participate, but remained quite uncomfortable with democracy. Therefore, despite their participation, these Egyptian Salafis more appropriately fall into our conditionalist Islamist category because their transformation stems more from political expediency than a natural ideological evolution. As a result, their commitment to the democratic process remains tenuous. More importantly, the acceptance of electoral politics quickly led to fragmentation of the Salafi Islamist landscape.[40]

In addition to being in a very nascent stage of development, Salafi political thought faces a major obstacle: It currently cannot reconcile participation in the democratic transition with its desire to implement a literal interpretation of Islamic law. However, some Salafi Islamists, particularly in smaller parties such as Hizb al-Watan (founded in December 2012), are more in line with MB thinking than Hizb al-Nour. Al-Watan is actually a more conservative version of the MB in the sense of its members' personal religious practices. In political terms, it has all but emulated the MB's program. This phenomenon is not surprising, for the MB itself contains members who are both Salafi (in religious terms) and MB (in political terms), some of whom were either originally Salafis or later embraced its religious thought. In fact, Hizb al-Watan founder Emad Abdel-Ghafour was originally head of Hizb al-Nour; he abandoned it partly due to disagreements over the restrictions imposed by al-Nour's parent group. This has allowed them to align with the MB to pursue two common goals: to weaken Egypt's autocratic structures and to contain the more radical Salafi tendencies.

Meanwhile, Hizb al-Nour has been trying to exploit the MB's milder ideological views to weaken its support among religious voters. This party accuses the MB of compromising religious ideals and presents itself as an alternative that will uphold Islamic principles. It has also taken advantage of the government struggle with jihadists by styling itself as an interlocutor at the expense of the MB. These tactics helped the party and its allies capture a quarter of the seats in the 2011-12 parliamentary elections.

Hizb al-Nour ran for elections based on the following party platform[41]:

- Supporting Article 2 of the Egyptian Constitution, which states that Islam is the religion of the state and the Islamic law is the main source of legislation.
- Preserving fundamental rights and public freedoms in the framework of Islamic law.
- Calling for Islamic law to serve as the guiding principles for all political, social, and economic issues.
- Supporting separation between the legislative, judicial, and executive powers and independence of the judiciary.
- Preserving the right to private property and free economic competition as long as it does not harm the interests of society.
- Reducing unemployment through state provision of jobs.
- Recognizing health care as a basic human right.
- Calling for the complete independence of al-Azhar from the government and restoration of its prominent role throughout the Islamic world.
- Improving education and establishing training programs throughout Egypt.
- Advocating for a greater state role in the institutions of Zakat and Waqf.
- Supporting religious freedom for the Copts and separate personal status laws for non-Muslims.

The party's second-place finish was a major accomplishment, considering that it had come into existence only a few months earlier. Salafi Islamists thus proved themselves far more organized than the secularist parties. While lacking the MB's political machine, the Salafis' long-term historic social roots allowed them to demonstrate that its rival not have a monopoly over the Islamist vote.[42]

Replacing the secularists as the MB's main rival represented a pivotal moment for Hizb al-Nour, for its new status as one of the most significant political parties gave it a crucial stake in the transitional process. Yet al-Nour also cooperated with the MB to achieve two key common objectives: (1) to make sure that the presidency did not fall into the hands of the Mubarak-era clique and (2) to use its sizeable presence in Parliament to influence the constitution-writing process. Al-Nour focused on the first objective because the presidential election's outcome would be decided well before the drafting of the charter. Furthermore, the judiciary torpedoed all efforts to forge a new constitution in an April 2012 ruling, a move that led to the dissolution of the first Constituent Assembly (CA).

Although knowing that it could not win the presidency on its own, and aware of the MB's declaration that it would not field a presidential candidate, al-Nour did not want to see its rival gain control of the presidency due to its majority in Parliament. Yet the party needed to align with the MB to prevent the secularists from winning the presidential election. In late March 2012 the MB, in a surprise move, announced the candidacy of its deputy supreme guide and most influential leader: Khairat El-Shater. In mid-April, the candidacy of the lone Salafi candidate, independent Hazem Salah Abu Ismail, was disqualified. Hizb al-Nour then decided to put its weight behind former MB stalwart Abdel-Monem Aboul Futouh, who was emerging as a non-partisan independent and a favorite. When El-Shater's disqualification caused the MB to replace him with Mohamed Morsi, the head of its political arm and a weaker candidate, al-Nour hoped that Aboul Futouh would win. But in the first round held during late May, Morsi, in an upset vote, came out in first place (25 percent) followed by Mubarak's last prime minister and ex-air force chief Ahmed Shafik in close second place (24 percent); al-Nour's preferred candidate came in fourth (18 percent). The run-off elections between Morsi and Shafik forced the party to support the lesser of the two evils.

The judiciary's decision to dissolve the Lower House of Parliament a mere 48 hours before the second round of the presidential vote was a major blow to al-Nour, for this move stripped the party of the only formal role it held in the post-Mubarak political system. The dissolution of the People's Assembly was also a setback for the MB, as it lost the opportunity to dominate both the executive and legislative branches. Morsi's narrow victory over Shafik forced al-Nour to align with the MB, as this was the only way the Salafi party could retain any influence within the emerging system. This was especially crucial for al-Nour, which by now had set its eyes on the constitution-writing process. But the party had to wait for this process to play out before it could have another shot at parliamentary elections, which were to be held after the new charter was finalized. In exchange for supporting Morsi, the largest Salafi party received a sizeable share of seats in the second Constituent Assembly. In its desire to see a charter which gave shari'a precedence, al-Nour backed Morsi's controversial November 2012 decree that gave himself sweeping powers. After the charter was finalized via a referendum in December, al-Nour received the second largest share of the 90 seats in the Upper House.

As a rival party, al-Nour of course did not want to remain in the MB's shadow. It also was facing competition from the many Salafi parties that had arisen by this time (viz., al-Islah, al-Amal al-Gedid, al-Fadilah, al-Shaab, and al-Islami), which were eroding the party's monopoly over Salafi Islamism. Many of these Salafi entities had secured key positions in the Morsi administration. Furthermore, al-Nour was dealing with severe internal trouble, so much in fact that its leader departed that same month. When 2013 began, al-Nour found itself in a state of decline. In January, Ghafour formed a separate Salafi party, al-Watan, which supported the MB. In early February, the independent Salafi leader and ex-presidential contender Abu Ismail, building on his own grassroots support base, formed al-Raya, which also backed Morsi. Elsewhere, GaI's political arm, the Construction and Development party, which had been part of the al-Nour alliance in the annulled parliamentary election, had also drifted into the MB orbit.

However, by this time the MB's inability to govern by consensus had already laid the seeds for a major mobilization on the part of its secular opponents. Al-Nour saw this as an opportunity to stage a comeback by carving out a unique position in the anti-Morsi movement, and by the spring of 2013 had skillfully positioned itself as a mediator between the Morsi government and the secularist camp. Al-Nour was not interested in defusing the crisis as much as it was in trying to present itself as a mainstream group at a time when the MB was being attacked for its Islamist partisanship. Just as al-Dawah al-Salafiyah did not join the protests against Mubarak until it had become clear that he would not survive, al-Nour steered clear of the late June Tamarrod demonstrations against Morsi and adopted a definitive (negative) position only after the military coup.

Its support for the coup and the MB's subsequent suppression has given this Salafi party an opportunity to establish itself as the country's main Islamist force. While trying to attain this new status, however, al-Nour has alienated many Islamists and is having its own internal problems. The main one is that since the secularists now dominate the post-Morsi process, the party has just one seat on the 50-member constitutional committee.

## Salafism and Democratization

This chapter began with a brief discussion of the historic origins of Salafi thought, which over the past two centuries gradually evolved into the full-fledged ideology known today as Salafism. As a religious community, Salafis have always represented a small subset of the wider Sunni population. Tracing their evolution since the mid-eighteenth century reveals that they have largely remained outside the bounds of Islamism. Their experience with democratization has taken place within three contexts since the early 1990s, a time when some Salafi groups started to shed their apolitical past and slowly became Islamists. During this period certain Salafis made limited but notable attempts to partake in electoral politics. The first was in

Algeria, when the FIS was on its way to a landslide victory in the 1990–91 parliamentary elections; the military denied its right to govern by annulling the process and taking power. In the post-Sept 11 period, Salafis had to come to terms with a hostile global environment that conflated them with jihadists. Feeling the need to respond to these generalizations, they sought to distance themselves from the insurrectionists. In addition, the MB's attempts to position itself as the Islamist mainstream at the expense of Salafis and jihadists also drove the former's difficult but necessary transformation.

The second Salafi democratic encounter took place in two separate Gulf Cooperation Council states.[43] The first one occurred during the 1990s in Kuwait via the appearance of the Islamic Salafi Association (ISA), which is still increasing its presence in Parliament. The second one took place in Bahrain, where the al-Asalah Party was founded in 2002 and remains a key player in the legislature. Both of these small parties have only limited influence, due to the fact that the royals have allowed them space only for specific geopolitical reasons. Thus neither case offers much insight on how Salafism and democratization can interact, although one scholarly work suggests that the former has behaved more democratically than the latter.[44] Many Salafis understood that their traditional apolitical policy was no longer tenable, and yet how they could become political actors without tarnishing their religious credentials remained unclear. The Arab Spring created a fait accompli that forced Salafis to not only get involved in politics, but also to deal with democratization.

The third and most significant development was Mubarak's fall from power. Prior to the Arab Spring, Salafis barely figured in the country's political landscape; however, they stormed onto the scene by capturing 25 percent of the seats in the 2011-2012 democratic election. Similarly, their rapid rise in Tunisia surprised many, given the country's relatively relaxed atmosphere toward religion.[45] In the three years following the Arab Spring's outbreak, Salafis have engaged in a complex mix of ideological and pragmatic behavior, which shapes the contours of conditionalist Islamism. As was the case with participatory Islamists, their conditionalist counterparts also come in multiple shades. But because conditionalist Islamism is a far more recent development, there are fewer manifestations. Egypt's Hizb al-Nour is clearly the standard-bearer of this trend; however, other Salafi parties that disagreed with al-Nour and each other regarding the appropriate degree of pragmatism they would have to employ joined it fairly quickly.

While al-Nour has experienced competition within Egypt from rival conditionalist Islamists and is still in its formative years, like-minded Salafis elsewhere (e.g., Tunisia, Morocco, Algeria, Gaza, Jordan, and Yemen) who are reportedly forming political parties see it as a model. In fact, a growing number of Salafi Islamist groups are emerging because staying on the sidelines is no longer an option, given the growing political problems in the Arab world. Even though many Salafis continue to steer clear of politics, the post-Arab Spring climate has made their journey toward political activism easier. The more difficult part is how to engage, given that accepting democracy remains conceptually difficult for most of them. Yet despite their discomfort with it, they know that they cannot ignore democratization. But the resulting gridlock is also opening up space for conceptual innovation, which we have recently seen in the behavior of al-Nour and smaller conditionalist Islamist factions.

Conditionalist Islamism is in its very early stages of development. In the future, other apolitical religious groups and even rejector Islamists could conceivably transition into this camp, especially if democratization gains traction. Hizb al-Nour and the other current conditionalists emerged in a context where participatory Islamists had already saturated the political space. For this reason, they have not yet articulated a position distinct from that of the MB, except for a generic claim that they are better placed to uphold the Muslims' religious interests. Salafis have long stressed that they have a more authentic understanding of the religion and also accuse the MB of compromising religion for political gains. Their entry into the discussion on religion and politics, along with their reservations regarding democracy, further add to this debate's contentious nature.

The MB has had decades to internalize the compatibility of Islam and democracy, as well as of practical experience in confronting autocracy. For this reason it has been more focused on power politics, especially given its experience with political bargaining. The Salafis, however, will continue to struggle for quite a while to balance their ideological imperatives with the need to be politically pragmatic. That said, by supporting the coup al-Nour is trying to make the case that it is more pragmatic than the MB. Considering that Salafis only recently began their move toward politics, there is always the danger of recidivism. The example of al-Nour' founder Emad Abdel Ghafour might be emblematic of future pathways for some Salafis. Ghafour, an advisor to ex-president Morsi, left politics in the aftermath of the 2013 coup and his subsequent brief detention and returned to the traditional Salafi position.

Ghafour's case is instructive, because he is perhaps the country's most pragmatic Salafi politicians. If he has pulled out of politics, albeit temporarily, the more ideological Salafis are more likely to do so and maybe even reject democracy altogether; others could opt for the insurrectionist path. Thus there are serious questions about the conditionalists' future trajectory, especially since democratization in Muslim countries is likely to be an extremely bumpy and non-linear process. Will they keep moving forward? If so, where will they stop? Some could move into participatory Islamism, whereas many others will remain in the conditionalist camp for the foreseeable future. Thus, in many ways conditionalist Islamism is an unsustainable position and may well prove to be a temporary stepping-stone on the path of democratization. In fact, it is quite likely that some of its adherents will agree with some aspects of democracy while objecting to others. But these will be the exceptions, for one can expect many conditionalists to gravitate slowly but surely toward greater acceptance of democracy as a value.

Salafis want to—but ultimately cannot—avoid fully emulating the MB, because they have no alternative approach to politics. In fact, even as conditionalists they are rejecting only certain aspects of democracy. The reality is that they will need to come to terms with their conceptual ambiguity concerning democracy and may find themselves adopting the MB position. In theory, conditionalist Islamists can remain Salafis in religious terms and continue along the democratization path.

In practice, however, this is not tenable because Salafi doctrine is less accommodating to the idea of democracy. Attempts to adjust theological positions have resulted in intra-conditionalist disagreements, most notably between Ghafour and Yasser Burhami, the leader of the al-Nour's parent body. During a December 2011 talk show, Ghafour responded to a question on why al-Nour had not fielded Christian candidates that he regretted the Copts' absence on the party list but hoped that they would run on al-Nour's ticket in the future. The remark elicited a sharp rebuke from Burhami, who strongly reiterated that only Muslims could hold "positions linked to the objectives (*maqasid*) of the Muslim state."[46] Similarly, when al-Nour announced that it might enter into a parliamentary alliance with secularist groups such as Free Egyptians, led by prominent Coptic businessman Naguib Sawiris, Burhami once again declared that "any alliance with groups that oppose God's Law is absolutely forbidden."[47]

Prior to the Arab uprisings, the majority of Salafis considered democracy un-Islamic because electing legislators to create laws infringes upon the sovereignty of God, the only valid sovereign.[48] Therefore, establishing the supremacy of democracy as well as legislative bodies violates the core Islamic belief that only God has the right to legislate and make laws. The burgeoning new Salafi parties across the Middle East, however, have launched a monumental shift away from this doctrinaire position.[49] Although they share a common core religious doctrine, they differ on how to operationalize their principles to address modern policy issues. Thus, conditionalist Islamism's different groups will continue to exhibit a multiplicity of attitudes.[50] Even within a single party there are often disagreements on the degree of flexibility one can exercise in reinterpreting religious texts in order to progress toward democratization. In this regard, al-Nour's slogan, "The only reform we desire is the reform we can achieve," is very telling,[51] for it contrasts sharply with the very literal Salafi understanding that Islam is a comprehensive framework for religion and state. The tensions between Burhami and Ghafour underscore al-Dawah al-Salafiyah's fears that the compromises by its political wing will eventually undermine it adherents' religious doctrines.

Since 2012, Egypt has witnessed a rapid mushrooming of Salafi parties. The emergence of new parties, the splintering of preexisting ones, and the creation of multiple new coalitions are all underway as this book goes to press. In general, such a reality indicates that Salafis are seeking a more active role in politics. The conditionalist Islamist landscape is still in the making, and thus it is quite hard to say exactly how many groups are out there. Furthermore, at this point any significant degree of insight about their internal ideological differences is lacking. However, we can discern two general trends: (1) there is a clear distinction between the more pragmatic (e.g., al-Watan) and the more conservative Salafis (e.g., al-Nour) and (2) they are trying to outdo each other by attempting to maintain their bona fide theological credentials while displaying their new political sophistication. Thus the landscape remains in flux. To get a sense of how dizzying the Salafi dynamic is, one only needs to look at how al-Nour supported the coup against Morsi while many of its smaller rivals continued to support the MB.

The Egyptian Salafis' embrace of parliamentary politics in 2011 was not unprecedented. What is surprising, as William McCants astutely points out, is that their support for this course of action has waxed and waned with their changing perceptions of the elections' fairness and the risk of sitting on the sidelines.[52] An examination of these shifting views reveals that many of them, especially after Mubarak's fall, have accepted parliamentary party politics for one specific reason: the benefit of shaping the new government's nature and activities outweighs the cost of compromising their principles and leaving the work to their competitors (e.g., secularists and less conservative Islamists).[53] Similar calculations will likely be made when there are open and fair elections in other Muslim-majority countries with large Salafi populations who wish to protect their own institutional clout. Such political participation has reduced—and may continue to reduce—the appeal of jihadist Salafis and their message of violent government overthrow.[54]

Under authoritarian systems, Salafis either steered clear of any political activism (e.g., political activism against the autocrats was tantamount to creating chaos [*fitnah*]) or appropriated the jihadi discourse to justify armed struggle. Even though they have now jumped into the political fray, the question of how they can steer the transition toward their envisioned "Islamic" state remains wide open. Decades of avoiding any political discourse and inexperience in political activism, and then suddenly being forced to play on a turf where their rivals perform far better, has put them at quite a disadvantage. Since politicized Salafis lack any kind of roadmap, their strategy is to take one step at a time. For now they are comfortable with engaging in politics to secure a major say in drafting a new constitution that will more or less adhere to their vision of shari'a.

But while they are figuring out how to attain this goal, they also have to ensure that they do not leave their communities behind. Since the Arab Spring, these groups have fractured even more and along multiple lines. Those who have joined the political mainstream, and are now riven by internal disagreements, have managed to alienate those who wish to adhere to their traditional apolitical ways. At the heart of this debate is what kind of compromise political Salafis will strike to reconcile ideology with political engagement. The possibility that the ongoing arguments might divert many from democratization should not surprise anyone, for after all these Salafis are dealing with an alien system that forces upon them a stark choice, one that does not face the MB: to leap beyond their traditional ideological boundaries or adhere to their traditional intellectual limits.

Several factors—all of them rooted in Salafism's origins as a religious doctrine instead of a political creed—will limit progress along this path. Given that it is a religious trend, as opposed to a coherent political ideology spearheaded by an organizational vehicle, for much of its history Salafism has been a non-Islamist force that still suffers from a chronic poverty of political thought. Initially this factor resulted in a great many Salafis becoming jihadists. But now this deficit is pushing the more flexible Salafis toward the MB model, and so for now Salafis in general either remain rejectors or conditionalists. Since the FIS's participation in the ill-fated 1990–1991 Algerian parliamentary elections to the emergence of Egypt's Hizb al-Nour, a significant number of Salafis have accepted electoral politics but not necessarily democracy. At best, this can be considered a very raw form of procedural democracy.

As we have seen, Egypt is the main arena for the interplay between Salafism and democratization. But any discussion of these two dynamics would not be complete without discussing this interplay's implications for Saudi Arabia, Salafism's birth-place and largest hub. Riyadh, like most Arab monarchies, has thus far escaped the chaos of Arab Spring. However, it is afraid that the turmoil, and especially the influence of the MB movements, will eventually cross its borders. In fact, the MB poses a major challenge on two levels: (1) it provides an alternative religious worldview to Saudi Arabia's apolitical Salafism and, more importantly, (2) seeks a democratic polity, which makes it hard for the Saudis to legitimize their monar-chy. Thus the Saudis, very soon after the outbreak of the 2011 uprisings, sought to contain the MB mainly through encouraging the rise of Salafi parties. The events of the past three years, particularly the anti-Morsi coup, suggest that Riyadh may have succeeded in neutralizing the MB threat. In addition, so far the kingdom has remained immune to the Arab Spring because of the dominance of apolitical Salafism.

However, the al-Saud cannot maintain its monarchical order while the sur-rounding countries are experiencing the rise of conditionalist Islamism among Salafis. Its efforts to use conditionalist Islamists against the MB represents a double-edged sword in that the kingdom cannot promote Salafi parties outside its border without incurring some blowback within its own borders. The cross-pollination of Salafi and MB ideas, which we discussed earlier, has also taken place in the kingdom, where a significant group of ulema and other intellectuals have been receptive to MB ideology. Prominent among them is Salman al-Awdah, a former leading figure of the 1990s *sahwa* (awakening) movement in Saudi Arabia. During July 2012 he posted the following on his Twitter and Facebook page: "Democracy might not be an ideal system, but it is the least harmful, and it can be developed and adapted to respond to local needs and circumstances."[55] Given his status, this pronouncement is a significant acknowledgment of the region's chang-ing political landscape. Undoubtedly, the rise of politically oriented Salafis will be the Saudi royals' main challenge even as they try to manage a difficult generational transition.

In this chapter we attempted to unpack the complexities of conditionalist Islamism and its relationship with democratization. Salafi Islamists represent the middle ground between participatory and rejector Islamism. We now turn our attention in the next two chapters to the central forms of rejector Islamism, namely, nationalist and transnational jihadists.

# 6

# Rejector Islamists: al-Qaeda and Transnational Jihadism

Over the last three decades, Muslim religio-political resurgence has undergone a significant metamorphosis insofar as its approach to establishing an "Islamic" polity is concerned. Disillusioned with what they perceived as their forerunners' passivity, in the late 1960s and early 1970s a much younger and radical generation of Islamists adopted a more violent and combative posture toward the region's incumbent pro-Western, secular, nationalist regimes and the Western governments that supported them.[1] A small segment of Islamists[2] were radicalized and became militant in the aftermath of the Arab defeat in the June 1967 war with Israel. This event, along with the general suppression of mainstream Islamists by the autocratic Egyptian state in the 1950s and 1960s, prompted certain individuals and groups to turn to armed insurrection as a means to establish an Islamic state. To justify their new militant approach, they incorporated the concept of jihad into the body of their political discourse. Consequently, over the last three decades the world has witnessed the emergence of a new type of Islamist political grouping: *jihadist* movements.[3]

Words like "jihad," "jihadist," and "jihadism" have become an integral part of the lexicon used by journalists, government officials, and academics, and yet they are often misunderstood. For example, "jihad" is usually mistranslated as "holy war" waged by "Islamic fundamentalists" in an effort to forcibly convert non-Muslims to Islam. Clearly, there is a crucial need to distinguish between two very different types of jihad, for the classical Islamic concept is far removed from the jihadist ideology and modus operandi of certain contemporary militant Islamist political groups. "Jihad" linguistically emanates from the Arabic root "ja-ha-da," which in generic sense means to struggle for a cause. Aside from its linguistic understandings, jihad in the classical period of Islam was understood as a state enterprise. The consensus among jurists was that "*jihad* is an attempt to assert state control over military activity against" non-state actors. As Heck shows this understanding prevailed from the Umayyad through Abbasid caliphal eras. In his view, "*Jihad* in its classical form can thus be understood as an instrument of foreign policy."[4] Classical scholarship generally viewed jihad, in its military sense, as being either *al-jihad al-mubada'ah* (offensive jihad) or *al-jihad al-dafa'ah* (defensive jihad). The Hadith literature also distinguishes between *al-jihad al-akbar* (the greater jihad) and *al-jihad al-asghar* (the lesser jihad): the former connotes the struggle for self-discipline according to the shari'a, and the latter refers to fighting to repel an invasion or end an occupation.[5] As Heck explains, the classical Islamic concept of jihad was formulated by the jurists of the time to specifically outlaw the ad hoc use of violent means by non-state actors. Contemporary Islamist militant groups justify their actions as jihad but clearly their interpretation falls outside the classical view of lawful jihad. That said, it is essential to make sense of the jihadist use of violence by evaluating their claims of being engaged in a legitimate armed struggle against forces they deem hostile to Islam and Muslims. The jihadists have reinterpreted the classical concept of jihad as a means by which to establish an Islamic state(s). This understanding is unprecedented. Qutb argued that jihad must be regarded as a "permanent condition, not an occasional concern," one that, given the current circumstances, requires deeds rather than words, struggle rather than contemplation, and revolution at home as well as resistance abroad.[6] In the premodern period this was the duty of the caliph, emir, or sultan; however, the post–Ottoman Empire geo-political vacuum[7] allowed non-state actors to justify that in the absence of a religiously legitimate state authority jihad had become an individual and/or group effort.

Jihadism, as Brackman correctly points out, is a "clumsy and controversial term." As it is a modern neologism, it is foreign to Islamic history and has little religious significance to Muslims. Those who use it do so out of convenience because, despite its inherent problems, it does communicate a vital point: militants and groups like al-Qaeda are distinguished from other Islamists by their singular focus on violent jihad.[8] Jihadism is, therefore, an ideology espoused by disparate militant groups operating on the periphery of the Islamist spectrum, groups that have appropriated the notion of jihad to legitimize non-state actors' use of force to reestablish a transnational "Islamic" polity. Intuitively, "jihadist" functions as an adjectival reference to this approach as well as to those individuals and/or groups who adopt this ideology to achieve their stated aim: overthrowing the Muslim world's current political order, which they see as dominated by pro-Western secular, nationalist, and authoritarian regimes busily implementing various hybrid capitalist or socialist economic systems. Clearly, therefore, *jihad* and *jihadism* are not the same thing.

The roots of jihadism can be traced back to its cradle: post-1948 Egypt.[9] The Arab defeat in the 1948 war with Israel, coupled with the growing anti-British sentiment, led to widespread civil unrest in Egypt. In response to the loss of Palestine, the MB launched a campaign to develop a broad-based anti-government movement. Led by founder Hasan al-Banna (d. 1949), the MB gained immense popular respect for the group's active participation in the 1948 war. It subsequently emerged as a powerful political force. The government's fear of an MB-led revolutionary takeover of the state was exacerbated by the group's ability to stage large-scale anti-government demonstrations in major cities. It thus decided to curtail the movement. Nokrashy Pasha, the then prime minister of Egypt, immediately ordered its dissolution. Three weeks later, on December 28, 1948, he was assassinated by allegedly an MB member. Ibrahim Abdul Hadi, a member of a faction of the Wafd party, succeeded Pasha and, after consolidating his power, also sought to crush the movement. Thousands of its members, workers, and, supporters were arrested, tortured, and held in desert camps without trial. In addition, the assassination of al-Banna on February 12, 1949 caused the group to fall into further disarray. As a result, the organization was driven underground and led many of its members toward radicalism. The ensuing leadership vacuum had more ideological than administrative repercussions. While Hasan al-Hudaybi succeeded al-Banna as the organization's General Guide, several ideologues began writing and came to be seen as carrying the ideological torch, among them Abdel-Qadir al-Awdah, Muhammad al-Ghazali, and Sayyid Qutb. This latter figure would have the most enduring influence on future generations of Islamists.[10]

In the midst of this turmoil within the MB, the Free Officers Society led by Colonel Gamal 'Abd al-Nasser ousted King Farouk in a coup d'état on July 23, 1952. Although relations between Nasser's regime and the MB had been uneasy from day one, the alleged attempt on Nasser's life by an MB member on October 26, 1954, gave the regime a pretext for a massive crackdown. This second phase of suppression involved arrests, torture, and executions. In an effort to make sense of Muslims seeking to advance the cause of Islam being attacked by fellow Muslims, Qutb advanced his controversial thesis of *jahiliyyah* and the belief that jihad should not be restricted to self-defense:

> If we insist on calling Islamic jihad a defensive movement, then we must change the meaning of the word "defense" and mean by it "the defense of man" against all those forces that limit his freedom ... When we take this broad meaning of the word "defense," we understand the true character of Islam, in that it proclaims the universal freedom of every person and community from servitude to any other individual or society, the end of man's arrogance and selfishness, the establishment of the sovereignty of Allah and His Lordship throughout the world, and the rule of the divine shari'a in human affairs.[11]

His central argument in his book *Milestones* furnished the intellectual framework for the jihadist groups that surfaced decades later. The government's anti-MB campaign reached its peak when Qutb, charged with subversion, terrorism, and inciting sedition, was executed on August 29, 1966. The following June, the Israeli defense forces inflicted a humiliating defeat on the combined forces of Egypt, Syria, and Jordan during the third Arab-Israeli war.[12]

These events ultimately gave rise to several proto-jihadist groups: Munazzamat al-Tahrir al-Islami, Gamaah al-Islamiyah, Takfir wa al-Hijrah, Tandheem al-Jihad.[13] Jihadism thus grew out of the MB's suppression during the 1950s and 1960s, but only in the 1970s did the *takfeeri* (excommunication) ideology take hold, a development that led to the emergence of sustained jihadist activity. The first major jihadist action took place when junior officers affiliated with Tandheem al-Jihad assassinated President Anwar Sadat in 1981. Muhammad Abd al-Salam Faraj provided the seminal manifesto *The Neglected Duty*, which would become the standard reference for the first generation of Egyptian jihadists.[14] Faraj argued that the present-day Muslim rulers, particularly in Egypt, had forsaken their religious duty to apply shari'a and had taken non-believers as their allies: "The rulers of these days are apostate. They have been brought up at the tables of colonialism, no matter whether of the crusading, the communist, or the Zionist variety. They are Muslim only in name, even if they pray, fast, and pretend that they are Muslims."[15] Therefore, waging jihad against them until they either repented or were killed was seen as the personal duty of every Muslim who could fight.[16]

Another major boost to revolutionary Islamists everywhere was Iran's 1979 revolution. By ousting the pro-Western Shah and replacing him with an Islamic republic, Iran's new Islamist regime became the champion of the worldwide Islamist cause by supporting a variety of Islamist groups in the Arab world and elsewhere.[17] In that same year, the Islamist insurgency began in Afghanistan against a fledgling communist stratocracy supported by Soviet troops. This proxy war attracted thousands of Islamist volunteers worldwide, all of them anxious to join the jihad against what was seen as godless communism. They were funded by Saudi money, armed with American weaponry, and furnished with Pakistani logistics acting in consortium.[18] The ensuing war (1979–1989) served as the incubator for the formation of al-Qaeda and enabled the rise of major jihadist figures (viz., Osama bin Laden, Ayman al-Zawahiri, and Abu Musab al-Zarqawi) as well as those who would form the rank and file of the jihadist groups that surfaced during the 1990s. The Afghan war, along with the American-led 1991 Persian Gulf War, encouraged many radicalized Salafis from Gulf Arab countries to join the jihadist movement, which provided yet another extremist component to its ideology. This meeting of Salafi socio cultural conservatism and Qutbi political radicalism produced the militant variety of Islamism that characterizes al-Qaeda. Bin Laden, its financier and figurehead, represented the organization's Salafi strain, and al-Zawahiri, leader of a faction of Egypt's Tandheem al-Jihad and al-Qaeda's chief ideologue, represented its radical Qutbi heritage.[19] This Salafi–Qutbi alliance incubated in Afghanistan largely due to the anarchy prevailing there during the 1990s. After the Soviet withdrawal, the Salafi–Qutbi radicals gained an ideal base of operations under the banner of what was emerging as al-Qaeda. As the ultra-conservative Taliban movement took over the war-torn country in 1996, al-Qaeda began pursuing a transnational agenda.

Transnational jihadism was a response to a perceived failure of jihadist groups seeking to topple the regimes in their respective countries.[20] Those who called for creating an international jihadist movement argued that the Arab/Muslim world's regimes could not be overthrown from within as long as they were supported by the West. In addition, this new genre of jihadists advocated responding to American military action against Muslim countries—either directly citing the example of the 1991 Gulf War or American support for Israel, which was seen as occupying pivotal Muslim land. Transnational jihadists thus prioritized fighting the *far enemy* as opposed to the *near enemy*.[21] This ideological transformation from the late 1980s to the early 1990s played a key role in the genesis of al-Qaeda. One factor that facilitated its rise was the weakening of those nationalist jihadists who had been active decades earlier in countries such as Egypt and Syria. These original jihadists had rejected the MB's approach of using constitutional/electoral means to realize an Islamic polity. To a great degree, the eventual shift toward militancy was based on an ideological disagreement with the MB, especially in terms of rejecting democracy as a Western and un-Islamic concept. An equally (if not more) important factor was the secular autocratic Arab rulers' brutal suppression of non-violent Islamists, which drove many younger Islamists away from the MB's acceptor approach and toward insurrection.

Much has been written about how the ideas of radical MB ideologue Sayyid Qutb played a key role in shaping the jihadist worldview, especially after his 1966 execution. But not enough attention has been paid to how secular authoritarianism served to push many Islamists away from mainstream politics and toward violent extremism. It is true that Qutb's journey from a secular civil servant and literary figure to a radical Islamist ideologue began with his trip to the United States in the late 1940s. A late-comer to the MB, his years with it coincided with the period of its systematic suppression of the organization by the Nasser regime. The result of the regime's autocratic nature, coupled with its heavy reliance on coercive means, was that many MB leaders were jailed and tortured. This ongoing suppression of dissent also brought the viability of the MB's political approach into question. Furthermore, republican Egypt's violent methods had the unintended consequence of pushing many Islamists toward radicalism. Qutb managed to fill this leadership vacuum with his radical diagnosis of what was going on in Egypt and the wider Arab/Muslim world. But he never truly embraced the movement's ideology, partly because of the time he began to associate with it and partly because he was an intellectual in his own right. In fact, the combination of these two factors allowed him to produce a political prescription that contradicted the MB's gradualist transformation. In other words, the lack of an open democratic environment and the militaristic suppression of all opposition reinforced the conviction in armed struggle among those Islamists who were already opposed to participating in a democratic polity.

Such rational arguments as that the MB's participatory method was flawed because it assumed a nonexistent democratic environment played a critical role in shaping insurrectionist Islamism. The authoritarian state's use of force to impose its secular order and stamp out all peaceful calls for a political order in keeping with the majority population's religious ethos contributed to the discourse of *takfeer*, which eventually gave way to the idea that jihad had to be waged against the state itself. Herein lies the basis for the transformation of jihad's classical-era definition as a state enterprise into jihadism, a modern reinterpretation that calls for the use of military force to reestablish an Islamic state. Eventually jihadism evolved from its initial incarnation as a competing modus operandi within Islamism to become an ideology unto itself. Ideational factors also played a major role in its emergence. In addition, significant structural reasons related to the lack of democratization in large parts of the Muslim world have shaped the jihadists' opposition to democracy. Thus, in a paradoxical turn of events, the lack of a democratic environment produced the jihadist form of Islamism. Armed insurrection against secular autocratic regimes coupled with the rejection of democracy forged a new ideology. Jihadism sought to recreate earlier caliphates or emirates, which in essence represent an Islamist version of authoritarianism. Attempting to graft a medieval template onto a modern reality meant that the focus was not so much on political thought in terms of change, but increasingly on armed struggle. The path of insurgency necessitated the movement's clandestine nature that, in addition to rejecting the state, also steered clear of society as a whole. The use of violence to topple the incumbent order gave rise to what we identified in Chapter 2 as the insurrectionist form of Islamism. In addition, the jihadists' opposition to democracy on ideological grounds placed them in the rejector camp. In theory, however, *rejector* Islamists do not necessarily have to be *insurrectionist* as well. But *insurrectionist* Islamists did not only oppose the *acceptors'* approach on a rational basis. For them, it was not simply a matter of calling for armed struggle against powerful military-backed dictatorial states as the only logical way forward. Had that been the case, they could have behaved like other rebel groups that have used violence to replace entrenched authoritarian regimes with a democratic order or limit the use of force to freeing their lands from foreign occupation and, once in power, govern via democratic political systems. But for the jihadists, their opposition to the MB was a function of their rejection of democracy as an un-Islamic political system that violated the principles contained in the Qur'an and Sunna as well as those derived from them. Privileging select writings of certain classical jurists in their definitions of Islamic governance and how it needs to be revived were key to jihadism's growing focus on armed conflict. Furthermore, there was a great deal of blurring of the lines between fighting non-Muslim occupation and reestablishing a global Islamic polity.

## The 1990s

Bin Laden, al-Zawahiri, and al-Qaeda's military chief Mohammed Atef saw their organization as an international Islamist vanguard. While its roots can be traced back to the war against the Soviets in Afghanistan in the 1980s, al-Qaeda truly materialized as a transnational force only during the early to mid-1990s. Its primary goal was to fight what it saw as American-led aggression against Muslim countries; establishing an Islamic political order was no more than a secondary goal. There is a particular logic to this evolution: The 1990s represented a decline in the nationalist jihadists' fortunes particularly in Egypt and Algeria, where the state crushed their insurgencies. In both cases, the jihadist actors limited themselves to operating within the boundaries of their respective countries. At the same time, the ongoing internationalization of both jihad and jihadism began to move them away from establishing Islamic governments within the context of specific nation-states and toward globe-trotting jihadism. In many ways this shift had already begun during the internationally backed Islamist insurrection in Afghanistan. In that case, the shift was a 360° one because most of the Afghan Islamist insurgents were initially pursuing the aim of an Islamic state and consisted of all three types: acceptors, propagandists, and insurrectionists. The Soviet entry forced them to shift from establishing governance to defending Muslim lands against what they perceived as international communism's massive invasion of a Muslim land.[22] Only a decade later, when the Soviet forces withdrew, did the Afghan Islamists and many of their foreign allies return to their original goal.[23] Intuitively, this swinging of the proverbial pendulum from setting up an Islamic state to defending Muslim lands back to setting up an Islamic state was a natural adjustment of priorities based on ground realities.

This experience was highly instrumental in shifting the agenda away from Islamic governance within the boundaries of a given nation-state to fighting non-Muslim forces on a global scale that either directly control "Muslim lands" or seek to expand and consolidate their influence there. Much of this flowed from the logic of the post–Cold War era. The collapse of pro-Moscow regimes in Eastern Europe and the subsequent implosion of the Soviet Union itself led to Muslim forces in the Balkans (mainly Bosnia), Central Asia (e.g., Tajikistan), and the North Caucuses (Chechnya and the surrounding regions) finding themselves at war with those who were, until recently, their fellow citizens. Indeed, many Afghan war veterans were soon fighting in one or more of these new theatres. Emboldened by their success in Afghanistan and the USSR's subsequent fall shortly thereafter, some of these battle-hardened fighters returned home to confront their own national ruling regimes. As many were denied entry on the grounds that they were a security threat,[24] many either settled in Afghanistan or Pakistan and then joined al-Qaeda or region-specific causes or became involved with Pakistani groups. In this latter case, they furthered Pakistan's foreign policy toward Afghanistan and India.[25] It is important to recall that Muslim states leveraged the presence of these Islamist militants to make the case that their countries were not ready for democracy. The autocratic regimes used the jihadists as a tool to contain those groups that were calling for democratization, particularly the participatory Islamists. But these same militants soon became a threat, as was the case in Egypt during the 1970s and 1980s. Fortunately for the rulers, the Afghan war made it possible for them to export these insurrectionist Islamists.

Between exporting and using such groups as proxies to further their own national security goals, Muslim states were major shapers of transnational jihadism as they surely preferred that to fighting nationalist jihadists at home. Since both authoritarian Muslim states and Islamist militant groups opposed democracy (for their separate reasons), they pursued zero-sum outcomes in terms of military solutions, which left no room for political accommodation. Thus instead of Islamist militants being pulled back into the national mainstream, they were further pushed toward transnational causes. Meanwhile, other key developments throughout the decade contributed to this transnationalization, such as the American intervention in Somalia (1992), the first World Trade Center bombing (1993), bomb attacks on American military personnel in Saudi Arabia (1995 and 1996), bin Laden and al-Qaeda's relocation from Sudan to Afghanistan and the Taliban's rise to power (1996), suicide bomb attacks against American embassies in East Africa (1998), the Kargil war between Pakistani military-backed Islamist insurgents and Indian forces in Kashmir (1999), and the attack on the USS Cole in Yemen (2000). Each of these attacks was in part designed to shape Western perceptions of a new rising global threat from the Muslim world. Complementing this jihadist intent was the West's own reaction, which further magnified the threat. By proclaiming transnational jihadists as the main threat—it put them on the agenda and allowed them to take center stage—despite their minority status in the wider jihadist milieu. By the end of the 1990s, transnational jihadism had essentially supplanted nationalist jihadism. However, there were a couple of notable cases in 1999 when nationalist jihadists began giving up armed struggle, such as Egypt's Gamaah al-Islamiyah's renounciation of violence and a large number of Algerian jihadists laying down their arms in exchange for official offers of amnesty.

Al-Qaeda was able to advance a strategy of transnational jihadism based on two core objectives: (1) fighting and expelling American forces from Muslim lands and (2) replacing Muslim governments with a transnational caliphate. The transnational jihadist network emerged on the global scene by trying to fight the American-led Western presence in the Muslim world. Achieving this goal, however, would require a model that differed from that of the Afghan Islamist rebels and their Muslim supporters who forced the Soviets to withdraw from Afghanistan. Instead, al-Qaeda adopted terrorism on the grounds that unlike that war, a campaign against the United States would receive no backing from Muslim regimes. Therefore, a guerilla war was not feasible. Furthermore, these jihadists began to think that the only way they could fight the national regimes was to sever the links between them and their Western backers, particularly the United States. Analyzing how nationalist jihadist efforts during the 1970s and 1980s had been crushed, al-Qaeda posited that a direct attack on the United States would cause it to pull back. By attacking American targets, they hoped to lessen American support for Muslim states and thereby be in a better position to engage the regimes directly.

The jihadists had several expectations, among them (1) the American military's withdrawal from the Middle East would both rid Muslim lands of foreign occupation and liberate the holy cities of Mecca and Medina, and (2) the absence of American soldiers would make it easier for them to overthrow the secular regimes. After all, they had watched Islamist rebels in Afghanistan throw out the Soviet-backed Kabul regime only three years after the Soviets' departure. However, they knew that the conditions in Afghanistan—a weak state and strong local support for al-Qaeda's cause—could not be replicated in other Muslim countries. Moreover, the jihadists were not a social movement that could mobilize the masses and overthrow a sitting government. Their method of toppling governments required the creation of anarchy, which would not only weaken the governments but also help draw people out of their comfort zones and make them more willing to support the cause. Moreover, they had seen that chaos had been instrumental in forcing American troops to withdraw from Vietnam, Lebanon, and Somalia. But as al-Qaeda itself could not create the necessary anarchy. What it sought was an external intervention similar to the Soviets in Afghanistan during the 1980s. The transnational jihadist organization hoped to bait the United States into attacking a key Muslim country preferably Saudi Arabia to create the desired upheaval. For this to happen al-Qaeda need to stage a massive terrorist strike inside continental United States. The 9/11 plot was designed precisely for this purpose. That 15 of the 19 hijackers that participated in the 9/11 attacks were Saudi citizens indicates how al-Qaeda sought to create a crisis between Washington and Riyadh. It should be recalled though that al-Qaeda's earlier argument, that American military forces were occupying the kingdom, remained problematic because these forces were stationed at bases out of the public's sight and were not engaged in any hostile action within the country. Moreover, the Persian Gulf Arab states generally accepted the fact that their weakness necessitated the protection of the American security umbrella. While this last factor helped al-Qaeda delegitimize the national regimes, it also meant that denying American support to them would be very difficult. Al-Qaeda saw its main challenge as driving a wedge between the two, which it sought to do by revealing the national regimes' inability or unwillingness to crack down on those groups that wanted to attack American interests. In fact, al-Qaeda was eager to show that its members had support from powerful quarters within the Saudi state itself, a reality that would create a crisis of confidence and force the United States to take matters into its own hands. This strategy gave birth to a new idea: Attacking the United States on its own territory might elicit a retaliation against the Muslim world (preferably Saudi Arabia) that would be strong enough to eventually stir up Muslims worldwide. The outbreak of war between the United States and the Muslim world would ultimately weaken the autocratic Arab regimes. At some future point during this global war, the al-Qaeda leadership believed, Washington would eventually be forced to withdraw its troops leaving behind weakened states this making it easier for the jihadists to overthrow the various national regimes. In the aftermath, the vanguard of the struggle—meaning itself and its allies—would step in to fill the power vacuum and establish the desired "Islamic" dominion.

## The Post-9/11 Decade

Contrary to al-Qaeda's expectations, the American reaction did not trigger the hoped-for global Muslim uprising. Realizing al-Qaeda's strategy, Washington avoided striking at Saudi Arabia. Nevertheless, its strategy appeared to be so incoherent that even today questions remain as to why it chose to invade Iraq and oust Saddam's regime.[26] Ironically, these military campaigns lent credence to the jihadist claim and conspiracy theories about an American-led Western war against Islam and Muslims. But the outcome was far more manageable than what would have happened if the United States had responded as al-Qaeda had hoped.

The wars in Afghanistan and Iraq, along with the global intelligence dragnet and the more recent use of unmanned aerial vehicle (UAV) technology, were all part of the effort to prevent Muslim regimes from collapsing and thereby creating a vacuum. Through a combination of pressure and incentives, the Bush administration was able to secure the cooperation of the Muslim countries in its global war against jihadism. While there was a great degree of disbelief in the Muslim world about al-Qaeda and its capabilities, there was also a substantial desire to show that transnational jihadism was a fringe element. Significantly, even the nationalist jihadists and Salafis repudiated its agenda. Most telling has been the Afghan Taliban's recent attempts to distance itself from transnational jihadism while using al-Qaeda elements as force multipliers, even though they staunchly defended al-Qaeda after the 9/11 attacks.[27] It is true that al-Qaeda-related violence has increased exponentially in Iraq, Yemen, Pakistan, Syria, Somalia, Libya, Algeria,

Mali and elsewhere. But this development is not due to transnational jihadism gaining strength; rather, it is due to the weakening of those states as well as to al-Qaeda's fragmentation and devolution, both of which were unintended consequences of the American response to 9/11. Muslims have overwhelmingly rejected the notion of *takfeer*, and al-Qaeda's killing of innocent civilians has led to the declining support for jihadists among Muslims since the 9/11 attacks. Indeed, the majority of the Muslim world has rejected jihadism especially because of the internal chaos it has created and the tensions between western and Muslim countries.[28] Islamists of different stripes (e.g., nationalist jihadists, Salafis, and even such radical entities as Hizb al-Tahrir) have gone to great lengths to distinguish their views from those of al-Qaeda. Although there is a very strong aversion to accepting Western influence in shaping mainstream Muslim thought and practices, powerful calls have been made across the Muslim world to reject extremism.

The Bush administration will always be remembered for its "war on terror," as well as the great amount of energy it expended on its Greater Middle East Initiative, which made such a pivotal contribution to deconstructing autocracy in the region well before the outbreak of the Arab Spring. While far from making serious progress toward democratization because of its ethno-sectarian nature, Iraq has come a long way from the days of the Baathist state. Even Afghanistan has developed a modest level of political institutions, especially when compared to the state's erosion during the Marxist era and the subsequent intra-Islamist civil war period. In both countries, where the future of democracy remains mired in great uncertainty, al-Qaeda's erstwhile allies have turned against the transnational jihadist movement. Iraqi Sunnis are largely playing by the democratic rules, and the Afghan Taliban are trying to enter the political mainstream. Even though its policy was replete with problems, the Bush administration realized early on that military campaigns alone would only exacerbate the jihadist threat. It therefore concluded that fighting jihadism would require a shift in its decades-long stance on democracy in the Muslim world. In other words, the support for the authoritarian status quo had to give way to democracy promotion. In a way, 9/11 upended unqualified American support for Muslim regimes, but not in the way the global jihadist network had desired. After effecting regime change in Afghanistan and Iraq, the Bush administration used its democracy promotion initiative (albeit selectively) to press countries like Egypt and Saudi Arabia to begin limited political reforms.

Iraq represented the United States' first collaboration with Islamists to replace a secular authoritarian regime with a democratic one. Initially, Washington partnered with the country's Shia Islamists, ethno-nationalist Kurds, and a few MB-type Sunni Islamists to lay the foundations for a democratic Iraq. By 2007, as part of its efforts to end the Sunni insurgency threatening the nascent democratic regime, the Bush administration had negotiated with jihadists (who had parted ways with al-Qaeda and its transnational agenda) and brought them into the political mainstream. Since both Egypt and Saudi Arabia had effectively dealt with their internal jihadist problems, the United States concentrated on stability. Thus there was little appetite to push hard for real democratic reform beyond the usual rhetorical statements.[29] Certainly, Hamas's 2006 victory in the Palestinian

Legislative Council elections—brought a pause to some of the administration's enthusiasm for democracy promotion. On the one hand, democracy served as a useful tool, since participatory Islamists served as a counter to radical and militant jihadists. But on the other hand the rise of Hamas, a militant Islamist group that engaged in terrorism against Israel, was an unintended consequence of Washington's approach. Overall, the regional policy of democracy promotion had to be implemented on a case-by-case basis and in line with each country's circumstances. For example, Yemen's hybrid regime allowed political parties and held periodic elections, and yet the country was another major transnational jihadist hub. Therefore, the Bush administration's goal was to make sure that the regime could contain al-Qaeda within its borders, especially since both society and state (particularly the security establishment) contained jihadist sympathizers. Similarly, Jordan and Syria had no jihadist problem and ensuring their continued internal stability was essential to managing Iraq. Jihadists were not an internal threat to Morocco and Tunisia; however, as they did represent a threat to Europe's security, it was essential to keep them stable. In those days Tunisia, due to its small size, was considered inconsequential in terms of the region's wider dynamics. Morocco, on the other hand, had traditionally used participatory Islamists (JDP) to contain al-Adl wa al-Ihsan and Salafists as well as a variety of jihadist *rejector* movements. Prior to 9/11, Algeria, North Africa's largest state, had successfully contained a decade-long jihadist insurgency.[30] Furthermore, Algiers had developed a combination of democratic and autocratic measures that kept participatory Islamists weak and divided.[31] Most significantly, its elections gave secular parties a key edge over Islamists. In 2003, Libya's Qaddafi regime made a strategic decision to renounce its historic policy of state sponsorship of terrorism and gave up its weapons of mass destruction (WMD) program in exchange for better relations with the West. While Tripoli had decades of relations with many terrorist entities worldwide, it had zero tolerance for Islamist militancy at home. Had these two factors not been in play, it was quite possible that the United States would have aggressively pushed for democratization there as well.

Finally there was the peculiar case of Pakistan, which after 9/11 began to emerge as both al-Qaeda's new global headquarters and a sanctuary for other international jihadist entities. Historically, the United States had worked with this country's military regimes that had dominated it for more than half of its existence. If there was one country in which the United States needed stability, it was Pakistan, and so Washington paid lip service to the cause of democracy there. In terms of democratization and Islamism, Pakistan represents an odd case. Before 9/11, most Islamist groups in the country were participators, despite their radical policy agenda, and thus did not pursue extra-constitutional means to gain power. But since non-Islamist parties consistently outperformed them at the ballot box, they had remained marginal players. The largely secular military–intelligence establishment has promoted Islamist groups as tools of domestic and foreign policy, a practice that conflicted with American interests after 9/11. Washington, however, refrained from using democracy as a tool to shape the behavior of Pakistan because of its geopolitical and strategic position vis-à-vis Afghanistan. Furthermore, the

Musharraf regime portrayed itself as bringing about democracy in a bottom-up manner and championed the idea of "enlightened moderation." In a *Washington Post* op-ed, Musharraf proposed a two-pronged approach: (1) the Muslim world should shun militancy and extremism and adopt the path of socioeconomic uplift, and (2) the West, particularly the United States, should work to resolve all political disputes with justice and help improve the Muslim world's currently deplorable socioeconomic condition.[32]

Through a skillful display of constitutional and electoral engineering, the Musharraf regime for the first time allowed the MMA to emerge as Parliament's second largest political bloc in the 2002 elections. The Islamist coalition also took power in the North-West Frontier Province and was part of Baluchistan province's coalition government. Musharraf used this outcome to create the perception that only his secular military government could contain Islamist radicalism. But while shaping a civil–military hybrid regime, he inadvertently instituted policies that allowed the democratic forces to grow via the rise of private media, civil society forces, an assertive judiciary. In fact, towards the end of his reign a powerful legal movement gave birth to an independent judiciary that forced him to relinquish his position as military chief (2007) and resign from the presidency (2008). Running parallel to democratization was a potent jihadist insurgency predicated upon growing religious radicalism and extremism. As many as 40,000 Pakistanis have died in dozens of post-9/11 jihadist attacks, the majority of them since 2007, that have largely targeted the country's security forces. The Musharraf regime was replaced by a coalition government led by the left-of-center Pakistan People's Party, which along with the other main non-Islamist parties took the bulk of the seats in the 2008 elections. This first democratic government in over a decade, spent the bulk of its five-year term in office fighting jihadism. In June 2013, Pakistan made history when for the first time ever one democratically elected government handed power to another after Prime Minister Nawaz Sharif's right-of-center Pakistan Muslim League won elections. Despite this major development the future of democracy there remains uncertain, especially given the poor state of the country's economy and a massive jihadist insurgency. Traditional Islamist parties, which have always had a rather marginal influence, have been further weakened by the growth of propagandist and, more importantly, insurrectionist Islamist groups. Complementing this trend is the public's disillusionment with democracy because of the outgoing government's poor track record.[33] Pakistan thus represents an exceptional case of democratization and Islamism, for the interplay between the two dynamics continues to undermine its budding democracy.

## The Arab Spring and Beyond

In some parts of the Muslim world, democratization was occurring well before 9/11; in other places, the American response jump-started it. Nonetheless, the general view was quite pessimistic in regards to the Muslim world's hope for democratization, mainly because of the series of events, among them 9/11, the resulting "war on terror," and the Islamist militancy engendered by the American military and intelligence operations conducted in Muslim countries.

The Arab Spring took place at a time when the world was heavily preoccupied with al-Qaeda and jihadism. As Fawaz Gerges points out, for a decade al-Qaeda had "a hold over the Western imagination, in part because the West will not let it go."[34] Yet most Arabs and Muslims were not buying it. He suggested that "the Arab awakening of the spring of 2011—in Tunisia, Egypt, Libya, Yemen, Bahrain, Oman, and Syria—has not only shaken the very foundation of the regional authoritarian order but threatened to unravel the standard terrorism narrative. As the Arab revolutions gathered steam, al-Qaeda Central was notably absent. Neither jihadist slogans and rituals nor its violent tactics found a receptive audience among the millions of Arab protesters."[35] Instead the Arab masses opted for peaceful protests and successfully toppled long-entrenched autocratic rulers— a setback from the jihadist doctrine of armed struggle. By the time Mubarak had been ousted and the Libyan, Yemeni, Bahraini, and Syrian regimes found themselves grappling with the outpouring of street agitation, it became quite clear that the Muslim world's "silent majority" had rejected both jihadism and autocracy.

Nearly three years later, however, the region remains in a state of flux. Authoritarian rule is slowly unraveling and the outlook for democratization is uncertain. This tumultuous transition period has inadvertently produced a vacuum in which jihadists are finding considerable room to maneuver. Here it is important to distinguish among states with evolving regimes (e.g., Egypt and Tunisia), collapsed regimes (e.g., Libya), and resilient regimes (e.g., Syria).[36] The first group of countries offer fewer opportunities for jihadists because they have a robust societal presence of participatory and conditionalist Islamists. In contrast Syria, which lacks such opportunities for participatory and conditionalist Islamists, have proved attractive to jihadists. Thus, autocrats and jihadists are the two principal actors that stand to lose from democratization. While the former are trying to hold on to power and thus portray the upheaval as a recipe for anarchy, the latter fear a democratic transition will limit the space for them to operate. Autocrats are using all available resources in an attempt to preserve as much of the old order as they can. Meanwhile, jihadists are trying to exploit the uprisings to topple the autocratic regimes and prevent the establishment of democratic polities. Some autocrats are either accusing the opposition of being jihadists or are warning that any weakening of the incumbent state will benefit the jihadists. As the Syrian civil war highlights, both claims have some merit. But the latter claim is far more significant in terms of implications, for regime-collapse threatens the viability of the Syrian nation-state, which is based on complex ethno-sectarian demographics. And, any such breakdown can only facilitate transnational jihadism's agenda. Syria is the most obvious case. The regime's decision to use military force to crush the uprising has created an outright civil war, with competing rebel groups (largely different Islamists and jihadists) battling a regime that is also slowly devolving into a non-state actor. Exacerbating matters is the wider geo-sectarian struggle between an Iranian-led largely Shia bloc and its multiple opponents (e.g., the United States, European powers, Turkey, Saudi Arabia, and Qatar).

Jihadists of various types (transnational and otherwise) have long been fighting secular autocracies. Their opposition to democracy was less visible in light of the scant prospects for it. Now that the authoritarian systems are crumbling, jihadist opposition to democracy becomes extremely relevant. The jihadists will be able to create physical space for themselves in the transitional period through armed action given that they have the military experience and an edge over religious discourse of resistance. They can be expected to benefit during the stage of insurrection after which they will try to block efforts towards the creation of democratic orders. The non-Islamist forces' military and ideological weakness renders them incapable of successfully forging new democratic order after the *ancien régime* falls. The only forces that can block the jihadists and facilitate democratization are their Islamist competitors, whether participatory Islamists (i.e., the MB) or the *conditionalists* (i.e., the Salafis). The former's political experience can help develop democratic structures and processes especially in countries, such as Libya, that have to build political systems from scratch. It is also essential that such countries' Salafis be *conditionalist* in nature so they can counter the jihadists on the theological front. That said, their *conditionalist* attitude toward democracy poses a serious risk of recidivism,

As recent entrants to mainstream politics, many Salafis are quite likely to be easily disillusioned by democracy. The risks of such an outcome increase if the process is disrupted or if the Salafis feel that it is falling well below their minimalist demands as regards enacting shari'a. For them, establishing the rule of law is nowhere near as important as their desire to see their preferred interpretation of shari'a implemented. Therefore, some of them may decide that the way forward in such circumstances is to move toward jihadism as opposed to adopting the MB model, especially in tribal social conditions.

### Jihadism and Democratization

As we have seen, jihadists are the least likely to accept democracy. All evidence suggests that they have rejected it and they view the participatory Islamists' embrace of democracy as blasphemous. *Rejectors* argue that any government not ruling solely by shari'a is apostate; democracy is not just a mistaken tactic but an unforgivable sin, because it gives people, instead of God, sovereignty. Al-Zawahiri, who succeeded bin Laden as al-Qaeda's chief, calls it "the deification of the people." Abu Hamza al-Masri, the Egyptian born jihadist leader who for years presided over London's notorious Finsbury Park mosque, considers democracy "the call of self-divinity loud and clear, in which the rights of one group of people, who have put their idea to vote, have put their ideas and their decisions over the decisions of Allah." Abu Muhammad al-Maqdisi, whom a recent West Point study found to be the most influential living jihadist thinker, proclaims, "Democracy is obvious polytheism and thus just the kind of infidelity that Allah warns against, in His Book."[37] The fact that jihadists subscribe to the most extreme forms of Islamism suggests that they are the least likely to accept any notion of democracy. There is a remote possibility, however, that if armed struggle does not eventually produce tangible results, some of them may abandon violence and gradually move into the conditionalist camp. This idea is not so far-fetched when one considers that that a large number of Algerian jihadists laid down their weapons and accepted an official amnesty. Similarly, groups such as Egypt's Gamaah al-Islamiyah renounced violence altogether and since the Arab Spring have formed political parties.

It should be noted that the Afghan Taliban movement (which we will discuss in the next chapter), the only jihadist-style organization that was successful in obtaining power via insurrection (1996–2001) is also in the process of trying to enter the political mainstream.[38] Al-Qaeda remains defiant though and insists on pursuing armed struggle against Muslim states and the American-led West. This dissonance between the two former allies underscores the critical difference between transnational and national jihadist entities. The Taliban and other similar jihadist groups, among them Jabhat al-Nusrah currently fighting the Syrian regime and the various Sunni Islamist militant groups active during Iraq 2003–2007, are rooted in specific national contexts. Al-Qaeda, on the other hand, gave rise to a new transnational form of jihadism. A necessary first step for deradicalization is rejecting this transnational jihadist agenda and returning to nationalist form of jihadism. Limiting the scope of the attacks to one's homeland suggests an acceptance of the nation-state, which moves the jihadist actors closer to seeking power in a given national context as opposed to an idealistic agenda of an endless global war against multiple non-Muslim and Muslim actors. Nationalist jihadists are likely to have a more realistic view of their limits and thus the extent to which they can fight their way to authority. Being invested in a given country tends to push jihadists toward seeking a stake there, which causes them to deal with the question of Islamic governance as opposed to being a perpetual armed opposition force. This dynamic has recently been seen in Yemen where the country's branch of al-Qaeda (known as al-Qaeda in the Arabian Peninsula) has moved to establish outfits such as Ansar al-Shariah. These new entities are designed to deal with the issues of governance in areas under the jihadist control while the core group continues to push a transnational agenda. Thus, there can be cases where jihadists in a particular country or region are simultaneously behaving as transnational and nationalist actors.

Once refocused on "Islamic" governance, jihadists are more likely to reevaluate their insurrectionist approach toward establishing an Islamic political entity. The assumption here is the presence of a democratic political arena that offers nonviolent ways to realize their objectives. In addition, there must be competition from a real rival—conditionalist and, more importantly, participatory Islamists. It is unlikely that jihadists will learn from the MB, given the major differences between the two. But given their shared core theology with the Salafis, jihadists are more likely to be open to Salafi ideas. Therefore, it is essential that there are Salafis who have embraced mainstream politics and offer the jihadists a nonviolent political prescription. In countries where regime collapse does not occur and the democratic transition continues to move along (albeit slowly and with disruptions), jihadists face a dilemma of relevance. This was especially the case in Egypt when both Salafis and former jihadists gravitated towards the MB's approach. Furthermore, the willingness of Muslim states and the West to negotiate with jihadists who are willing to part with al-Qaeda's transnational jihadist agenda and confine themselves to the existing national framework could facilitate a return to nationalist jihadism.

While al-Qaeda's franchises continue to wreak havoc in Iraq, Yemen, Somalia, Nigeria more recently, in Mali and the Maghreb/Sahel regions, al-Qaeda prime has been severely weakened by the American war against it. Transnational jihadism thus suffers from both physical and intellectual threats, a reality that is bound to generate much internal debate about their future. This is even more the case since many former jihadists have turned toward political participation on the grounds that the conditions that justified insurrectionist Islamism no longer exist. One prominent former Egyptian jihadist who served decades in jail for assassinating Sadat in 1981, Abboud al-Zumar (Tandheem al-Jihad), now favors a political approach. His cousin Tarek al-Zumar, who suffered a similar fate and is now a prominent Gamaah al-Islamiyah leader, first came out with this strategy, in his *Al-Badil al-Thalith bayna al-Istibdad wa-al-Istislam* (*The Third Alternative between Despotism and Surrender*), which he coauthored with his cousin in 2009 while both of them were still in prison.[39] After their release less than a month after Mubarak's ouster, they stated in an interview with Reuters that the age of armed insurrection is over and the new democratic order would prevent Islamists from using violence against the state. According to Abbud, "The coming period does not at all require armed struggle with the ruler."[40] Arguing that past violence was a reaction to state oppression, Abbud was quoted as saying that "violence breeds violence." Tarek elaborated on this by saying that militancy was no longer applicable because the country has shifted toward a climate of freedom. In his own words, "Our concern in this period is to anchor the basis of a just political system which guarantees freedoms and the state of law"[41] and "The project of establishing the Islamic state as a political model will be determined by the ballot box ... and the thing that will determine its continuation in power is the choice of the people."[42] Al-Zumar pursued a law degree during his incarceration. Their statements clearly show that some jihadists could abandon political violence.

This abandonment occurred in Mubarak-ruled Egypt partially because of the authoritarian regime's hybrid nature. For example, it perpetuated the military-backed single-party state but also permitted a limited amount of political competition. Gamaah al-Islamiyah's imprisoned leadership declared a ceasefire in 1997, before some internal rogue elements killed 62 mostly foreign tourists at Luxor's Pharaonic temple complex. For the next five years, the group's jailed leaders began what would become an intellectual metamorphosis that would lead them away from political violence. By the time of the 9/11 attacks, al-Gamaah was publishing "The Initiative for Stopping the Violence," which eventually grew into a series of books entitled *The Concept Correction Series*. In 2007 Sayyid Imam Abd al-Aziz Imam al-Sharif, the most renowned jihadist theoretician, as well as the leader of Tandheem al-Jihad and one of al-Zawahiri's mentors, published *Tarshid al-Jihad fi Misr wa al-Aalam* (*Rationalizations on Jihad in Egypt and the World*). In it, he essentially recanted all of his prior treatises justifying violence to establish an Islamic state.[43] These Gamaah al-Islamiyah and Tandheem al-Jihad ideologues based their arguments on juristic and rational reasoning. In other words, these two groups have moved from rejector to conditionalist Islamists. While a world of difference still remains between them and the MB, these former insurrectionist Islamists have now entered the conditional category.[44] A key reason for this is that while both groups were insurrectionists as regards establishing an Islamic polity, in doctrinal terms they were not hardcore Salafis. In contrast, many Salafi-jihadist groups could have a hard time renouncing violence due to their underdeveloped political thought, and an even harder time accepting democracy because of its Western origins.[45] In most cases, such jihadists are unlikely to either give up violence or embrace democracy, in which case they will remain at the "militant Islamists" end of our political spectrum. Those who give up violence yet remain opposed to democracy will have moved along the spectrum to the left and entered the "radical Islamist" category. Groups such as Gamaah al-Islamiyah. and to some extent Tandheem al-Jihad, have made their way rather easily from the "militant" end of the Islamist spectrum to the "conservative Islamist" category, as have those Salafis who have joined electoral politics. Following the Arab Spring, Gamaah al-Islamiyah officially established itself as a political party—Hezb al-Banna' wa al-Tanmiya (The Building and Development Party). Initially denied a license by the Political Parties Affairs Committee on the grounds that its platform was "purely religious," it was officially recognized during October 2011.[47] It even provided a political and socioeconomic platform that highlighted some of its reservations about secular democracy and insisted that religion must be an integral part of the state. Some of its key highlights were[48]

- Supporting a new political system based on the principles of freedom, justice, plurality, equality, and peaceful rotation of power.
- Promoting legal, constitutional, and political reform, such as greater judicial oversight over the national security apparatus.
- Supporting solutions to social, political, economic, and strategic challenges that come from Islam and the modern application of Islamic law.
- Preserving Egypt's Islamic and Arab identity and challenging any attempts at Westernization and secularization.
- Establishing strong Islamic values in society to combat injustice, corruption, and moral decay.
- Establishing Islamic *hudud* or criminal punishments including the cutting off of hands for theft, stoning to death of adulterers, and lashing of those who drink alcohol.
- Supporting the roles of the family and women in society in accordance with Islamic principles.
- Spreading the political concepts and values of Islam and combating smear campaigns against Islam.

There could be some cases in which jihadists give up violence and return to being apolitical Salafis engaged in religious preaching and thus would exit Islamism altogether. But it is difficult to see too many jihadists giving up politics, which means that renouncing jihadism as a way to establish an Islamic state will be difficult. But if jihadism is renounced and the jihadist actor(s) does not abandon politics, there are two options: (1) try to enter mainstream politics and align with Gamaah al-Islamiyah, Hizb al-Nour, or similar groups, or (2) steer clear of constitutional politics and engage in vigilante activism to influence the political process from the outside. Many Tunisian Salafi-jihadists have adopted the latter approach. In this current age of democratization, jihadists will be pressured to offer alternative political models. Even if they deem democracy un-Islamic, they might accept the concept of elections. Under a limited franchise system, only religious scholars, tribal leaders, and military commanders would be allowed to help select the emir. Paradoxically, al-Qaeda and its form of transnational jihadist agenda can both promote and undermine democratization. Many radicals and militants were rethinking the entire notion of fighting Muslim states even before 9/11. Al-Qaeda's attacks on the United States facilitated the process of ideological and behavioral transformation. In contrast, the Arab Spring has created renewed opportunities for the growth of jihadism, specifically in Syria where civil disobedience has given way to armed insurrection. Elsewhere, in Egypt following the 2013 coup that ousted President Morsi and the subsequent suppression of the MB, there is the risk that many of these conditionalist and even participatory Islamists could engage in insurrectionist behavior. Indeed there has been an increase in attacks in the Sinai and to a lesser degree in mainland Egypt. What is interesting though is that Gamaah al-Islamiyah has assumed a cautious position where it condemns the coup but is also critical of the MB's hardline stance against the putsch.

Having discussed transnational jihadism, in the next chapter we turn our attention to jihadists operating within national boundaries by examining the Afghan Taliban movement.

# 7

# Rejector Islamists: Taliban and Nationalist Jihadism

Like al-Qaeda, the Afghan Taliban are *rejector* Islamists who have not yet moved much beyond the idea that democracy is incompatible with Islam.[1] Like other jihadist groups, they are insurrectionist Islamists, waging an insurgency against Western forces and the Afghan state. Yet, unlike Al-Qaeda which is a transnationalist, the Taliban is a nationalist jihadist group. As a nationalist jihadists group the Taliban accept the framework of the Afghan nation-state. This still begs the question why devote an entire chapter to relatively small group of largely militant Pashtun Islamists who reject democracy. The case of the Taliban provides unique insight into an ultraconservative manifestation of Islamism that cannot escape the geopolitical context it finds itself. Indeed, the Afghan Taliban's behavior in the post-9/11 decade increasingly shows that they have cautiously adjusted their behavior and ideology in order to remain relevant at a time when the country continues to democratize.

Democratization in Afghanistan is a long, slow work in progress that has inched along for over a decade. Yet during this time, the process has created a political reality that the Taliban are unlikely to militarily dismantle. Well aware of this, the insurrectionist Islamist movement has been forced to seek accommodation with the state it has been battling. Indeed, the Afghan jihadists realize that their armed struggle has had limited impact and their goal of establishing an Islamic state will have to be pursued through political means. Thus, through their negotiations, especially those with the United States, the Taliban have been forced to seek a power-sharing arrangement for a post-NATO Afghanistan.[2] Meanwhile, the far more militant Pakistani Taliban, who share al-Qaeda's transnational jihadist agenda, are undermining—even while being shaped by—the democratization process in Pakistan that began anew with the fall of General Pervez Musharraf's military regime in 2007–2008.[3] This distinction between the Afghan Taliban and the Pakistani Taliban is important, especially in terms of its implications for democratization. Neither group is ready to fully embrace democracy, but the former one is a nationalist jihadist force that has limited its political ambitions to Afghanistan and has stated that it is ready to share power.[4] Furthermore, since 9/11 'the Afghan Taliban movement has increasingly distanced itself from the transnational al-Qaeda jihadist network.

The Afghan Taliban's ascent to power in the mid-1990s was the result of unique circumstances. The jihadist movement emerged in the context of the intra-Islamist civil war (1992-1996) between the various Islamist insurgent groups, which had toppled the Marxist regime in 1992 but then began fighting each other. Fifteen years of civil war had destroyed the political and economic institutions of the country – a vacuum that allowed the Taliban to quickly seize control of most of the country. Those circumstances no longer exist, because American and international efforts have helped to develop the country's infrastructure over the past decade and significantly weaken the Taliban. A military seizure of power is not a viable option and the Taliban have no choice but to negotiate a power-sharing arrangement. In a communiqué issued in August 2011 on the occasion of Eid al-Fitr, the Afghan Taliban chief Mullah Mohammed Omar stated, for the first time that his group was not seeking to monopolize power and referred to the "Islamic Emirate of Afghanistan" as a non-state actor instead of an alternative shadow regime: "Our manifesto is that Afghanistan should have a real Islamic regime which is acceptable to all people of the country. All ethnicities will have participation in the regime and portfolios will be dispensed on the basis of merits."[5] He stated that: "Contrary to the propaganda launched by the enemies, the policy of the Islamic Emirate is not aimed at monopolizing power. Since Afghanistan is the joint homeland of all Afghans, so all Afghans have right to perform their responsibility in the field of protection and running of the country."[6] Undoubtedly, the underlying geopolitical circumstances and Mullah Omar's own pronouncement will necessitate that the Taliban accept some key aspects of the democratic political system.

A future Afghan political dispensation in which the Taliban represent a key component would be very different from the Taliban regime of 1996 to 2001. At that time the Taliban attempted to establish a political system based on their outdated understanding of an Islamic emirate established through territorial conquests against rival Muslim groups.[7] The loss of that state soon after 9/11 has led to a considerable—and ongoing—change in their political thought. Thus the Taliban have not yet offered a blueprint of their envisioned political system for post-NATO Afghanistan. The group's expressed readiness and desire to share power suggests that its members could accept some form of constitutional electoral political process, but one based heavily upon a strict reading of *shari'a*. The Taliban seek a political arrangement in which religious scholars maintain oversight over the political leadership. As a result, the Taliban's envisioned polity would be a Sunni version of Iran's hybrid regime. The jihadists' desire for such a religious dominated state is based on ideological motivations as well as political calculations. The Taliban understand that they are not likely to perform well at the polls even if they were to accept the democratic rules of the game. The Taliban by nature are an insurrectionist Islamist group and thus cannot simply end their armed struggle and enter electoral politics. In this regard, the Taliban cannot be compared to their insurrectionist Islamist counterparts in Egypt such Gamma al Islamiyah and Tandheem al-Jihad, which transitioned from insurrectionist to the conditionalist Islamist camp. GaI was a social political movement for decades before it took up arms and had years to transform itself after renouncing violence in 1997. In contrast, the Taliban are a product of civil war and have not known any other means of seeking power except through armed struggle. They are bound to take much longer to transition into the acceptor camp. Even if they accept the Afghan state without reservation it is still not clear where they stand on democratic politics. Therefore, it will be a while before the Taliban make their way into the conditionalist Islamist camp, if at all. It is no coincidence that in recent months reports have surfaced that the Taliban in their back-channel talks have said they would not compete in elections for many years to come. Therefore, the only way for the Taliban to ensure their place in a future Afghan government is to insist from the outset that the constitution be amended to grant them a pre-defined share of power in all three branches of government as well as the security apparatus. Regardless of its actual shape or form, if the Taliban and their opponents can agree upon a system of governance, the resulting state will likely be far more theocratic than democratic. It is important to understand that Taliban political thought is just one factor driving the negotiations, which we address in greater detail later in this chapter. But first, we provide a historical overview of the country's political development in the modern era and the many obstacles it has faced.

Afghanistan emerged as a sovereign entity, separate from both the Safavid and Mughal empires, with the founding of the Durrani dynasty (1747–1823). During the days of the Emirate of Afghanistan, Emir Abdur Rahman Khan (r. 1880–1901) began to modernize the country, while Emir (later King) Amanullah Khan (r. 1919–1929) began to Westernize and secularize Afghanistan. Religious conservatives resisted Amanullah's westernization policies and eventually forced him to abdicate. Monarchical rule continued until the mid-1960s. During this period, Afghanistan's longest reigning king Mohammed Zahir Shah (r. 1933–1973) instituted the country's first democratic reforms. In 1964, a new constitution that allowed the people to elect one-third of the representatives to a bicameral legislature. The king appointed one-third of the representatives, and the provincial assemblies indirectly selected the final one-third. This experiment initiated two key changes to the country's political structure: Political parties at both ends of the spectrum were permitted to operate. In addition, members of the royal family were not allowed to hold political office.[8] It was, however, short-lived because his cousin Sardar Mohammed Daud Khan, who had served as prime minister (1953–1963), overthrew the king and established a secular republic with himself as its first president. Daud came to power with the help of the military and, more critically, the country's communist movement: the People's Democratic Party of Afghanistan (PDPA). Under the latter's heavy influence, he introduced socialist policies and, more importantly, pushed for the nationalistic reunification of Pashtunistan (split between Afghanistan and Pakistan). The government of Pakistan's first democratic leader, Zulfikar Ali Bhutto, retaliated by supporting some of Daud's Islamist opponents, such as Gulbadin Hekmatyar, Burhanuddin Rabbani, and Ahmed Shah Massoud.

The Afghan Islamists emerged during the struggle over Pashtunistan. By the mid-1970s, the tension between secular and religious forces, which had started during Amanullah's reign, intensified. Islamist groups among the Pashtuns (e.g., Hekmatyar's Hizb-i-Islami) and the Tajiks (e.g, Rabbani's Jamiat-i-Islami) were initially composed of university students. The watershed event, however, was the April 1978 military coup, which led to Daud's killing and the PDPA's seizure of power marking the establishment of the Democratic Republic of Afghanistan, a communist regime, which ideologically polarized the country. In December 1979, the Soviet Union militarily intervened to secure this Marxist stratocracy, amid the infighting between its two rival wings (viz., the Parcham and the Khalq). The entry of Soviet troops into the country led to an upsurge of Islamist forces nationwide and the mobilization of Islamist fighters from across the Muslim world who flocked to Afghanistan. Democratization had already been derailed by Daud's establishment of an autocratic republic followed by the communist coup. For the next 10 years a major Islamist insurgency ravaged the country and laid the foundations for its major turn toward insurrectionist Islamism.[9]

## The 1990s

In 1987, there was an attempt to transform the single-party state established by the April 1978 Saur Revolution[10] into a more democratic one. The country's fourth communist president (and former intelligence chief) Mohammad Najibullah called for a ceasefire between Kabul and the seven-party Islamist rebel alliance and initiated a process of national reconciliation. A new constitution was drafted and a three-chamber legislature was established, composed of the traditional *loya jirga* (grand assembly), a senate, and a house of representatives. This latter institution would replace the PDPA's revolutionary council. The one-party system was abolished and the word "democratic" was removed from the country's official name. Once again it was known as the Republic of Afghanistan and Islam was once again declared the official state religion.

The Islamist rebel alliance rejected these concessions for its leaders, encouraged by their battlefield gains, concluded that they had more to gain from fighting than from reaching a power-sharing deal with the communists. In addition, the Afghan Islamists' ongoing radicalization had made them uncompromising in their attitude. Thus they rejected Najibullah's peace proposals and the fighting continued. The Soviet withdrawal was a major boost to their morale. What further emboldened both them and their foreign Arab/Muslim allies was the Soviet implosion less than two years after the last Soviet soldier's departure.

Afghanistan has had only limited experience with democracy, transforming, almost overnight, from a monarchy to an authoritarian republic. In addition, the country underwent rapid a ideological shift. In under three decades it went from an uneasy blend of religious and secular state identity to a heavy dose of communism followed by a near total tilt towards insurrectionist Islamism. During this period, an ideological transformation was occurring among the country's Islamists, many of whom went from viewing jihad as a way to end the Soviet occupation to a means of establishing an "Islamic" state. This led to jihadism becoming the dominant trend in Afghanistan, even though the contours and exact nature of this Islamic state had neither been articulated nor fully thought through. Thus the Soviet withdrawal left the Islamists without a roadmap of how to construct their cherished Islamic polity. The two major Islamist rebel organizations, Hizb-i-Islami and Jamiat-i-Islami, modeled after Egypt's Muslim Brotherhood and Pakistan's Jamaat-i-Islami initially subscribed to the electoral/constitutional process as a means of achieving power. The Cold War context, which aggravated ideological opposition, helped transform them from acceptors to insurrectionists. Put differently, they sought the incumbent state's total demolition and thus were pushed toward using armed struggle to construct their Islamic polity. Compounding this situation was the fact that both Afghan Islamist groups cooperated closely with Pakistan's Jamaat-i-Islami, which pursued electoral politics as a way to power at home but insisted that the Afghanis could only achieve their goal through jihad. In addition, Jamaat-i-Islami encouraged its own cadre to go there and join the fight.[11] Whatever little commitment to democratic politics the Afghan Islamist groups had, soon evaporated as they began interacting with the Arab jihadists on the battlefield. The Soviet collapse further reinforced the belief that armed struggle offered more dividends than any peaceful approach. This idea played a key role in their decision to reject the communist regime's national reconciliation program, as did the constant encouragement from their American, Saudi, and Pakistani backers, not to mention that of the militant foreign fighters. Another element reinforcing this view was the centuries old Afghan tribal tradition of doing "politics by other means," In fact, imposing military defeat was the means of transfer of power between different dynastic groups in the Muslim world since the founding of the Umayyad dynasty.

The United States ended its support after the Soviet withdrawal; the Saudis and the Pakistanis, however, continued on with the project due to their policymakers' view that toppling the Marxist regime was a key national security interest. The Najibullah government, contrary to many estimates, actually survived its patron's collapse and the discrediting of communism as an ideology. In fact, a plan conceived by then ISI chief Lt. Gen. (retd.) Hamid Gul to have the Afghan Islamist rebel alliance capture Jalalabad from the Afghan army failed, thereby demonstrating the communist state's resilience despite the departure of nearly 100,000 Soviet troops.

The war would rage on for a little over three years until Moscow under the government of President Boris Yeltsin was forced to end fuel and food supplies given the post-Soviet economic crisis in Russia. The shortages in Afghanistan led to defections within the Afghan army. A key defection was that of Afghan army commander Abdul Rashid Dostum whose forces played a pivotal role in the capture of Kabul after Najibullah lost control of the capital. Soon after Najibullah sought refuge in the United Nations office in Kabul in 1992, the several Islamist factions began fighting each other. In fact, the manner in which they entered the capital set the stage for an intra-Islamist civil war between those who had been allies for over a decade. The Peshawar Accords, an ill-fated attempt to formulate an acceptable power-sharing arrangement, could not prevent this new type of civil war. The intra-Islamist struggle following a decade of insurrectionist Islamism, were key factors that only intensified this four-year tragedy.

The main belligerents were the two major Islamist parties: Hizb-i-Islami and Jamiat-i-Islami. Other factions would align with one of them and, in many cases, later switch sides, as was the case with Dostum's group. The civil war was sparked by Hekmatyar's Hizb-i-Islami, backed by the Pakistani intelligence service, wanted to dominate the post-communist regime. Several attempts to revive the Peshawar Accords failed, as Hizbi-i-Islami had begun a vicious bombardment of the capital. These warring Islamist rivals, divided by ethnicity, sect, and foreign backers (e.g., Pakistan, Saudi Arabia, Iran, India, Russia, and Tajikistan), quickly spread across the country. Rabbani and Massoud's Jamiat-i-Islami, in conjunction with some of the smaller factions, set up the Islamic State of Afghanistan. But since this latest regime spent most of its term fighting, most of the country quickly succumbed to anarchy, which gutted the urban centers that had until then largely escaped the essentially rural-based communist-Islamist civil war.

Two years into the intra-Islamist war, the Taliban, based in Kandahar, came on the scene as a new force that hoped to end the infighting and stabilize the country. The predominantly Pashtun segments of society initially supported their emergence. At the time, Islamabad, disappointed with the performance of their main proxy, Hizb-i-Islami, and impressed by the Taliban's battlefield successes, threw its weight behind this new and far more radical militia composed of mullahs, tribal elders, and younger Islamist militiamen loyal to the Kandahar-based Mullah Mohammed Omar. After two years of fighting various factions, which included a brief alliance with the Rabbani government in Kabul, the Taliban gained control over much of the country's southern, eastern, and western regions. In September 1996, it seized Kabul and proclaimed the Islamic Emirate of Afghanistan, a development that triggered a re-alignment among the main Islamist factions. For example, Hekmatyar finally agreed to cooperate with Rabbani. But by this time the old factions, now weaker and with little (or no) credibility, were forced to flee the capital. The Taliban, which had emerged as the main Pashtun group, forced Hekmatyar to go into exile in Iran. With the Taliban in control of the Pashtun areas in the south and east, the non-Pashtun minorities set aside their previous differences and formed the Northern Alliance, a coalition largely representing the Tajik, Uzbek, Hazara, and other ethnic minorities.

The Taliban's ultraconservative interpretation of Islam led it to seek allies among al-Qaeda and the foreign fighters who had long been in Afghanistan and had come from other Muslim countries, the areas of the Former Soviet Union and even Europe. These foreign fighters, along with Pakistani, Saudi, and UAE assistance, enabled the Taliban to push the Northern Alliance into a small area in northern Afghanistan bordering Tajikistan. The Northern Alliance, led by the Tajik group Jamiat-i-Islami, continued to claim that the Islamic State of Afghanistan was the country's legitimate government and was recognized as such internationally, particularly by the United Nations. By the end of the 1990s, the ground reality was that the Taliban controlled some 90–95 percent of country and were imposing the most draconian Islamist rule ever seen in contemporary times.

Essentially, the Taliban symbolize the upshot of the trend toward jihadism as well as the more mainstream Islamist forces' failure to reach a power-sharing formula within the framework of a Muslim democracy after having toppled a leftist autocracy. At the onset of the new millennium, Afghanistan had drifted toward an extreme form of Islamism, one that was incompatible with democracy.

### The Post-9/11 Decade

In 2000 the Taliban regime, faced with widespread international sanctions, embarked on a diplomatic initiative to ease its isolation. Its harsh rule had already turned the population, which had initially welcomed it as the restorer of internal security, against it. The United States was pressuring it relentlessly for harboring al-Qaeda, especially after the 1998 bombings of the American embassies in Kenya and Tanzania. Even its relationship with Saudi Arabia was growing tense, for Mullah Omar would not hand bin Laden over to Saudi authorities, even after Prince Turki al-Faisal, the kingdom's intelligence chief, visited Kandahar and met with the Taliban founder. The hijacking of an Indian Airlines flight from Nepal to Kandahar caused the regime to be put under the spotlight and labeled as a supporter of international terrorists. Likewise, Islamist militant rebels from Central Asia (mainly Uzbeks) and China's northwestern Xinjiang (aka Eastern Turkistan) province had found a launch pad in Taliban-ruled Afghanistan. The Taliban temporarily flirted with transnational jihadism more because of tactical needs as opposed to any strategic alignment. In the end, they remained a nationalist jihadist group even though they were doing business with al-Qaeda and others. In fact, there is little evidence that the Taliban had any ambitions beyond Afghanistan.[12] The provision of sanctuary to foreign militant forces was motivated by three factors: (1) assisting like-minded Muslims engaged in similar struggles in their home countries, (2) benefiting from their financial and technical assistance at a time when it had very few sources of external support, and (3) using them as force multipliers in their attempt to fully defeat the Northern Alliance and complete their takeover of the country.

A lack of political development, coupled with the Pashtun cultural norm of transferring power through military means, pushed the Taliban to fight with non-state actors that had different agendas.[13] Their most important objective was to consolidate power, which they could do only by imposing a complete defeat on the Northern Alliance holed up in the northern region of Badakhshan province. The alliance survived only because of the support coming in from Russia, India, and Iran, all of which were assisting those members of the alliance based in Tajikistan. Pakistan, the Taliban's principal backer, had already reached the limits of the support it could provide, for it was also busy on its eastern border with India due to the 1999 Kargil mini-war. The Taliban thus allowed the transnational jihadists to operate in their country in exchange for human and material battlefield assistance against the alliance.[14] There is no conclusive evidence to suggest that they were aware of al-Qaeda's plans to attack the United States on September 11, 2001. It was such a well-guarded secret that even key senior al-Qaeda officials were unaware of this plot. Therefore, it is highly unlikely that al-Qaeda shared what it was about to do with the Taliban, for despite the sharing of certain ideas their agendas were completely different.

The 9/11 attacks and the American response, which toppled the regime in a matter of weeks after the bombing began on October 7, 2001,would have a profound impact on the Afghan Taliban in terms of its relationship with al-Qaeda over the course of the subsequent decade and of its eventual embrace of geopolitical pragmatism. The American move to carry out regime-change had a sobering impact on them, for they could see that their decision to allow al-Qaeda to set up its global headquarters on their soil had very quickly taken them from being on the verge of consolidating power to being forced to give up everything they had accomplished and go into hiding just to survive.

The Taliban initially thought that the United States would stage a ground invasion, which they hoped would rekindle the national spirit of jihad that had sent the Soviet army packing. But when Washington devised a strategy that combined massive air power, intelligence cooperation with Iran, financial incentives, and anti-Taliban militias as its ground forces, the Taliban realized the futility of going up against such overwhelming odds. They therefore made the strategic decision to decline combat and return at a later time to launch an insurgency against the foreign forces and the Karzai regime.[15] The Taliban spent the early years following the fall of their regime to regroup.. The leadership, which had remained largely intact, went into hiding either in their core turf in the south or in the east or (and mainly) in Pakistan. Reviving the organization, let alone organizing an insurgency, proved difficult for Mullah Omar and his top associates in the movement's Majlis al-Shura.

During their first attempt to rise to power, the Taliban had the benefit of anarchy and the discrediting of the Islamist militias that had fought the Soviets. Foreign forces had departed the country five years before, and the collapse of the Najibullah government had left the Afghan state virtually non-existent. Moreover, they had the benefit of overt assistance from Pakistan and it was a pre-9/11 world in which the United States had not yet declared a global war against radical Islamism. In contrast, the Taliban's attempt at resurgence has taken place in an environment that contained a large number of American-led Western forces. NATO forces have enjoyed considerable local support from Afghans who sought liberation from Taliban rule. Almost immediately, the international community began to erect a new system of democratic governance. Meanwhile Pakistan, now under intense American pressure to crack down on the Taliban and al-Qaeda, could offer no more than limited assistance. In addition, Islamabad was engaged in a delicate balancing act between its interests on its western border and the need to cooperate with the world's sole—and now thoroughly enraged—post-9/11 superpower. Thus, it took a good three to four years for the Taliban to truly reconstitute itself in the form of a major insurgency.

While focused on advancing the insurgency, the Afghan Taliban leaders were largely cut-off from its al-Qaeda counterpart, much of which had survived the American assault on their facilities in Afghanistan by relocating to northwestern Pakistan. This created considerable distance between the two leaderships, which allowed the Taliban to re-assess their relationship with the transnational jihadist movement. The distanciation from al-Qaeda and fighting what they considered an American occupation of their homeland allowed the Taliban to emphasize their nationalist credentials. Al-Qaeda not only cost the Taliban their government, but it was also a liability undermining the latter's credibility among fellow Afghans. Furthermore, the Taliban leadership was bitter that, after its rout in Afghanistan, al-Qaeda invested far more resources in Iraq after Saddam was toppled. Another key factor that created a rift between the two movements was al-Qaeda's exploitation of Pakistan's internal tension between the state and Islamist militants over Islamabad's decision to side with the United States and largely freeze its militant proxy project in both Afghanistan and India. This dynamic led to the rise of the Pakistani Taliban, which differed from the original Afghan movement in regards to its ultimate goal: toppling the Pakistani state through armed insurrection. Al-Qaeda found allies among Pakistan's Taliban rebels in the tribal areas, parts of the Pashtun-dominated northwestern province, and other Pakistani Islamist militant elements based in the core province of Punjab. From the point of view of the Afghan Taliban, Pakistan was a source of support and thus should not be fought. More importantly, the insurgency in Pakistan distracted from the fight against the western-backed Karzai administration, which for the Afghan Taliban was the only legitimate cause. Furthermore, if Pakistan had to fight its own jihadist insurgency, less resources would be available to help the Afghan Taliban because of the overlapping battle space.[16] The insurgency in Pakistan did not really intensify until 2007 but it has taken the lives of some 40,000 Pakistanis including several thousand security forces personnel who have been the target of the al-Qaeda backed Pakistani Taliban rebels. After trying to manage this domestic insurgency through tactical-level offensives and negotiations, in the spring of 2009 Islamabad made a strategic decision to wage an all-out counterinsurgency offensive in both the Greater Swat region and South Waziristan.[17]

The offensives have since widened to include anti-extremism and deradicalization programs. These undertakings have severely impacted the Pakistani economy, which has been teetering on the verge of bankruptcy since 2008. More importantly, it has caused Pakistan to change its attitude toward the entire Taliban phenomenon, which has significant implications for the Afghan Taliban. Unlike the 1990s, Pakistan no longer views the group's return to power in a post-NATO Afghanistan as something positive. Facing an unprecedented Taliban threat within its own borders, any Taliban comeback next door could aggravate Pakistan's own domestic security problem. As a result, Pakistan would now like to see any Taliban resurgence kept within the limits of a broad-based power-sharing agreement. To this end, Islamabad has reached out to the Karzai administration and elements of the former Northern Alliance that are not part of the current Afghan government. At the same time, it is encouraging the Taliban to negotiate with its former enemies and join the political mainstream.

## The Arab Spring and Beyond

The Afghan Taliban insurgency has grown considerably since 2003, forcing Washington to seek a negotiated settlement with the Afghan jihadist movement.

The process has gained considerable momentum since 2010 to the point where both the Obama administration and the Taliban leadership have acknowledged that they have been in back-channel talks. In 2013 Washington sought formal public negotiations with the Taliban movement. They had been given an opportunity to open a political bureau in Qatar to facilitate this process. Part of the aim was to accord legitimacy to the insurrectionist movement. However, this effort did not gain traction and quickly led to the closure of the Doha office. As the Middle East began to unravel due to the Arab spring, the United States accelerated its efforts to try and bring the war to a close. Washington now needed to focus its attention elsewhere. The difficult democratic transition underway in the Arab world had direct implications in the efforts to mainstream the Taliban with the hopes to bring them into the political process. Furthermore, an agreement with the Taliban would facilitate the planned drawdown of NATO forces by the end of 2014. Regardless of how the negotiations proceed, the United States and the international community will not abandon the country as it did after the Soviet withdrawal. Considerable support will continue to be made available to the post-NATO Afghan state, especially in terms of military backing, along with Washington's latest military doctrine: keep a leaner physical presence in country and rely heavily on air power augmented by UAV technology and special operations forces. The Taliban are cognizant of this American intent and realize that this is not the mid-1990s when they were able to fill a security vacuum. Furthermore, if the Marxist regime held out for three years after the Soviets left, despite the loss of substantial external support and the presence of a well-armed insurgent force, then it is very likely that the Afghan state will be able to hold its own after the NATO drawdown. This is even more the case since the geopolitical conditions existing in 2014 will be the exact opposite of those that existed in 1989.

The aforementioned circumstances have softened the Taliban's ideological rigidity by instilling a sense of pragmatism. For one thing, they realize it is unlikely that they will be able to take power through force. Although they will be able to expand their domestic influence and control, the Taliban will experience a stalemate as soon as it pushes beyond its core turf in the south and east. The result would likely be a long civil war at a time when the movement is already exhausted. These multiple constraints have forced the leadership to negotiate with the United States in an attempt to secure as much power as they can and have the international community officially legitimize the group. As this legitimation must come before the NATO withdrawal, for the past several years the Taliban have offered to help the NATO forces withdraw in an orderly manner. In exchange, the Taliban have several demands, one of which is to be internationally recognized as a legitimate Afghan national political movement. In 2009, they issued a statement in which they depicted themselves as "nationalist actors upholding the undeniable Islamic right to self-defense . . . their objectives [were] defined as 'independence, Islamic social justice, human dignity and national identity.' "[20] In addition, they call for the release of prisoners and the removal of their leadership from the international terrorist lists. The United States would be willing to meet these demands if the Taliban (in addition to verifiably ensuring that they will no longer provide sanctuary to transnational jihadists) agree to a power-sharing arrangement with the Karzai regime and the other Afghan stakeholders who are not part of the current government. But the Taliban, while not averse to a coalition, is not willing to simply join the current political system. Rather, they want to alter the Afghan state in two ways: (1) to amend the constitution so that it conforms with their understanding of an "Islamic state"; and (2) to ensure that as the single-largest group representing the largest ethnic community (viz., the Pashtuns), it has a significant stake in any future political pie. This is where the negotiations intersect with the slow process of democratization underway in Afghanistan.

Meanwhile, Pakistan is trying to shepherd the Afghan Taliban along the path of political mainstreaming. At the same time, Islamabad seeks to roll back the domestic "Talibanization," which has led to the state's loss of sovereignty over its frontier regions from where the jihadists have been projecting power to all the major urban centers. The Pakistani approach is based on a two-prong strategy: 1) To physically eliminate as many of the jihadist elements who cannot be separated from al-Qaeda's transnational agenda with the hope is that this effort will diminish the strength of the Pakistani Taliban; 2) To force the remaining elements to accept a negotiated settlement within the framework of the Pakistani constitution. Ultimately, any reconciliation with the Pakistani Taliban intersects with the country's democratization process. Pakistan has begun the trek towards democratic consolidation whereas Afghanistan remains in a nascent stage of democratization. Pakistan's 2013 elections resulted in the first ever transfer of power between two democratic governments. In addition, the Pakistani judiciary is increasingly becoming assertive and there is a growing civil society activism and a vibrant independent media. Most importantly, there is a steady march towards civilian control over the military. All of these factors together have forced the new government in Islamabad to be more responsive to a significant public support for negotiations with the jihadist rebels. As a result, the increasingly democratic Pakistani state is having difficulty pressing the Afghan Taliban towards reconciliation with Kabul while pursuing a military solution with its own Taliban rebels. The right of center federal government of Prime Minister Nawaz Sharif and the further right party of Imran Khan, which governs the majority Pashtun, Khyber-Pakhtunkhwa province, are both pushing for talks with the country's main Taliban rebel alliance, the Tehrik-i-Taliban Pakistan (TTP). The TTP, however, emboldened by the state's defensive posture, has escalated attacks designed to force Islamabad to enter into negotiations from a position of weakness. This situation has led to considerable disagreements among the civil-military elite as well as the wider society over the political leadership's unanimous decision to pursue the path of dialogue. The government is under growing pressure to delay any talks until after it has militarily gained an upper hand. It is not clear how Islamabad will move forward with the talks but any talks with the TTP are unlikely to succeed. In essence, the Pakistan's transnational insurrectionist Islamists are trying to exploit the democratization in the country as well as the international efforts towards a negotiated settlement with their nationalist Afghan counterparts.

## The Taliban and Democratization

The Taliban do not believe in a deliberative political process, least of all in democracy. Generally speaking, those on both sides of the Durand Line subscribe to the idea that democracy is un-Islamic. While there may be some variance among the different Taliban elements, their view of democracy as a Western secular notion based on the West's Judeo-Christian heritage that grants sovereignty to people as opposed to the Almighty remains a core tenet. Furthermore, the Taliban believe that only God can legislate. Thus Western-style democracy, which empowers people and their representatives in legislative bodies (parliaments) as legislators, impinges upon God's exclusive domain. As a result, the entire democratic process is a sin. Ahmed Rashid's 2001 interview with the Taliban's foreign minister Mullah Wakil, conducted at a time when the Taliban still ruled most of Afghanistan, makes this point very clearly. Wakil referred to Mullah Omar in his capacity as *Amir ul-Mumineen* (commander of the faithful).

> Decisions are based on the advice of the Amir ul-Mumineen. For us consultation is not necessary. We believe that this is in line with the Sharia. We abide by the Amir's view even if he alone takes this view. There will not be a head of state. Instead there will be an Amir al- Mumineen. Mullah Omar will be the highest authority and the government will not be able to implement any decision to which he does not agree. General elections are incompatible with Sharia and therefore we reject them.[21]

It should be noted that Mutawakkil softened his view after the regime's fall. In fact, he is no longer an official part of the movement. For many years he has been part of the process of trying to bring the Taliban into the political mainstream by acting as a mediator. Importantly, he is only one of many former senior Taliban officials who have moderated slightly or reevaluated their views and political stances. But those waging the insurgency do not share their former colleagues' pragmatism and largely remain rejectors. Therefore, it is unlikely that the Taliban will readily accept the notion of democracy even if they are engaged in talks towards a power-sharing agreement. A general lack of political thought beyond implementing the shari'a, especially the *hudud laws* (pertaining to the most egregious crimes and thus most severely punished), limits the extent to which democracy can be appreciated with an Islamic qualifier. Furthermore, the Taliban remain insurrectionist Islamists in that their view is that their armed confrontation has been able to force their opponents to the table. It is important to point out that a qualitative difference between the Taliban and their predecessor groups. The seven groups that comprised the anti-communist insurgent alliance were political forces before they took up arms and were able to expend considerable energies on develop their ideas. Born in war, the Taliban's evolutionary trajectory, however, is very different from that of the insurrectionist Islamists who fought the Soviets.

The Taliban ideology sprang from the amalgamation of several intellectual and political developments: (1) the ultraconservative tribal Pashtun culture's established the broad normative boundaries of the desired order, (2) a militia composed of madaris students and exposed to a medieval curriculum taught by radical Deobandi clerics, (3) the understanding of as a war of liberation against a foreign non-Muslim military force, (4) a civil war among rival ideological and ethnic forces, and (5) the need to fight fellow Muslims seen as western collaborators. These are the main factors that have shaped the Taliban's specific flavor of insurrectionist Islamism. This would explain why the group sought to impose an archaic religio-political order. The Afghan Taliban did not have the time to fully develop their ideas when they took power in the mid-1990s. In the last dozen years the Taliban, while, trying to wage an insurgency, the movement's leadership has had more than ample time to re-assess how it governed during the five years they were in power in Kabul. While condemning its domestic opponents for having sided with the West to establish an un-Islamic democratic order in the country, the Taliban leadership realize how the country has moved far beyond the 1996–2001 period.

Indeed the Afghan state that has emerged since the 2002 Bonn Conference remains weak and the Taliban are hoping to take advantage of its weaknesses in the military sense. What the Taliban cannot do is to sell the model they implemented during the years they were in power. On the contrary, the Afghan Taliban have been forced to shift their position. Publicly the Taliban have skirted the issue of democracy but it is unlikely that the movement has remained unscathed by the democratization process gripping the country. The Taliban realize that they are behind the curve and that Afghanistan has moved ahead on the path towards democratization. What's more is that their opponents have advanced democratically and now retain considerable public support. The Taliban understand that not only were they reviled when their regime fell but over the past twelve years the Afghan nation has undergone political development to the point where it is not prepared to go back to the 1996–2001 political climate. For this reason, large segments of the population will align with it against the Taliban. Of course, the Afghan security apparatus remains weak and Taliban has penetration into them; nonetheless, they remain a formidable challenge. What this does is make it even more unlikely that the Taliban will be able to fight its way into power. As a result, the Taliban leadership has been forced to moderate itself and emphasize its role as a nationalist force seeking an end to the presence of foreign forces in the country (as opposed to its ideological agenda).

In a December 2011 interview, former prime minister and now key supporter of the Taliban in Kabul, Ahmed Shah Ahmedzai, suggested that Mullah Omar is open to an "Islamic democracy" (with heavy emphasis on the "Islamic" qualifier) once foreign forces leave the country.[22] Mullah Omar's own words from his communiqué are indicative of this view.[23]

Professors, students, writers and the intelligentsia should individually and collectively wage a practical struggle for obtainment of complete independence; for protection of national and Islamic values and for solidarity of the Afghans. We should remain united for the sake of a common goal and wipe out all hypothetical and superficial gaps. It is the Islamic values that can do away with all lingual and geographical differences among the Afghans. We advise all global actors involved in the issue of Afghanistan to seek a real and pragmatic solution of the Afghan issue instead of focusing on factitious and superficial solutions. They should realize the ground realities of Afghanistan; The Afghans have a splendid tradition for the solution of problems and understanding among themselves. But it is in a condition when foreign intervention does not exist. Considering it its legitimate right, the Islamic Emirate wages a lawful struggle for the defense of its religion, country and soil. The only reason for that being the presence of foreign invaders in the land. If the global invading coalition ends occupation of our land, the Islamic Emirate, as a peace-loving and responsible regime, will maintain positive relations with countries of the region and the world.

It can be argued that the Taliban finally started to develop their current views after losing power and while fighting the NATO forces and the Western-backed Karzai government. As a result, it has spent the past two or three years trying to establish itself as an Afghan nationalist jihadist force. Its negotiations with Washington underscore the ongoing moderation of its behavior, but not necessarily its ideology. Their willingness to talk with Washington and their enemies, especially from the former Northern Alliance in an early 2013 meeting in Paris, as well as to discuss a power-sharing arrangement, shows that the movement is slowly moving away from its status as an *insurrectionist* Islamist movement. That may happen once the movement is removed from the international terrorist list and gains recognition as a legitimate Afghan political entity. If there is substantial progress in the ongoing power-sharing talks, it could eventually become an *acceptor* Islamist movement. By entering into negotiations and forming a political bureau the Taliban have made the initial steps towards the acceptor category. But they are not yet there because they are still trying to use their military leverage to force their opponents to make changes to the current constitutional setup. It is not clear the Taliban will succeed in forcing changes in the current setup. Depending on the outcome of the talks and the balance of power on the battlefield after next year they may or may not succeed.

Regardless of the sequence of events, when the Taliban movement agrees to operate within the constitutional parameters of the Afghan political system it could become an acceptor Islamist entity. That said, the Taliban is primarily a militia, with a small political wing and thus disarming will long be an issue even after it has moved from the insurrectionist to acceptor Islamist category. It will want to use the militia capabilities as leverage to bargain for certain changes to the current republican setup. What they really want to do is to alter the current state's very nature so that an unelected body of ulema can implement the shari'a, which is already a demand of those ultraconservative forces within the existing political system. We have talked about how a future Afghan state could resemble Iran's hybrid system. But unlike Iran's system of electing members of Parliament and the president, the Taliban's preferred system would likely keep all elected bodies weak, thereby further undermining democratization. Many former senior officials hold positions in the post-Taliban state, and many others are collaborating with them and acting as conduits between the Taliban leadership and the Afghan and various Western governments. Although such a situation tends to bring about some level of political learning, the Taliban, unlike the elite that emerged during the war with the Soviets, have had negligible experience with Western-style institutions. For example, Hekmatyar's Hizb-i-Islami is both an insurgent movement led by its founder and has significant power within the Karzai government through its several MPs and Cabinet members. In Hizb-i-Islami's case, though, it used to be the Afghan/Pashtun counterpart to Pakistan's Islamist political party Jamaat-i-Islami, which, in turn, is based on the MB model. Before joining the armed struggle against the Soviet army and the forces of Afghanistan's Marxist government, Hizb-i-Islami was a political movement. As its leadership is politically quite sophisticated, it can oscillate between mainstream politics and insurgency. In contrast, the Taliban has only in the last three years or so begun to take the initial steps toward mainstream politics. Thus, it is likely to remain in the insurrectionist Islamist category for quite some time. Even if the Afghan Taliban become an acceptor type Islamist group, it will struggle to be a conditionalist entity as far as democratization is concerned. Getting the Afghan Taliban to enter the political mainstream underscores how the situation in neighboring Pakistan will be even more difficult. Even though Pakistan is at a more advanced stage of democratization, the transnational jihadism of the Pakistani Taliban in many ways is more dangerous to Islamabad's stability than the nationalist jihadism is to Kabul.

# 8

# Participatory Shia Islamism: The Islamic Republic of Iran

Thus far, we have examined four trends of Sunni Islamism on the basis of their approaches to power and their attitudes to democracy. This exercise suggests that the Muslim Brotherhood (MB) is comfortable with democratic politics, while the other groups are either participating with reservations (e.g., Salafis) or rejecting democracy outright as un-Islamic (e.g., some Salafi, Taliban, and al-Qaeda-style transnational jihadists). In this chapter, we will explain how the Shia Islamist trend in Iran has responded to the democratic political system. By examining the historical development of Shia political thought, we will show how contemporary Shia political ideas and behavior, regarding the state, adhere to the acceptor form of Islamism. Additionally, Iran's Shia Islamists, like the MB, are participatory in regards to democracy. In fact, in some respects they are more acceptor and participatory than the MB, which is rather surprising given the origins and nature of Shia theology.[1] Unlike Sunni Islamists, over the centuries Shia Islam has gravitated toward a clerical hierarchy. Intuitively, this should mean that the minority branch of Islam would be far more resistant to what prominent contemporary Iranian philosopher Abdolkarim Soroush calls "extra-religious" ideas.[2] On the contrary, there has been an evolution in Shia religio-political thought and practice—facilitating an embrace of presidential–parliamentary republicanism that is lacking among several of their Sunni counterparts.

All things being equal, the main schism within Islam's body politic, based on the disagreement over the nature of succession to Prophet Muhammad, should have resulted in Sunnis, over time, accepting democracy whereas the Shia should have resisted it. After all, from the earliest days onward it was the Sunnis who insisted that the caliph is a political leader chosen by consensus of the community's representatives. Meanwhile, the Shia doctrine of Imamate defined political leadership as divinely ordained and limited to the Prophet's descendants.[3] Over the centuries these views reversed. Within three decades after Muhammad's death, Sunnis moved toward hereditary rule and, within three centuries, toward orthodoxy. This resulted in intellectual and hence political-economic stagnation, which in the modern era led to numerous forms of republican authoritarianism and, in some key cases, the perpetuation of dynastic rule.[4]

Meanwhile, Shia political thought struggled during the early centuries largely due to governmental persecution.[5] This was especially true of the Abbasids, under whose rule many of the 12 Imams were, according to the Shia, assassinated. After the death of Hassan al-Askari, the 11th Imam, loyalists reportedly hid his son, Muhammad al-Mahdi (the 12th [and final] Imam) to protect him from the authorities.[6] This situation gradually paved the way for the doctrine of occultation (*ghaybah*),[7] which states that the 12th Imam absented himself from the physical plane sometime during the mid-tenth century after promising his representative that he would return near the end of time to establish justice.[8] This concept, a response to the harsh political realities of that time, stemmed from the need to deal with severe oppression. But it also created an intellectual dilemma and, by extension, a political vacuum, for the clergy argued that the Imam's political responsibilities could not be assumed by anyone until the 12th Imam (aka the Mahdi) returned.[9] In order to deal with the ensuing leadership crisis, many Shia clerics were forced to engage in intellectual innovation.[10]

Building upon a saying attributed to Muhammad that the ulema are inheritors of the Prophet, during the late-tenth and early-eleventh centuries the clerics began developing the theory that Islam called for jurists to have custodial authority over the masses.[11] Between the eleventh and fourteenth centuries this custodianship was limited. Initially confined to collecting religious taxes, it later on expanded from organizing the Friday prayers to implementing the penal codes and then to the outright declaration that the jurist was a deputy of the 12th Imam. The dominant Akhbari school of thought, which rejected *ijtihad*, arrested the evolution of Shia political theory and prevented this notion from gaining much traction. By the advent of the second millennium, however, Shia ulema had decisively moved beyond the classical idea of the Imamate.[12] Even the Akhbaris, who were uncomfortable with the jurists serving as the political authority until the 12th Imam's return, for all practical purposes were comfortable with allowing Shia dynastic regimes (e.g., the Buyids and later on the Safavids) to take care of the community's geopolitical affairs during the 12th Imam's occultation.[13]

The idea of the *velayat-e-faqih* (guardianship of jurists), however, remained peripheral and only fully took off politically after Muhammad Baqir Bihbihani (1706–1791) led the Usulis, who privileged a rational appreciation of the religious texts, to victory over the Akhbaris.[14] During the eighteenth century the latter school experienced a near-total decimation, which helped give rise to the concepts of *velayat-e faqih* and *marjaa-i-taqleed* (the locus of a mass following).[15] Two of Bihbihani's students, Mullah Ahmad Naraqi (1771–1829) and Murtadha Ansari (1781–1864), furthered their master's *ijtihad* to formulate the theory of *velayat-e faqih;* however, it took another 150 years for it to be operationalized in the form of the world's first Islamist state: the Islamic Republic of Iran.[16]

The struggle between the two rival schools of thought over the clergy's role in politics, which led to a synthesis, played a key role in modern Shia Islamism's move toward the acceptor and participatory form of Islamism. The Akhbaris' opposition to reason only aggravated the crisis generated by the doctrine of occultation, for it created a situation in which all political affairs were de facto left to secular dynastic rulers. In other words, under the Akhbaris the Shia had no particular preferences insofar as political systems were concerned. But the Usulis, who sought to address the political dilemma created by the 12th Imam's occultation, were open to discussing what would be the best way to operationalize governance based on shari'a.[17] Their need to find a way to give the *fuqaha* (jurists) a critical role in government and politics led them to adopt, in the twentieth century, a Western-style parliamentary democracy. By the time of the Usulis' victory, Persia was ruled by the Qajar dynasty (1796–1925). Under this dynasty, the development of religious thought was complemented by the adaption of Western political thought. And thus began the struggle between monarchical and constitutional forms of rule, which continued under the Pahlavi dynasty (1925–1979).[18]

The 1979 revolution, which ousted the pro-Western monarchy of Mohammad Reza Shah Pahlavi, enabled Ayatollah Ruhollah Khomeini, the preeminent revolutionary leader, to translate theory into practice.[19] Nearly a decade earlier, building upon the works of Naraqi and Ansari, he had developed the theory further in his *Islamic Government: Governance of the Jurist.*[20] One critical aspect facilitated the implementation of the Guardianship of the Jurist: Its amalgamation with Western parliamentary democracy, in the form of the republic's constitution, which provided a unique form of acceptor Islamism. Under Khomeini, Iran became the world's first Islamist attempt at democracy. In fact, its democratic components were made possible by the country's Constitutional Revolution (1906–1911), which established the first legislature.[21] The republic was also influenced by Marxist thought, given the short-lived cooperation between the Khomeini-led Islamist movement and the communist Tudeh Party in their joint efforts to oust the shah.[22] The post-revolutionary Iranian polity, therefore, was a hybridization of Shia and Western political thought.[23] A lengthy and complex evolution of this religio-political thought played a critical role in allowing Shia Islamists to establish a form of Muslim democracy well before their Sunni Islamist counterparts. Since its inception in 1979, the Iranian state remains part democratic and part theocratic, or what the South Asian Islamist ideologue Sayyid Abul Alaa Maududi referred to as a *theo-democracy.*[24]

Over the past 35 years, Iran has evolved into a complex polity of competing institutions dominated by clerics, politicians, and military officers. But it remains a unique case even among the Shia, as the other Shia Islamists (which we will examine in Chapter 9) have not adopted the doctrine of *velayet-e-faqih.* While Iran represents the rare case of an Islamist state actor, many Shia Islamist non-state actors have adopted democracy via a different route. Among these actors are the Shia Islamist forces in Iraq, especially in the context of the post-Saddam era, and Hezbollah in Lebanon,[25] both of which we will discuss in Chapter 9 as well.

## The 1990s

When the 1990s arrived, the Islamic Republic had assumed an unmistakable oligarchic characteristic. A small group of like-minded conservative ayatollahs began to wield a disproportionate amount of power through their control of key clerical and political centers of power.[26] These included Khamenei, who, after serving as president (1981–1989) assumed the system's highest post: the Supreme Leader; Ali Akbar Hashemi Rafsanjani, who after being a speaker of parliament (1980–1989) became president (1989–1997), chairman of the Expediency Council (1988–present) chairman of the Assembly of Experts (2007–2011); Ahmad Jannati, who after years as its senior member, took over the chairmanship of the Guardian Council (1988-present) and was also a leading member in the Assembly of Experts; and the late Ali Meshkini, who had been chair of the Assembly of Experts (1983–2007) since its founding after the constitution was approved in 1980. Thus the state's democratic organs were carefully circumscribed by a constellation of clerical bodies.[27] Although the Assembly of Experts is popularly elected, its membership is restricted to clerics. Furthermore, Parliament is dominated either by clerics or nonclerics who can pass the litmus test of the Guardian Council's gatekeepers.

This heavy theocratic character is not the only factor that constrains democracy. The 1980–1988 Iran–Iraq war also created several civil–military issues. Iran has an unusual form of civilian supremacy over the military, for the Supreme Leader is commander-in-chief of the armed forces, including the elite military force, the Islamic Revolutionary Guards Corps (IRGC), which derives its legitimacy from the clergy as the republic's protector. As the constitutional commander-in-chief of the armed forces, the Supreme Leader has a major say in the appointment of the heads of such security organs as the interior and defense ministries (in the case of the latter, it is usually a serving general of the IRGC). The fact that the intelligence minister is always a cleric further strengthens the hands of the Supreme Leader and his clerical associates. The IRGC's central role in the war with Iraq facilitated the rise of this elite military force as the most influential center of power (after the clerics) in the political system.[28] Preventing the nascent republic's defeat by the far more militarily powerful Iraq catapulted the IRGC over the larger Artesh (the regular armed forces) and transformed it into the core of the security establishment. And, because the IRGC was given a lead role in the postwar reconstruction efforts, it gradually gained control over the state's economic sectors and thereby acquired even greater political influence.

Meanwhile, on the political front the pendulum was swinging away from the hardliners toward more liberal and reform-minded leaders who would gain control of both the presidency and the legislature. Like his predecessor, Rafsanjani also served as president for two terms, the hallmark of which was economic development along free-market lines. On the political front he tried to create a democratic space within the polity, but only in a guarded way. His presidency, coupled with the fact that reformists increasingly performed well in the 1992 and 1996 parliamentary elections, led to the 1997 election of the reformist Mohammad Khatami as president.[29] It is quite remarkable that Khatami, a relatively political unknown, garnered 70 percent of the vote and thus defeated Ali Akbar Nategh-Nouri, the establishment candidate who had been speaker of the parliament for the previous five years. The Rafsanjani years had produced a climate of great political efficacy, as evidenced by the over 75 percent voter turnout in the 1997 elections. The progress made during his years in office raised hopes that the republic could move toward greater democratization.[30]

The fact that Khatami was elected twice while his reformist allies dominated Parliament even before his election, underscores that Iran was democratic to the extent that even clerical and political forces severely disliked by the conservative establishment could be elected to power and actually wield it. Advocating the freedom of expression and tolerance that made the growth of civil society possible, the Khatami presidency represents the high point of the republic's more democratic turn. But there was serious resistance to substantive systemic reform. Khatami sought reform by working within the constitutional parameters; however, the system's conservative custodians viewed any change as a threat to their ideological and material interests.

To varying degrees, the conservatives subscribed to a highly procedural view of democracy: In their view democracy has to be guided, and the elected officials have to be overseen, by those who are knowledgeable in matters of religion. Therefore, they believe that reformists will not simply seek more freedoms within the existing system, but that they will gradually sacrifice *velayat-e-faqih* in favor of democracy. From the point of view of the conservatives, the reformists were far more dangerous than the secularists, for the former were seen as "out to subvert" the Islamic Republic from within. Although ideology is a major driving force shaping the conservative establishment's behavior, interests also represent a significant motivating factor for those clerics at the core of the system, especially those who are unelected (e.g., on the Guardians Council and in the judiciary). Even the Assembly of Experts, a popularly elected institution, would be called into question if a greater emphasis were placed on democratization. Opening this body to even a limited number of nonclerics threatens to weaken the clerics' hold over the system. Such a development might actually have transpired if the conservatives had not neutralized the reformists who, in the 2000 parliamentary elections, had gained so much ground that the conservatives were only able to hold on to 54 of the 290 seats.

That said, the establishment was not prepared to rush matters and upset the system; rather, its members knew that the situation had to be managed constitutionally. In other words, the reformists' influence had to be rolled back through the ballot box. This required holding the line until the next parliamentary election by using the Guardian Council and the right-wing-dominated security establishment to block any major policy changes. After all, Khatami had been reelected in the 2001 presidential election with an even greater majority than he had secured in 1997.

### The Post-9/11 Decade

The 9/11 attacks occurred when the reformists still controlled both the executive and legislative branches. On the foreign policy front, the Khatami administration reduced tensions with the United States especially through his "Dialogue of Civilizations" initiative. Furthermore, 9/11 created a temporary convergence of interests between the United States and Iran in the form of American efforts to effect regime-change in Afghanistan. This would be a popular move in Iran, given its rather tense relationship with the Taliban due to its political and theological opposition to al-Qaeda. This convergence of interests manifested itself not just in the usual back-channel conversations, but also in the form of limited but direct public talks, despite President George W. Bush's referring to Iran as part of the "axis of evil" in his 2002 State of the Union address. Even with the increasing tension over Iran's nuclear enrichment program that came to light in mid-2002, both countries were engaged in a complex set of dealings designed to help Washington effect regime-change in Iraq.

These unusual dealings further increased Khamenei and the conservatives' desire to reassert their control over the now-reformist-run two branches of government. Already deeply concerned about the impact of the reformists' domestic strength, the conservatives also knew that the rise of Tehran's Shia allies in post-Baathist Iraq and the nuclear controversy would increase dealings with the United States. They feared that the reformists, in their attempts to improve relations with the United States, would compromise easily and thus render the system vulnerable to a "colored revolution" move toward greater democratization. The establishment accelerated its efforts toward a conservative revival primarily via the Guardian Council's attempt to disqualify approximately 2,500 reformist candidates (including 80 outgoing lawmakers) from running in the election. Along with the resulting low voter turnout, a dramatic shift in the composition of Parliament took place: The conservatives increased their bloc by 102 seats, while the reformists lost 150 seats. With Parliament back in their hands, the conservatives set out to regain control over the presidency. The following year's presidential elections brought Mahmoud Ahmadinejad to power and returned control of the executive and legislative branches to the conservatives. But his ascension did not mean that the clerics had regained control over the system. On the contrary, the election of the new president set the stage for a complex intraconservative power struggle that, as of the writing of this book, is reshaping Iran in ways that the reformist versus conservative competition could not do.

Ahmadinejad, the republic's first nonclerical president in nearly a quarter of a century, was not part of the Tehran establishment and had run a populist campaign on the theme of eliminating corruption among the old clerical elite. Throughout his first term, he faced growing opposition from most major conservative circles but nevertheless managed to maintain a close relationship with Khamenei. In fact several months before the June 2009 election, the Supreme Leader gave the incumbent president a very overt endorsement for a second term. Ahmadinejad shared Khamenei's conservative outlook on most policy issues, and the opposition he faced from rival conservatives rendered him dependent on the Supreme Leader. Such realities strengthened the clerics' hand within the system. There was the cost of growing intraconservative rivalry between Ahmadinejad and his opponents. But Khamenei found this cost acceptable, for during his years as Supreme Leader his mastery of the art of playing off various factions had allowed him to remain above the fray and ensure that the system did not veer too much off course.

Intra-elite power struggles, however, went critical in the aftermath of the 2009 presidential election. Reformist forces in the form of the Green Movement disputed Ahmadinejad's victory. Protests and demonstrations continued until the end of the year, the first major popular uprising in the country since the 1979 revolution. Yet this public display of dissatisfaction was limited because it occurred largely in Tehran and a few other urban centers. Furthermore, while its leadership was spearheaded by various reformist tendencies, many grassroots elements were antisystem and thus pushed the unrest in a more radical direction. This was especially true after the regime launched a major IRGC-led crackdown. Ultimately, since the movement was divided internally and the regime had its support base, the unrest was contained.

While the world was focusing on the Green Movement as a third revolutionary moment that would lead to greater democratization, a far more critical evolutionary process was underway. Even as the regime was quelling the Green Movement, the intraconservative rift was exacerbating and this time Ahmadinejad, having won a second term, became very assertive. His appointment of his closest associate, Esfandiar Rahim Mashaie, as first vice-president elicited a strong response from the clergy. Mashaie, who had served in various capacities in the government, was head of the Cultural Heritage and Tourism Organization and one of the several vice-presidents during Ahmadinejad's first term. But beyond that, he has been a controversial figure given his rather secular and nationalist leanings. Over the years his actions and statements had earned him the ire of the regime's key clerics. On more than one occasion, Mashaie had stated that Iranians are friends with everyone, including Israelis, and that the problem was with the Israeli government. Ahmadinejad's own intelligence and culture ministers opposed Mashaie's appointment, and Khamenei was forced to jump into the fray when he overruled it.

Ahmadinejad gave a major jolt to the system by refusing to comply with the Supreme Leader's order for a little over a week. In two back-to-back Friday prayer sermons, top clerics chastised him for this disobedience. Despite knowing that he would ultimately comply, Ahmadinejad proved that the presidency could assert some independence from the Supreme Leader. Eventually, he gave in and had Mashaie resign, only to immediately appoint him as his adviser and chief of staff. At the same time, he fired his intelligence chief and forced the culture minister to resign. Here again Ahmadinejad was pushing the boundaries of the president's constitutional powers to the fullest extent possible. This entire incident made it clear that, at least so far, Ahmadinejad has been the republic's most ambitious president. Being neither a cleric nor someone from the military, he relied upon his popular support base and conservative credentials to assert himself in the system and make the case that a popularly elected leadership is the one that has decision-making authority. Khamenei tried to contain the president primarily by building up resistance to him throughout the legislative branches that have been brought under the control of the Larijani clan, the principal rival of Ahmadinejad's camp. Ali Larijani, whom Ahmadinejad had forced to resign as national security chief in 2007, was elected speaker of parliament after the 2008 elections. At the time, Parliament was already split between conservatives who either supported or opposed Ahmadinejad. After the 2009 election, Khamenei appointed a younger brother of parliamentary speaker Mohammad-Sadegh Larijani as head of the judiciary, even though the younger Larijani was not a full ayatollah. He also used the Supreme National Security Council and the foreign ministry to block Ahmadinejad's second-term attempts to try and reach a negotiated settlement with the United States. Another key weapon in the Supreme Leader's hands is his control over the IRGC-dominated security establishment; however, the IRGC remained divided over the Khamenei-Ahmadinejad power struggle. Fighting back, Ahmadinejad dismissed Foreign Minister Manouchehr Mottaki while he was on a foreign tour, based on the facts that he was an ally of Khamenei and an obstacle to the president's policies. Further, he has tried to use the intelligence ministry to weaken Khamenei and his opponents.

## The Arab Spring and Beyond

When popular agitation broke out in the Arab world, many observers thought that it would enable Iran's Green Movement to revive itself. After all, it had only been contained for a little over a year. Such expectations were based on a mis-understanding of the nature of the republic as well as of the Green Movement, and also disregarded the intra-elite schism fermenting within Tehran's conserva-tive establishment. Unlike the Arab republican regimes, Iran had gone through its own revolutionary experience 30 years earlier. Similarly, the Green Movement and its struggle with the government elites were not comparable to the youth-led uprisings in Tunisia, Egypt, and Libya given the difference in the scale of unrest. Furthermore, Iran is dealing with its own unique form of dissent, which was not taking place in the streets but within the corridors of power. In fact, the situation in Iran is much more significant in that we are dealing with a critical metamorphosis of the Islamic republic. For the past eight years, those driving this process were not the average moderate or liberal or reformist Islamists. During the Ahmadinejad years, the former president's non-clerical faction in an unprece-dented manner was at odds with the Khamenei led clerical establishment – even though the two sides had much in common in terms of ideology. Ahmadinejad's ideological commitment to greater democratization was at best unclear. But the fact that he derived his power from the ballot box and asserted himself against the top cleric was lending strength to the democratic side of the Iranian political system.

By the time the Arab Spring was well underway in Syria and the Saudi-led Gulf Cooperation Council (GCC) military intervention had quelled Shia-majority Bahrain's opposition movement, Iran's rival conservative factions were experi-encing another intraregime crisis: Ahmadinejad's April 2011 attempt to get rid of the second intelligence chief since his reelection.[31] Under pressure from the president, Minister of Intelligence and Security Heydar Moslehi resigned. This time Khamenei reacted in a very direct way by rejecting Moslehi's resignation and reinstating him. Ahmedinejad's two predecessors were content on accept-ing these encroachments by the supreme leader on the executive branch. The maverick president, on the other hand, was clearly trying to limit the Supreme Leader's role to oversight as opposed to direct intervention. In fact, during the

April 2011 fiasco over the intelligence ministry, Ahmadinejad's public relations adviser Ali Akbar Javanfekr proclaimed that the Supreme Leader's statements served as general guidance and advice as opposed to obligatory edicts. Javanfekr was likely responding to a Friday prayer sermon comment made by Ayatollah Ahmad Khatami, a senior member of the Assembly of Experts. Delivered after the fiasco, he had said that the president should "know that the majority vote for him was not absolute but conditional on his obedience toward the orders by the Supreme Leadership," adding, "The top of the system is the constitution, which has clarified the power structure." Javanfekr's remark represents the most serious public challenge from the elected leadership to the clergy and relates to the fault line hardwired into the republic: grafting the *velayat-e-faqih* theocracy onto a Western parliamentary democracy. This is not a new struggle, as we discussed earlier, given the history of the liberal Islamists from the time of the republic's founding up to when reformists controlled the legislative and executive branches. But what was significant about this tug of war was that conservatives were leading the charge.

For Khamenei, the clerics, and their supporters, Ahmadinejad and his allies were far more dangerous than the reformists because the latter do not attack the clergy directly. Rather, they adroitly linked their ideas and actions with Khomeini's teachings. Ahmadinejad's presidency represented a unique case of growing complexity within Islamism at a time of democratization. Normally, liberal Islamists are stressing democracy over theocracy, but in Ahmadinejad's case it was the rise of a new conservative political class that was not just nonclerical but was actually seeking to limit the clerics' power. In the context of Iran, Ahmadinejad and his faction represented a major realignment within the conservative spectrum. In his first term, Ahmadinejad, as a new entrant into the nation's political elite and anxious to establish his own conservative credentials, was seen as the figurehead of the ultra-conservatives (or ultra-cons) while his conservative opponents (e.g., Rafsanjani, Larijani, and others) were seen as pragma-cons who opposed his hardline policies. In his second term, the situation changed: Ahmadinejad assumed the mantle of pragmatic conservatism, while his opponents struggled to maintain themselves as pragmatic actors. This shift happened because the anti-Ahmadinejad conservatives, many of whom are nonclerics (e.g., the Larijani clan), did not seek to alter the clerics' privileged position within the system. On the contrary, they rely on Khamenei and the clerics to secure their own positions. Even though they hold pragmatic views on different issues, especially the need to negotiate with the United States, their alignment with the clerics gives the perception that they are more hardline than they really are. In contrast, it can be argued that Ahmadinejad was not as hardline as he appeared to be, given the statements and behavior of his top aides. At the same time, the ex-president was not a moderate in the reformist sense, but more of a radical reformer in that he was willing to press hard against the system. His economic measures geared toward cash handouts to middle- and lower-income people are well known. In addition, his social policies have earned his camp the ire of the clerics.

Javanfekr, who previously was head of the official news agency IRNA, was jailed in September 2012 on the charge of insulting the Supreme Leader. In April 2011, he had stated that the Supreme Leader's statements were not of an obligatory nature. More importantly, he was also charged with publishing material deemed to be against Islamic moral codes. This was a reference to an article in the magazine section of the state-run daily *Iran* that criticized forcing women to wear the headscarf. During his interview with Mehdi Kalhor, Javanfekr, a former senior Ahmadinejad adviser who is also a close associate of Mashaie, claimed that the black-colored chadors favored by the hardliners was something that the Qajar king Nasser al-Din Shah (1831–1896) had brought to Iran after seeing young women in Paris wearing black clothes at lavish nighttime parties. The article quoted Kalhor as saying that "from a philosophical viewpoint chador is the worst type of hijab." This article incensed the clerics, and Javanfekr defended his assertions by arguing that the "people of Iran have rights as citizens.... We should not give an impression to the world that here society is strangled. We respectfully express our minds."[32] This was perhaps among the most serious incidents of clerics clashing with the Ahmadinejad administration. But such clashes have been the hallmark of his time in office, for he has consistently advocated policies that are out of step with the clergy's wishes. These policies stem from Ahmadinejad's constant efforts, especially during his second term, to spread his voter base among the economically underprivileged to those who oppose restrictive social codes. When asked during a June 2010 television interview about why women were the prime target of the religious authorities' attempts to enforce social morality, Ahmadinejad replied, "Let me say in one word, this has nothing to do with the government. The government does not meddle in these things. We consider these things to be insults." He went on to say, "to have a man and a woman walking in the streets and then someone comes up and asks, 'What's your relation to each other?' None of your business! We don't have the right, no one has the right to ask." Similarly, when national police chief Brig.-Gen. Esmail Ahmadi Moghaddam was asked why the police do not confront women with "bad" hijab, he explained that the president had ordered them "not to bother the young people." Female public attire and social norms are not the only taboo issues that Ahmadinejad and his allies openly flouted. They also engaged in celebrating Iran's pre-Islamic heritage, such as Nowruz (Persian New Year) and figures like Cyrus the Great.[33] Such moves are unprecedented in the republic's history, but Ahmadinejad, as well as Mashaie and others in the president's inner circle, have nevertheless openly promoted an Islamism that is deeply steeped in Iranian nationalism. The president's faction was clearly promoting an alternative ideological narrative to that of Khamenei and the clerics. In an August 2010 speech, Mashie remarked that "without Iran, Islam would be lost" and that if "we want to present the truth of Islam to the world, we should erect the Iranian flag. Countries are scared of Iran, because the truth of Islam is here." These comments elicited a sharp rebuke from the country's top military officer, Maj.-Gen. Hassan Firouzabadi (commander of the Joint Armed Forces Command that oversees both the IRGC and the Artesh) who described them as a "crime against national security."[34] The Supreme Leader disagreed with Firouzabadi and was actually forced to defend Mashaie by saying that the latter was not placing Iranian nationalism in opposition to religion. This shows that Khamenei was trying to play a balancing game and that the clergy's seemingly reactionary nature only emboldened the president and his allies. In this case, Mashaie went on the offensive and questioned whether Iran should follow its own interpretation of Islam or accept all of the understandings found in the Arab countries and the wider Muslim world.

But what had the clerics far more worried than these unorthodox views about religion was Ahmadinejad's invocation of the Mahdi, with whom he claims to have a close relationship.[35] Clerics both within the regime and in Qom feared that their position would be rendered moot if a nonclerical political leader somehow manages to become the medium through which the public can access the Mahdi. Thus Ahmadinejad's opponents accused his administration of being controlled by a "deviant current" but did not accuse him personally of deviance. In fact, many of them had actually expressed hope that the president would return to the revolutionary fold and to the ideals upon which the republic was founded. Khamenei thus focused on using the legislative and judicial branches to shape the behavior of the Ahmadinejad-led executive branch. This created a great deal of friction between the three branches, resulting in increasing power struggles that upset the Supreme Leader's traditional modus operandi of seeking to balance the various centers of power and factions to maintain his own position at the system's apex. In order to compensate for these increased systemic tensions, in July 2011 Khamenei created a new state body: the Supreme Board of Arbitration and Adjustment of Relations among the Three Branches of Government. Headed by the former judiciary chief Ayatollah Mahmoud Hashemi Shahroudi, this ineffective body only exacerbated the already problematic hyperinstitutionalization of the state. Another key factor informing Khamenei's strategy of dealing with Ahmadinejad was that the establishment didn't want to risk deposing him, as doing so would have undermined the system itself. What makes this whole matter so interesting was that Khamenei, along with the clerical- and IRCG-dominated establishment, actually had gone to great lengths to get Ahmadinejad elected in the first place—and even more so to get him reelected. Since the June 1981 impeachment of the republic's first president, Abulhassan Banisadr, no sitting president had been forced from office. If the clerics and the IRGC could tolerate a reformist like Khatami, then getting rid of their fellow conservative Ahmadinejad would be all the more damaging to the system. This is why Ahmadinejad's opponents did their best to ensure that he was followed by a conservative president who would fall in line and align his policies with the Supreme Leader. Towards this end, the Guardian Council disqualified Mashaie's candidacy in the 2013 elections. Hassan Rouhani's electoral victory in the 11th presidential election on June 14, 2013 has further diffused power within the Iranian political system. The presidential race itself highlighted the fact that all the candidates were pragmatists to varying degrees who campaigned on an agenda of reform – promising improvements to the rule of the law and more importantly the economy battered by crippling sanctions. In 2012, the Islamic republic experienced a 40 percent slump in its revenues caused by U.S.-led sanctions that targeted Tehran's ability to export crude. A key fallout was the plummeting of the value of the Iranian Rial by over 70 percent and the Iranian foreign exchange reserves dropping from 110 billion to 70 billion during the December 2011 to December 2012 period. To a great extent the final slate of presidential candidates reflected the desire within the establishment to steer the country away from the maverick policies of Ahmadinejad.

After the eight tumultuous years of Ahmadinejad, Khamenei sought a president who could reform the political economy of the country standing at the precipice and yet remain loyal to the clerical foundations of the country. But as we explained earlier in the chapter, the supreme leader's ability to influence the outcome of elections is quite limited. His first preference was former foreign minister (1981–97) and his longtime foreign affairs adviser, Ali Akbar Velayeti but the technocrat did not have the votes. While Rouhani was not his first choice, he is an old associate of the supreme leader tracing back to the pre-revolutionary days who from the mid 1980s till 2005 served as the country's top national security official. A cleric himself, Rouhani will not likely push hard against the theocratic centers of power as as his predecessor had done. As a pragmatic conservative politician with a soft corner for the reformists, Rouhani is trying to expand democracy in the country but will balance this agenda with the need to work with both the clerical and security establishments. As is evident from the domestic political reactions to Rouhani's efforts to improve ties with the United States, the new president is not facing as much resistance from Khamenei and the clerics as he is from the military, specifically the IRGC. On Sept 17, 2013, while addressing the 20th annual assembly of the corps, both Rouhani and Khamenei called on the revolutionary guards to steer clear of partisan politics. Curbing the political power of the corps, however, will be difficult given that the IRGC's influence in the state has grown by leaps and bounds in the quarter of a century since the end of the disastrous war with Iraq. It is true that the veterans of the Islamic Revolutionary Guards Corps do not represent the views of the current commanders whom themselves have variant political leanings. Furthermore, the corps derives its legitimacy from the clerics and is a much smaller entity than the regular military. Indeed, there exists a peculiar form of civilian control over the military but it has been eroding over the last two decades. Initially it was because of the need of the Rafsanjani presidency (1989–97) to use the state's most organized institution to rebuild the country. When the Khatami administration took over, the clerical establishment relied on the IRGC to rein in the government's agenda, which was well outside Khamenei's preferential boundaries. Finally, during the Ahmedinejad era, the regime became even more dependent on the corps - both to counter opposition and to rein in the maverick presidency. Rouhani knows he needs to give incentives to the IRGC, which is why in addition to asking for the corps help in reviving the economy, he has appointed a former IRGC naval chief and defense minister Ali Shamkhani as head of the National Security Council. Ultimately, the Rouhani administration, working with the clerical establishment, seeks to strengthen the power of the elected government. This is something that all stakeholders within the Islamic Republic want to see. There is a realization among the clerical and security elites that large segments of the Iranian public are dissatisfied with the way the country has been managed especially given the economic hardships. But neither the clerics nor the IRGC wants to see the democratic centers of power strengthen at their own expense.

Consequently, the 2013 election might prove be the most important election in the republic's history for it will shape the future of the state's democratic and theocratic pillars.

### Iranian Shia Islamism and Democratization

The Islamic republic represents the unique case of an Islamist state actor. Iranian Shia Islamism, however, is not monolithic, as is clear from the ideological schisms over the question of democracy among the factions that make up the state. As we have shown, there is a great degree of dissonance even among the conservatives. Ideology is a critical factor informing this chasm, but it goes beyond ideological differences. The key tension is that the concept of *velayat-e-faqih*, remains highly contested, centering on how it should be operationalized in terms of clerical oversight of the political system. There is also the issue of how much authority the president has in formulating policies, especially when the constitution states that the Supreme Leader is to provide the general parameters for the president's actions. The president has a considerable degree of flexibility, but only if his preferred policies do not come into direct conflict with the Supreme Leader's wishes. Elected officials are also able to maneuver within the Supreme National Security Council. The president not only heads the council, but also appoints its secretary, who is the country's de facto chief national security officer. The president, depending upon his ability to navigate the system in which he essentially shares influence over top officials with the Supreme Leader, can steer policymaking. The 12-member council includes four top Cabinet members (viz., the foreign, defense, interior, and intelligence ministers) as well as the top IRGC and Artesh commanders. The president could use his influence among this group to shape a consensus among more than half of the council members, who, in turn, could sway some of the remaining (e.g., the joint chief, parliamentary speaker, judiciary head, and the Supreme Leader's representatives) members. Since the Supreme Leader has to approve any council decision, a large number of members who favor a certain policy could shape his thinking and behavior.

Currently a number of unelected clerics control the system. At the center is the Guardian Council, which consists of six members (theologians) appointed by the Supreme Leader and six others (jurists) appointed by head of the judiciary (himself a Supreme Leader appointee). These latter six appointees must also receive parliamentary approval. Given that the current judiciary chief and the parliamentary speaker are brothers suggests that the Guardian Council is currently insulated from public scrutiny. As we noted earlier, the popularly elected Assembly of Experts only includes clerical members. On paper, this body has the power to hold the Supreme Leader accountable. However, it has never exercised this role because doing so would undermine the Supreme Leader's position and establish a precedent for subjecting him to public criticism. The republic's history highlights the constant struggle to balance the theocratic and democratic aspects of the political structure in order to ensure governance. Contrary to the hopes of its founders and their supporters, the systemic architecture and its functioning has actually exacerbated the debate over the clerics' role. Put differently, even those who accept the *velayat-e-faqih* continue to search for the right balance between clerics and nonclerics, especially since the latter group dominates the executive and legislative branches. Iran is a unique case in our acceptor category, as the notion of acceptor Islamism was built upon the idea of Islamic state via democracy. In the case of Iran, we are not dealing with non-state actors seeking to realize their preferred Islamic state. The issue of how the state should be established is therefore moot. Unlike their Sunni counterparts, Iranian Islamists have had their state since 1979. Thus the more pertinent issue is the degree to which they embrace democracy. We have shown how Iranian Islamism is of the participatory type. That said, Iran's Shia Islamist ideology, based upon *velayat-e-faqih*, has limited the degree to which it is participatory. Competing intra-elite preferences over the clerics' role underscores the divisions within the participatory nature of Iranian Islamists. Not even the most reformist faction is calling for a form of participatory Islamism that would replace theocrats with democrats, for under the current constitution this is not permitted. In fact, the real issue is about political capability and systemic stability. Those who favor the status quo are far more powerful than those who seek to alter the balance of power between theocracy and democracy. Even if this were not the case and the latter had more power, they would lack the political will to radically steer toward greater democratization. The fear here is that such a move could destabilize the state and plunge the country into chaos. This is why the more liberal Islamists seek gradual change. They are anticipating a future situation in which the establishment would be willing to accept some reforms due to extenuating circumstances. Even those individuals that seek this vision do not wish to eliminate the clergy altogether, given the society's religious nature and the social relations between the clerics and the laity.

There is a great deal of diversity among the Iranians' attitudes toward democracy. In fact, only a small minority of clerics favors a total theocracy and thus could be categorized as rejectors. Most of the clerics realize that they cannot govern and that the political leadership must be popularly elected, which places them between conditionalist and participatory types of Islamists. Right now, the challenge is how to ensure that the government adheres to their vision of an Islamic state, which entails a cleric-guided democracy. Very few political figures, such as Rafsanjani, Khatami, and Rouhani are both clerics and politicians who see the need for greater democratization in order to bridge the gap between the public and the ruling clerical elite. But they continue to face significant opposition from the bulk of the establishment. With clerics losing political ground and a non-clerical political class arising over the past decade, it is likely that the theocratic versus democratic debate will become more acute. The clerics will want to ensure that only those politicians who accept their role as overseers are elected. The problem, as demonstrated during Ahmadinejad's presidency, is that even those who are very close to the clerics want to govern with minimal interference. As even factions that consider themselves reformists are marginalized and the secularists have no presence in the system at all, most of the Iranian political elite (both clerics and nonclerics) fall within the moderate and conservative bands of our spectrum. They all agree that democracy in Iran should be a religious one, but contest the political application of *marjaa taqleed* and the current understanding of how the doctrine of *velayat-e-faqih* ought to be operationalized.

The struggle between those in favor of a more democratic polity and those wanting to sustain clerical dominance over the state is approaching a historic crossroads.[36] The presidency of Ahmadinejad has shown that the reformist versus hardliner dichotomy does not adequately explain the cleavages within in the country. In the long run, Ahmadinejad is one individual leading a partisan movement with a limited shelf life. His camp, however, has discreetly but potently challenged the notion of *velayat-e-faqih* and from within the conservative milieu. Ahmedinejad's actions while he was president will likely have lasting repercussions for Iranian Shia Islamism and its practical manifestation, the Islamic republic. In a way, this conservative faction is not different from others that preceded it. Indeed, as the historical analysis in this chapter demonstrates, the hallmark of Iranian domestic politics since the revolution has revolved around the struggle between those who wish to sustain the upper hand of theocrats and those who seek greater democratization. From clerics like Ayatollah Shariatmadari and political forces such as Mehdi Bazargan's Freedom Party during the earliest days of the regime to the reformists led by President Khatami all the way to the present, if there has been one constant, it is the push against the clergy dominating the state.

Until the rise of Ahmadinejad, however, the establishment maintained the upper hand against these dissenting voices. It accomplished this by making the case that its opponents were liberal left-leaning forces enamored by the west who were sorely lacking in their commitment to the ideals of the revolution. However, the regime could not easily dismiss Ahmadinejad and his allies without considerably damaging the system itself as is evident from Khamenei's Feb 16, 2013 remarks criticizing the rival factions for infighting, which highlight the sense of vulnerability on the part of the supreme leader.[37] After Ahmadinejad's efforts to enhance the power of the presidency, his successor, President Hassan Rouhani seeks to enhance the quality of democracy in the country (albeit without ruffling the feathers of the theocrats). Rouhani is nothing like his predecessor but the need to govern will naturally steer him towards policies that will create problems between the elected government and the clerics. Conducting both domestic and foreign policies will entail compromises, especially given that the latest round of sanctions, which have severely weakened the economy at home and thus increased the need for compromise with the United States. Ahmadinejad's behavior and that of his associates has already created a precedent for the executive branch to assert itself against the clerical institutions designed to oversee policy-making. The two terms of Ahmadinejad created an atmosphere where top government officials publicly expressing opinions contrary to those of the clergy is no longer beyond the pale. Now that that rubicon has been crossed, it is only a matter of time this type of disagreement gradually becomes a norm. Rouhani's ascension to the presidency has indeed harmonized the political system but the splits among the conservatives remain. Furthermore, a lack of a robust culture of political parties shapes the complex fragmentation among the various shades and hues of those elements that identify themselves asconservatives.

Meanwhile, the IRGC is also heavily involved in politics and actually makes the current situation exponentially more complicated. The clerics fear that, if this trend continued, the time when the IRGC could become even more powerful than the clerics may not be far off. Khamenei has held the office of the supreme leader for a little under a quarter of a century and he is nearly 75 and soon will be replaced by the republic's third supreme leader. We have written about how the position suffered when Khamenei ascended to it given that he possessed significantly less scholarly or political credentials of his predecessor. We have also detailed how the evolution of the Islamic Republic over the past 24 years has further weakened the position in political terms. Khamenei's successor, if he is a much more established grand ayatollah, could restore some measure of religious legitimacy to the office. That said, from a political point of view, the new Supreme Leader will be much weaker than even Khamenei and could very well end up being a figurehead for the IRGC. There is also the fact that most of the senior clerics in the system are also aging. The heads of the main clerical organs, the Guardian Council, Expediency Council, and the Assembly of Experts, all are in advanced ages and likely to leave office (either due to death or incapacitation)around the same time. Most of them are likely to be replaced by less than qualified individuals, as is the case with the current judiciary chief, Mohammad-Sadegh Larijani, who was a junior cleric with the Hojjat-ol-Islam title up until a few months prior to his appointment in July 2009.

This scenario suggests that the clerics in general will face a decline in influence. In fact, the notion of velayat-e-faqih, which even during its heyday was an anomalous concept among the majority of the Shia clergy, may undergo a revision in how it is operationalized. It would not be surprising to see the office of the supreme leader at some point in the future being replaced by a council of top *marjaa* with far less direct authority over the government.[38] In fact, Article 111 of the Iranian constitution states, that in the interim period between the departure of the incumbent supreme leader and the election of a new one by the Assembly of Experts, a leadership council composed of the president, the judiciary chief, and a jurist from the Guardian Council would provisionally assume the duties of the supreme leader. It is quite possible that this leadership may not be as provisional as originally envisioned and could discharge the constitutional responsibilities of the supreme leader indefinitely.[39] This is especially the case given that the Assembly of Experts has become factionalized and may not be able to reach a decision for quite some time. The weakening of the clerical institutions implies that the IRGC could likely be the deciding factor in the election of future supreme leaders.[40] In addition to exercising influence over the theocratic leadership, the IRGC could also gain control over the political leadership by supporting the election of a retired commander as president. Such a behind the scenes role as kingmaker is preferred by the IRGC. Cognizant of growing public sentiment in favor of an elected leadership and the need to manage a weak economy, the corps has an interest in maintaining the democratic facets of the state. In this sense, the shift would be that the IRGC could for all intents and purposes replace the clergy in having oversight over the state. Since the IRGC currently derives its legitimacy from the clergy it will be difficult for the corps to sustain it should the supreme leader become a pawn in the hands of the generals of the elite force. Such a situation could provide for political forces to press for greater democratization.

Regardless of how future civil-military relations pan out, at present the clergy has overwhelming control. Yet as we have seen the Iranian polity has strong democratic dimensions with a heavy dose of religion woven throughout.

# 9

# Arab Shia Islamism: Iraqi Shia Islamists and Hezbollah

The Iranian model of a Shia Islamist state was made possible only through the convergence of unique circumstances that do not exist in the Arab Shia milieu. For example, Iran has an overwhelming majority Shia population (slightly over 90 percent) and its 1979 revolution completely dismantled the monarchical order and established the Islamic republic. Moreover, the proponents of *velayat-e-faqih* were the most coherent and organized revolutionary faction. As the only fully Shia state, Iran became the de facto leader of the global Shia community. The geopolitical context of countries with significant religious and ethnic diversity has set Arab Shia Islamists apart from their Iranian counterparts. This chapter focuses on Lebanon's Hezbollah and Iraq's Hizb al-Dawah, the al-Sadrite movement, and the Islamic Supreme Council of Iraq (ISCI) Islamists. A third group, Bahrain's Jamiyat al-Wefaq al-Watani al-Islamiyah, is less consequential and only discussed in a cursory manner.[1] Each is based on the acceptor model of Islamism regarding the state and is predominantly participatory Islamist in regards to democracy. Clerics have played a major role in their development but, for the most part, do not seek a theocratic state. In fact, without the *velayat-e-faqih*, Arab Shia Islamism is more acceptor and participatory in nature than the Iranian incarnation.

Lebanon's Hezbollah movement, founded as a terrorist entity in the early 1980s, quickly became Iran's premier regional proxy. By the 1990s it had evolved into a political movement and the preeminent player in mainstream Lebanese politics. Since January 2011, it has been the major driving force behind the Beirut government. Despite embracing the mainstream, Hezbollah holds on to its armed wing—the only group in the country with one. For the most part, it has used its military capabilities against Israel. Hezbollah represents the first Arab Shia Islamist non-state actor to become a major state-level player. In the last decade, Arab Shia Islamism gained further ground as the Shia Islamists have gained power in Iraq. While Hezbollah faces no major competition from within the Lebanese Shia community (Islamist or otherwise) and does not dominate the state, Iraqi Shia Islamism represents a fragmented lot at the intra-Islamist level but has come to dominate the state. Iraq Shia community' has a virtual absence of secular groups. The three principal political players, namely, Hizb al-Dawah, the al-Sadrite movement, and the Islamic Supreme Council of Iraq, are all Islamist.[2] All are rooted in the original Hizb al-Dawah founded in 1957 but have evolved along different trajectories. Each engaged in armed struggle during the periods of military and Baathist rule, but has adapted to democratic politics and evolved vis-à-vis its preference for an Islamic state.[3]

Arab Shia Islamists have not adopted Iran's *velayat-e-faqih* partially because of their consociational political arrangements, in which power is shared among Christians, Shia and Sunni Muslims. But in Iraq and Bahrain, where the Shia are the single largest communal group, they ideologically disagree with the Iranian model. Instead, their modus operandi and evolutionary trajectory has resembled that of the main Sunni Islamist movement, the MB: coming to power through electoral politics, compromising on their ideological agenda in the face of political constraints, and evolving from being opposition groups to the governing party. Furthermore, Arab Shia Islamists developed years prior to the 1979 revolution. Clerics like Lebanon's Musa al-Sadr, Iraq's Baqir al-Sadr in Iraq, and Bahrain's Abdul-Amir al-Jamri formed their own religio-political ideas long before Khomeini developed his theocratic doctrine, and also founded political groups and participated in mainstream politics decades before Iran's 1979 revolution. Yet because their political principals were Islamists, Iran has influenced them. Although Arab Shia groups have not embraced the *velayat-e-faqih*, this serves Iran's interests since it does not face competing centers of Shia power across the region.[4]

## The 1990s

### Hezbollah

In order to understand Hezbollah's move toward mainstream electoral politics during the 1990s, one must consider the context from which it emerged as a militant entity. After Lebanon's independence in 1943, Maronite Christians and Sunni Muslims dominated the confessional state; the Shia had a marginal share of power commensurate at the time with its size. Over the next four decades, however, their numbers increased dramatically and eventually accounted for 41 percent of the population, making it the largest religious group.[5] They began to assert themselves as a political force well before the outbreak of civil war in 1975 under the leadership of the country's legendary cleric Musa al-Sadr.[6] He led them toward the formation of social and political groups, most importantly, Afwaj al-Mouqawama al-Lubnaniyah, better known as Amal, the first major Lebanese Shia political entity. After the cleric's sudden disappearance while on a trip to Libya in 1978, Amal was run by a more elitist secular leadership, which undermined its social standing among the largely poor and religiously oriented Shia community. Given its role as a belligerent in the civil war further complicated matters for Amal, for this created space for the emergence of competing and more religiously motivated factions. In addition, the 1982 Israeli invasion of Lebanon in response to PLO attacks from there catalyzed the actions of these religious militants largely based in the south, who assumed different public names but were essentially proto-Hezbollah cells and networks. After about three years of attacking American, French, and Israeli civilian and military targets, in 1985 these groups coalesced into Hezbollah.[7] This organization, in turn, would eventually develop into a major Lebanese and regional force within this complex context of communal marginalization, civil war, and the Israeli invasion.[8] With critical assistance from Iran's elite ideological military force, the IRGC, the group transformed itself into a major guerilla movement by the end of the 1980s. Much has been written about Hezbollah as a terrorist/guerilla organization and not so much on its evolution into a political entity. We will assess the extent to which it has become a participatory Islamist group during Lebanon's democratization process.

The 1989 Taif Accords, which ended the nearly 15-year civil war, provided Lebanon with a new power-sharing agreement and created the conditions that facilitated Hezbollah's transformation into a political movement.[9] Both Amal and Hezbollah had participated in this complex civil war involving American, French, Syrian, Israeli, Saudi, Iranian, and Iraqi proxies. Given its highly fractured landscape along both communal and partisan lines, as well as foreign involvement, alliances shifted continually among the various intercommunal militias. Hezbollah, having emerged earlier in the decade in opposition to Amal, rapidly became a powerful competitor. By the end of the war intracommunal fighting broke out between them for control over shared turf: the Shia community. The fighting ended with an arrangement that has more or less existed ever since. Hezbollah began establishing itself as a national organization representing the Shia as early as 1985, after the Israeli Defense Forces' (IDF) withdrawal from Beirut to the security zone just north of the Israeli-Lebanese border. However, the civil war and fighting the IDF in the south kept Hezbollah's focus mainly on military, as opposed to political, activities. During the three-year interval between the Taif peace treaty and the 1992 elections, Hezbollah made a major move toward becoming a political movement.[10] In 1989 Sheikh Subhi al-Tufayli became its first secretary-general. A cleric, he opposed the group's evolution in mainstream Lebanese politics. Tufayli's position conflicted with Hezbollah's main patron, Iran,[11] which had approved of the Taif Accords and wanted their proxy to participate in upcoming parliamentary elections. The struggle ended with Tufayli being replaced by Abbas al-Musawi.[12] It is not clear as to what degree al-Musawi favored joining the mainstream, but within nine months he was assassinated in an Israeli airstrike.

Al-Musawi was succeeded by Hassan Nasrallah, who still holds the post and under whose leadership Hezbollah eventually became the most influential political movement in Lebanon. Since his teenage years in the late 1970s, Nasrallah had ample experience in Shia political, religious, and military matters with Amal. His exposure to religious education in the Najaf Hawza indoctrinated him in Hizb al-Dawah's participatory Islamism.[13] A key founder of Hezbollah in 1985, he also played a leading role in developing the organization at the grassroots level. Nasrallah spent about two years in the Iranian seminary town of Qom, where he had an opportunity to closely understand *velayat-e-faqih*, the core principle of Iranian Shia Islamism. He accepted Khamenei as the transnational *vali-e-faqih* of the global Shia community, but balanced it with the need for participatory Islamism in Lebanese national politics. When al-Musawi was killed, Nasrallah was well positioned to assume Hezbollah's leadership. Within a year he successfully led the group through the country's first elections in 20 years. Although independents won 92 of the 128 seats, Hezbollah won eight seats (the most that any group would win), and four of the independents were affiliated with the movement.

During the 1990s, Hezbollah's focus was divided between fighting Israeli occupation and participating in Lebanese politics. In 1985 the IDF had withdrawn from Beirut and much of the Lebanese south to a security zone from where Israeli troops, in concert with its Lebanese Christian proxy the South Lebanon Army, fought Hezbollah militiamen. Over time Hezbollah developed the capability to fire rockets into northern Israel, which led to a major IDF offensive, Operation Grapes of Wrath, in 1996. IDF forces struck across the entire Shia geography in Lebanon, namely, the south, Beirut, and Baalbek, in an attempt to force Beirut to dismantle Hezbollah's armed wing. Given the sociopolitical capital Hezbollah had accumulated over the decade since its founding, the Israeli offensive ended in a UN-sponsored ceasefire that left the group's military wing free to conduct attacks from inside Lebanese territory. The war prevented Hezbollah from improving upon its electoral performance in the previous poll; it actually lost a couple seats. Even after the 1996 elections, Hezbollah was consumed with fighting the Israelis in the southern security zone. Toward the end of the 1990s the strategy paid off when Israel, under Ehud Barak's new Labor government withdrew from the south in the spring of 2000. Hezbollah's stock rose tremendously, as it had forced the Israeli withdrawal, but this did not translate into too many seats during the parliamentary elections later that year. Unable to fully dominate the Lebanese Shia political landscape because it shared power at the intra-Shia level with Amal, its status as a political movement with a large militia transformed it into a state within a state by the end of the 1990s.

## Dawah, the al-Sadrites, and ISCI

Iraq's invasion of Kuwait critically weakened the Baathist state. Already exhausted from the 1980–1988 war with Iran and devastation from the 1991 war with the United States, allowed its Shia opposition—both at home and abroad—to reassert itself. The 12 years of sanctions following the war and the no-fly zones severely limited Baghdad's ability to contain the country's Shia majority.

Saddam Hussein had neutralized the main Shia threat, Hizb al-Dawah, a decade earlier. Furthermore, the war with Iran had prevented the main Iranian proxy, the Supreme Council of the Islamic Revolution in Iraq (SCIRI) and its militia, the 10,000-strong Badr Brigade, from seriously penetrating into the country.[14] The rather dormant presence of the two organizations in the Shia south was a key reason why the Baathist regime was able to crush the uprising triggered by the 1991 war, in which Shia military units mutinied against the regime. Such was the scale of the mutiny, however, that Baghdad complemented coercion with encouraging the rise of a new Shia Islamist force under the leadership of Grand

Ayatollah Mohammed Sadiq al-Sadr, father of the current leader of Sadrite movement, Muqtada al-Sadr.[15] The death of Grand Ayatollah Abu al-Qasim al-Khoei (Al-Sistani's mentor), Iraq's most senior cleric, in 1992 further helped Sadiq al-Sadr to emerge as a major *marja'ah taqleed* (highest-ranking jurists of Twelver Shia community). The Baathist regime saw the senior al-Sadr as a potential way to keep the Shia community divided among the various clerical, ideological, and nationalist rivalries and counter any potential Iranian moves to take advantage of Iraq's weakened state.[16] Sadiq al-Sadr also steered clear of provoking the authorities while he secretly developed an underground movement among the more impoverished urban and rural Shia.[17] Desiring to see an Islamic state in Iraq, he felt that it needed a strong popular base, which he built through offering social and religious services.[18]

Toward the latter half of the 1990s he began to openly criticize the regime, particularly for its inability to provide the poor with basic services, and call for an Islamic state. He revived the Friday prayers, a break with Shia doctrine that deems them as nonobligatory in the Mahdi's absence, and his approximate four dozen sermons drew a couple of hundred thousand worshippers.[19] His growing popularity was seen as a major threat by the Saddam regime, and in 1999 he and his two sons were gunned down by agents of the Baath Party. After his death his core followers went underground and another of his sons, Muqtada, was placed under house arrest. Although Sadiq al-Sadr's political career as leader of the Iraqi Shia had lasted for only eight years, he had laid the foundations of a robust movement that his son would lead after the regime-change.[20] What added to the movement's aura was the fact that Sadiq al-Sadr was a cousin of Baqir al-Sadr, the founder of the Dawah Party, who along with his sister had also been killed by the Saddam regime in 1980. In fact, Sadiq al-Sadr's efforts in many ways had a greater impact than those of his cousin in that the Dawah Party of today is a shell of its former self, whereas Sadiq al-Sadr's movement constitutes Iraq's largest Shia Islamist party.

## The Post-9/11 Decade

### Hezbollah

Israel's withdrawal from the security zone was a major victory for Hezbollah, as reflected in the fact that its electoral alliance with Amal won all of the south's 23 seats in the 2000 elections. Yet with the Israeli withdrawal, the basis upon which Hezbollah had maintained its armed wing evaporated. Neither the Lebanese Shia Islamist movement nor its Iranian and Syrian patrons, however, wanted to see it disbanded. Hezbollah also resisted that option because Israel was still occupying the Shebaa Farms, a 25-square kilometer piece of real estate that the UN maintains is part of Golan Heights. Both Syria and Lebanon assert that this land, occupied by Israel during the 1967 war, belongs to Lebanon. Furthermore, Hezbollah insisted that its militia existed to defend the country from Israel. The Israeli withdrawal from Lebanon also energized the anti-Syrian Lebanese factions to demand the withdrawal of Hezbollah's patrons, the Syrian military and intelligence forces, who had been in Lebanon since the outbreak of its 1975 civil war. They were also unhappy with Syria's manipulation of the Lebanese elections to ensure that its Lebanese allies would maintain their majority in Parliament.

Matters came to a head when Syria tried to engineer parliamentary approval for a three-year extension of the term of President Emile Lahoud, a key ally of the Assad regime in 2004. Lebanon's Prime Minister Rafic al-Hariri, a top Sunni leader with close ties to Saudi Arabia, opposed this. The resulting dispute prompted an American-French initiative in the form of UNSC Resolution 1559 (approved in September 2004) that called for the Syrian forces to withdraw from Lebanon, for Syria to end its interference in Lebanese politics, and for Hezbollah to disarm its militia. Incensed by the resolution, the Syrians were able to coerce al-Hariri and his allies to vote for the extension in October 2004. After the extension was approved, al-Hariri resigned. In February 2005, he was assassinated in a large-scale bomb attack in Beirut believed to be the handiwork of Syrian intelligence operatives. This event triggered massive anti-Syrian protests that finally forced Damascus to withdraw its forces in April 2005. It also polarized the Lebanese landscape, as the factions converged between the anti-Syrian March 14 coalition, led by al-Hariri's Future Party and now headed by his son Saad, and the pro-Syrian March 8 coalition led by Hezbollah.

In the May 2005 elections, the March 14 coalition won 72 of the 128 seats in Parliament; Hezbollah and its allies came in second with 57 seats. Hezbollah and Amal, forming a single bloc, won all 23 seats in the south and garnered a total of 28 seats (14 each). Under domestic, regional, and international pressure, Hezbollah decided to join the government, particularly since the new al-Hariri faction-led government would be pushing for its armed wing to be disbanded. By joining the Cabinet of Prime Minister Fuad Siniora, formed in July 2005, Hezbollah was able to secure government recognition that its armed wing was not a militia, but a "national resistance force" that would not be disbanded. Its ministers boycotted Cabinet meetings for six weeks until this demand was met. In early 2006, Hezbollah sought to strengthen its position by allying with the largest Christian political group in Lebanon, the Free Patriotic Movement (FPM) of retired General Michel Aoun (who had returned to Lebanon after a 15-year exile in France), which had won 21 seats but did not join the government. Meanwhile, in the wake of the departure of the Syrian forces, Hezbollah's military wing began assuming greater security responsibility. Although the government agreed to accept its armed wing as a resistance movement, there was a great deal of pressure to disarm the group especially in the form of the March 2006 National Dialogue talks that involved all major factions. Three key issues were addressed: future relations with Syria, the international tribunal investigating the al-Hariri assassination, and implementing UNSC Resolution 1559, which calls for disbanding militias. To demonstrate its resistance credentials, Hezbollah initiated the July 2006 war with Israel through a complex cross-border raid that captured two Israeli soldiers and killed three others. After 34 days of fighting a ceasefire was brokered, which essentially showed that Hezbollah had prevented Israel from defeating it militarily. However, Lebanese opponents and their international backers criticized it for this "unnecessary" war and continued to press for disarmament. Three months later, five Hezbollah and Amal Cabinet members and a sixth (FPM) one resigned, citing the failed national dialogue process. Two weeks later Hezbollah and its allies launched a major protest campaign, and Nasrallah demanded a national unity government with the Hezbollah-led opposition bloc filling one-third of the Cabinet positions, which would give it veto power in the Cabinet and enable it to collapse the government.

The American- and Saudi-backed government, led by the March 14 alliance, rejected these demands. Hezbollah and its allies kept pushing for early parliamentary elections in order to undo the March 14 majority in parliament while the ruling bloc was anxious to hold a fresh presidential vote to remove the pro-Syrian incumbent Emile Lahoud. But this required a two-thirds vote in Parliament, which could not be convened due to the crisis. The stand-off led to clashes between Sunni and Shia gunmen in the capital in January 2007; Nasrallah intervened and prevented matters from escalating into armed conflict. On May 7, 2008, the government shut down Hezbollah's communication network, which the Shia movement declared as an act of war and deployed its forces. For the first time since end of the civil war, Hezbollah used its military wing against rival Lebanese factions. Gun battles in the streets of Beirut and elsewhere lasted for two weeks and killed many. Hezbollah seized control of large parts of the capital from rival factions' gunmen and handed them over to the army. Subsequently, the Lebanese armed forces played a key role in rescinding the decision to shut down Hezbollah's communication network. This incident underscored a significant exception to Hezbollah's general stance of pursuing domestic power via democratic means while fighting Israel. Hezbollah demonstrated that it would use force domestically to retain its intelligence and military capabilities. Thus it is the same as other armed groups, such as the Irish Republican Army (IRA), that have used their military prowess to carve out political space. But what sets Hezbollah apart is that even after having entered the political mainstream, it keeps its arsenal and thus its preeminent position in the political system. Moreover, it is willing to risk civil war to defend its disproportionate amount of influence. The belligerents signed a Qatar-mediated agreement on May 21, which ended the 18-month-long impasse that had led to civil war-like conditions. The Doha Agreement acknowledged Hezbollah's armed wing and the Lebanese military as separate forces sharing security responsibility. Additionally, the Hezbollah-led opposition got the 11 ministries (a third of the Cabinet portfolios) it was seeking, which was reflected in the new government formed two months later, led by former army chief Michel Suleiman as a consensus president.

Two months after the July 2008 formation of the new national unity government led by Siniora, Parliament passed a new electoral law that divided the country into smaller electoral districts (another stipulation of the Doha Accord to level the playing field between the two sides). Elections held in the following June resulted, five months later in November 2009 in a national unity government led by Saad al-Hairi, whose March 14 bloc received 15 Cabinet posts; the Hezbollah-led alliance got ten, and another five were given to the neutral president Suleiman. What was key here is that Hezbollah's opponents were not the majority. This government lasted for only 14 months, as tensions mounted over the UNSC-backed Special

Tribunal for Lebanon (STL) that was trying to indict several Hezbollah members for their alleged involvement in the Rafic al-Hariri assassination. Blocking the STL from issuing the indictments was a key factor in Hezbollah engineering the collapse of Saad al-Hariri's government. On January 12, 2011 ten members of Hezbollah-led coalition resigned, and the Shia Islamist movement convinced one of Suleiman's five ministers, a fellow Shia, to follow suit. Now it had the minimum requirement of 11 ministerial resignations to collapse the Cabinet. But there was more to it than just that, for Hezbollah had now acquired enough influence to topple and form governments. Five months after the al-Hariri government's collapse, a new government—minus the March 14 coalition led by Prime Minister Najib Mikati, a Sunni—was formed in June 2011. What made this possible was the Druze faction, headed by Walid Jumblatt's Progressive Socialist Party (PSP), with 11 seats in Parliament had broken with the March 14 back in August 2009 and reduced the latter's seats from 71 to 60. Initially, the PSP supported the Hezbollah-backed Mikati Cabinet, thereby giving Hezbollah and its allies a parliamentary majority that allowed it to dominate the Lebanese government for the first time.

## Dawah/al-Sadrites/ISCI

Much has been said about how the Arab Spring enabled Islamism and democratization to come together. These two trends first impacted each other during Washington's move to topple Saddam Hussein's regime. Certainly, the Iraqi case is a limited one in which the Islamists in question represent the minority (Shia) Muslim sect and is seen through the lens of the U.S. invasion of the country. This has led to an underappreciation of the event as a case study of political Islam and democratization interacting in a unique and complex way. Over the past decade, Iraq offers insights into how Shia Islamists who remain very close to Iran focus less on Islamist issues than on democratic ones and those related to sustaining their power in a political atmosphere where ethno-sectarianism is hardwired into the fabric of both state and society. On the intercommunal level they have had to deal with Kurdish demands for greater autonomy and manage the Sunni minority, which had ruled Iraq for close to a century. There is also a great deal of acrimonious competition among the three main Shia Islamist factions. This dual-level context means that each main group has to be examined both individually and as part of the overall fragile Shia coalition, which has to deal with the other two main communal groups. Both the Dawah and ISCI, despite their dormancy, had years of support from Iran and then worked closely with the United States for many years in the lead up to the 2003 invasion and thus dominated the building of a democratic Iraq. In contrast, the al-Sadrite movement, even though it had assumed the de facto leadership of the Iraqi Shia during the 1990s, was neither in the Iranian orbit nor part of the American-led regime-change process. It thus found itself outside the system.

Muqtada al-Sadr and his associates were bitter that their movement had suffered under Saddam while those who had chosen exile were benefiting from the new post-Saddam order. Even worse, the al-Sadrites had no role in the embryonic system that consisted of the 25-member Iraqi Governing Council (ICG) appointed by the American-controlled Coalition Provisional Authority (CPA). Despite its massive civil society presence in Baghdad and the Shia south, the al-Sadrite movement had no seat at the table, thanks to opposition from Dawah and ISCI, as well as the Americans and the Iranians. Therefore in April 2004, when Sunni nationalist insurgents and jihadists launched a major campaign to prevent the United States and its largely Shia and Kurdish partners from erecting a new state on the ashes of the old, the al-Sadrite also deployed its militia, the Mehdi Army, against the emerging new order. To distinguish his movement, al-Sadr emphasized resistance against foreign occupation and its role in shaping the new state. This placed his group in the same light as that of the Sunni insurgents and the Iraqi node of al-Qaeda. But unlike the Sunni militants, the al-Sadrite goal was to gain recognition as a major player without whose participation the transition could not move forward. The al-Sadrites resorted to armed struggle to position their group to take advantage of unprecedented opportunities in the post-Baathist era but also to counter threats.[21] The spring 2004 uprising in Baghdad, Kufa, Karbala, and Najaf was triggered by CPA Administrator Paul Bremer's issuance of an arrest warrant for al-Sadr and to shut down *al-Hawza,* the movement's mouthpiece publication. A short-lived truce was reached by the end of May, but fighting broke out again in August when the militia attacked a US Marine patrol, which the Shia group thought was sent to arrest Muqtada al-Sadr. A second truce was established, this time with the mediation of al-Sistani. Many have viewed the 2004 uprising as a failure, especially since the al-Sadrite militia underwent a complex fragmentation over the next three years. Indeed the Mehdi Army was no match for the American troops, but this fighting revealed al-Sadr's broad and deep support among the Iraqi Shia grassroots, a fact that allowed it to gain recognition within the Shia and national mainstream. Aware that they had to co-opt the al-Sadrites, the Shia religious and political establishment brought the group into a fragile alliance with Dawah and ISCI; however, the movement continued to compete with both.[22]

After being absent from the process that created the ICG as well as its successor, the Interim Government established in June 2004 and headed by Ayad Allawi, the al-Sadrites wanted to participate in the elections scheduled for early January 2005. Those elections would create a Transitional Government that would draft the country's new constitution that was to replace the provisional Transitional Administrative Law crafted by the ICG under American and UN supervision. The al-Sadrites had a lot of catching up to do with their two rivals, who had been involved in the ICG and the Interim Government as well as coordinating with the United States for several years to oust the Baathist regime. The movement had one edge over its two more sophisticated and politically mature competitors: nationalist credentials, which helped it develop ties across the political spectrum. But compared to ISCI and Dawah, which had spent years working with Iran, Syria, United Kingdom, and the United States, as well as with the country's Kurds, the al-Sadrites had to balance their anti-American and religious radicalism with pragmatism. Initially the al-Sadrite movement was not a formal part of the Shia United Iraqi Alliance (UIA) dominated by SCIRI and Dawah.[23] However, its affiliates won 23 out of the 140 seats that the UIA gained in the January 2005 elections, which established the transitional legislature tasked with drafting the new constitution and an interim government led by Dawah chief Ibrahim Jaafari.[24] Having gained recognition at the intra-Shia level, the al-Sadrite movement sought to advance itself to the status of a national movement, especially given its Iraqi nationalist orientation.

The al-Sadrite opposition to a federalist state that allowed provinces to come together into autonomous regions with significant self-rule powers during the constitutional debates enabled the movement to gain major respect from the Sunnis and nonsectarian centrist forces. Given its weak presence in Parliament and government, the movement resorted to public demonstrations to highlight opposition, a tactic that also led to clashes with ISCI, initially its principal Shia rival. This campaign helped the al-Sadrites distinguish themselves from ISCI and Dawah, who favored a federalist political structure (the former more so than the latter) for the new Iraqi state. After an excruciatingly painful negotiation process at multiple levels (e.g., intra-Shia, Shia-Sunni, Arab-Kurdish, secular-Islamist, and federalist-centralist), a deal was reached and the constitution was approved in a national plebiscite held on October 15, 2005. This referendum paved the way for a second round of parliamentary elections in December 2005, in which the Shia were a far more coherent bloc with the al-Sadrites a formal part of the UIA. This body also contained several other much smaller Shia factions, most significantly the Basra-based Islamist al-Fadhila Party (a splinter of the al-Sadrite movement that opposed Muqtada al-Sadr's leadership).[25] The al-Sadrite movement formally joined the UIA in late October. Al-Sadr had sought to do so when he could derive maximum concessions from his Shia rivals; however, the timing of this decision was also informed by the need for intra-Shia harmony to counter the Sunnis, who had largely boycotted the January elections were now gearing up for the December ones in the form of two blocs.[26]

The Sunnis' participation in the December 2005 elections, which were called to elect the first constitutional legislature, led to the expected decrease of the Shia and Kurdish seats. The UIA won 128, the Kurds 53, and the two Sunni blocs (the Tawafoq Iraqi Front and the Iraqi Front for National Dialogue), which won 44 and 11 seats, respectively. Within the Shia alliance, ISCI controlled 36, the al-Sadrites 32, Dawah 25, Fadhila 15, and the independents 32 seats. In those early days, the main rivalry was between the al-Sadrites and SCIRI, which Dawah exploited in order to balance between the two and thus sustain its lead position. The prior arrangement of having Dawah's leader serve as prime minister continued, but there was significant opposition from the Kurds, Sunnis, and the United States to Jaafari becoming a full-term prime minister. Eventually Dawah retained the premiership but the post went to Jawad al-Maliki, a Jaafari deputy and compromise candidate, mainly because of his relative independence from Iran. After al-Maliki assumed office in April 2006, he reverted to his original name (Nouri al-Maliki) and began consolidating the Shia-dominated Iraqi state. A final power-sharing agreement was not clinched until June 2006, when the three security ministries were handed out: the Shia got the interior and national security portfolios, while the Sunnis got defense.[27] The three-member presidency council continued with Jalal Talabani, leader of the Patriotic Union of Kurdistan, as president with Adel Abdul-Mahdi of ISCI and Tariq al-Hashmi of the Iraqi Islamic Party (IIP). The IIP, the Iraqi branch of the Muslim Brotherhood, was part of the larger of the two Sunni parliamentary blocs: the Islamist-dominated Iraqi Accord Front.[28] Mahmoud al-Mashhadani, a Salafi member of the Iraqi Accord Front, was elected speaker of the parliament, replacing Hajim al-Hassani (from the Iraqi Brotherhood) and served during the transitional setup.

All-Maliki's first term as prime minister (2006–2010) was the critical formative period for the post-Baathist republic, for it was the al-Maliki administration that had to deal with Iraq's security, stability, and economic and infrastructure reconstruction. Thus both the intercommunal and intra-Shia power-sharing arrangements underwent significant shifts. For example, the prime minister also assumed leadership of the Dawah Party, with which he had a long affiliation. Under al-Maliki's leadership, this party retained its Islamist orientation but assumed a more centrist, secular, pragmatic, and Iraqi nationalist outlook. At a strategic level, al-Maliki had to balance the United States and Iran, both of which were competing to shape the new Iraqi state. On the domestic front, he had to deal with his Shia competitors, ISCI and al-Sadr, both of which were far more ideological than his party. His main worry was the Sunnis, who were neither prepared to accept the Shia's rise nor the Shia Islamism aligned with Iran and thus were waging a major insurgency. Furthermore, the secular Kurds were concerned about preserving and enhancing the autonomy they had enjoyed since the first Gulf War. But before he could deal with such matters, al-Maliki first needed to become the preeminent Shia actor. With ISCI as an ally and the al-Sadrites as an opponent with a militia, the prime minister sought to defang the latter. One of his first orders of business was to disband the militias. The Sunni landscape was full of militant outfits and thus a long-term project. His first target was the Mehdi Army still retained by the al-Sadrites, even though they had joined the mainstream Shia alliance.

What helped was that al-Sadr was slowly losing control of it, as different factions were already operating independently. The sectarian war that transnational jihadists had been trying to foment since the 2003 began after the February 2006 bombing in Samarra that destroyed the 11th Shia Imam's mausoleum (viz., Hasan al-Askari). Militants from the various al-Sadrite militia factions were reportedly involved in the ensuing anti-Sunni retribution killings. Furthermore, Muqtada, given his lack of scholarly credentials, had many opponents among those who had been loyal to his father. This process gained momentum when he joined the political system in 2005. Iran exploited this situation to bring the movement under its control. It supported the splinter groups, and its IRGC-QF developed the Special Groups, which served as a lever against the United States. Iranian actions helped al-Maliki who used the actions of these rogue outfits to move against the al-Sadrite militia and other armed and criminal outfits in Baghdad and the south, especially in Basra. Al-Sadr thus had to find a way to preserve his militia, so he enhanced his share of power beyond the minor ministries his group had acquired via the political process. He was competing with ISCI and Dawah, who had far greater political power and authority over the security forces. His militia, however, was increasingly becoming a liability given that it was involved in unauthorized attacks that threatened his movement as a whole.

Between the government crackdown on his militia and his own fighters going rogue, al-Sadr fled to Iran in early 2007, reportedly due to threats to his personal safety. The relocation not only offered al-Sadr security but also a way to manage the crisis he faced with Iranian help. Thus Tehran finally brought the movement, which had long defied it, under its tutelage. This move actually accelerated the movement's transformation from being a Hezbollah-like political group that maintained an armed wing to a purely political party. Iran reorganized the Mehdi Army into smaller cells that were beholden to it and also gained influence over the movement's core. Al-Sadr also knew that while he needed Iran, Iran needed him to give it some influence among the deeply divided Iraqi Shia community. After all, his movement provided a counter to al-Maliki, who was never as pro-Iran as his predecessor had been. Furthermore, al-Sadr's anti-American stance allowed Tehran to keep the new prime minister in check, especially as al-Maliki had to work with Washington. Thus in exchange for aligning with Iran, al-Sadr secured Iranian religious and political support. He also sought to continue his clerical studies there in order to become an ayatollah, which remains a work in progress, and, ultimately with Iranian assistance, secure a permanent political stake in Iraqi politics. Iran envisaged using the stand-off between Baghdad and al-Sadr to press for a timetable for the withdrawal for American forces, which converged with al-Sadr's interests to prevent a crackdown on his militia. As mentioned earlier, he was focused on salvaging his militia from both the crackdown and the internal rebellion because it was his main leverage to compete with his Shia rivals who had a major head-start in terms of consolidating their own political power.

Thus he pressed for this timetable and once again pulled his ministers out of the Cabinet in April 2007. He also threatened to withdraw his 32 MPs from the Shia alliance if his demands were not met. The goal here was to squeeze al-Maliki, who had just lost the support of the 15 al-Fadhila MPs who had left the UIA, for both sides knew that if the al-Sadrites defected, al-Maliki could lose even more support in Parliament.[29] The ploy did not work, however, for al-Maliki called al-Sadr's bluff and appointed replacements for those al-Sadrites who had resigned. Al-Sadr could not afford to simply stay out of Iraq, for this would weaken his movement even further. After working out a deal involving Tehran, Baghdad, and Washington, al-Sadr returned to Iraq the following month after agreeing, in principle, to disband his militia. In August he ordered a six-month freeze on Mehdi Army activities, after his militiamen clashed with the local ISCI-dominated security forces at two major shrines in Karbala; 52 people died. While the Shia Islamist forces were fighting with each other, the United States quietly worked out a deal with the tribal principals of Sunni nationalist insurgents. After four years of fighting, Washington reached a settlement with the Sunnis in al-Anbar and other Sunni-dominated central provinces: They would turn their guns toward al-Qaeda-led jihadist forces operating in their midst. Financially underwritten by the Pentagon, the Sunni insurgent forces became the Awakening Councils (aka Sons of Iraq) and were given responsibility for security in their areas. The United States brought back the Sunnis to counterbalance the Shias and Iran, as the three main Shia groups, with Tehran's assistance were working towards greater intra-communal cooperation.

In a subsequent Iranian brokered deal, ISCI and the al-Sadrite movement announced a truce in early October. The Shia, including al-Maliki, reacted sharply to the American decision to support Sunni militias, which further accelerated the efforts to disband all Shia militias so that the battle-lines would be between the Shia-dominated state and the Sunni militias operating beyond its writ. Iran increased its pressure on all Shia groups to get their act together because their infighting was hurting its strategic imperatives. As a result, al-Sadr began transforming his militia into a purely political organization. Given that the al-Sadr movement/Mehdi Army was al-Maliki's largest challenge, the disbanding of the al-Sadrite militia was a major victory for the pm. Having neutralized this threat, the al-Maliki-led Dawah emerged as the undisputed Shia leader. This was also important because al-Maliki received Iranian recognition for the intra-Shia arrangement as well as for the Baghdad–Washington agreement according to which the United States would withdraw all of its forces by December 31, 2011. Coopting al-Sadr into accepting the internal Shia balance of power was a major development that al-Maliki was able to push ahead on several other fronts in 2009, such as emerging as a national leader. Several developments that year helped him gain a disproportionate amount of influence. Moreover, the way the Iraqi security forces took on the Shia militants (in addition to the jihadists) underscored just how effective the Shia-dominated state's intelligence and domestic capabilities had become.

Since al-Maliki had presided over the development of the state security organs, he essentially became the leader of the post-Saddam establishment. With security under control, especially in the Shia south, he set about developing Iraq's long-neglected oil sector and thereby managed to strengthen his hold over power. Backed by his security forces and the incoming oil income, he also coopted many members of the Sunni militias. Now that al-Maliki and Dawah had become Iraq's largest Shia Islamist force, in the lead-up to the provincial elections he established a new Shia coalition led by his Dawah party—the State of Law (SoL), which did not include ISCI or the al-Sadrite movement. The results of the provincial elections held in late January 2009 highlighted al-Maliki's strength: SoL won 126 out of a total of 440 seats, the ISCI-led coalition won 52 seats, and the al-Sadr movement only won 43 seats.[30] The extent to which Dawah had overtaken ISCI became clear during the last elections in 2005: ISCI had 192 and Dawah had 42 seats. ISCI's decline enabled al-Maliki to assert a measure of independence from Iran, which was reflected in his decision to contest the 2010 parliamentary elections under the banner of his SoL coalition, which by now included Sunnis. Al-Maliki's rise led to a realignment of the Shia Islamist landscape, for the al-Sadrites joined forces with its archrivals to form the Iraqi National Alliance (INA), a more Islamist pro-Iranian coalition. The results of the March 7 elections, however, were a setback for al-Maliki, who had miscalculated the strength of Allawi's new al-Iraqiyah coalition, which now included most of the key Sunni players and a time when the Sunnis were not boycotting the polls. Al-Iraqiyah won 91, SoL won 89, and INA won 70 seats. Al-Maliki failed to win the election for several reasons, such as the Shia Islamist sectarian vote was divided between SoL and INA, al-Maliki could not shake his decades-old image as a sectarian and an Islamist, and al-Iraqiyah won-over many Shias in the various districts and in the south who were opposed to sectarianism and Islamism. Forced to go back to his former allies in the INA and forge a post-election alliance, he formed a super Shia Islamist bloc that held 159 seats and thus became the largest group in Parliament. And yet it still took him nine months to form a coalition government via a great deal of wheeling and dealing at the intra-Shia level and at the intercommunal level with al-Iraqiyah and the Kurds.[31] Al-Maliki gained a second term as prime minister, and the Iraqi Shia Islamists retained their hold on the post-Baathist state after reaching a power-sharing agreement on December 21, 2010—a mere few weeks before the Arab Spring erupted.

## The Arab Spring and Beyond

With the minor exception of Bahrain, the Arab Shia Islamists were largely unaffected by the Arab Spring. The limited protests in Beirut and Baghdad were largely sympathy rallies as opposed to the major uprisings found in other Arab countries. Both Lebanon and Iraq had already had their respective democratic experiences and thus lacked the strong desire for transformation found in Tunisia, Egypt, Yemen, and Libya. Governance was an issue, but the delicate power-sharing agreements achieved in both Lebanon and Iraq over the previous decade insulated them from any major public unrest. Neither country had a serious opposition that wanted to dramatically change the status quo. Furthermore, Hezbollah and the Iraqi Shia had very recently gained comfortable political positions. Hezbollah had skillfully engineered the constitutional coup against the Sunni-dominated al-Hariri government and by June 2011 had put in place a coalition government dominated by the Lebanese Shia Islamist movement. In Iraq, the Shia Islamists had once again closed ranks to prevent the Sunnis from translating their electoral victory into political power. Things were looking fine for Shia Islamists in both countries until Syria caught the Arab Spring contagion in March 2011. The weakening of President Bashar al-Assad's regime threatens the power of Shia Islamists in both countries. Those regional and international groups trying to weaken the influence of their common patron, Iran, are hoping that Assad's fall will somehow undermine the dominant position of Hezbollah and the Iraqi Shia Islamist groups. Both sets of Shia Islamist actors are working with their allies in Tehran to isolate themselves from Syria's meltdown. While they hope to limit the fallout from the geosectarian proxy war in Syria, both Hezbollah and the Iraqi Shia Islamists have fresh elections coming up in 2014, which will test their strength. Hezbollah's situation is far better in that the various stakeholders on both sides of the Lebanese divide do not wish to suffer through another civil war. The situation in Iraq is much more complex, for it is not as divided like Lebanon and Shia Islamists share an interest with the Kurds in making sure that Sunni empowerment in Syria does not lead to a Sunni resurgence in Iraq. But al-Maliki's aggressive behavior against both the Sunni and Kurdish coalition partners complicates matters for the Shia, now that the American forces have departed. Over the past nearly two years the al-Maliki administration has tried to implicate several senior Sunni government officials in terrorism cases. Similarly, his hardline policy toward Kurdish efforts to enhance their autonomous status has led to a dangerous stand-off between Baghdad's security forces and those of the northern Kurdistan region. Meanwhile, since the 2010 election the al-Sadrite movement has emerged as the main challenger to the al-Maliki-led Dawah and is exploiting the rift with both minority communities to weaken his hold on power. The al-Sadrites, however, are constrained by the fact that the evolving situation in Syria threatens Shia power in Iraq and the region as a whole. Therefore, it is unwilling to make any serious move against al-Maliki that might undermine Shias' collective communal interests. It is unclear how things will evolve in this post–Arab Spring decade vis-à-vis Arab Shia Islamists. A lot depends on what happens in Syria, especially given that in 2013 the position of the regime has improved. Hezbollah as well Iraqi Shia militias working with Iranian military and intelligence forces have been aiding the al-Assad regime against the rebels. Clearly, sectarian interests are driving the Arab Shia Islamists more so than ideological ones..

### Arab Shia Islamism and Democratization

The evolution of Hezbollah, Hizb al-Dawah, the Islamic Supreme Council of Iraq, and the al-Sadrite movement clearly shows that they had no ideological aversion to democracy. This sets them apart from many of their Sunni counterparts, who are either conditionalists or rejectors. This fact, however, does not automatically imply that they have wholeheartedly embraced democratic politics and thereby have become participatory Islamists. What is most important to note here is that unlike the Muslim Brotherhood, the Arab Shia Islamists' religious and ideological ideals were not as instrumental in steering them toward democracy. Instead, geopolitical considerations were far more important in their decision to participate in democratic politics. At a general level, their participatory attitude stems from their current acceptor view of the state and society.

But as the previous sections have shown, the actions of Hezbollah since its inception during the civil war and those of the Dawah, ISCI, and al-Sadrites during the periods of autocratic rule—both military (1958–1968) and Baathist (1968–2003)—show that both sets of actors did not always behave as acceptors, especially not during the 1980s and 1990s. As Lina Khatib discusses, Hezbollah "learned the value of pragmatism (or at least the perception of pragmatism) early on. Although it declared its key objective to be establishment of an Islamic state, and that it did not recognize the Lebanese state as legitimate, in 1985, it soon changed its tone and began selling its mission in patriotic terms, branding itself as a national resistance movement."[32] Their behavior was based not on ideological factors, but on the circumstances in which they were established and evolved. Thus, regime-type (or the absence of one altogether as is the case of Hezbollah) shaped the development of their modus operandi. Like the Muslim Brotherhood, they only sought the right to participate in mainstream politics. However, they faced far more structural obstacles than the Muslim Brotherhood, (which was suppressed but still tolerated), ever did. Thus, we opine that the Iraqi and Lebanese Shia Islamist groups were acceptors because of structural reasons, as opposed to any specific Islamist view. Lebanon's civil war had consumed the state, and the Iraqi state was a single-party edifice largely off-limits to the Shia majority. In other words there was no state to accept, much less to participate in. The Shia's marginal stake in Lebanon's political system complicated this situation, especially after they had emerged as one of its largest communities.

Under Saddam, the majority Shia community was shut out of the single-party authoritarian system. In fact, the Sunni-dominated Baathist regime specifically targeted it as a hostile entity. Thus, in contrast with Lebanon, Iraq had a very fierce state that was not only autocratic but also actively denying the Shia any political role. As a result, both actors adopted violence to varying degrees in order to ensure their physical survival and pursue their political aims. In other words, the polity's very nature shaped the behavior of the Lebanese and Iraqi Shia Islamists during their formative period. Clearly, the use of violence was informed by on-the-ground realities as opposed to any ideological factors.

Hezbollah remains caught between the ideals of *velayat-e-faqih* and the confessional Lebanese state, which proportionally distributes power between the Muslim and Christian communities and their various internal sects. The al-Maliki-led regime, despite coming to power through a democratic process, is behaving autocratically in dealing with the Sunnis and the Kurds. What we have here is a situation in which expediency drives participation in democratic politics, and both the Lebanese and Iraqi Shia Islamists have their respective motivations. The Arab Shia actors' perceptions of religion's role in politics are also based far more on geopolitical factors than on ideological grounds. The fact that they hail from the minority branch of Islam and are situated in pluralist societies pushes them toward a system of power-sharing because they cannot push policies based on their religious ideology. Thus this is far more than a simple Islamist versus secularist ideological struggle.

As Lina Khatib points out, Hezbollah's 1985 Open Letter document "called on Lebanese people to accept an Islamic state" and "aspires to an Islamic democracy under Iran's Guardianship of the Jurist (*velayat-e-faqih*) model," which it reiterated in a 2004 declaration establishing an "Islamic Republic."[33] As recently as 2008, Secretary General Hassan Nasrullah stated in an interview with journalists that the party's commitment to *velayat-e-faqih* has not changed. But the 2009 manifesto did not mention establishing an Islamic state, arguably because, as Khatib posits, Hezbullah realized that for practical reason such a position would be unlikely to attract at least half the population. Thus its omission can be interpreted not as a sign of abandoning this goal, but rather of pragmatism given the current reality of Lebanon's sectarian politics.[34] For this reason, neither Hezbollah nor the Iraqi Shia groups have sought to impose shari'a law. In many ways, for both of them the issue is not their ideology, but their communal interests and need to ensure their share of power and slowly enhance it as much as possible.

Hezbollah's participation is motivated by several long-term goals, among them the desire to replace its current consociational system with a majoritarian democracy along the lines of what Iraq now has.[35] In December 2004

Hezbollah MP Mohammad Raad announced his belief that a referendum would show that the majority of Lebanese supported the continuation of the "resistance" and that one question should be "whether the presidency should still be reserved for the Maronites."[36] Hezbollah Deputy Secretary-General Naim Qassem said in 2008 that "the Party's final objective, in its political jihadist vision and program of work, is not to reach ultimate ruling power within the current sectarian system."[37] Its 2009 manifesto explains why the party wants a majoritarian democracy.

> The main problem in the Lebanese political system, which prevents its reform, development and constant updating is political sectarianism . . . The fact that the Lebanese political system was established on a sectarian basis constitutes in itself a strong constraint to the achievement of true democracy where an elected majority can govern and an elected minority can oppose, opening the door for a proper circulation of power between the loyalty and the opposition or the various political coalitions. Thus, abolishing sectarianism is a basic condition for the implementation of the majority—minority rule.[38]

A majoritarian system would allow Hezbollah to rule and give the group far more leverage within the political system. Their status as a "sect," despite outnumbering the Sunnis, means that they face resistance within the Islamist and Muslim contexts. Furthermore, it must always weigh its ongoing relationships with other ethnic and religious communal groupings, including the Druze, the Alawites and the various Christian denominations. Given all of these realities, they cannot impose their ideological worldview or shari'a law.

The history of Hezbollah speaks volumes about political Islam's complexity. This entity is both a political party engaged in national politics and a paramilitary organization engaged in transnational geopolitics. Along with Hamas, but not exactly in the same way, Hezbollah defies our typological framework because it cannot be placed neatly into any category of the typologies that we have offered. Despite having a militia and engaging in terrorism, it does not belong in the insurrectionist category because it rarely uses violence to achieve its domestic political goals. Yet it cannot be described as an acceptor group, for it refuses to subordinate itself to the state security forces and insists upon retaining its militia. In terms of democracy it is a participatory Islamist group, but this needs to be qualified since its militia gives it leverage over all other groups, be they allies or opponents.

Our goal in this book is to present a conceptual framework for understanding the Islamists' behavior in relation to democracy. Yet Hezbollah is a clear exception, which becomes rather apparent when one analyzes how it has used its militia to garner domestic political support. In its early days Hezbollah fought the Israeli occupation forces but also engaged in terrorist attacks on Western targets. During the civil war it also fought factions aligned with the West and/or Israel. By the end of the civil war it was also fighting Amal, a fellow Shia group, which had started out an Islamist-oriented entity but eventually gone secular. After the Taif Accords, Hezbollah was caught between being an Iranian proxy and a Lebanese group fighting the Israeli occupation. The peace agreement that ended the 15-year civil war also forced the group to redefine itself vis-à-vis mainstream politics, which by then had become something that it could do.

After the Taif Accords, there was a great deal of internal deliberation and consultation with Ayatollah Ali Khamenei, as well as influence from Lebanon's Grand Ayatollah Muhammad Hussein Fadhlallah about participating in the national political system.[39] Hezbollah provided a great deal of religious justification for doing so, even though he had earlier considered un-Islamic and sought to change it. By this time, its own leadership as well as their Lebanese and Iranian *marjaa* deemed such participation necessary in order to achieve Hezbollah's original goals: resistance against Israel and furthering its own political interests. The group has found it rather hard to maintain this delicate balancing act.

In the 1990s, Israel's occupation of southern Lebanon made it easy for Hezbollah to be a party with an armed wing. The only actor it fought was the South Lebanese Army, a Christian militia that served as Israel's proxy. Its resistance helped strengthened the political clout it had gained in the 1992 and 1996 elections. When Israel gave up its security zone in 2000, it became harder for Hezbollah to justify retaining its armed wing, which had done so much to enhance its communal and partisan fortunes. Leveraging its anti-Israeli stance enabled the group to enhance the Shia communal influence far more than its predecessor, competitor, and ally Amal had been able to do. In fact, Hezbollah's resistance allowed it to overtake all other Lebanese forces in terms of political power. The 2005 al-Hariri assassination was a major development in terms of understanding Hezbollah's dual-track strategy. Since the STL has not concluded its investigation into the former premier assassination, Hezbollah's involvement in it remains extremely unclear. But the murder happened in the midst of an international effort to disarm Hezbollah and force its patron, Syria, to withdraw its forces. Whether or not Hezbollah was involved, the consequences, especially the Syrian withdrawal, greatly unnerved the group. Based on these new geopolitical circumstances, Hezbollah was forced deeper into the political system—it joined the government for the first time since the 2005 elections.

Now part of the government, Hezbollah could influence any attempts to disarm its militia. There is a view that Hezbollah considers resistance, particularly against Israel, as its primary mission and thus participates in mainstream politics so that its militia will remain intact. This line of reasoning suggests that being a participatory actor is a means toward an end—resistance is important, especially in the transnational context, since Hezbollah perceives itself as a vanguard movement furthering the interests of the Muslim world. As Khatib points out, "[f]rom its 1985 Open Letter to its 2009 manifesto, the party has consistently presented its vision as transcending Lebanon. The Open Letter was primarily addressed to Muslims world-wide, and the manifesto frames Hezbollah's outlook as global in scope: 'The Resistance in Lebanon has evolved from a Lebanese national value to an Arab and Islamic value and has become today an international value that's taught all over the world.' "[40]

However, its participatory role is linked to its status as the principal group representing the country's largest sectarian community. One cannot deny that its militia allows it to augment the influence it has garnered via electoral politics. But relying on the ballot box can take Hezbollah only so far. Its political bloc has yet to win the majority of seats in Parliament. The closest it has come to this was after the 2009 elections, when post-electoral realignments allowed its allies to claim more seats in the legislature and thus form the current government back in June 2011. Having a militia lets it force concessions and eventually affect political change without having a majority. This was seen clearly in the 2008 Doha Accords. This agreement resulted from Hezbollah's first use of its militia against its rivals when Beirut dismantled the movement's telecommunication network. This domestic use of military force to settle a political dispute underscores the group's reliance upon its militia to maintain its edge especially as the Syrian civil war casts a shadow of uncertainty over Lebanon's future.

In Iraq, ISCI got its armed wing (the Badr Corps) incorporated into the state security organs because it dominated the state. Such an accomplishment is likely beyond Hezbollah, since it does not enjoy a similar status. A more likely scenario would be Hezbollah's armed wing becoming an elite military force separate from the Lebanese Armed Forces, along the lines of the IRGC in Iran. Such a development would require a special political dispensation giving Hezbollah a lead share of power in Beirut and allowing its armed wing to enhance the movement's power far beyond that which it can acquire via political participation. In Iraq, the fact that the Shias constitute a demographic majority is a key incentive for its three main Islamist forces to participate in democracy. Of course, nearly 40 percent of the country is a combination of Kurds and Arab Sunnis. But because the Kurds are more interested in political autonomy, the Shias are able to better dominate the central government.

When the Sunnis finally participated as a community in the 2010 elections and the intra-Shia differences led to Dawah competing separately from ISCI and the Sadrites, the Sunni-backed party al-Iraqiyah came in first place. Realizing that not running on a joint Shia platform undermined their communal position, al-Maliki quickly began working for a post-election realignment merger of the two Shia groups to form a coalition government. The Iraqi Shia Islamists are only participatory because it is in their collective sectarian interest to do so. Furthermore, their commitment to democracy and the rule of constitutional law is weak, given the post-Baathist state's attempts to marginalize the Sunnis and limit the Kurds' autonomy. Dawah, ISCI, and the al-Sadrites, while being part of an alliance still have their partisan differences. The most intense rivalry is that between al-Maliki and al-Sadr, for the latter controls the largest number of Shia seats in the legislature. The al-Sadrites would like to replace al-Maliki's party as the leader of the Shia and the country, especially since ISCI's power is not what it used to be. On numerous occasions al-Sadr has sided with the Sunnis and Kurds to weaken al-Maliki. But each time he has been careful not to topple the government for he knows that this will not necessarily result in his party becoming the new ruling party. His MPs would be outnumbered in any alliance with the Sunnis and the Kurds. It is likely that the Shia seats would fragment and that the majority community would lose power. Thus he is waiting for Dawah to weaken, as has already happened with ISCI, so that his group can assume the lead position among the Shias and take over the government.

It is unlikely that Hezbollah will rule Lebanon anytime soon, because Lebanon's demographics are not going to change anytime soon. In addition, the crisis in Syria threatens to sharpen Lebanon's internal religious divides. The same is true of Iraq, but on a much longer timeframe and to a lesser degree because its Shias are a much larger majority and have more direct Iranian support, given the two countries' common border. Beyond rhetoric, neither Hezbollah nor Iraq's Shia Islamists have really pushed for religion to have a prominent role in public affairs, mainly because their sectarian identity arouses other groups' resistance. Shia Islamists adopt new norms when the surrounding realities cause them to reshape their own world-views. Hezbollah's closest allies, the Maronite Christians, are not even Muslim. Likewise al-Maliki, having gained the leadership of his own Shia community, needs to deal with the secular Kurds and Sunnis and thus cannot appear to be a purely sectarian official. As we have seen, sectarianism has thus led to a transformation in which accentuating their Islamism is not a priority.

# 10

# Post-Islamism: The Case of Turkey's AKP

Each of the case studies covered thus far has involved an Islamist actor. In this chapter, we examine a secular party that is the successor of a long line of Islamist groups. Turkey's ruling Justice and Development Party (Adalet ve Kalkinma Partisi, AKP) is a prime example of a post-Islamist group making the journey out of Islamism.[1] Any discussion of political Islam and democratization would be incomplete without a closer look at this key post-Islamist actor. Some observers insist that the AKP remains very much an Islamist group and argue against classifying it as secular. They suggest that its retreat from its Islamist agenda is a tactical move designed to avoid the fate of its more open predecessors that were eventually declared illegal. However, the party's behavior over the past decade underscores a genuine transformation that has seen it jettison its Islamist roots and thus it can no longer be considered part of Islamism.[2]

The AKP's principal founders are former Islamists who embraced secularism and established this post-Islamist party.[3] The binary view of the Turkish political landscape, which describes the struggle between the AKP and its Kemalist opponents as one between an Islamist-rooted party and an adamantly secular camp, prevents many from recognizing this significant transformation. This perspective also prevents an appreciation of the complexity of the party's ideology. The AKP has been pushing for American style "passive" and moderate secularism as opposed to the "assertive" French laicist model of radical (and perhaps even militant) secularism that the Kemalists have imposed since the republic's founding.[4] But the Kemalist experience may have also inadvertently played a key role in ensuring that Turkish Islamists were not radical like their counterparts elsewhere and have given them the space in which to mobilize during the period when the main domestic and international threat came from left-wing radicalism. The Kemalist republic was more committed to secularism and nationalism than it was to democracy, which would explain the single-party state that lasted until the 1950s and the military interventions since the 1960s.

As Banu Eligur argues, the Kemalist military served as an inadvertent elite ally of the Islamists by introducing and insisting on a Turkish nationalism with an element of Sunni Islam as the official state ideology, which opened up a sociopolitical space for Islamist mobilization.[5] In his words, this "represented a fundamental shift in state ideology away from the Kemalists' understanding of secularism, which used state control to relegate religion to the private sphere."[6] We do not fully agree with this inference because it by no means reflects the Kemalists altering their historical aversion to religious forces, as they made clear by closing down Necmettin Erbakan's second political vehicle, the National Salavation Party, in 1981. Rather it was a tactical move by the military, which saw Islamists as the lesser threat when, after the 1980 coup, they sought to eliminate leftist forces and repress ultranationalists. This was an extraordinary time, for the Soviet Union had invaded Afghanistan and Turkey, as a NATO member state located so close to the USSR, was extremely vulnerable. Moreover, the military had taken direct control of the state and had to avoid alienating the religious Right at the same time it was battling the Left.

To understand how Turkey's Islamism evolved into post-Islamism, one must first appreciate its unique historic nature. Mustafa Akyol argues, contrary to conventional wisdom, that the roots of Turkish democracy and the country's unique form of Islamism predate the republic.[7] During the nineteenth century the Ottoman Empire launched a major reform initiative to catch up with an ascendant Europe. The Tanzimat reforms spearheaded by Sultan Mahmud II led to the creation of the 1876 constitution and the establishment of Parliament. Furthermore, as Ihsan Yilmaz argues, Turkish Islamists were never persuaded by hardline Islamist views so dominant in other Arab and Muslim countries, for Sufi Islam had taken root throughout the Turkic core during the Ottoman era. As a result, radical Islamists have always had a negligible presence in Turkey. As Metin Heper highlights, radical Islamists also have no recognized charismatic leader who was Turkish or Sunni, similar to what one might find in Iran or Arab countries. Furthermore, they had always been dispersed into relatively marginal Islamist groups, such as the Giriim (Enterprise), the Buyuk Dogu (Grand East), the Vahdet (Unity), and Hezbollah (the Party of God), which are not linked by any unifying central structure.[8] Turkish radical Islamists sought to spread ideas that were alien to the country's religious communities—they were imports from the wider Arab/Muslim context—and thus could not find a receptive audience.

The efforts toward a constitutional order during the late Ottoman period were thus attempts to reinterpret Islam in the light of modernity. The difference was that while the Ottoman Empire and its various sociopolitical forces began trying to reconcile their Islamic heritage with modern Western secularism in the late nineteenth century, Mustafa Kemal (d. 1938) and his associates adopted French laicism. The empire's collapse and the rise of the Kemalist state essentially meant that the latter's ultrasecularism prevailed over the milder form sought by the Ottomans. As a result, Kemal himself enforced a culture that drastically reduced the space for religion in public life by instituting a series of laws. Even after his death, his successors developed such a level of intolerance for religion that they ousted the democratic government of Prime Minister Adnan Menderes in the first-ever coup in 1960. Menderes, although not an Islamist, did adopt more tolerant policies toward religion, an attitude that the Kemalist establishment saw as a threat.

His center-right Democrat Party was disbanded, and Menderes was executed a year later.

This coup effectively laid the foundations for an autocratic Kemalist order that would, beginning in the 1970s, shut down two political parties founded by Erbakan: the National Order Party (outlawed in 1971) and the National Salvation Party (disbanded after the 1980 military coup). When the army returned to the barracks three years later, another center-right political force led by Turgat Ozal, a devout Muslim, came to the fore and, under the banner of the Motherland Party, instituted liberal economic policies. During his two terms as prime minister and nearly one as president (he died in his first term), a social space was created for religion at the same time that Turkey was pursuing a pro-Western orientation. As Akyol notes, Ozal hailed from a Sufi family and was a practicing Muslim on a personal level. But because of his career in the World Bank and the private sector, he was also an ardent believer in Western-style market economy. For this reason, the Kemalists tolerated this devout Muslim political leader. Therefore, it was not the AKP that merged personal piety with laissez-faire economy; rather there was a major precedent in the form of the Ozalian decade (1983–93) that came to an abrupt end with Ozal's death in office in 1993, ushering in an era of unstable coalition governments.

## The 1990s

During these years of coalition governments, Refah came to power after the December 1995 elections. For the first time in modern Turkey's history an Islamist party won the most seats in parliamentary elections: 158 seats. However, two other center-right parties (viz., former prime minister Tansu Ciller's True Path Party and the Motherland Party now headed by Mesut Yilmaz) each had about 130 seats as well. After the initial coalition government formed by the two secular parties collapsed, Erbakan became prime minister and, in June 1996, he formed a new coalition government with Ciller's party. His Islamist rhetoric, decision to invite top leaders of Sufi orders to a Ramadan banquet, and efforts to reorient foreign policy toward the Muslim world angered the military, which forced him to resign in June 1997.

Erbakan's fall triggered a challenge to his leadership of the Islamist movement from a younger generation of moderate Islamist figures, such as Recep Tayyip Erdogan and Abdullah Gul. With the January 1998 closure of Refah and the founding of Fazilet a month earlier, Erbakan no longer enjoyed a monopoly over the party's ideological direction. Erdogan and Gul stressed that Turkish Islam had always been unique and thus their party should differ from the region's Islamist parties. They called for democracy, free-market economy, and human rights. It was important for this newly emerging reformist wing to not only reject the laicism of the Kemalist state, but also the Islamism of the party. Erdogan stressed that individuals (and not the state) who followed one religion or another.[9] Yilmaz, again using discursive analysis, tries to make the case that these reformers within Fazilet were influenced by the ideas of Fethullah Gulen. The prominent religious thinker had long been arguing that the sphere of religious activity was society and not the state. According to Gulen, the state should remain neutral.[10] There is no denying that Gulen's socio-religious movement has influenced individual AKP members' thinking, but the party has maintained its independence from it.

While this internal struggle was underway, in May 1999 the Kemalist judiciary began proceedings on a case to ban Fazilet on the grounds that it was merely a new label for Refah and was pursuing the same Islamist agenda of its predecessor. Two years later Fazilet was declared illegal. But by this time the reformist wing had gained considerable ground and, under the leadership of Erdogan, Gul, and Bulent Arinc, founded the center-right conservative AKP in August 2001. Erdogan and his supporters understood that Islamist political vehicles were a liability within the Turkish political context and therefore resorted to more secular oriented mechanisms to further their political goals. Many critics will read this as a temporary opportunistic move that does not represent a fundamental ideological shift. The past twelve years suggest otherwise. These post-Islamists soon joined hands with key elements from other centrist and nationalist groups, such as the Motherland and Democratic parties who came into the fold of the AKP. The departure of Erdogan and his allies left Erbakan and his Islamist movement significantly weakened. Erbakan moved on to establish a new and now much smaller group: the Sadet Partisi (Felicity Party).

AKP was founded as a quintessential centrist group: conservative in terms of its social policies, liberal vis-à-vis the economy, and supportive of a secular democratic order. It sought to establish civilian supremacy over the military, a tall order considering its origins and the entrenched Kemalists' power, and thus avoided any confrontation with the establishment. Thus shortly before 9/11, Turkish Islamism had given way to post-Islamism.

## The Post-9/11 Decade

Founded in 2001, the AKP quickly became the country's most powerful party. At this same time, the country was experiencing a major economic crisis that had been in the making for several years and culminated in the February 2001 stock market crash. The poor economic conditions were conducive to the emergence of a new party. While the Kemalists were deeply suspicious of the AKP, the economic crisis prevented them from undertaking any action against the new party out of fear that it would further destabilize the country. In November 2002, Turkey experienced a political revolution when the AKP won an overwhelming majority in the parliamentary elections and swept out the political parties and Kemalist figures who had dominated Turkish politics for the past 40 years.[11] While it only won slightly over 34 percent of the popular, it gained 363 seats, a two-thirds majority in Parliament. Only the Republican People's Party (CHP) managed to cross the required 10 percent threshold by winning slightly under 20 percent of the popular ballots.[12] All the other parties failed to secure their presence in the legislature because their share of the votes fell well below the 10 percent threshold. Significantly, Erbakan's Felicity Party secured only 2.5 percent. The AKP victory ended the years of coalition governments that had been in place since 1987. Now in power, it focused on reviving the economy. In the municipal elections held two years later, its success on that front helped it win over 40 percent of the vote, which further deepened its grassroots-level support.

The AKP's success came a little over a year after the Sept 11 attacks. 9/11 had triggered an international search for acceptor Islamists who could potentially help counter the insurrectionists and propagandists. While the AKP had long moved beyond the boundaries of Islamism, it was still identified as an "Islamist lite" party and seen by many in the West as a model for the region's Islamists. The AKP's leadership was careful to balance its Western support with the need to cater to the nationalist mood at home, especially as it refused Washington's request, after a bipartisan vote in Parliament, to use Turkish soil as a staging ground for the 2003 invasion of Iraq. Meanwhile, within weeks of coming to office, the AKP began to work with the CHP to build consensus within Parliament to implement legal reforms that were prerequisites for Turkey's application for European Union (EU) membership. This move initially led to tactical gains: A December 13, 2002, vote in Parliament amended Article 76, which barred individuals convicted of ideological crimes to run for public office. As a result of this change, party chief Erdogan was allowed to assume the post of prime minister that he had won in a March by-election. Until this time, Gul had been serving as prime minister. Erdogan, now in the capacity of both party chief and prime minister, helped consolidate the AKP in government. The accelerated drive toward EU membership was a skillful way for the party to undercut the Kemalist establishment. Having appropriated the historic secularist agenda of orientation toward Europe/the West, the AKP could counter any opposition against its Islamist roots. More importantly, this drive helped the AKP consolidate its power at the expense of the Turkish Armed Forces (TSK), the bastion of Kemalism. By embracing secularism, this now post-Islamist party could compete with the Kemalists on an ideological platform that the latter had monopolized since the republic's founding. Erdogan and his AKP knew that their preferred American-style moderate secularism would run into competition from the French-style Kemalists who had the advantage of being embedded in the state for nearly 80 years. The AKP had an edge in the democratic arena, but the TSK-led Kemalist establishment had always managed to turn Turkey into a "graveyard of parties" by closing down any party deemed to be following policies that could unravel the republic's secular fabric. The AKP knew from the case of Menderes and his Democratic Party that even secular parties were not immune to such moves.

Although the EU was unlikely to approve Turkey's application for membership, the AKP pushed on because it was not after membership per se, but rather after using the accession process to deepen democracy at home. As the Kemalists had long privileged secularism over democracy and supported EU membership, they could not oppose the changes to the legal system. Thus, in a very adroit manner, the AKP began to shift the imbalanced civil–military relationship. It also needed to enhance its control over the political system, which meant moving beyond the legislative branch and countering the Kemalist influence within the civilian bureaucracy, especially the judiciary. At the same time, the AKP's core voter base was religious-minded and wanted to see an easing of restrictions against religious practices in the public domain. While the party was not in the mood to give the Kemalists a pretext that could be used against it, the ruling party also could not ignore the demands of those who had brought it to power. But before the AKP could respond to the demands from its core electoral base , the party had to capture the presidency. All throughout the first AKP government (2002–2007), Ahmet Necdet Sezer, a prominent former judge and an ex-head of the Constitutional Court, was president (the only one to have come from the judiciary). A hardcore Kemalist, Sezer was a major obstacle to the AKP enhancing its power. But his term was set to expire in May 2007 just when the AKP obtained its biggest majority in Parliament, the body that elected the president. On April 24, 2007, the party announced that its number two figure, Abdullah Gul, who had been serving as foreign minister since Erdogan became prime minister in March 2003, would be its presidential candidate. The resulting tension between the government and the TSK was immediate, and there were even rumors of a potential coup. It seemed like the AKP, despite its abandonment of Islamism, would be ousted from power. It was one thing for the Kemalists to have a parliament and government run by former Islamists who were still practicing Muslims, but it was another thing entirely for the president to be a religiously observant man as well and, even worse, married to a woman who wore the headscarf. This was just too much for the radical secularist establishment. After months of gridlock during which Erdogan and TSK chief, General Yasar Buyukanit, engaged in a public war of words, the AKP decided to hold early parliamentary elections and acquire a fresh vote of confidence from the public before attempting to elect Gul as president.[13] Thus early elections were held in July 2007 and the AKP increased its vote share by over 12 percent, gaining nearly 47 percent and 341 seats in Parliament.[14] Yet it earned 22 fewer seats than the first time around because a third party, the Nationalist Action Party (MHP), an ultra-nationalist group, was able to cross the 10 percent threshold. Nonetheless, with a greater public mandate than 2002, the following month the AKP got Gul elected as president, although after three rounds of polling.[15]

With both the presidency and parliament in its hands, the AKP now sought to more effectively transform the country's laicism into an American-style secularism, whereby religion in public affairs could be tolerated. In January 2008, Erdogan announced that his party would introduce a bill to reverse the ban on headscarves in universities instead of pursuing the issue via a constitutional amendment. The Kemalists could not allow the AKP government to proceed with what it perceived as the slow weakening of the country's secular character. Two months later, the Kemalists moved to have the ruling party outlawed by letting the country's top prosecutor file a case in the Constitutional Court accusing Erdogan and Gul of antisecular activities and demanding their dismissal. Before it would hear the case, in June the 11-member highest court struck down the lifting of the ban on headscarves in universities as unconstitutional in a 9–2 decision, which at the time was an indication that the ruling party was on its way to being disbanded. At the end of July, however, the AKP narrowly escaped this fate through a 6–5 vote in the top court, which showed that divisions had emerged within the radical secularist establishment over the nature of secularism. This also revealed that the AKP had made considerable gains in changing the historic viewpoint, which had always been extremely intolerant of religion in public affairs. With the court verdict behind it, the AKP moved to further consolidate its power, but more cautiously, especially in terms of domestic policies on religious matters. So it began another campaign, one designed to weaken the Kemalists' grip over the media, judiciary, and military. The goal was to subordinate the military to civilian rule, an undertaking that it accomplished by arresting several retired and serving commanders and officers on the grounds of alleged coup plots against the government. In a major turning of the tables, democratization under AKP rule had reached the point where the military could no longer mount coups and could be subjected to prosecution for any attempt to do so. By the time of the Supreme Military Council's annual meeting in August 2010, the military could no longer on its own effect appointments and promotions—it was now required to seek the prime minister's input.[16]

### Beyond the Arab Spring

The Arab spring came about just when the AKP had achieved major successes in democratizing the Turkish polity and the economy had survived the 2008 global financial crisis. Initially Ankara was considering an IMF loan but its relatively strong economic standing allowed it to forego the option in March 2010. The decision helped the AKP's domestic political calculus when in June 2011 the party won its third consecutive election by securing nearly 50 percent of the popular vote. Despite winning approximately half of the ballots cast, the AKP was unable to reach the two-thirds figure of 367 seats, which would have allowed the party to unilaterally amend the charter. The AKP fell three seats short of the 330 mark that would have allowed it to push through a new constitution via a national referendum. The AKP wanted to build upon the gains of the September 2010 constitutional referendum and further undo the 1982 charter that was crafted under military rule. The outcome of the 2011 election forced the AKP to work with at least one of the other parties in parliament to effect any changes to the document.

The military had seen how the AKP had gained considerable ground domestically since the failed 2008 attempt to have the ruling party outlawed. The regional and international climate characterized by democratization further helped the AKP deepen democracy at home reducing the TSK's ability to rein in the ruling party. The top brass of the armed forces knew that the 2011 annual Supreme Military Council meeting would be pivotal event for the government to further enhance its control over the military establishment through the process of appointments and promotions. Already the TSK had been the target of investigations into two alleged coup plots, *Ergenekon* and *Balyoz*, and had been placed on the defensive and badly needed leverage against the government. The commanders sought to do this through a collective resignation move in which the three services chiefs along with the joint chief quit their posts a few days before the top military meeting. The hope was that the move would create a crisis for the government, which would be forced to negotiate with the four commanders. However, the government responded by accepting the resignations and appointing a new set of commanders thereby averting a potential crisis. The manner in which the AKP government check-mated the generals and without any repercussions underscored that civilian supremacy over the military had taken root in the Turkish republic, which had historically been dominated by the Kemalist military.

Relieved of the threats of military intervention, the AKP has been pushing an ambitious policy agendas – both internally and externally. On the home front in addition to amending the constitution, the AKP has been pushing a peace process trying to bring an end to decades old Kurdish separatist insurgency. The Arab Spring, and the rise of participatory Islamists in the Arab world, provided the AKP government a key opportunity to enhance its foreign policy agenda of furthering Turkey's geopolitical clout. The rise of participatory Islamists in the 2011 elections in North Africa was a key development in this regard. However, problems faced by participatory Islamists governing Egypt, Tunisia, and Morocco in 2012 placed limits on the AKP's influence. While AKP's allies in North Africa were increasingly facing domestic unrest, the situation in the Levant had taken a turn for the worse. The Syrian civil war had quickly turned into a regional sectarian conflict. Insurrectionist Islamism and Kurdish separatism south of the border had turned opportunity into a threat for Turkey. By 2013, the Erdogan administration was clearly struggling on the foreign policy front. In late May it ran into trouble domestically as well with the unprecedented anti-government protests that broke out in Istanbul's Taksim Gezi Park. Demonstrators angry over the AKP's curbs on freedoms, heavy-handed response to the protests, and fears that the ruling party was pushing the country towards authoritarianism, aggravated the situation. However, having failed to undermine the AKP's core support base, the unrest by July had largely fizzled out. Erdogan had managed to pull through at a time when his ally in Egypt was forced out of office.

## The AKP and Democratization

While, historically Islamism had a significant presence in Turkey, the emergence of the AKP in 2001, has rendered it insignificant. The reason for this is that propagandist and insurrectionist forms of Islamism never took root in the country. The majority of Turkey's Islamists have been acceptors despite the fact that they have been operating in a militant secularist state. Furthermore, since January 1970, when Erbakan founded the National Order Party, Islamists have been of a participatory type. Much of the manifestations of Islamism in Turkey over the past few decades may be rooted in the differences between the historical religious experiences of the Turkish and Arab subjects of the Ottoman Empire. Additionally and more significantly, notions of secularism and democracy had been adopted, especially in the Turkish context, a century before the empire's dissolution. In fact, it was the imperial polity that had sought to learn from Europe and dispatched students there to bring back modern Western thought to begin fusing Islamic tradition and Western modernity. There is also the unique Kemalist experience, building upon the Tanzimat period, that played a key role in secularizing Turkish society as opposed to the purely state-driven secularization that took place in most other Arab and Muslim countries, which did not reach large parts of society. In Turkey, the question was not so much whether democracy was compatible with Islam. The establishment of the Ottoman parliament in the late nineteenth century meant that any debates over democracy's theological compatibility with Islam had already been settled. Instead the debate over democracy had to do with the balance of power between the sultan and the legislature, which was highlighted when Sultan Abdul Hamid II dissolved Parliament in 1878. Similarly, during the early republican era, the resistance to secularism was not because of the outright rejection of the concept but rather a reaction to the Kemalist elite's near-total suppression of religion.

This explains why the Erbakan-led Islamists did not seek to build their envisioned Islamic polity by completely dismantling the secular state. They were a product of the intellectual evolution that began in the late Ottoman era and continued through the early decades of the Turkish republic. Their participation in the democratic process, despite being countered by the military, as well as their experiences in Parliament and governance (especially at the municipal level) continued to transform the movement from within. The predecessors to the AKP were predominantly participatory Islamists. Based on our model, participatory Islamism is one step shy of post-Islamism, which partially explains the genesis of the AKP, which is located between participatory Islamists and secularists. The Turkish ruling party's proximity to both set of actors explains the AKP's support for secularism while also showing strong affinity for Islamists. In 2011 on his first trip to Egypt after the Arab spring, the Turkish prime minister called on the Brotherhood to accept secularism. Two years later, Erdogan is one of the most vocal and staunch supporters of the Brotherhood in the wake of the coup that toppled former Egyptian president, Mohamed Morsi.. The past Islamist experience of Erdogan and his allies have shaped their current secularism to such an extent that the ruling party neither seeks to impose religion via the state nor to oppose its presence in society. For the AKP, its understanding of moderate secularism offers the balance that allows the more overtly observant religious elements in the country to coexist with those who subscribe to the Western idea that religion is a private matter.

This novel interpretation of secularism conforming to Islamic principles raises a question: To what degree does the AKP serve as a model for Islamists in the Arab countries and the wider Muslim world? Ahmet Kuru advances the idea of passive and assertive secularism as a template for Islamist democratization in the wider Muslim world. He feels that even though the AKP represents a unique journey from Islamism to secularism, applicable lessons can be drawn from its experience.[17] Indeed, certain forces beyond Turkey are in a similar place, such as Morocco's ruling PJD, Tunisia's Ennahda Party, and Egypt's Hizb al-Wasat,. Each of these actors is an Islamist, , who could gradually gravitate toward post-Islamism. The AKP, however, stands out due to its unique circumstances and ability to supplant Islamism in Turkey.

As shown above, Turkish Islamists since their emergence in the early 1970s and subsequent mobilization in the 1980s have been acceptors of the secular state as well as active participators in the democratic process. The AKP expanded upon this preexisting reality and took it to the next level of embracing secularism but insisting upon religious neutrality for the state, instead of its traditional "assertive secularism" and antipathy toward religion. "The AKP through its efforts to enact legal reforms especially those related to the public sector is attempting to expand the public space for religion and in doing so it is also gauging the extent to which the Kemalist establishment is willing to accept the role of religion in public affairs."[18] Unlike Islamists who seek to implement shari'a, the AKP is trying to pull Turkey back from the radical and even militant secularism that does not allow religious freedoms. By maintaining the secular nature of the state, in the sense that it remains neutral to societal developments (be they religious or irreligious), the AKP is underscoring its own post-Islamism.

In our opinion, the AKP best exemplifies the concept of "post-Islamism". Coined by Asef Bayat in 1996 to explain the transformation of post-Khomeini Iran during the Rafsanjani presidency, post-Islamism has been understood differently by others.[19] The French Islamicist scholar Gilles Kepel, in an *Harvard International Review* article used the term to note the rise of the reformist presidency of Mohammad Khatami in Iran.[20] Another major French luminary on Islamism, Olivier Roy, sees the term as confirming his 1994 *Failure of Political Islam* thesis that the Islamists' ideology could not solve the problems of Muslim societies and therefore Islamists are headed towards post-Islamism.[21] In 2005, Henri Lauzire used the concept to interpret the political thought of Abd al-Salam Yasin, Morocco's most prominent Islamist thinker and founder of its more conservative Islamist movement.[22] Amel Boubekeur examined the notion in cultural terms and as it applies to sociopolitical mobilization.[23] In a more recent work on Iran, Mojataba Mahdavi from the University of Alberta identified the phenomenon in the Islamic republic's trajectory since its founding.[24] Husnul Amin, a professor at the International Islamic University in Islamabad, has analyzed the issue in his PhD thesis on certain significant post-Islamist religio-political currents within Pakistan.[25] Although the term "post-Islamism" has been used for nearly two decades, there is still little agreement on its meaning. Bayat offers the clearest definition: Post-Islamism "represents both a condition and a project, which may be embodied in a master movement. It refers to political and social conditions where, following a phase of experimentation, a rethink about the Islamist project takes place, leading to emphasizing rights instead of duties, plurality instead of singular authoritative voice, historicity rather than fixed scripture, and the future instead of the past."

Ihsan Yilmaz of Istanbul's Fatih University has done the most to apply this idea to Turkey by examining the AKP's evolution from the Milli Gorus (National Vision) movement that spawned the Islamist political parties that preceded the current ruling party. In addition, he looks at the role of the Turkish-led international socio-religious Gulen Movement and its role in influencing the rise of the AKP. Yilmaz draws an interesting distinction between post-Islamism and what he calls *non-Islamism*: The former is a combination of Islamism and democracy, whereas the latter is a discarding of Islamist values in order to more firmly embrace democratic ones. In Yilmaz's view, Fazilet Partisi (Virtue Party), which succeeded the Refah Partisi (Welfare Party) in December 1998, is an example of a post-Islamist group, whereas the AKP that succeeded Fazilet is a case of a non-Islamist party. Yilmaz considers post-Islamism as a stage in which the actors can either move forward and leave Islamism altogether or revert to Islamism. He argues that the AKP was created as a break with Erbakan, the founder of the modern Turkish Islamist movement. While Erdogan and his allies founded the AKP, Erbakan reverted to Islamism by found Saadet. While Yilmaz points out that Fazilet's discourse was no longer Islamist, in practice Fazilet was never any-thing more than a slightly milder version of Refah, for it constituted both the reformist elements led by Erdogan and Gul and the old guard led by Erbakan, who never really left Islamism. Therefore, there was no reverting, as Yilmaz claims. The group still included Erbakan and was actually led by his long-time associate Recai Kutan, who later on led Saadet as well. That Erdogan and his faction parted ways with their ideological leader only after Fazilet was outlawed further shows that Fazilet was a somewhat modified version of Refah. In other words, it was not really post-Islamist, which brings us back to the issue of how to define this particular term.

We agree with Bayat that post-Islamism is a secularizing process, as opposed to a mid-point between Islamism and secularism. In fact, it is a rejection of Islamism because it does not call for the establishment of an Islamic state. To use Yilmaz's preferred terminology, post-Islamism *is* non-Islamism, which in a gen-eral sense can also be referred to as secularism. But as we have demonstrated throughout this book, certain Islamists can renounce Islamism, but they are unlikely to cease being observant Muslims as well. Bayat, in his examination of Iran, shows how the post-Islamists are those who have realized through experi-ence that there is a need to go beyond religious texts in order to address the social, political, and economic problems facing modern societies.[26] He does, however, distinguish between secularization and secularism; the former is the process of acknowledging the need for extrareligious ideas, whereas the latter is the marginal-ization of religion.[27] Therefore, post-Islamism is exiting Islamism and possibly heading toward a secularism that is not based on rejecting religion's role in public affairs. Instead post-Islamists, as Bayat points out, have recognized the inadequa-cies inherent in their ideological formulations and hence the need to adopt secular modalities. Post-Islamists have therefore reinterpreted both Islamic religious prin-ciples and revised their older view of secularism as being antireligion. For them, secularism is not something un-Islamic, and embracing it does not necessarily mean that they have to compromise on their religious principles. Post-Islamists can thus be defined as former Islamists who have relinquished their rigid ideolog-ical positions on enforcing Islamic principles through the state, and now they seek to realize their religious ideals through democratic politics and a secular state.

Take, for example, Turkey's headscarf ban in government buildings. Despite being in power for over 10 years and consolidating democracy, the AKP has not attempted to forcibly reverse this ban imposed by Ataturk in 1925, despite the fact that observant women working in the private sector are presently able to wear it. On March 21, 2013, deputy prime minister Arinc, said that the government is waiting for a sociopolitical "maturing" of the issue before engaging in the necessary legal steps to remove the ban. Clearly, the AKP sought to create a national consensus on this and other contentious issues. An Islamist government would more likely impose the headscarf in public, whereas the AKP has framed the issue as a matter of personal freedom. In its most recent efforts to reverse the ban on headscarves the AKP has resorted to doing so through legal means. This is evident from the very recent lifting of the ban on headscarves in the public sector workplace as part of a reform package. Furthermore, in recent years the AKP has established a great degree of civilian control over the military, which has been the traditional mainstay of opposition to any public display of religiosity.[28] As Metin Heper observed at the time of Erbakan's rise to power, "[t]he marriage between Islam and democracy in Turkey can be consummated if the radical secularists stop trying to impose their preferred life-style and set of values upon the Islamists, and if the latter do not attempt to undermine by word or deed the basic tenets of the secular democratic state in Turkey."[29] It seems that the AKP has learned this lesson and is trying to forge a relationship that will make the marriage between secularists and Islamists a lasting one.

# 11

# Conclusion: Prospects for Muslim Democracies

This book has sought to assess the role of religion in politics within Muslim societies, especially in light of the transformational changes taking place since the Arab Spring.[1] Most Western scholars have long asserted that religion has no place in a democratic polity. Our goal here was to determine the validity of this claim in Muslim-majority countries with a focus on the Middle East and North Africa (MENA) region. Our central argument is that Islamists have played a decisive role and will continue to do so in the years and decades ahead as the region transitions through this democratization process. As scholars, we have gone to great length to approach this subject objectively and with sensitivity to avoid the polemic tensions on both ends of the spectrum. This is especially necessary on a topic as contentious and oft-politicized as this one. Undoubtedly there will be critics that disagree with the merits of our argument while others will oppose it on ideological grounds. We look forward to a lively and constructive discussion with the former while we find the polemic nature of the later more difficult to engage.

By providing democratization as the theoretical framework and in-depth historic case studies, we examined the role that Islamists have played in the transition from authoritarianism. As the case studies in this book highlighted, Islamists of varying shades become major players as authoritarian states break down and autocratic leaders lose their grip on power. Their widespread support may wax and wane, but it is not likely to disappear. This reality reflects the deeply held view that Muslims reject the Western notion that religion has no place in the political arena. Therefore, they will choose those political forces that they think will (in addition to securing their material needs) ensure their desire for religion to shape the character of their envisaged democratic state. Many Western theorists of democracy, who continue to misread Islamism, have yet to understand or fully appreciate religion's historically prominent role and centrality to the region's struggle for democracy. First, by focusing on political Islam, we assess the relationship between Islamists and democratization. More importantly, we examine how these two trends interact to produce Muslim democracies. We argue that religion will likely play an important role in Muslim politics as this democratization process unfolds. In so doing, we add to the recent contributions by such scholars as Alfred Stepan and Nader Hashemi, both of whom challenge the conventional Western wisdom that religion is largely irrelevant to democracy. Second, we illustrate the growing diversity within Islamism, a reality of which both the scholarly community and the general public remain largely unaware. Third, we make the case that the outcome of Islamist democratization will likely lead to Muslim *democracies*, as opposed to a Muslim *democracy*.[2] In many ways, this book represents an attempt to fill the gap in the existing literature on political Islam and democratization. It is our hope that future appraisals of political Islam will no longer be discussed in abstract and will require a parallel evaluation of democratization in the Muslim world. The case studies presented herein showed that secular autocratic regimes spent decades suppressing the growing popular demands for religious expression. With the advent of the Arab Spring and the dramatic transformations across MENA, the democratization process now underway enabled popular sentiments to shape the newly emerging democratic polities. Even though Islamists have seen an erosion of their initial post-Arab Spring gains, this process only furthers the dynamic of religion's entrance into the public sphere.

In one of the most comprehensive global surveys of Muslim attitudes toward religion and politics – 38,000 face-to-face interviews in over 80 languages with Muslims across the world – the Pew Research Center found overwhelming support for religion's central role in politics. The 2013 Pew Global Attitudes survey found strong support for making shari'a the law of the land in the vast majority of Muslim countries. In fact, it points out that the majority of respondents in those countries with constitutions or basic laws that already include Islam say that shari'a should be enshrined as the official law. The highest percentages of people who support this view are found in Afghanistan (99 percent) and Iraq (91 percent). Arab countries at the center of the ongoing democratic transitions have equally high support levels: Morocco (83 percent), Egypt (74 percent), Palestine (89 percent), and Tunisia (56 percent). Similarly, there was strong support among Muslims for religious leaders having a "some" or a "large" say/influence in political matters: Afghanistan (82 percent), Jordan (80 percent), Egypt (75 percent), Tunisia (58 percent), and Iraq (57 percent). The survey also found high support for instituting shari'a in the domestic-civil sphere. When asked whether religious judges should decide family or property disputes, 94 percent of Egyptians, 93 percent of Jordanians, 78 percent of Afghans, and 73 percent of Iraqis replied "Yes."[3]

H. A. Hellyer adds that the weakening of public support for Islamists should not be interpreted as the masses seeking a secular polity.[4] Citing fresh polling date in Egypt, he suggests that while support for Islamist parties has declined, conservative religious attitudes remain steady. Gallup and Tahrir Squared surveys show that 98 percent of Egyptians see religion as very important in their day-to-day affairs. Even many secularists in the Middle East and the wider Muslim world favor some role for religion in state and society, although they are unclear about its precise parameters. In this area, at least, secularists in the Muslim context differ from their Western counterparts. In fact, given the public affinity for religion, states in the Muslim world do not seek to eliminate religion from public affairs, but to manage this demand by implementing an "official" Islam.[5] As we have seen above and in the analyses throughout the book, religion cannot be ignored when it comes to shaping the politics of Muslim countries. This is especially clear in the region's continued democratization effort.

The United States' ongoing conflict with jihadists has had both intended results and unintended consequences, one of which was the altering of Islamism from within. The American need to isolate extremists from the wider Muslim landscape created opportunities for mainstream Islamists as well as those who, at one time, subscribed to armed struggle. The ensuing democratic openings have accelerated this shift for previously violent groups. Although insurrectionist Islamists such al-Qaeda and its allies still pursue violence, others (e.g., al-Gamaah al-Islamiyah and Tandheem al-Jihad) renounced violence long ago and decisively entered democratic politics after Mubarak's overthrow. Thus even insurrectionist Islamists have embraced electoral politics because of specific circumstances within the country or because the Arab Spring has shown them the benefits of moderation and abandoning violence.

This current phase of moderation differs considerably from what we saw in the past. Islamists have moved from being largely societal forces to entering the corridors of power. Their complexity as non-state actors has become even more complicated by the fact that democratization has allowed Islamism in general to become a state phenomenon. We argued that religion will have a greater role in Muslim politics as the secularist autocratic order continues to meltdown, thereby creating space for religio-political forces to operate. Being the most organized and coherent sociopolitical force, Islamist groups were the initial beneficiaries of the democratic openings. But even though they were the best positioned to take advantage of the new climate, they have had to deal with considerable resistance from their secular opponents. Thus they are not simply influencing democratization; rather, they are being influenced by it as well. Moving from society into the state requires pragmatism and, in the case of very few agreed-upon rules, a great deal of compromise. The events of the past year has shown that Islamists will embrace pragmatism to varying degrees, as we have shown with the Egyptian MB, Hizb al-Nour, and Ennahda. Regardless of these distinctions, what we have witnessed is an unmistakable trend toward pragmatism. As the French sociologist and scholar of Islamism Olivier Roy states in his *Journal of Democracy* article (July 2012), Islamists will be unloading a great deal of ideological baggage. While we agree with him, we maintain that his conclusion does not capture the full range of the shift underway. Indeed, Islamists will temper their ideologies in order to deal effectively with on-the-ground realities in their specific societies. Some may eventually even cease to qualify as Islamists. Regardless of their level of moderation, however, they will not cease to be who they are in essence: observant Muslims. As practicing believers, they will want their religious values reflected in the public sphere, as shown by the Pew surveys. It is safe to say that many will continue to be Islamists who seek to mobilize the average devout voter to advance their political aims. Thus we can expect Islamism, as an ideology, to persist for a long time. But more importantly, it will be in a state of intense evolution. This realization is the first step toward understanding the type of democratic polities that are likely to emerge.

Therefore, the first step toward understanding what is going on must be to deconstruct the complexity of Islamism and create a system that can help scholars navigate the Islamist bayou. Toward this end, we began our book by clarifying the terminological chaos that plagues the discourse on Islamism. We identified the problems associated with the popular vocabulary used even by experts and offered an alternative nomenclature. Clarifying the language in and of itself, however, is not enough. One needs to make sense of the actors populating the Islamist space–time continuum. Our three-tiered taxonomy of classifying organized groups according to their behavior toward the status quo (state and society) attempts to do just that. Obviously, and as our case studies show, there will always be exceptions to any model. But we feel that our model offers a general rule that goes a long way toward making sense of the ever more complicated Islamist maze.

Building on our taxonomy, we advanced a four-level spectrum that offers a way to understand the different types of Islamists and their secularist counterparts based on their specific views of religion's role in politics. Having sorted out the Islamist landscape, we then introduced our theoretical framework: democratization. Our extensive literature review showed how mainstream Western theorists define democracy and democratization from the point of regime types and the behavior of groups leading the transition. We then demonstrated how the assertions of Western scholars, many of whom claim that the Muslim world's inability to democratize is partially due to its people's adherence to Islam, lack evidence. Such essentialist readings are informed by the fact that Western social scientists by and large insist that democratization requires secularization as an a priori condition. This was followed by an examination of the diverse and nuanced Muslim opinions on democracy and religion. Many in the West are confused by the Muslims' desire to seek democracy and apply Islamic law at the same time.[6] In addition, we highlighted the dissonance among Islamists by means of our typology, which organizes Islamists of different flavors based on their attitude toward democracy. Such an approach serves as a conceptual tool to capture the great deal of nuance within Islamist opinions regarding democracy. It categorized Islamists as belonging to three types: (1) *participators*, who have fully embraced democracy as a system of governance because they view it as being in accord with Islam; (2) *conditionalists*, who have opted to partake in electoral politics but are not fully comfortable with democracy due to what they perceive as a conflict between human and divine sovereignty; and (3) *rejectors*, who unequivocally denounce democracy as an un-Islamic system. This categorization shows that far from being monolithic, Islamism is composed of devout believers holding many opinions that are rather fluid in nature.

We then applied this model of Islamist democratization to seven different case studies. Our main category was the Muslim Brotherhood genre, which constitutes the bulk of Islamist groups. The second most significant grouping, the Salafis, is a recent entrant to Islamism and has joined the electoral fray after years of rejecting democracy. Next we turned to al-Qaeda-style transnational jihadism, which remains among the most vehement opponents of democracy. We then looked at the Taliban, who represent the classic case of nationalist jihadists who have exhibited signs that they are willing to join the political mainstream but still question the validity of democracy. Our fifth case was the only one involving a state actor, namely, the Islamic Republic of Iran, whose political system is a hybrid between parliamentary democracy and a unique type of Shia theocracy. Case number six involved Arab Shia Islamist groups in Iraq and Lebanon, whose engagement with democratic politics is a function of pursing their sectarian interests within multi-communal contexts. Lastly, we explored the lone case of former Islamists who have embraced secularism, namely, Turkey's ruling Justice and Development Party (AKP).

By testing our theory of Islamist democratization on these seven cases, we draw the following key conclusions:

(1)  The majority of Islamists are participatory in regard to democracy. This is proven by the fact that the Muslim Brotherhood-style organizations, which represent the classic case of participatory Islamists, constitute the largest grouping of Islamists. Second, the Arab Shia Islamist actors have also opted for the participatory route. Finally there is Iran, which, despite its increasing restrictions on participation in recent years, nevertheless continues to popularly elect presidents, parliaments, municipalities, and a key clerical body. Lastly, there are signs that a small group of pragmatic Salafis, Egypt's al-Watan party, may be moving away from the conditionalist camp and toward the participator camp, given that they have parted ways with their more hardline former colleagues in al-Nour. Even al-Nour is exhibiting signs of greater accommodation with secularists and democratic process, for it supports the post-Morsi roadmap.

(2)  Conditionalist Islamists form the second largest class, as the surge of Arab Salafi groups to form political parties in order to participate in elections and shape the emerging democratic political system has shown. In fact Egypt, which has the most significant Salafi political force, continues to see a growth in the number of Salafi parties. Following Egypt's lead, their counterparts in Morocco, Algeria, Jordan, and Yemen are rushing to form parties. In addition, we have seen former jihadist groups in Egypt (e.g., al-Gamaah al-Islamiyah and Tandheem al-Jihad) form parties and enter the political arena. Both these Salafis and ex-jihadists have accepted electoral politics as the way forward; however, their more conservative interpretations of Islam conflict with the needs of democratic politics.

(3)  Rejector Islamists form the smallest class of actors. In our seven case studies, only al-Qaeda and its transnational jihadist allies completely reject democratic politics. There is also the case of the nonviolent propagandist group Hizb al-Tahrir. While both groups represent two very different sets of actors, both are opposed to the nation-state and seek to establish a transnational caliphate. This goal is a key reason why they reject the democratic political system. The Afghan Taliban is also a case of rejector Islamists, but for a different reason. They are a nationalist jihadist force in the process of seeking to enter mainstream politics via negotiating a post-NATO power-sharing agreement. That said, they have yet

to prove their willingness to participate in electoral politics. There is a precedent for nationalist jihadist forces to leave the rejectors for the conditionalists: Egypt's al-Gamaah al-Islamiyah and Tandheem al-Jihad. Furthermore, we have seen how those Iraqi nationalist jihadist forces that had tactically aligned with al-Qaeda during the early years of the American occupation embraced mainstream politics in 2007 via negotiations with the United States. Therefore, it is possible that large parts of the Taliban movement could, in the future, join the conditionalist camp.

Our case studies also revealed significant exceptions to our conceptual framework: Hezbollah, Hamas, and the Iraqi Shia Islamist groups do not neatly fit within any of our three categories because our typology is based on Islamist groups' theological view of democracy. These groups' commitment to democracy is largely informed by their unique political conditions. Hezbollah has to function within Lebanon's consociational and therefore sectarian-based political system, as well as the wider regional context of geopolitical sectarianism. This has become even more true due to civil war in Syria, which shapes the group's behavior. Likewise, the Iraqi Shia groups' commitment is driven by their sectarian interests and because, as the majority community, democracy works in their favor. Hamas, on the other hand, is dealing with the subnational context of Gaza and Israeli occupation in the West Bank. While the Iraqi Shia groups have transformed themselves from militias to political parties, neither Hamas nor Hezbollah is willing to give up its military wing and become a pure political force. Both groups will, of course, cite the Israeli threat, but there is also the reality that their armed wings are a source of domestic political power. Therefore, we cannot regard them as purely participatory Islamist actors.

We also examined the case of the post-Islamist AKP, a group founded by former Islamists who have embraced secularism.[7] Emulating its trajectory will be difficult even for the most developed participatory groups, such as Tunisia's Ennahda, which, despite being closer to the AKP than the MB, will likely have ongoing issues with secularism. A key factor to note here is that it was the Turkish state's radical (and often militant) secularism coupled with the military's dominance of the political system, as opposed to Islamists' religious ideology, that prevented the AKP's predecessors from political participation. In other words, these Islamist forerunners were also participatory Islamists.

The democratization process has been altering the Islamist landscape in a way not seen since the ideology's emergence in the early twentieth century. After long decades of being in the opposition, some now find themselves entrusted with governing the state. Given this new reality, they can no longer afford to deal with Islam and democracy in an abstract manner. Democratic openings are influencing their behavior, and they, in turn, are influencing the transition process. The Islamists and the states in which they operate are experiencing major change, a situation that is likely to persist for generations. Democratization in the heart of the Muslim world will take place along unfamiliar lines and religion will play a role, one way or another.

## Outlook for Muslim and Islamist Democratization

Muslim societies will face many challenges while moving from authoritarianism to democracy. In fact, these political transitions will be even more disorderly because of the religious factor. Given that it usually takes at least several election cycles to consolidate democracy, we can say with some confidence that in most Arab/Muslim countries this will likely be a nonlinear multigenerational process. The normal process of inculcating a democratic ethos becomes even more complicated when there is an intense debate over religion and its role in public affairs. This will be a major—if not *the* major—issue for observant non-Islamist Muslims and for those who are not so observant but cannot be considered Western style secularists. Moreover, in places where Islamist political forces are playing the lead role and facing strong resistance from secularist forces, the path to democracy is bound to be exponentially longer and more complicated. What is going on in Egypt as this book goes to press is a case in point.

And then there is the fragmentation of both camps into various Islamist and secularist forces, as we have shown through our spectrum, which only makes things even more complicated. The secularist camp still has some semblance of a unified purpose, at least in terms of ensuring that Islamists do not end up dominating the emerging political systems. On the other side is a great deal of intra-Islamist contention, which has a crucial bearing on democratization. Both the participators (MB) and the conditionalists (Salafis) are trying to influence the outcome. Their common demand that religion play a public role alone creates numerous problems, especially since they do not agree on (or even know themselves) what its precise role should be. Additionally, one needs to remember that both camps have significant internal disagreements along partisan and intra-party factional lines.

Moreover, their perspectives on democracy remain in flux partly because of the ongoing evolution—yesterday's rejectors have become today's conditionalists, and some of these conditionalists will become tomorrow's participators. Movement in the reverse direction is also likely, especially among the Salafi newcomers, some of whom may not be able to reconcile their view of religion with democracy and thus go back to being rejectors. Still other Salafi Islamists will join their brethren as staunch apolitical Muslims who will once again see the very idea of engaging in politics as un-Islamic. In addition to ideological issues, unique geopolitical and contextual circumstances are shaping attitudes.[8] For example, the crackdown on the MB in the aftermath of the Morsi ouster, bankrolled by Saudi Arabia and its GCC allies, may push some participatory Islamists (MB members) into the rejector camp. Some of these demoralized MB members may conclude that political participation is futile and thus could be influenced by the insurrectionist stance. Indeed, al-Qaeda chief Ayman al-Zawahiri has been trying to recruit such dejected MB affiliates. In essence, all groups are adjusting their views. Taken together, all of these mentioned disagreements will make the process of reaching a consensus that much harder.

The predominant view among both Muslims and non-Muslims is that Muslim democratization is a difficult concept to digest. Average Muslims wonder to what extent democratization will compromise their core religious values. Likewise many non-Muslims, especially those in the West, cannot imagine democratization with a religious tinge. Regardless of each side's respective arguments, however, all of them ultimately revolve around the concept of secularism. For most Westerners, democratization can succeed only if religion is confined to the private realm. Conversely, many Muslims believe religion must have a role in the public domain. In short, both sides are asking whether democracy's definition can be expanded to include states in which religion plays a role in politics. While not new, this question has become even more relevant as the Islamist-led and increasingly messy transition toward democracy continues to unfold.

Even though democracy is a universal value, it will manifest itself in different ways because all societies have their own unique geopolitical, cultural, and civilizational characteristics. Great lessons can be learned from the Western experience; however, it is essential to realize that its modernization trajectory is unique. Shmuel Eisenstadt makes this point in his work on "multiple modernities".[9] Eisenstadt argues that Western-style modernity is not applicable to all modernizing societies because each one privileges its own socio-cultural characteristics that, in turn, shape their alternative modernities. While he focuses on the example of Marxist ideologies, his ideas can be extended to Muslim contexts as well. Like the socialists before them, Muslims are trying to develop themselves based on a critique of classic notions of Western modernity. In keeping with Eisenstadt's view, they have accepted modern institutions and themes to varying degrees but resist the Western concept of modernity and thus seek to reinterpret the classical notion to fit their own societies. His idea of new modern movements based on socio-philosophical, religious, or ethnic identities sheds light on the behavior of Islamists as well as Muslims in general. Islamists and the average conservative Muslim, both of whom are subject to societal transformations, are currently negotiating with the modern contextual settings. While struggling with the Western notions of modernity, they are also engaging with competing narratives (various secularist and Islamist prescriptions) that have developed locally. Regardless of their internal debates, however, Muslims in general, are now shaping their modernities and distinguishing them from those found in the West.

In keeping with Ernest Gellner's view that Muslims are resistant to secularization, many Western observers continue to speak of "Islamic exceptionalism," meaning thereby that the Muslim world is somehow incapable of democratization. This assertion is based on the assumption that all "democratic" societies must adhere to Western standards. But when the West's own historical path and the resulting types of democracies are analyzed, the uniqueness of its path becomes very clear. As Nader Hashemi correctly points out, it is erroneous to assume that all cultures will evolve in the same way as the West did. We have tried to show, both through our theoretical framework and its application to the seven case studies, how democratization in Muslim contexts will differ considerably as regards religion's role in politics and in line with Alfred Stepan's "Twin Tolerations" theory.[10]

In 1994, Roy famously pronounced *The Failure of Political Islam.*[11] Two decades later, he reiterated his central thesis, arguing that it has not changed, in a *Journal of Democracy* (July 2012) article entitled "The Transformation of the Arab World"[12]:

> [T]he collapse of Islamism's revolutionary momentum would be followed by two trends: (1) a wave of 'neofundamentalism' that stressed a strict return to purely religious norms (the call to implement shari'a), replacing Islamism's ideological-political agenda (building an Islamic state and institutions, setting up an 'Islamic economy,' striving to build a transnational ummah, and so on); (2) There would be a move toward a 'Muslim democracy' (along the lines of an assertive Christian democracy) that endorses nationalism and recasts Islamic norms as moral and cultural values with appeal to a larger conservative constituency. [13]

According to him, "[t]his is exactly where we are today" and "the [Muslim] Brotherhood itself is torn between these two trends."[14] But why must there only be those two choices? We agree with him that the ideology of the MB and other Islamist groups does not currently provide a roadmap for an ideal Islamic society or a guidebook for good governance. This may *currently* be the case as Sunni Islamists begin to govern for the first time, but it does not necessarily have to *always* be the case. We should not automatically assume that Islam is unlikely to play a role in the final formulation as Islamists learn how to better integrate their "Islamic" ideas into practical and pragmatic policy options. Roy assumes that they have a specific ideology to begin with, whereas the ideology of any group (Islamist or otherwise) is always evolving. Ideology is, by definition, not something that can be implemented as policy, for the latter is distilled from the former. In fact, the landscape suggests a very different picture. In his index of state-religion regimes for 46 Muslim-majority countries, Ahmet Kuru argues that 11 are Islamic states (the ulema and courts control the legal system), while another 15 have adopted Islam as the official religion but do not enforce religious laws through institutional mechanisms. He classifies the remaining 20 as secular states in which religious authorities are not involved in the legislative process or enforcing the law. Islamists have a say in the 15 countries in which Islam is an established religion.[15] More important questions need to be asked here: What types of states are likely to emerge due to the momentous changes taking place? Will this transition lead to stable, consolidated democracies? If so, will they be secular or religious? In a related question, what role will Islamists play (if any) in shaping modern Muslim societies?

Democratization is about grassroots sentiments being channeled into the political process. Thus far, despotic leaders and their authoritarian states disenfranchised conservative Muslims and allowed them no role in their country's governance. Moving forward, however, polities will now be shaped by the demands of the common citizens, for whom religion has great meaning—one that goes beyond rituals and is often a central part of their identity. Unlike in the Judeo-Christian tradition, as we observed in our case studies, large majorities of people living in Muslim-majority countries generally support a type of democracy that includes Islam. Recent polls on attitudes toward religion and politics suggest that the majority of Muslims in these countries want religious authorities to have a greater role in politics. As confining Islam to the private sphere is unlikely, their new democratic systems will not be exact copies of those in the West. In fact, there will be a plurality of democracies, just as there are in the West: the American, British, French, and other Western forms of democracy are hardly monolithic in nature. Why, one might ask, given their unique experiences, should Egyptian democracy resemble those found in Turkey and Pakistan as well as from those emerging in such monarchical countries as Morocco and Jordan? Furthermore, it is important to note that not all Muslim countries will necessarily undergo democratization. Those riven by factionalism and unable to agree upon a new social contract will most likely remain in the "gray zone" for years, if not decades. But these will tend to be the exception rather than the rule, and Muslim democracies will likely emerge over time.

As highlighted throughout this book, democracy in the Muslim world will continue on the unique path it has already forged. Several types of Muslim democracies will likely take root. Religion's role in the public policy sphere does not disqualify them as democracies; rather, their quality could be gauged on the basis of Robert Dahl's criteria of a "polyarchy": (1) free and fair elections, (2) inclusive suffrage, (3) the right to run for office, (4) freedom of expression, (5) the right of political leaders to compete for support and votes, (6) the availability of alternative information, (7) the freedom to form and join organizations, and (8) the existence of institutions that make government policies depend on votes and other expressions of preferences. Dahl extricates liberal democracy's basic institutional requirements and suggests that "ideal democracies" are not fully realizable. Thus he speaks of a "polyarchy" instead. Similarly, "Muslim democracies" may fall short of the ideal definition. But in line with Dahl's prescription, if they meet the minimum criteria they should qualify as democracies. But despite this evolution, Islamists and many Muslims are unlikely to accept the Western practice of confining religion to the private sphere or to dilute their worldview so much that they cease to believe that Islam has a certain role to play in public affairs— even though the nature of this role is not exactly clear and thus likely to remain a point of contention.

Ultimately, none of the Islamist actors involved in the democratization process knows where they will end up from an ideological point of view. If they themselves are subject to an uncertain evolution, then certainly we cannot say what the outcome will look like. The only certain things are that it will be very difficult to return to the status quo ante, that democratization is a work in progress, and that it will remain so for decades to come. Both the process and the end product will not resemble the Western "template." As we have argued all along, religion will play a role in any type of Muslim democracy that emerges from the interplay between participator and conditionalist Islamism and democratization. These new democracies will be characterized by religion informing the public sphere in line with their societies' specific national contexts. But that sphere will also contain secular sectors. Some scholars agree with Hashemi that the Muslim world's passage through the gates of democratization will produce liberalism and secularism. That may happen, but because religion will retain a key role in informing its sociopolitical development, liberalism and secularism will also join the litany of what W. B. Gallie refers to as "contested concepts."

Until the Arab Spring, Islamists had proposed their ideas from the outside and therefore could neither test them or translate them into governance. Now that they are in power and actively engaged in governing, they will have the chance to do so. Surely this will not happen overnight. Furthermore, we expect it will go through many iterations and setbacks before a workable formula emerges. This should not mean, however, that Islamists will abandon their endeavor to integrate religion into the political arena. While one cannot be sure how this will play out over time, one can be certain that Islamists will remain an integral part of democratization and strive to capitalize on the popular sentiment to integrate Islam into the political arena. No doubt they will learn from their mistakes and in time find ways to translate their ideological positions into practical policy options.

# Notes

## Foreword

1. Richard Mitchell, *The Society of the Muslim Brothers* (New York: Oxford University Press, 1969; 2d ed. 1993); Lisa Brynjar, *The Society of the Muslim Brothers in Egypt: The Rise of an Islamic Mass Movement, 1928–1942* (Ithaca,: Ithaca Press, 1998); Francois Burgat, *The Islamic Movement in North Africa*, trans. William Dowell (Austin: University of Texas Center for Middle East Studies, 1997, new ed.); Nazih Ayubi, *Political Islam: Religion and Politics in the Arab World* (New York: Routledge, 1991); Olivier Roy, *Globalized Islam: The Search for a New Ummah* (New York: Columbia University Press, 2004); Sami Zubaida, *Islam, the People and the State: Political Ideas and Movements in the Middle East* (London and New York: I.B. Tauris, 2001); Raymond William Baker, *Islam without Fear: Egypt and the New Islamists* (Cambridge, MA: Harvard University Press, 2003); Said Amir Arjomand, *The Turban for the Crown: The Islamic Revolution in Iran* (New York and Oxford, NY: Oxford University Press, 1988); and Seyyed Vali Reza Nasr, *The Vanguard of the Islamic Revolution: The Jama'at-i Islami of Pakistan* (Berkeley and Los Angeles: University of California Press, 1994).
2. Stathis N. Kalyvas, *The Rise of Christian Democracy in Europe* (London: Cornell University Press, 1996), 258.
3. Ibid., 261.
4. George M. Marsden, *Fundamentalism and American Culture: The Shaping of Twentieth-Century Evangelicalism: 1870–1925* (Oxford, New York: Oxford University Press, 1980).
5. Jillian Schwedler, *Faith in Moderation: Islamist Parties in Jordan and Yemen* (Cambridge, New York: Cambridge University Press, 2006), 3 and 16.

## 1   Introduction: The Role of Religion in Politics

1. Abdullahi A. An-Na'im, *Islam and the Secular State: Negotiating the Future of Shari'a* (Cambridge: Harvard University Press, 2008). Also see Bassam Tibi, *Islamism and Islam* (New Haven: Yale University Press, 2012).
2. Azza Karam, "Democracy and Faith: The Continuum of Political Islam," in *The Struggle over Democracy in the Middle East: Regional Politics and External Politics*, ed. Nathan J. Brown and Emad El-Din Shahin (London and New York: Routledge, 2010), 62. Bernard Lewis, *The Crisis of Islam: Holy War and Unholy Terror* (London: Weidenfeld and Nicholson, 2003). Also see Jeffrey Bale, "Islamism and Totalitarianism," *Totalitarian Movements and Political Religions* 10, no. 2 (2009): 73–96.
3. Emmanuel Sivan, *Radical Islam: Medieval Theology and Modern Politics* (New Haven: Yale University Press, 1985); Katerina Dalacoura, *Islamist Terrorism and Democracy*

*in the Middle East* (New York: Cambridge University Press, 2011); Edward Mortimer, *Faith and Power: The Politics of Islam* (New York: Faber and Faber, 1982).

4. Lorenzo Vidino, *The New Muslim Brotherhood in the West* (New York: Columbia University Press, 2010).

5. Carl L. Brown, *Religion and State: The Muslim Approach to Politics* (New York: Columbia University Press, 2000).

6. Robert D. Lee, *Religion and Politics in the Middle East: Identity, Ideology, Institutions, and Attitudes* (Boulder: Westview Press, 2010), 267; Nazih Ayubi, *Political Islam: Religion and Politics in the Arab World* (London: Routledge, 1991), 35–47; Anoushiravan Ehteshami, "Islam, Muslim Polities, and Democracy," *Democratization* 90, (2004): 90–110. Also see Talal Asad, *Formations of the Secular: Christianity, Islam, Modernity* (Stanford: Stanford University Press, 2003).

7. Dale F. Eickelman and James Piscatori, *Muslim Politics* (Princeton: Princeton University Press, 1996), 46.

8. Barbara A. McGraw and Jo Renee Formicola, eds., *Taking Religious Pluralism Seriously: Spiritual Politics on America's Sacred Ground* (Waco: Baylor University Press, 2005). For an excellent account of this contentious struggle in Latin America, see Anthony Gill, *Rendering unto Caesar: The Catholic Church and the State in Latin America* (Chicago: University of Chicago Press, 1998).

9. Nader Hashemi, *Islam, Secularism, and Liberal Democracy: Towards a Democratic Theory for Muslim Societies* (New York: Oxford University Press, 2009), 2.

10. Robert Audi, *Democratic Authority and the Separation of Church and State* (New York: Oxford University Press, 2011); Robert Audi, *Religious Commitment and Secular Reason* (Cambridge, UK and New York: Cambridge University Press, 2000).

11. Kent Greenawalt, *Religious Convictions and Political Choice* (New York: Oxford University Press, 1991); Frederick C. Harris, "Something Within: Religion as a Mobilizer of African-American Political Activism," *Journal of Politics* 56, no. 1 (February 1994): 42–68.

12. Hashemi, *Islam, Secularism, and Liberal Democracy*, 24.

13. Eric O. Hanson, *Religion and Politics in the International System Today* (Cambridge, UK: Cambridge University Press, 2006); Elizabeth Shakman Hurd, *The Politics of Secularism in International Relations* (Princeton: Princeton University Press, 2008); Stathis N. Kalyvas, "Democracy and Religious Politics," *Comparative Political Studies* 31, no. 3 (June 1998): 292–320; Corwin Smidt, "Religion and Civic Engagement: A Comparative Analysis," *Annals of the American Academy of Political and Social Science* 565 (September 1999): 176–92; Craig Calhoun, Mark Juergensmeyer and Jonathan VanAntwerpen, eds., *Rethinking Secularism* (New York: Oxford University Press, 2011).

14. For an excellent account of this contentious struggle in Latin America, see Gill, *Rendering unto Caesar*. Hashemi, *Islam, Secularism, and Liberal Democracy*, 171. For the most compelling critique of this view, see Alfred Stepan, "Religion, Democracy, and the 'Twin Tolerations,' " *Journal of Democracy* 11 (October 2000): 27–57.

15. Owen Chadwick, *The Secularization of the European Mind in the Nineteenth Century* (Cambridge, UK: Cambridge University Press, 1975); Jonathan Laurence, *The Emancipation of Europe's Muslims: The State's Role in Minority Integration* (Princeton: Princeton University Press, 2012).

16. Larry Diamond, Marc F. Plattner and Daniel Brumberg, eds., *Islam and Democracy in the Middle East* (Baltimore: Johns Hopkins University Press, 2003).

17. Lee, *Religion and Politics in the Middle East*, 267; Donald Eugene Smith, *Religion and Political Development* (Boston: Little, Brown, 1970).

18. Ronald Inglehart and Christian Weizel, *Modernization, Cultural Change, and Democracy: The Human Development Sequence* (New York: Cambridge University Press, 2005).

19. Bernard Lewis, *What Went Wrong: The Clash Between Modernity and Islam in the Middle East* (New York: Harper Perennial, 2003). For a more detailed discussion about the debate about Orientalism, see Zachary Lockman, *Contending Visions of the Middle East: The History and Politics of Orientalism* (Cambridge, UK and New York: Cambridge University Press, 2004).

20. Lee, *Religion and Politics in the Middle East,* 268.

21. Hashemi, *Islam, Secularism, and Liberal Democracy,* 2.

22. Marc Lynch, *The Arab Uprising: The Unfinished Revolutions of the New Middle East* (New York: Public Affairs, 2012).

23. Larbi Sadki, *Rethinking Arab Democratization: Elections without Democracy* (Oxford, UK: Oxford University Press, 2009). Also see Ayubi, *Political Islam,* 35–47.

24. Lynch, *The Arab Uprising.* For a historical perspective, see Larbi Sadiki, "Popular Uprisings and Arab Democratization," *International Journal of Middle East Studies* 32, no. 1 (2000): 71.

25. Henry E. Hale, "Hybrid Regimes: When Democracy and Autocracy Mix," in *The Dynamics of Democratization: Dictatorship, Development, and Diffusion,* ed. Nathan Brow (Baltimore: Johns Hopkins University Press, 2011), 23–45.

26. For a discussion of hybrid regimes, see Terry Lynn Karl, "The Hybrid Regimes of Central America," *Journal of Democracy* 6, no. 3 (July 1995): 72–87. Also see Larry Diamond, "Thinking about Hybrid Regimes," *Journal of Democracy* 13, no. 2 (April 2002): 21–35.

27. Fareed Zakaria, *The Future of Freedom: Illiberal Democracy at Home and Abroad* (New York: W.W. Norton & Co., 2003).

28. Marina Ottaway, *Democracy Challenged: The Rise of Semi-Authoritarianism* (Washington, DC: Carnegie Endowment for International Peace, 2003).

29. Daniel Brumberg, "The Trap of Liberalized Autocracy," *Journal of Democracy* 13, no. 4 (October 2002): 56–68.

30. Thomas Carothers, "The End of the Transition Paradigm," *Journal of Democracy* 13, no. 1 (January 2002): 5–21.

31. David Collier and Steven Levitsky, "Democracy with Adjectives: Conceptual Innovation in Comparative Research," *World Politics* 49, no. 3 (April 1997): 430–51; Steven Levitsky and Lucan A. Way, "The Rise of Competitive Authoritarianism," *Journal of Democracy* 13, no. 2 (April 2002): 51–65; Andreas Schedler, "Elections without Democracy: The Menu of Manipulation," *Journal of Democracy* 13, no. 2 (April 2002): 36–50; Andreas Schedler, "The Nested Game of Democratization by Elections," *International Political Science Review* 23, no. 1 (2002): 103–22; Andreas Schedler, *Electoral Authoritarianism: The Dynamics of Unfree Competition* (Boulder: Lynne Rienner, 2006); Nicolas van de Walle, "Elections without Democracy: Africa's Range of Regimes," *Journal of Democracy* 13, no. 2 (April 2002): 66–80.

32. Council on Foreign Affairs, *The New Arab Revolt: What Happened, What It Means, and What Comes Next* (New York: Council on Foreign Affairs, 2011).

33. Mark Tessler, "The Origins of Popular Support for Islamist Movements," in *Public Opinion in the Middle East: Survey Research and the Political Orientations of Ordinary Citizens,* ed. Mark Tessler (Bloomington, IN: Indiana University Press, 2011).

34. Ernest Gellner, *Conditions of Liberty: Civil Society and Its Rivals* (London: Hamish Hamilton, 1994).

35. Myron Weiner, "Political Change: Asia, Africa, and the Middle East," in *Understanding Political Development,* ed. Myron Weiner and Samuel Huntington (Boston: Little, Brown, 1987); Ernest Gellner, "Islam and Marxism: Some Comparisons," *International Affairs* 67, no. 1 (1991): 1–6. Also see Lewis, *What Went Wrong?*; Bernard Lewis, "Islam and Liberal Democracy," *Atlantic* 271 (February 1993): 89–94. Nader Hashemi strongly refutes this argument in his *Islam, Secularism, and Liberal Democracy.*

36. Kamran Bokhari, *From Islamism to Post-Islamism* (Austin: Stratfor, 2005).

37. Irfan Ahmed, *Islamism and Democracy in India: The Transformation of Jamaat-e-Islami* (Princeton: Princeton University Press, 2009).

38. This ongoing contentious relationship between the state and society has aptly been articulated by Joel S. Migdal, *State in Society: Studying How States and Societies Transform and Constitute One Another* (New York: Cambridge University Press, 2001).

39. 2010 Pew Report (Pew Research Center, 2010) as referenced in Amitai Etzioni, "Should We Support Illiberal Religious Democracies?" *The Political Quarterly* 82, no. 4 (October–December 2011): 567–73.

40. Ibid.

41. Ibid.

42. Jillian Schwedler, *Faith in Moderation: Islamist Parties in Jordan and Yemen* (New York: Cambridge University Press, 2006).

43. Quintan Wiktorowicz, *The Management of Islamic Activism: Salafis, the Muslim Brotherhood, and State Power in Jordan* (New York: State University of New York Press, 2001); Quintan Wiktorowicz; Ali Riaz, *God Willing: The Politics of Islamism in Bangladesh* (Lanham, MD: Rowman and Littlefield, 2004); Doug Ramage, *Politics in Indonesia: Democracy, Islam, and the Ideology of Tolerance* (London: Routledge, 1997).

44. One of the few scholars trying to provide this type of comprehensive theoretical framework is Julie Chernov Hwang, *Peaceful Islamist Mobilization in the Muslim World: What Went Right* (New York: Palgrave Macmillan, 2009), 3.

45. Sadki, *Rethinking Arab Democratization.*

46. Juan Linz and Alfred Stepan, *Problems of Democratic Transition and Consolidation: Southern Europe, South America, and Post-Communist Europe* (Baltimore: The Johns Hopkins University Press, 1996); Guillermo O'Donnell, Philippe Schmitter and Laurence Whitehead, eds., *Transitions from Authoritarian Rule: Prospects for Democracy* (Baltimore: The Johns Hopkins University Press, 1986); Alfred Stepan, *Rethinking Military Politics: Brazil and the Southern Cone* (Princeton: Princeton University Press, 1988); Larry Diamond, Juan J. Linz and Seymour M. Lipset, eds., *Democracy in Developing Countries: Comparing Experiences with Democracy* (Boulder: Lynne Rienner, 1995); Dietrich Rueschemeyer, Evelyne Huber Stephens and John D. Stephens, *Capitalist Development and Democracy* (Chicago: University of Chicago Press, 1992); Adam Przeworski, *Democracy and the Market: Political and Economic Reforms in Eastern Europe and Latin America* (Cambridge, NY: Cambridge University Press, 1991); John Higley and Richard Gunther, *Elites and Democratic Consolidation in Latin America and Southern Europe* (Cambridge, NY: Cambridge University Press, 1992); Scott Mainwaring, Guillermo O'Donnell and J. Samuel Valenzuela, eds., *Issues in Democratic Consolidation: The New South American Democracies in Comparative Perspective* (South Bend, IN: University of Notre Dame Press, 1992); Diamond and Plattner, *The Global Resurgence of Democracy*; Richard Gunther, *Politics of Democratic Consolidation* (Baltimore: The Johns Hopkins University Press, 1995); Larry Diamond and Marc F. Plattner, *Democratization in Africa: Progress and Retreat* (Baltimore: The Johns Hopkins University Press, 2010). For a review of these works, see Gerardo L. Munck,

"Democratic Transitions in Comparative Perspective," *Comparative Politics* 26 (1994): 355–75.

47. These three words were used by former CIA director and top military commander, retired Gen. David Petraeus, during an April 2009 talk at Harvard, when he acknowledged that the United States government lacked the "rigorous, granular, and nuanced understanding" to distinguish between "the reconcilables and the irreconcilables" among the Afghan Taliban movement.

## 2  Understanding the Complexity of Political Islam

1. John Esposito, ed., *The Iranian Revolution: Its Global Impact* (Gainesville: University of Florida Press, 1990).

2. Nikki R Keddie, *Roots of Revolution: An Interpretive History of Modern Iran* (New Haven, CT: Yale University Press, 1981); Shaul Bakhash, *The Reign of the Ayatollahs: Iran and the Islamic Revolution* (New York: Basic Books, 1984); Dilip Hiro, *Iran Under the Ayatollahs* (London: Routledge, 1985).

3. For a detailed examination of this incident within the broader context of Islam in Saudi Arabia, see James P. Piscatori, "Ideological Politics in Saudi Arabia," in *Islam in the Political Process*, ed. James P. Piscatori (Cambridge, New York: Cambridge University Press, 1983); Farouk A. Sankari, "Islam and Politics in Saudi Arabia," in *Islamic Resurgence in the Arab World*, ed. Ali E. Hillal Dessouki (New York: Praeger, 1982), 178–95; William Ochsenwald, "Saudi Arabia and Islamic Revival," *International Journal of Middle East Studies* 13, (1981): 271–86.

4. Nazih Ayubi, *Political Islam: Religion and Politics in the Arab World* (London: Routledge 1991); Joel Beinin and Joe Stork, eds., *Political Islam: Essays from Middle East Report* (Berkeley, CA: University of California Press, 1997); John L. Esposito, ed., *Political Islam: Revolution, Radicalism, or Reform?* (Boulder, CO: Lynne Rienner, 1997); Graham Fuller, *The Future of Political Islam* (New York: Palgrave Macmillan, 2003); Olivier Roy, *Globalized Islam: The Search for the New Ummah* (New York: Columbia University Press, 2004); Peter Mandaville, *Global Political Islam* (London and New York: Routledge, 2007); Mohammed Ayoob, *The Many Faces of Political Islam: Religion and Politics in the Muslim World* (Ann Arbor, IL: University of Michigan Press, 2008).

5. See Peter Bergen's op-ed on CNN in February 2011. http://edition.cnn.com/2011/OPINION/02/23/bergen.revolt.binladen/index.html?iref=allsearch.

6. Daveed Gartenstein-Ross from the Fund for the Defense of Democracies is perhaps the most prominent voice among those who continue to caution against the idea that al-Qaeda has been dealt a death blow. See his October 3, 2012, "Reports of al-Qaeda's Death Have Been Greatly Exaggerated," *Foreign Policy*.

7. At the time of writing this book, Egypt had over six different Salafist parties.

8. Martin Kramer, "Coming to Terms: Fundamentalists or Islamists?" *Middle East Quarterly* (spring 2003): 65–77. Also available online at http://www.meforum.org/541/coming-to-terms-fundamentalists-or-islamists.

9. Guilain Denoeux, "The Forgotten Swamp: Navigating Political Islam," *Middle East Policy* 9, no. 2 (June 2002): 61.

10. Fuller, *The Future of Political Islam*, xi.

11. Mohammad Ayoob, "The Future of Political Islam: The Importance of External Variables," *International Affairs* 81, no. 5 (2005): 951–60.

12. Denoeux, "The Forgotten Swamp," 61.

13. Kamran Bokhari, "A Divided Epistemic Community and Political Islam: A Constructivist Approach to Understanding the Making of United States Foreign Policy," *The American Journal of Islamic Social Sciences* 19, no. 3 (summer 2002), 11–30.

14. Denoeux, "The Forgotten Swamp," 61.

15. Schwedler, *Faith*, 8.

16. Fuller, *Future of Political Islam*, xi.

17. Wickham, *Mobilizing Islam*, 95.

18. Ayoob, "The Future of Political Islam," 952; Denoeux, "The Forgotten Swamp," 61.

19. Fuller, *Future of Political Islam*, 45.

20. "Making Sense of the Post-Sept. 11 'Islamist' Terminology," October 28, 2005. Available via subscription at http://www.stratfor.com/search/site/Makings%20sense%20of%20 post%20terminology.

21. The London-based Institute of Strategic Dialogue elucidated upon such European radical groups in its February 2012 briefing paper "The New Radical Right: Violent and Non-Violent Movements in Europe." Available online at http://www.strategicdialogue. org/ISD%20Far%20Right%20Feb2012.pdf.

22. There is some debate among those who follow Hizb al-Tahrir as regards its relationship to political violence. While the party itself does not engage in violence, its modus operandi does entail mass protests calling for a military coup against the incumbent order. This approach carries a high risk of violence. Moreover, it is not unknown for individuals to leave the group and begin to blend its antidemocracy and anti-nation-state ideas, as well as its calls for reestablishing a transnational caliphate, with the jihadist view of armed struggle—all of which leads to militant offshoots. Both of these aspects are problematic, but by and large the group is still very different from jihadist forces and hence radical but not militant. That said, some scholars subscribe to the conveyer belt theory about Hizb al-Tahrir, namely, that it serves as an intermediary forum for radicalized youth who then graduate from nonviolent radicalism to militancy. See Zeyno Baran, "Fighting the War of Ideas," *Foreign Affairs* 84, no. 6 (November/December 2005): 68–78.

23. Holly Fletcher, *Militant Extremists in the United States* (New York: Council on Foreign Relations, April 21, 2008), http://www.cfr.org/publication/9236/.

24. Ayman al-Zawahiri, al-Qaeda's second in command, pointed out this difference in a 2005 communication to al-Qaeda's former leader in Iraq, Abu Musab al-Zarqawi, in an attempt to moderate the latter's uncompromising Salafi/Wahhabi views.

25. We do not examine Hizb al-Tahrir as a case study in this book due to space limitations and because the group has not demonstrated a potent enough presence in the Arab/Muslim world. Yet, its modus operandi remains a critical method of political change especially in the wake of the Arab Spring. For example, in Egypt, the Mubarak and Morsi governments were overthrown by mass uprisings leading to military coups. While Hizb al-Tahrir has not had success with this method of change, secular forces seem to have adopted it. This practice threatens the democratization process because it relies on mass demonstrators and coups as a means for change rather than the electoral process.

26. Fawaz Gerges, *The Far Enemy: Why Jihad Went Global* (New York: Cambridge University Press, 2009).

27. In popular parlance, Egypt's anti-Islamist forces are often identified as liberal secularists. However, the manner in which the secular camp forced President Morsi out of office via a military putsch prevents us from labeling them all as liberals. The reality is that Egyptian secularists have always fallen into all three of our categories (radical, liberal, and moderate). The elements within the Egyptian civil military establishment

who are intolerant of Islamists are an example of radical secularists. Secularist notables like Mohamed El Baradei represent liberal secularists especially in his opposition to the violent crackdown on the Brotherhood. Amr Hamzawy is an example of moderate secularists that are far more receptive to working with Islamists.

## 3   Theoretical Framework: Democratization and Islamism

1. For examples, see Guillermo O'Donnell, Philippe Schmitter and Laurence Whitehead, eds., *Transitions from Authoritarian Rule: Prospects for Democracy* (Baltimore: The Johns Hopkins University Press, 1986); Alfred Stepan, *Rethinking Military Politics: Brazil and the Southern Cone* (Princeton: Princeton University Press, 1988); Larry Diamond, Juan J. Linz and Seymour M. Lipset, eds., *Democracy in Developing Countries: Comparing Experiences with Democracy* (Boulder: Lynne Rienner, 1995); Dietrich Rueschemeyer, Evelyne Huber Stephens and John D. Stephens, *Capitalist Development and Democracy* (Chicago: University of Chicago Press, 1992); Adam Przeworski, *Democracy and the Market: Political and Economic Reforms in Eastern Europe and Latin America* (Cambridge, New York: Cambridge University Press, 1991); John Higley and Richard Gunther, *Elites and Democratic Consolidation in Latin America and Southern Europe* (Cambridge, New York: Cambridge University Press, 1992); Scott Mainwaring, Guillermo O'Donnell and J. Samuel Valenzuela, eds., *Issues in Democratic Consolidation: The New South American Democracies in Comparative Perspective* (South Bend: University of Notre Dame Press, 1992); Larry Diamond and Marc F. Plattner, eds., *The Global Resurgence of Democracy* (Baltimore: The John Hopkins University Press, 1993); Richard Gunther, *Politics of Democratic Consolidation* (Baltimore: The Johns Hopkins University Press, 1995). For a review of these works, see Gerardo L. Munck, "Democratic Transitions in Comparative Perspective," *Comparative Politics* 26 (1994): 355–75.
2. Guillermo O'Donnell, "The Perpetual Crises of Democracy," *Journal of Democracy* 18, no. 1 (January 2007): 8–9.W. B. Gallie, "Essentially Contested Concepts," *Proceedings of the Aristotelian Society* (Blackwell Publishing1955): 167–98.
3. Laurence Whitehead, quoted in Larbi Sadiki, *Rethinking Arab Democratization: Elections without Democracy* (Oxford, New York: Oxford University Press, 2011), 2.
4. Joseph Schumpeter, *Capitalism, Socialism, and Democracy* (New York: Harper, 1947). Other scholars, most notably Adam Przeworski and his collaborators (Alvarez et al. 1996; Przeworski et al. 2000), have also maintained a more minimalist definition that centers on contested elections and electoral turnover.
5. Steven Levitsky and Lucan A. Way, *Competitive Authoritarianism: Hybrid Regimes after the Cold War* (Cambridge, New York: Cambridge University Press, 2010), 4. For further discussion about democracy's definition, see Philippe C. Schmitter and Terry Lynn Karl, "What Democracy Is . . . and Is Not," *Journal of Democracy* 2, no. 3 (Summer 1991): 75–89; Larry Diamond, *Developing Democracy: Toward Consolidation* (Baltimore: The Johns Hopkins University Press, 1999), 7–15. Also see Samuel P. Huntington, "The Modest Meaning of Democracy," in *Democracy in the Americas: Stopping the Pendulum*, ed. Robert Pastor (New York: Holmes and Meier, 1989); Samuel P. Huntington, *The Third Wave: Democratization in the Late Twentieth Century* (Norman, OK: University of Oklahoma Press, 1991), 5–13; David Collier and Steven Levitsky, "Democracy with Adjectives: Conceptual Innovation in Comparative Research," *World Politics* 49, no. 3 (April 1997): 430–51; Scott Mainwaring, Daniel

Brinks and Aníbal Pérez Liñan, "Classifying Political Regimes in Latin America, 1945–1999," *Studies in Comparative International Development* 36, no. 1 (Spring 2001): 37–65.

6. Levitsky and Way, *Competitive Authoritarianism,* 4. Also see Collier and Levitsky, "Democracy with Adjectives."

7. The most articulate assessment of this view comes from Nader Hashemi, *Islam, Secularism, and Liberal Democracy: Towards a Democratic Theory for Muslim Societies* (New York: Oxford University Press, 2009).

8. Huntington, *The Third Wave.* For a theoretical assessment of democratization, see Laurence Whitehead, *Democratization: Theory and Experience* (New York: Oxford University Press, 2009).

9. Diamond and Plattner, eds., *Global Resurgence.*

10. Huntington, *The Third Wave,* 21–6; Larry Diamond, "The Globalization of Democracy," in *Global Transformation and the Third World,* ed. Robert Slater, Barry Schultz and Steven Doerr (Boulder: Lynne Rienner, 1993), 32–8; Juan Linz and Alfred Stepan, *Problems of Democratic Transition and Consolidation: Southern Europe, South America, and Post-Communist Europe* (Baltimore: The Johns Hopkins University Press, 1996); Higley and Gunther, *Elites and Democratic Consolidation;* Mainwaring, O'Donnell and Valenzuela, eds., *Issues in Democratic Consolidation;* Larry Diamond and Marc F. Plattner, *Democratization in Africa: Progress and Retreat* (Baltimore: The Johns Hopkins University Press, 2010); Michael Bratton and Nicholas van de Walle, *Democratic Experiments in Africa: Regime Transitions in Comparative Perspective* (Cambridge: Cambridge University Press, 1997).

11. For useful typologies of transition from authoritarianism, see Scott Mainwaring, *Transitions to Democracy and Democratic Consolidation: Theoretical and Comparative Issues,* Working Paper #130 (Helen Kellogg Institute for International Studies, University of Notre Dame: 1989); Terry Karl, "Dilemmas of Democratization in Latin America," *Comparative Politics* 23 (1990): 1–21; Terry Karl and Philippe Schmitter, "Democratization around the Globe: Its Opportunities and Risks," in *World Security: Trends and Challenges at Century's End,* ed. Michael T. Klare and Dan Thomas (New York: St. Martin's Press, 1993).

12. Francis Fukuyama, *End of History and the Last Man* (New York: Free Press, 2006).

13. Andreas Schedler, *Electoral Authoritarianism: The Dynamics of Unfree Competition* (Boulder: Lynne Rienner, 2006), 3–7.

14. Juan J. Linz and Alfred Stepan, eds., *The Breakdown of Democratic Regimes: Crisis, Breakdown, and Reequilibration* (Baltimore: The John Hopkins University Press, 1978).

15. Schedler, *Electoral Authoritarianism,* 3–7.

16. Thomas Carothers, "The End of the Transition Paradigm," *Journal of Democracy* 13, no. 1 (January 2002): 5–21.

17. Daniel Brumberg, "The Trap of Liberalized Autocracy," *Journal of Democracy* 13, no. 4 (2002): 56–68.

18. Fareed Zakaria, *The Future of Freedom: Illiberal Democracy at Home and Abroad* (New York: W.W. Norton & Co., 2003).

19. For a discussion of hybrid regimes, see Terry Lynn Karl, "The Hybrid Regimes of Central America," *Journal of Democracy* 6, no. 3 (July 1995): 72–87; Collier and Levitsky, "Democracy with Adjectives," 430–51; Andreas Schedler, "Elections Without Democracy: The Menu of Manipulation," *Journal of Democracy* 13, no. 2 (April 2002): 36–50; Andreas Schedler, "The Nested Game of Democratization by Elections," *International Political Science Review* 23, no. 1 (2002): 103–122; Schedler, *Electoral Authoritarianism;* Nicolas van de Walle, "Elections Without Democracy: Africa's Range

of Regimes," *Journal of Democracy* 13, no. 2 (April 2002): 66–80. Also see Larry Diamond, "Thinking about Hybrid Regimes," *Journal of Democracy* 13, no. 2 (April 2002), 21–35; Steven Levitsky and Lucan A. Way, "The Rise of Competitive Authoritarianism," *Journal of Democracy* 13, no. 2 (April 2002), 51–65; Marina Ottaway, *Democracy Challenged: The Rise of Semi-Authoritarianism* (Washington, DC: Carnegie Endowment for International Peace, 2003).

20. Schedler, *Electoral Authoritarianism*, 3–7.
21. Ibid.
22. Ibid.
23. Ibid.
24. Ibid.
25. Brumberg, "The Trap," 56–68.
26. Sadiki, *Rethinking Arab Democratization*, 3.
27. Peter Mandaville, *Global Political Islam*, 103. Also see Brumberg, "The Trap," 56–68.
28. Amr Hamzawy, "The Key to Arab Reform: Moderate Islamists," in *Policy Brief 40* (Washington, DC: Carnegie Endowment for International Peace, 2005), 4.
29. Mandaville, *Global Political Islam*, 103. Also see Brumberg, "The Trap," 56–68.
30. Levitsky and Way, *Competitive Authoritarianism*, 10.
31. David Epstein, Robert Bates, Jack Goldstone, Ida Kristensen and Sharyn O'Halloran, "Democratic Transitions," *American Journal of Political Science* 50, no. 3 (July 2006): 551–69.
32. Levitsky and Way, *Competitive Authoritarianism*, 10.
33. Ibid., 4.
34. Ibid., 15.
35. Schedler, *Electoral Authoritarianism*, 3–7.
36. Collier and Levitsky, "Democracy with Adjectives."
37. Ibid., 3–7; Also see Levitsky and Way, "Competitive Authoritarianism"; Howard and Roessler, "Post-Cold War Political Regimes."
38. Andreas Schedler, *Electoral Authoritarianism*, 3–7.
39. Ibid.
40. Recent example of normative work is M. A. Muqtedar Khan, ed. *Islamic Democratic Discourse: Theory, Debates, and Philosophical Perspectives* (Lanham, MD: Lexington Books, 2006); Abdelwahab El-Affendi, *Who Needs an Islamic State?* (London, Malaysia Think Tank, 2008); Abdelwahab A. El-Affendi, "The Islamism Debate Revisited: In Search of 'Islamist democrats,' " in *Europe, the USA, and Political Islam: Strategies for Engagement,* ed. Michelle Pace (London: Palgrave, 2010), 125–38; Abdelwahab A. El-Affendi, "The Modern Debate(s) on Islam and Democracy," in *Islam and Democracy in Malaysia: Findings from a National Dialogue,* ed. Ibrahim Zein (Kuala Lumpur: International Institute of Islamic Thought and Civilization, 2010), 3–68; Abdelwahab A. El-Affendi, "On the State, Democracy, and Pluralism," in *Islamic Thought in the Twentieth Century,* ed. Suha Taji-Farouki and Basheer M. Nafi (London: I.B. Taurus, 2004), 172–94; Abdelwahab A. El-Affendi, David Beetham and Neil Walker, "Democracy and the Islamist Paradox," in *Understanding Democratic Politics: An Introduction,* ed. Ronald Axtmann (London: Sage, 2003), 311–20; Abdelwahab A. El-Affendi, "The Elusive Reformation," in *Islam and Democracy in the Middle East,* ed. Larry Diamond, Marc F. Plattner and Daniel Brumberg (Baltimore: The Johns Hopkins University Press, 2003), 252–7.
41. There were several contributions to *Annals: Journal of the American Association of Political Science,* no. 524 (November 1992), most notably by Lahouari Addi and I. William Zartman. Similarly, the *Journal of Democracy* devoted an entire issue to Islam and

democracy, which was later published as a book: Diamond, Plattner and Brumberg, eds., *Islam and Democracy*. The discussion within the context of democracy promotion was outlined by Graham Fuller in his "Islamists and Democracy," in *Uncharted Journey: Promoting Democracy in the Middle East*, ed. Thomas Carothers and Marina Ottaway (Washington, DC: Carnegie Endowment for International Peace and Democracy, 2005).

42. The conceptual debate about democracy in the Middle East is nicely outlined in Ghassan Salame's *Democracy without Democrats?: The Renewal of Politics in the Muslim World* (London: I.B. Taurus, 1994). His survey of the region takes a nuanced look at the problems of democratization and links them to the social changes of the last three decades. A contrasting theoretical perspective is provided in Rex Brynen, Bahgat Korany and Paul Noble, *Political Liberalization and Democratization in the Arab World* (Boulder: Lynne Rienner, 1995). Also see Muhammad Muslih and Augustus Richard Norton, "The Need for Arab Democracy," *Foreign Policy* 83 (Summer 1991); Dale Eickelman and James Piscatori, *Muslim Politics* (Princeton: Princeton University Press, 1996). A most significant contribution is Richard Norton, ed., *Civil Society in the Middle East*, 2 vol. (New York: E. J. Brill, 1995). The work's primary task is to define "civil society" in that particular context so that the extent of its usefulness (descriptively rather than merely prescriptively) can be established in each country. In terms of specific case studies, the most notable are Sheila Carapico, *Civil Society in Yemen* (Cambridge, UK: Cambridge University Press, 1998) and Denis Sullivan, *Private Voluntary Organizations in Egypt: Islamic Development, Private Initiative, and State Control* (Gainsville: Florida University Press, 1994). Carapico refutes the argument that Muslims cannot be civil and encourages a dynamic rather than static view of how people organize their social lives. Sullivan examines the relationship between charitable associations and the Egyptian government by analyzing whether these associations support or threaten the current regime's underlying legitimacy. Iftikhar Malik, *State and Civil Society in Pakistan* (London: MacMillan Press, 1997); Eva Bellen, "Civil Society in Formation: Tunisia," in *Civil Society in the Middle East*, ed. Augustus Richard Norton (New York: E. J. Brill, 1995), 120. Jillian Schwedler ed., *Towards Civil Society in the Middle East?* (Boulder: Lynne Reinner, 1995).

43. Robert W. Hefner, ed., *Shari'a Politics: Islamic Law and Society in the Modern World* (Bloomington and Indianapolis: Indiana University Press, 2011), 4.

44. Azzam S. Tamimi, *Rachid Ghannouchi: A Democrat within Islamism* (New York: Oxford University Press, 2001).

45. For further reading on this view, see Abdolkarim Soroush, *Reason, Freedom, and Democracy in Islam* (New York: Oxford University Press, 2002).

46. Bernard Lewis, "The Roots of Muslim Rage," *Atlantic* 266 (September 1990): 47–54, 56, 59, 60; Bernard Lewis, "Islam and Liberal Democracy," *Atlantic* 271 (February 1993): 89–94; Elie Kedourie, *Democracy and Arab Political Culture* (Washington, DC: Washington Institute for Near Eastern Policy, 1992); Martin Kramer, "Islam vs. Democracy," *Commentary* 95, no. 1 (January 1993): 35–42.

47. Irfan Ahmad, *Islamism and Democracy in India: The Transformation of Jamaat-e-Islami* (Princeton: Princeton University Press, 2009), 11.

48. Ibid.

49. Humeira Iqtidar, *Secularizing Islamists? Jama'at-e-Islami and Jama'at-ud-Da'wa in Urban Pakistan* (Chicago: University of Chicago Press, 2011), 13.

50. Ernest Gellner, *Muslim Society* (Cambridge, New York: Cambridge University Press, 1981); Ernest Gellner, "Islam and Marxism: Some Comparisons," *International Affairs* 67, no. 1 (1991): 1–6; Ernest Gellner, *Postmodernism, Reason and Religion* (London:

Routledge, 1992); Ernest Gellner, *Conditions of Liberty: Civil Society and Its Rivals* (London: Hamish Hamilton, 1994). Referenced in Ahmad, *Islamism and Democracy in India* 11.

51. Sayyid Qutb, *Ma'alim fi'l-Tariq* (Cairo: Kazi Publications, 1964). Also see Sayyid Qutb, *Social Justice in Islam* (Oneonta, NY: Islamic Publications International, 1953).

52. While Qutb is often cited as a prime example of an antidemocratic Islamist thinker, Taqi al-Deen al-Nabhani (founder of Hizb al-Tahrir), Abu Muhammad al-Maqdisi (a contemporary Jordanian Salafist-jihadist theoretician), and others have detailed why they reject democracy. Furthermore, Qutb's ideas on divine sovereignty were influenced by such South Asian Islamist thinkers as Sayyid Abul Ala Maududi and, to a lesser extent, Abul Hasan Ali Nadwi. See Barbara Zollner, *The Muslim Brotherhood: Hasan al-Hudaybi and Ideology* (London: Routledge, 2008). It should be noted that Maududi eventually went from supporting theo-democracy to embracing democracy, especially since he signed off on the 1973 Pakistani constitution, crafted by a secular democratic government, as being in line with Islamic precepts.

53. Qutb, *Ma'alim*. For a theoretical formulation of Islamist authoritarianism, see Husayn ibn Muhsin ibn 'Ali Jabir, *Al-Tariq ila Jama'at al-Muslimin*, 3rd ed. (al-Mansura, Egypt: Dar al-Wafa', 1989). For a critique, see 'Abd Allah Fahd al-Nafisi, ed., *Al-Haraka al-Islamiyya: Ru'ya Mustaqbaliyya: Awraq fi al-Naqd al-Dhati* (Cairo: Maktaba Madbuli, 1989).

54. Amaney Jamal

55. Iqtidar, *Secularizing Islamists?*. Also see Ellen Lust-Okar and Amaney A. Jamal, "Rulers and Rules: Reassessing the Influence of Regime Type on Electoral Law Formation," *Comparative Political Studies* 35, no. 3 (April 2002): 336–66.

56. Giacomo Luciani, "The Oil Rent, the Fiscal Crisis of the State and Democratization," in *Democracy without Democrats? The Renewal of Politics in the Muslim World*, ed. Ghassan Salamé (London: I.B. Tauris, 1994), 130–55; Also see Giacomo Luciani, "Allocation vs. Production States: A Theoretical Framework," in *The Arab State*, ed. Giacomo Luciani (Berkeley: University of California Press, 1990), 65–84; Giacomo Luciani, "Economic Foundations of Democracy and Authoritarianism: The Arab World in Comparative Perspective," *Arab Studies Quarterly* 10, no. 4 (1988): 457–75.

57. Christian Welzel, "Theories of Democratization," in *Democratization*, ed. Christian W. Haerpfer, Patrick Bernhagen, Ronald F. Inglehart and Christian Welzel (Oxford, UK: Oxford University Press, 2009), 80.

58. For further elaboration, see, Elie Kedourie, *Democracy and Arab Political Culture* (Washington, DC: Washington Institute for Near Eastern Policy, 1992); Lewis, "The Roots of Muslim Rage," 47–54, 56, 59, 60 and Lewis, "Islam and Liberal Democracy," 89–94; Martin Kramer, "Islam vs. Democracy," *Commentary* 95, no. 1 (January 1993): 35–42.

59. Iqtidar, *Secularizing Islamists?* 13.

60. Tamimi, *Rachid Ghannouchi*.

61. Much of the discussion on democracy and democratization was informed by the analysis on secularism in relation to the west in Iqtidar, Humeira. 2011. *Secualrising Islamists? Jama'at-e-Islami and Jama'at-ud-Dawa in Urban Pakistan*. University of Chicago Press, pp.12–17. For further elaboration on Ghannouchi's understanding of democracy within the Muslim context see Tamimi, Azzam. 2001. *Rachid Ghannouchi: A Democrat Within Islamism*. Oxford University Press.

62. Ibid., pp.12–17

63. Iqtidar, *Secularizing Islamists?*.

64. Abdolkarim Soroush, *Reason, Freedom, and Democracy in Islam* (New York: Oxford University Press, 2002).

65. Saba Mahmood, "Is Liberalism Islam's Only Answer?" in *Islam and the Challenge of Democracy*, ed. Khaled Abou El Fadl (Princeton: Princeton University Press, 2004).

66. Graham Fuller, "Islamists and Democracy," in *Uncharted Journey: Promoting Democracy in the Middle East*, ed. Thomas Carothers and Marina Ottaway (Washington, DC: Carnegie Endowment for International Peace and Democracy, 2005).

67. Robert W. Hefner, ed., *Remaking Muslim Politics: Pluralism, Contestation, Democratization* (Princeton, NJ and Oxford, UK: Princeton University Press, 2005), 26.

68. We have consciously avoided the more thrown-about "Islamic democracy" in favor of "Muslim democracy," because this book deals with the behavior of Islamists and Muslims, as opposed to examining the issue from a normative religious standpoint. Our stance on the word "Islamic" is elaborated upon in greater detail in Chapter 4.

69. Hashemi, *Islam, Secularism, and Liberal Democracy*, 2.

70. For a detailed discussion please see Louay Safi, "Islam and the Secular State: Explicating the Universal in Formative Islamic Political Norms" (paper delivered at the 2nd annual conference of the Center for the Study of Islam and Democracy, Washington, DC: 2001).

71. Stepan's "Twin Toleration" model gives due credit to religion's role in a democracy. Alfred Stepan, "The Multiple Secularisms of Modern Democracies and Autocracies," in *Rethinking Secularism*, ed. Craig Calhoun, Mark Juergensmeyer, and Jonathan VanAntwerpen (Oxford, New York: Oxford University Press, 2011).

72. Zakaria, *The Future of Freedom*.

73. Sadiki, *Rethinking Arab Democratization*, xii.

74. Ibid., viii.

75. As referenced in Hefner, ed., *Shari'a Politics*, 4; John L. Esposito and Dalia Mogahed, *Who Speaks for Islam: What a Billion Muslims Really Think* (New York: Gallup Press, 2007); Moatazz A. Fattah, *Democratic Values in the Muslim World* (Boulder: Lynne Rienner, 2006); Riaz Hassan, *Faithlines: Muslim Conceptions of Islam and Society* (Karachi: Oxford University Press, 2002); Pippa Norris and Ronald Inglehart, *Sacred and Secular: Religion and Politics Worldwide* (Cambridge, New York: Cambridge University Press).

76. Hefner, *Shari'a Politics*, 4.

77. Ibid.

78. Schwedler notes in her 2011 World Politics article on Islamist moderation that in recent years, scholarship on Islamism has moved away from abstract debates about the compatibility of Islam and democracy and toward empirical studies of the practices and commitments of Islamist groups.

79. Emmanuel Sivan, *Radical Islam: Medieval Theology and Modern Politics* (New Haven, CT: Yale University Press, 1985).

80. Iqtidar, *Secularizing Islamists?* 13.

81. Ahmad, *Islamism and Democracy in India*. Also see John L. Esposito, "Introduction: Islam and Secularism in the Twenty-first Century," in *Islam and Secularism in the Middle East*, ed. John L. Esposito and Azzam Tamimi (London: Hurst and Co.), 1–12.

82. Iqtidar, *Secularizing Islamists?* 13.

83. Ibid.

84. Schwedler, *Democratization in Middle East*, 57.

85. Eberhard Kienle, "More Than a Response to Islamism: The Political Deliberalization of Egypt in the 1990s," *Middle East Journal* 52, no. 2 (Spring 1998): 227.

86. Mohammad Ayoob, "The Future of Political Islam: The Importance of External Variables," *International Affairs* 81, no. 5 : 951–61.

87. In addition to the 444 elected members of Parliament, the president appoints ten parliamentarians, thereby bringing to 454 the total membership of the People's Assembly.

88. International Crisis Group interview, Deputy General Guide Muhammad Habib, Cairo, March 2008. "Islamism in North Africa II: Egypt's Opportunity," *Crisis Group Middle East/North Africa Briefing* 13 (April 20, 2004).

89. *Observer*, January 19, 1992; John Esposito and John Voll, *Islam and Democracy* (New York: Oxford University Press, 1996). For further reading on Ghannoushi's thoughts, see Tamimi, *Rachid Ghannouchi*.

90. Ellen Lust-Okar, "Elections under Authoritarianism: Preliminary Lessons from Jordan," *Democratization* 13, no. 3 (June 2006): 459.

91. Larbi Sadiki, "Bin Ali's Tunisia: Democracy by Non-Democratic Means," *British Journal of Middle East Studies* 29, 1 (2002): 57–78. Also see Mark Gasiorowski "The Failure of Reform in Tunisia," *Journal of Democracy* 3, no. 4 (1992): 85–97.

92. Albert Hourani, *Arabic Thought in the Liberal Age: 1798–1939* (Cambridge, New York: Cambridge University Press, 1983).

93. Giacomo Luciani, "Economic Foundations of Democracy and Authoritarianism."

94. Nathan Brown, Amr Hamzawy, and Marina Ottawa, *Islamist Movements and the Democratic Process in the Arab World: Exploring the Gray Zones* (Washington, DC: Carnegie Endowment for International Peace, 2006), 5–6.

## 4    Participatory Islamists: The Case of the Muslim Brotherhood

1. Roxanne L. Euben and Muhammad Qasim Zaman, *Princeton Readings in Islamist Thought: Texts and Contexts from al-Banna to Bin Laden* (Princeton: Princeton University Press, 2009), 49. Banna's life has been extensively documented in his own memoirs and by various scholars. See, for instance, Christina Phelps Harris, *Nationalism and Revolution in Egypt: The Role of the Muslim Brotherhood* (The Hague: Mouton, 1964) and Hasan al-Banna, *Mudhakkirat al-Da'wa wa'l-Da'iyya* (Cairo: Dar al-Kitab al-Arabi, 1974).

2. Albert Hourani, *Arabic Thought in the Liberal Age: 1798–1939* (Cambridge, NY: Cambridge University Press, 1983).

3. Malcolm H. Kerr, *Islamic Reform: The Political and Legal Theories of Muhammad 'Abduh and Rashid Rida* (Berkeley: University of California Press, 1966).

4. The best and most comprehensive historic account of the Muslim Brotherhood since its founding remains Richard Mitchell, *The Society of the Muslim Brothers* (Oxford, NY: Oxford University Press, 1993).

5. For a detailed examination of its influence in Europe and North America, see Lorenzo Vidino, *The New Muslim Brotherhood in the West* (New York: Columbia University Press, 2010); Brigette Marechal, *The Muslim Brothers in Europe: Roots and Discourse* (Leiden and Boston: Brill, 2008); Gilles Kepel, *Allah in the West: Islamic Movements in America and Europe* (Palo Alto: Stanford University Press, 1997); Gilles Kepel, *The War for Muslim Minds: Islam and the West* (Cambridge, MA: Harvard University Press, 2004); Larry Poston, *Islamic Da'wah in the West* (New York: Oxford University Press, 1992). Also see Alexandre Caeiro and Mahmoud al-Saibl, "Qaradawi in Europe, Europe in Qaradawi? The Global Mufti's European Politics," in *Global Mufti: The Phenomenon of Yusuf al-Qaradawi,* ed. Bettina Graf and Jakob Skovgaard-Petersen (New York: Columbia University Press, 2009), 109–48.

6. Barry Rubin, ed., *The Muslim Brotherhood: The Organization and Policies of a Global Islamist Movement* (New York: Palgrave Macmillan, 2010), 1. Some scholars have argued that during the late 1940s, early 1950s, and 1960s, the Muslim Brotherhood adopted radicalism and militancy. However, an overwhelming amount of evidence suggests that these were exceptions to the rule and that the movement's core has continued to shed radical splinter groups.

7. Ibid.

8. Egypt is the birthplace of both Islamism and its militant incarnation: jihadism. In addition to containing the Muslim Brotherhood, from the 1970s and until the 1990s Cairo was battling as many as five different radical and militant outfits.

9. Olivier Roy details the region's complex divisions and among Islamists triggered by Iraq's invasion of Kuwait and the subsequent war to liberate the GCC state. Olivier Roy, *The Failure of Political Islam* (Cambridge, MA: Harvard University Press, 1996).

10. Carrie Rosefsky Wickham, *Mobilizing Islam: Religion, Activism, and Political Change in Egypt* (New York: Columbia University Press, 2002).

11. Lisa Blaydes, *Elections and Distributive Politics in Mubarak's Egypt* (New York: Cambridge University Press, 2011), 162.

12. Ibid.

13. Yahya Sadowski, *Political Vegetables: Businessman and Bureaucrats in the Development of Egyptian Agriculture* (Washington, DC: Brookings Institution, 1991), 130.

14. Blaydes, *Elections and Distributive Politics,* 162. It should be noted that the increased space for the movement in the 2005 elections was also the result of the George W. Bush administration's pressure on the Mubarak regime as part of its Greater Middle East Partnership initiative.

15. Blaydes, *Elections and Distributive Politics,* 153.

16. Gilles Kepel, *Muslim Extremism in Egypt* (Berkeley: University of California Press, 1986).

17. Gelles Kepel, *Jihad: The Trial of Political Islam* (Cambridge, MA: Harvard University Press, 2002).

18. This phrase was first used by Assistant Secretary of State for Near Eastern Affairs Edward Djerijian in an April 1992 speech in Washington, DC. It became quite popular among those who argued that even those Islamists who embraced democracy saw it as a tool to gain power and establish an Islamist autocracy.

19. Carrie Roshefsky Wickham, "The Path to Moderation: Strategy & Learning of the Formation of Egypt's Wasat Party," *Comparative Politics* 36, no. 2 (January 2004): 205–28.

20. Mohammed Zahid, *The Muslim Brotherhood and Egypt's Succession Crisis: The Politics of Liberalization and Reform in the Middle East* (New York: I.B. Tauris, 2010), 18.

21. Ibid., 19.

22. Ibid., 18.

23. Janine A. Clark, *Islam, Charity, and Activism: Middle-Class Networks and Social Welfare in Egypt, Jordan, and Yemen* (Bloomington: Indiana University Press, 2004) as quoted in Zahid, *The Muslim Brotherhood and Egypt's Succession Crisis,* 19.

24. Nathan J. Brown, *Jordan & Its Islamic Movement: Limits of Inclusion?* (Washington, DC: The Carnegie Endowment for International Peace, November 2006).

25. Ziad Abu Amr, "Hamas: A Historical and Political Background," *Journal of Palestine Studies* 22, no. 4 (Summer 1993), 5–19.

26. Jean-Pierre Filiu, "The Origins of Hamas: Militant Legacy or Israeli Tool?" *Journal of Palestine Studies* 41, no. 3 (Spring 2012): 54–70.

27. Ibid., 55.

28. Andrew Higgins, "How Israel helped to Spawn Hamas," *Wall Street Journal*. January 29, 2009. http://online.wsj.com/article/SB123275572295011847.html.

29. Azzam Tamimi, "Palestine Question and Islamic Movement: The Ikhwan (Muslim Brotherhood) Roots of Hamas," *Kyoto Bulletin of Islamic Area Studies* 1, no. 1 (2007): 30–51.

30. Ibid.

31. Kamran Bokhari and Farid Senzai, "Defining a Moderate," in *Debating Moderate Islam: The Geopolitics of Islam and the West*, ed. M. A. Muqtedar Khan (Salt Lake City: University of Utah Press, 2007).

32. The RAND Corp was heavily criticized for what many saw as a project to set the standards for acceptable Muslim values. See Cheryl Bernard, *Civil Democratic Islam: Partners, Resources, and Strategies* (Santa Monica: RAND, 2004).

33. Lawrence Wright, *The Looming Tower: Al Qaeda and the Road to 9/11* (New York: Knopf, 2006).

34. A number of policy papers from the American Enterprise Institute (AEI), the Washington Institute for Near East Peace (WINEP), the Hudson Institute, and other conservative think tanks continue to promote this view.

35. See Marina Ottaway and Thomas Carothers, *Greater Middle East Initiative: Off to a False Start* (Washington, DC: The Carnegie Endowment for International Peace, March 2004). Policy brief no. 29.

36. Zahid, *The Muslim Brotherhood and Egypt's Succession Crisis*, 20.

37. Caveat: the June 2007 takeover of Gaza and the civil war with Fatah.

38. This was one of the unique and isolated cases in which the Muslim Brotherhood and the Salafis, contesting the election on separate platforms, aligned against the Shia bloc and engaged with each other.

39. Yoram Cohen and Matthew Levitt, with Becca Wasser, "Deterred but Determined Salafi-Jihadi Groups in the Palestinian Arena," *Policy Focus* 99 (Washington, DC: The Washington Institute for Near East Policy, January 2010).

40. Rashid al-Ghannoushi, *Al-Hurriyyat al-'Amma fi al-Dawla al-Islamiyya* (Beirut: Center for Arab Unity Studies, 1993).

41. Stephen Cook, *Ruling but not Governing: The Military and Political Development in Egypt, Algeria, and Turkey* (Baltimore: The Johns Hopkins University Press, 2007). Here, Cook lays out the notion on how militaries prefer to rule from behind the scenes as opposed to assuming the cumbersome day-to-day governance.

42. Larbi Sadiki, "Re-constituting Egypt," *Al-Jazeera*, November 29, 2012, www.aljazeera.com.

43. Ibid.

44. Amr Hamzawy, *Party for Justice and Development in Morocco: Participation and Its Discontents* (Washington, DC: The Carnegie Endowment for International Peace, July 2008). Report no. 93.

45. Ibid., 2.

46. Ibid.

47. Zahid, *The Muslim Brotherhood and Egypt's Succession Crisis*, 21.

48. Hamzawy, *Party for Justice and Development in Morocco*, 2.

49. Karin Brulliard, "Amid Islamist Rise, Jordan's Muslim Brotherhood Pledges Caution," *Washington Post*, July 18, 2012. Accessed March 18, 2013 http://articles.washingtonpost.com/2012-07-18/world/35489461_1_muslim-brotherhood-hamza-mansour-egypt.

50. *Hamas Looks to Revive the Palestinian Muslim Brotherhood.* October 16, 2012. Stratfor: Austin, TX. Available online via subscription at: http://www.stratfor.com/analysis/hamas-looks-revive-palestinian-muslim-brotherhood

51. *Egypt: The Muslim Brotherhood's Disagreement on Hamas.* November 18, 2012. Stratfor: Austin, TX. Available online via subscription at: http://www.stratfor.com/analysis/egypt-muslim-brotherhoods-disagreement-hamas

52. This phrase is borrowed from the title of Azzam Tamimi's biography of Tunisian Islamist thinker. Azzam Tamimi, *Rachid al-Ghannouchi: A Democrat within Islamism* (New York: Oxford University Press, 2001).

53. *"Egyptians Increasingly Glum"* Pew Global Attitudes Survey (Washington, DC, Pew Research Center) May 16, 2013.

54. Robert S. Leiken and Steven Brooke, "The Moderate Muslim Brotherhood," *Foreign Affairs* 86, no. 2 (March–April 2007): 110.

55. Jillian Schwedler, "Can Islamists Become Moderates?: Rethinking the Inclusion-Moderation Hypothesis" *World Politics* 63, no. 2 (April 2011): 1. Also see Jillian Schwedler's earlier work *Faith in Moderation: Islamist Parties in Jordan and Yemen* (Cambridge, NY: Cambridge University Press, 2006), 166.

56. Michael Fournie, "Al-Wasat and the Destiny of Moderate Islamists in Egypt," *Civil Society* (September 2005).

57. Bruce Rutherford "What Do Egypt's Islamists Want? Moderate Islam and the Rise of Islamic Constitutionalism," *Middle Eastern Journal* 60, no. 4 (2006): 724.

58. Fournie, "Al-Wasat." Also see Blaydes, *Elections and Distributive Politics,* 151.

59. Bruce Rutherford, *Egypt after Mubarak: Liberalism, Islam and Democracy in the Arab World* (Princeton: Princeton University Press, 2008), 177.

60. Lecture by Amr Hamzawy, "Islamists in Electoral Politics: Politics and Strategies of the Egyptian Muslim Brotherhood," *UCLA International Institute*, April 20, 2006.

61. Lisa Blaydes, *Elections and Distributive Politics,* 149.

62. Lisa Blaydes, *Elections and Distributive Politics,* 149

63. Schwedler, *Faith in Moderation,* 156.

64. Ibid. Also see Blaydes, *Elections and Distributive Politics,* 151.

65. Abed-Kotob, "The Accommodationists Speak: Goals and Strategies of the Muslim Brotherhood of Egypt," *International Journal of Middle East Studies* 27, no. 3 (1995): 331.

66. Schwedler, *Faith in Moderation,* 172.

67. Ibid.

68. Magdi Khalil, "Egypt's Muslim Brotherhood and the Political Power: Would Democracy Survive?" *Middle East Review of International Affairs Journal* 10, no. 3 (March 2006): 44–52.

69. Sadiki, "Re-constituting Egypt."

70. "Egyptians Increasingly Glum" Pew Global Attitudes Survey (Washington, DC, Pew Research Center) May 16, 2013.

## 5  Conditionalist Islamists: The Case of the Salafis

1. Roel Meijer, ed., *Global Salafism: Islam's New Religious Movement* (New York: Columbia University Press, 2009). This book represents an attempt to capture the various manifestations of Salafism around the Islamic world.

2. Quintan Wiktorowicz, "Anatomy of the Salafi Movement," *Studies in Conflict & Terrorism* 29 (2006): 207–39.

3. As quoted in Jami'at Ihyaa' Minhaaj al-Sunnah, *A Brief Introduction to the Salafi Da'wah* (Ipswich, Suffolk, UK: Jami'at Ihyaa' Minhaaj al-Sunnah, 1993), 3. There are many variations of this hadith. See Tirmidhi, 2:89.

4. Wiktorowicz, "Anatomy," 209.

5. This narration, with slight variations, is quoted by five of the six major classical-era Sunni hadith scholars.

6. David Commin, *The Wahhabi Mission and Saudi Arabia* (London: I.B. Tauris, 2006); Christopher M. Blanchard, "The Islamic Tradition of Wahhabism and Salafiyya," *Congressional Research Service*, RS21695, January 25, 2006. Stephane Lacroix uses "Wahhabi" to distinguish from the later "Muslim reformists," who also refer to themselves as *salafi*. See Stephane Lacroix, *Awakening Islam: The Politics of Religious Dissent in Contemporary Saudi Arabia* (Cambridge, MA: Harvard University Press, 2011), 10.

7. Lacroix, *Awakening Islam*, 10.

8. For the best scholarly treatment of Ibn Abd al-Wahab and his thought, please see Natania J. Delong-Bas, *Wahhabi Islam: From Revival and Reform to Global Jihad* (London: I.B. Tauris, 2004).

9. Al-Fahad, Abdulaziz H. " From Exclusivism to Accommodation: Doctrinal and Legal Evolution of Wahhabism." *NYUL Rev.* 79 (2004): 485..

10. Lacroix, *Awakening Islam*, 11.

11. Yossef Rapoport and Shahab Ahmed, *Ibn Taymiyah and His Times* (New York: Oxford University Press, 2010). For further examination of Ibn Abd al-Wahhab's thought, see Commin, *The Wahhabi Mission*; Abdulaziz al-Fahad, "From Exclusivism to Accommodation: Doctrine and Legal Evolution of Wahhabism," *New York University Law Review* 79, (2004): 485–879.

12. Abdul-Hakim al-Matroudi, *The Hanbali School of Law and Ibn Taymiyyah: Conflict or Conciliation* (London and New York: Routledge, 2006).

13. Malcolm Kerr, *Islamic Reform: The Political and Legal Theories of Muhammad Abduh and Rashid Rida* (Berkeley: University of California Press, 1966). Also see Nikki Keddie, *An Islamic Response to Imperialism: Political and Religious Writings of Sayyid Jamal ad-Din "al-Afghani"* (Berkeley: University of California Press, 1983).

14. Bernard Haykel, "On the Nature of Salafi Thought and Action," in *Global Salafism: Islam's New Religious Movement*, ed. Roel Meijer (New York: Columbia University Press, 2009), 34.

15. Ibid.

16. Ibid., 34–5.

17. "Saudi Arabia and the Muslim Brotherhood: Unexpected Adversaries," March 5, 2012. Stratfor, Austin, TX. Available online via subscription at: http://www.stratfor.com/analysis/saudi-arabia-and-muslim-brotherhood-unexpected-adversaries.

18. Lacroix, *Awakening Islam*.

19. Wiktorowicz, "Anatomy of the Salafi Movement," 207–39.

20. Amel Boubekeur, *Salafism and Radical Politics in Postconflict Algeria* (Washington, DC: Carnegie Endowment for International Peace, 2008).

21. Hassan Mneimneh, "The Spring of a New Political Salafism?" *Current Trends in Islamist Ideology* 12 (Washington, DC: Hudson Institute, 2011), 21–36.

22. Rasheed Madawi, *Contesting the Saudi State: Islamic Voices from a New Generation* (Cambridge, NY: Cambridge University Press, 2007).

23. "Salafist Unrest and the Threat to Tunisian Democracy," November 8, 2012. Stratfor, Austin, TX. Available online at: www.stratfor.com/analysis/salafist-unrest-and-threat-tunisian-democracy.

24. Prior to the 1990s, the rare case of Salafis engaged in political activism was in Pakistan. Ehsan Elahi Zaheer, a protégé of Saudi Arabia's mufti Abdulaziz bin Baz, founded the Jamiat Ahle Hadith (JAH) there in 1986. This was a way for the Saudis to insert a political proxy into the nation, which by then had returned to electoral politics after martial law had been lifted. The JAH never really took off, for it splintered into factions and saw the emergence of rival Salafi groups.

25. Lacroix, *Awakening Islam*.

26. Mamoun Fandy, *Saudi Arabia and the Politics of Dissent* (New York: St. Martin's Press, 1999). Also see R. Hrair Dekmejian, "The Rise of Political Islamism in Saudi Arabia," *Middle East Journal* 48, no. 4 (Autumn 1994): 629.

27. Fandy, *Saudi Arabia*.

28. Brynjar Lia, *Architect of Global Jihad: The Life of Al-Qaida Strategist Abu Mus?ab Al-Suri* (New York: Columbia University Press, 2008), 134–6.

29. The Saudi regime benefited greatly when the core of religious establishment labeled these politicized Salafi scholars followers of deviant Surouri/Qutbi/Ikhwani trends.

30. Steve L. Monroe, "Salafis in Parliament: Democratic Attitudes and Party Politics in the Gulf," *Middle East Journal* 66, no. 3 (2012): 409–24.

31. William McCants, "The Lesser of Two Evils: The Salafi Turn to Party Politics in Egypt," *Middle East Memo* (Washington, DC: The Brookings Institution, May 2012), 1–8.

32. Boubekeur, *Salafism & Radical Politics*, 2008.

33. Laurent Bonnefoy, *Salafism in Yemen: Transnationalism and Religious Identity* (New York: Columbia University Press, 2012).

34. Zaydis are a Shia sect largely found in Yemen and is actually closer to Sunni Islam than mainstream Twelver Shiism.

35. For the most pioneering analysis of the *sahwa* movement, see Lacroix, *Awakening Islam*.

36. William B. Quandt, *Between Ballots & Bullets: Algeria's Transition from Authoritarianism* (Washington, DC: The Brookings Institution, 1998); Daniel Brumberg, "Islam, Elections and Reform in Algeria," *Journal of Democracy* 2, no. 1 (1991): 58–71.

37. Fandy, *Saudi Arabia*. Also see R. Hrair Dekmejian, "The Rise of Political Islamism," 629.

38. Lacroix, *Awakening Islam*, 238.

39. The Carnegie Endowment for International Peace (Washington, DC: accessed March 18, 2013). http://egyptelections.carnegieendowment.org/2011/09/21/al-nour-light-party.

40. Kamran Bokhari, "Salafism and Arab Democratization," October 2, 2012. Stratfor: Austin, TX. http://www.stratfor.com/weekly/salafism-and-arab-democratization.

41. The Carnegie Endowment for International Peace (Washington, DC: accessed March 18, 2013). http://egyptelections.carnegieendowment.org/2011/09/21/al-nour-light-party.

42. William McCants, "The Lesser of Two Evils: The Salafi Turn to Party Politics in Egypt," *Middle East Memo* (Washington, DC: The Brookings Institution, May 2012), 1–8.

43. Fred Lawson, "Demands for Political Participation in the Arab Gulf States," *International Journal* 49, no. 2 (1994): 378–407.

44. Monroe, "Salafis in Parliament," 6.

45. Christian Caryl, "The Salafi Moment," *Foreign Policy* (September 12, 2012).www.foreignpolicy.com/articles/2012/09/12/the_salafi_moment.

46. "Hawla *ta'assuf ra'is hizb al-Nur 'ala 'adam tarashshuh nasrani fi qawa'im al-hizb* (On the apology of the president of the Nour Party for the lack of Christians on the party's lists)," Sawt al-Salaf, January 1, 2012, <http://www.salafvoice.com/article.php?

a=5914>. As quoted in Lacroix, Stéphane. "Sheikhs and Politicians: Inside the New Egyptian Salafism." *Policy Brief* (Brookings Doha Center June 2012).

47. *Al-Fath* (official mouthpiece of the Salafi Da'wa), January 4, 2012. As quoted in Lacroix, Stéphane. "Sheikhs and Politicians: Inside the New Egyptian Salafism." *Policy Brief* (Brookings Doha Center June 2012).

48. Aaron Y. Zelin, "Democracy, Salafi Style," *Foreign Policy*, (July 20, 2012). www. foreignpolicy.com/articles/2012/07/19/democracy_salafi_style.

49. Ibid.

50. Quintan Wiktorowicz details how different types of Salafis interpret the same texts to reach different prescriptions for sundry political situations.

51. The Carnegie Endowment for International Peace (Washington, DC: accessed March 18, 2013). http://egyptelections.carnegieendowment.org/2011/09/21/al-nour-light-party.

52. Ibid.

53. Ibid.

54. Ibid.

55. Zelin, "Democracy."

## 6  Rejector Islamists: al-Qaeda and Transnational Jihadism

1. Fawaz Gerges, *The Far Enemy: Why Jihad Went Global* (New York: Cambridge, 2005). Ayman al-Zawahiri, al-Qaeda's second-in-command, wrote *Bitter Harvest* when he was involved with the Tanzeem al-Jihad group in Egypt during the 1970s. In this treatise, he critiques the Muslim Brotherhood's approach.

2. The late Kalim Siddiqui coined and defined the term "Global Islamic Movement" to identify the various contemporary Islamic groups seeking to establish an Islamic polity. For an elaboration, see Kalim Siddiqui, *Stages of Islamic Revolution* (London: The Open Press, 1996).

3. For an in-depth historical background on jihadist movements, see John L. Esposito, *Unholy War: Terror in the Name of Islam* (New York: Oxford University Press, 2002).

4. Paul L. Heck. "Jihad Revisited". *Journal of Religious Ethics* Vol 32 Issue 1 p95-18 March 2004.

5. Abul A'la A. Mawdudi, *Jihad in Islam* (Pakistan: Islamic Publication, 1998). For a comparative perspective, see J. Kelsay and J. T. Johnson, eds., *Just War and Jihad: Historical and Theoretical Perspectives on War and Peace in Western and Islamic Traditions* (New York: Greenwood Press, 1991). Also see David Cook, *Understanding Jihad* (Berkeley: University of California Press, 2005).

6. Sayyid Qutb, *Ma'alim fi'l-Tariq* (Beirut: Dar al-Shuruq, 1991; originally published in 1964), 67–8, 82, as quoted in Roxanne L. Euben and Muhammad Qasim Zaman, eds., *Princeton Readings in Islamist Thought: Texts and Contexts from al-Banna to Bin Laden* (Princeton: Princeton University Press, 2009), 41.

7. Hugh Kennedy, *The Armies of the Caliphs: Military and Society in the Early Islamic State* (New York: Routledge, 2001).

8. Jarret M. Brackman, *Global Jihadism: Theory and Practice* (New York: Routledge, 2009), 5.

9. Most of the literature dealing with the origins of jihadi organizations attributes their emergence to the circumstances in the post-1967 Middle East. But in order to understand the sociopolitical and ideological antecedents that led to their emergence, it is essential to examine the Muslim Brotherhood's history, especially its experiences with

violence as a means to achieve their political objectives. Hence it is crucial to discuss 1948, when its members participated in the first Arab-Israeli war.

10. John Calvert, *Sayyid Qutb and the Origins of Radical Islamism* (New York: Columbia University Press, 2010).

11. Sayyid Qutb, *Milestones* (Plainfield: American Trust Publications, 1990).

12. Ziad Abu-Amr, *Islamic Fundamentalism in the West Bank & Gaza: Muslim Brotherhood & Islamic Jihad* (Bloomington and Indianapolis: Indiana University Press, 1994).

13. R. Hrair Dekmejian, *Islam in Revolution: Fundamentalism in the Arab World* (Syracuse: Syracuse University Press, 1985) provides a highly detailed account of Arab Islamist groups.

14. Peter Mandaville, *Global Political Islam* (New York: Routledge Press, 2007), 241.

15. Mohammed Abd al-Salam Faraj, "The Absent Duty," in *The Militant Prophet: The Revolutionaries,* ed. Rifaat Sayed Ahmed (London: Riad El-Rayyes Books, 1991), 2:137–49. [in Arabic]

16. Gerges, *The Far Enemy*, 10.

17. John L. Esposito, ed., *The Iranian Revolution: Its Global Impact* (Miami: University Presses of Florida, 1990).

18. Barnett R. Rubin, "Arab Islamists in Afghanistan," in *Political Islam: Revolution, Radicalism, or Reform?* ed. John L. Esposito (Boulder: Lynne Rienner Publishers, 1997), 179–206.

19. Mohammed Ayoob, "Political Islam: Image and Reality," *World Policy Journal* 21, no. 3 (Fall 2004): 4. Also see Ayman al-Zawahiri, *Knights under the Prophet's Banner* [in Arabic] (serialized by *Asharq al-Awsat*, December 12, 2001).

20. Fawaz Gerges, *Journey of the Jihadist: Inside Muslim Militancy* (Orlando, FL: Harcourt, 2006).

21. Gerges, *The Far Enemy* is the best work on this topic.

22. Moscow's deployment of troops in Afghanistan was not an invasion or occupation, but a response to the Marxist government's request for help.

23. Even while they were fighting, the Islamist insurgents knew that the goal of their armed struggle was not simply to expel the Soviet troops, but also to replace the Marxist regime with an Islamic one. We will analyze their view toward the latter elsewhere.

24. In many cases, the home governments gladly sent them to Afghanistan to fight the Soviets because this allowed them to export their radicalism problem as well. They expected many of the radicals to be killed. In any case, countries like Egypt wanted them gone and gladly obliged the United States, which had a major interest in raising a large fighting force to oppose the Soviet armed forces.

25. The struggle to unify Yemen during 1990–1994 was another example of Islamist militants being used for national security purposes. Before this event, North Yemen deployed many jihadists to fight the forces of Marxist South Yemen, which later on wanted to retract its decision to accept unification. After the war, many of these jihadists were inducted into the reunified country's intelligence service and security forces.

26. Thomas Hegghammer, "Global Jihadism after the Iraq War," *Middle East Journal* 60, no. 1 (January 2006): 11–32.

27. Strong evidence suggests the presence of considerable friction between the Taliban and al-Qaeda even when the former was hosting the latter on Afghan soil. This was because the Taliban's nationalist jihadism conflicted with al-Qaeda's transnational agenda.

28. Fawaz Gerges, *The Rise and Fall of Al-Qaeda* (New York: Oxford University Press, 2011).

29. Thomas Hegghammer, *Jihad in Saudi Arabia: Violence and Pan-Islamism since 1979* (New York: Cambridge University Press, 2010).

30. Michael Willis, *The Islamist Challenge in Algeria: A Political History* (New York: New York University Press, 1996).

31. Ibid.

32. Pervez Musharraf, "A Plea for Enlightened Moderation," *Washington Post* (June 1, 2004): A23.

33. A January 2013 Pew study shows that some 60 percent of Pakistanis favor a strong ruler over democracy.

34. Gerges, *The Rise and Fall,* 4.

35. Ibid.

36. There is also a situation in which the regime is evolving but collapse is not inevitable (e.g., Yemen), given that institutions (especially the military) are weak but salvageable. Jihadists have a significant presence within both the withering Yemeni state and society. While the country has institutions, splits within the military could cause an institutional breakdown. Such a scenario could thus provide the kind of opening that jihadists hope to exploit.

37. Robert S. Leiken and Steven Brooke, "The Moderate Muslim Brotherhood" *Foreign Affairs* 86, no. 2 (March–April 2007): 111.

38. At best, the Taliban represent an exception to the jihadist paradigm in the sense that while they did establish an Islamic polity via an armed struggle, their ascension to power was more a result of the chaos that prevailed in Afghanistan since the beginning of the Islamic insurgency against the communist takeover in 1978. For a detailed account of the Taliban, see Ahmed Rashid, *Taliban: Militant Islam, Oil, and Fundamentalism in Central Asia* (New Haven: Yale University Press, 2001).

39. For a detailed treatment, see "The Forgotten Recantation" at http://www.jihadica.com/the-forgotten-recantation/ Posted: January 8, 2010 by Nelly Lahoud.

40. Tom Perry, Reuters, March 18, 2011, http://www.reuters.com/article/2011/03/18/us-egypt-islamist-militancy-idUSTRE72H62820110318.

41. Ibid.

42. Ibid.

43. Jarret Brachman, "Leading Egyptian Jihadist Sayyid Imam Renounces Violence" *CTC Sentinel* (December 15, 2007), http://www.ctc.usma.edu/posts/leading-egyptian-jihadist-sayyid-imam-renounces-violence

44. The fact that many current Muslim Brotherhood leaders such as Essam el-Erian and former leader Abdul-Monem Abul Futouh (who has become more liberal than the MB) came from Gamaah al-Islamiyah in the 1970s proves that the two groups' attitudes toward democracy were not so different.

45. Jordanian Salafi-jihadist ideologue Abu Muhammad al-Maqdisi's treatise "Democracy: A Religion!" is a key example of such thinking.

46. The Carnegie Endowment for International Peace (Washington, DC). For further detail, see http://egyptelections.carnegieendowment.org/2011/09/20/al-banna'-wa-al-tanmiyya-building-and-development-party

47. Ibid.

48. Ibid. Accessed on March 20, 2013.

## 7    Rejector Islamists: Taliban and Nationalist Jihadism

1. The Taliban's participation in the American-led international talks toward a post-NATO power-sharing agreement suggests that they are open to some form of mainstream political participation.

2. The *Wall Street Journal* reported on December 6, 2011, that Taliban chief Mullah Omar sent emissaries to Paris to meet with representatives of the movement's former foe: the Northern Alliance.

3. A December 6, 2012, Reuters report, quoting unnamed Pakistani military sources, states that the Pakistani Taliban rebel grouping known as Tehrik-i-Taliban is on the verge of changing its leadership. It is posited that a more moderate leadership will emerge, one that will facilitate reconciliation with Islamabad.

4. For a full treatment of the distinction between transnational and nationalist jihadists, see Fawaz Gerges, *The Far Enemy: Why Jihad Went Global* (New York: Cambridge University Press, 2005).

5. Mullah Omar's communiqué on the occasion of Eid al-Fitr in August 2011. http://www.informationclearinghouse.info/article28997.htm

6. Ibid.

7. According to classical Muslim political thought, an emirate is a geographically limited polity ruled by a particular dynasty. In contrast with the caliphate, it also has local authority.

8. Dennis O. Young, "Overcoming the Obstacles to Establishing a Democratic State in Afghanistan," *Report* (Carlisle: Strategic Studies Institute, 2007), 5–6.

9. The war against the Soviets and their Afghan proxy regime, or the "Afghan jihad" according to its supporters, empowered the Afghan *mujahideen* and played a pivotal role in the rise of national jihadism both in the Arab/Muslim world and in its international transnational form. See Vali R. Nasr, "The Rise of Sunni Militancy in Pakistan: The Changing Role of Islamism and the Ulama in Society and Politics," *Modern Asian Studies* 34 (2000): 139–80.

10. The Saur Revolution refers to the April 1978 communist takeover of political power from the government in Afghanistan.

11. The exact numbers are probably buried deep in the bowels of the Inter-Services Intelligence directorate's headquarters, Pakistan's foreign intelligence service. It is generally believed that hundreds (if not thousands) of Jamaat-i-Islami volunteers, mostly from its student wing (viz., Islami Jamiat-i-Talaba) fought in the Afghan war along with thousands of others from smaller but more radical Islamist outfits.

12. In a 1997 interview, an emissary of Taliban in London told the lead author that the movement did not see its government as a caliphate and that Mullah Omar was a local figure whose authority was confined to Afghanistan's political boundaries, as opposed to the leader of all Muslims.

13. Maulvi Wakil Ahmed Muttawakil, the Taliban foreign minister who surrendered to American military forces shortly after the regime's fall in late 2001, is on record as opposing the leadership's decision to allow al-Qaeda and other foreign jihadist groups a free reign in the country.

14. Northern Alliance leader Ahmed Shah Massoud was assassinated on September 9, 2001, by two al-Qaeda operatives of North African origin posing as a European media crew seeking to interview him. This is one of the more noteworthy examples of how al-Qaeda helped the Taliban, given that the latter at the time in question was a militia force and not versed in the art of urban terrorism—certainly not suicide bombing.

15. For a comprehensive treatment of the 2001 invasion of Afghanistan, see George Friedman, *America's Secret War* (New York: Doubleday, 2004).

16. "Afghanistan, Pakistan: The Battlespace of the Border," STRATFOR. October 14, 2008, https://www.stratfor.com/analysis/afghanistan-pakistan-battlespace-border.

17. The offensive launched in the fall of 2009 was initially confined to South Waziristan. By early 2010, however, it had expanded to all of the Federally Administered Tribal

Area's agencies except North Waziristan, where the Afghan Taliban's Haqqani Network is based. It also is home to tribal militia leader Hafiz Gul Bahadur, who has a neutrality agreement with Islamabad and whose fighters are busy in eastern Afghanistan.

18. Christine C. Fair, Neil Malhotra, and Jacob N. Shapiro, "Democratic Values and Support for Militant Politics: Evidence from a National Survey of Pakistan," *Report* (Princeton: Princeton University, November 27, 2012).

19. Fernando Lujan, "How to Get Afghans to Trust Us Once Again," *The Washington Post*, March 2, 2012, www.washingtonpost.com/opinions/how-to-get-afghans-to-trust-us-onceagain/2012/03/01/gIQAfhZ9mR_story.html.

20. Alia Brahimi, "The Taliban's Evolving Ideology," *Working Paper* WP 02/2010 (London School of Economics: July 2010), 5.

21. Pierre Tristam, "The Taliban in Its Own Words: Democracy and Negotiations Are against Sharia Law: No Deliberative Process, No Exceptions," http://middleeast.about.com/od/afghanistan/qt/me080903.htm.

22. Kamran Bokhari interview in Kabul with former Afghan prime minister Ahmed Shah Ahmedzai, December 2011.

23. Mullah Omar's communiqué on the occasion of Eid al-Fitr in August 2011, http://www.informationclearinghouse.info/article28997.htm.

## 8  Participatory Shia Islamism: The Islamic Republic of Iran

1. We confine our discussion to the mainstream Twelver Shia, because it is the dominant group and the only one with a vibrant Islamist tendency.

2. Abdolkarim Soroush, *Reason, Freedom, and Democracy in Islam: Essential Writings of Abdolkarim Soroush*, tr. Mahmoud and Ahmad Sadri (New York: Oxford University Press, 2002).

3. The doctrine as we know it today began to develop under the Abbasids. However, it grew out of the initial idea that Ali deserved to succeed Muhammad as the community's ruler because, among other reasons, of his closeness to the Prophet due to familial ties.

4. Antony Black, *The History of Islamic Political Thought: From the Prophet to the Present*, 2nd ed. (Edinburgh: Edinburgh University Press, 2011).

5. Allamah Sayyid Muhammad Husayn Tabataba'i, *Shiite Islam*, tr. Seyyed Hossein Nasr (Albany: State University of New York, 1979) offers a rather comprehensive account of the evolution of Shia thought.

6. Abdulaziz Sachedina, *Islamic Messianism: The Idea of the Mahdi in Twelver Shi'ism* (Albany: State University of New York, 1981).

7. Mohammad Ali Amir-Moezzi, *The Divine Guide in Early Shi'ism: The Sources of Esotericism in Islam*, tr. David Streight (Albany: State University of New York, 1994).

8. Abdulaziz Sachedina, *The Just Ruler in Shi'ite Islam: The Comprehensive Authority of the Jurist in Imamite Jurisprudence* (New York: Oxford University Press, 1998).

9. Mohammad Ali Amir-Moezzi, *The Spirituality of Shi'i Islam: Belief and Practices* (London: I.B. Tauris, 2011).

10. Andrew J. Newman, *The Formative Period of Twelver Shi'ism: Hadith as Discourse between Qum and Baghdad* (Richmond: Curzon2010).

11. Tamima Bayhom-Daou, *Shaykh Mufid* (Oxford: Oneworld, 2005).

12. Moojan Momen, *An Introduction to Shi'i Islam: The History and Doctrines of Twelver Shi'ism* (New Haven: Yale University, 1987).

13. Seyyed Hossein Nasr, Hamid Dabashi and Seyyed Vali Reza Nasr, *Expectation of the Millennium: Shi'ism in History* (Albany: State University of New York, 1989).

14. For a comprehensive background on Bihbihani's role in the Usuli triumph, see Zachary M. Heern, *Usuli Shi'ism: The Emergence of and Islamic Reform Movement in Early Modern Iran and Iraq* (Ph.D. diss. submitted to the University of Utah, 2011). Electronic copy available at http://www.scribd.com/doc/68940894/24/Mulla-Ahmad-Naraqi.

15. Linda S. Walbridge, *The Most Learned of the Shi'a: The Institution of the Marja' Taqlid* (New York: Oxford University Press, 2001).

16. Said Arjomand,. *The Shadow of God and the Hidden Imam: Religion, Political Order, and Societal Change in Shi'ite Iran from the Beginning to 1890* (Chicago: The University of Chicago Press, 2010).

17. Said Arjomand, ed., *Authority and Political Culture in Shi'ism* (Albany: State University of New York, 1988). This book traces the historical evolution of Shia political thought.

18. For a rendition of the intellectual developments during the Qajar period, see Nikki R. Keddie, *Qajar Iran and the Rise of Reza Khan: 1796–1925* (Costa Mesa: Mazda Publishers, 1999); and Ervand Abrahamian, *A History of Modern Iran* (Cambridge, New York: Cambridge University Press, 2008). This latter book focuses on the Pahlavi dynasty and links the Islamic republic with the defining epoch of the Qajars.

19. Nikki R. Keddie, *Religion and Politics in Iran: Shi'ism from Quietism to Revolution* (New Haven: Yale University Press, 1984).

20. Ruhollah Khomeini, *Islam and Revolution: Writings and Declarations of Imam Khomeini (1941–1980)*, tr. Hamid Algar (New York: Mizan Press, 1981).

21. Said Arjomand, *Iran between Two Revolutions* (Princeton: Princeton University Press, 1982).

22. Ali Shariati had a profound influence on the revolution and continues to inspire Iran's democratic-minded forces. He therefore deserves far greater space than the scope of this book allows. For a better appreciation of his contribution to the discourse, see Ali Rahnema, *An Islamic Utopian: A Political Biography of Ali Shariati* (London: I.B. Tauris, 2000); and Kingshuk Chatterjee, *'Ali Shari'ati and the Shaping of Political Islam in Iran* (New York: Palgrave MacMillan, 2011).

23. Hamid Enayat, *Modern Islamic Political Thought* (London: I.B. Tauris, 2005) devotes considerable space to contemporary Shia political thought.

24. Being a Sunni Islamist theoretician, Maududi's view of theo-democracy differed from Khomeini's vision of *velayat-e-faqih*, especially since Sunni Islam does not view the ulema as a clergy in the sense of a go-between for God and humanity.

25. There are some key omissions, however. Azerbaijan, although a major Shia-majority country, is by and large a secular state and society owing to its historical experience as part of the former Soviet Union. Its Islamists constitute an insignificant minority. We therefore decided not to include it in our study. Likewise, there are multiple Shia Islamist forces in Saudi Arabia, Pakistan, Afghanistan, and elsewhere. In each case, this branch of Islam and, more notably, its ideological actors represent a minority. Hence we felt that a full treatment of them was not necessary; however, some of them will be mentioned parenthetically.

26. Said Amir Arjomand, *After Khomeini: Iran under His Successors* (New York: Oxford University Press, 2009).

27. http://www.stratfor.com/analysis/iran-presidential-election-and-metamorphosis.

28. http://www.stratfor.com/analysis/islamic-revolutionary-guard-corps-part-1-unconventional-military.

29. In the 1992 election, the reformist Combatant Clergy Association won 150 of the 270 seats, while the remaining 120 went to independents. In other words, the conservatives were not just a numerical minority but also were not organized in the form of a party. In the 1996 polls, the reformists made further gains when the Combatant Clergy

Association won 110 seats while the Servants of Iran's Construction won another 80 seats.

30. Gilles Kepel, "Islamism Reconsidered," *Harvard International Review* 22, no. 2 (2000): 22–8.

31. http://www.stratfor.com/analysis/iranian-leaders-square-over-intelligence

32. http://www.pbs.org/wgbh/pages/frontline/tehranbureau/2011/08/what-to-wear-state-run-daily-stirs-controversy-with-special-section-on-hejab.html

33. http://www.pbs.org/wgbh/pages/frontline/tehranbureau/2011/05/opinion-ahmadinejad-khamenei-rift-deepens-to-an-abyss.html

34. http://www.bloomberg.com/news/2010-08-10/iran-forces-chief-of-staff-criticizes-ahmadinejad-aide-over-islam-remarks.html

35. http://www.aei.org/article/foreign-and-defense-policy/regional/middle-east-and-north-africa/ahmadinejad-versus-the-clergy/

36. Kamran Bokhari. "Geopolitical Journey: Iran At Crossroads" *Stratfor*. Austin, TX. Sept 27, 2011.

37. "Iran's Khamenei Says Irked by Officials Infighting" . *AFP*, Tehran. Feb 16, 2013.

38. Having a council replace the supreme leader is something that Rafsanjani has long been advocating. See Nader, Alireza, David E. Thaler and S. R. Bohandy. The Next Supreme Leader: Succession in the Islamic Republic of Iran. Santa Monica, CA: RAND Corporation, 2011. http://www.rand.org/pubs/monographs/MG1052. Also available in print form.

39. Mehdi Khalaji. " Supreme Succession: Who Will Lead Post-Khamenei Iran?" *Policy Focus* 117 (Washington, DC: The Washington Institute for Near East Policy). February 2012.

40. Mazyar Mokfi and Charles Recknagel. "How Could Iran's Hard Liners Choose The Next Supreme Leader?" Radio Free Europe/Radio Liberty. July 04, 2009

## 9   Arab Shia Islamism: Iraqi Shia Islamists and Hezbollah

1. Bahrain's largest Shia movement, Jamiyat al-Wefaq al-Watani al-Islamiyah, which is also its largest political group, represents yet another case of Arab Shia Islamism in the making. Founded in 2001 and led by a cleric, it has aligned with secular groups seeking greater democratization. In the two elections it has participated in since 2006, it has emerged as the largest bloc in parliament. In the wake of the Arab Spring, it tried to leverage its position in Parliament and via the protests to seek a constitutional monarchy. Other more radical Shia Islamist elements within the opposition wanted to replace the monarchy with a republic. Given the country's geographical, sectarian, and ideological proximity to Iran, the Arab Spring in Bahrain quickly devolved from a struggle for democracy into a geopolitical sectarian struggle. Not wanting to see Iran gain a geopolitical outpost on its side of the Persian Gulf, Saudi Arabia and its Gulf Cooperation Council (GCC) allies intervened militarily to quell the largely Shia-led protests. Along with the Sunni mercenaries recruited by the royal family from non-GCC Arab states and Pakistan, the protests were quelled violently within a few months. Despite the major crackdown, however, al-Wefaq has steered clear of employing any extraconstitutional means. Thus the government in recent months has renewed dialogue with the Shia Islamist movement. That said, the movement is only 12 years old and, given the geosectarian stakes, its future trajectory remains unclear. Thus we will not attempt to provide an in-depth examination. We merely note that it is an example of a budding Shia Islamist democratic movement.

2. Many secular Shias were involved in the Baath Party, but there was never a substantive secular force that represented Shia communal interests. Even after Saddam's overthrow, there was no room for secular Shia parties because Islamists dominated the opposition and filled the political vacuum. There are a few prominent secular Shia politicians, such as former interim premier Iyad Allawi, whose nonsectarian centrist stance has forced him to align his Iraqi National Accord party with largely Sunni factions in order to challenge the Shia Islamists. His bloc is known as al-Iraqiyah. Ahmed Chalabi, another prominent secular Shia figure who until 2004 was very close to Washington, has all along been aligned with the Islamists, given his sectarian leanings and his ties to Iran.

3. Juan R. Cole, "The Ayatollahs and Democracy in Iraq," *ISIM Paper* 7 (Leiden: Amsterdam University Press, 2006).

4. During the 1990s Grand Ayatollah Mohammed Sadiq al-Sadr, the founder of the Iraq's Sadrite movement who otherwise resisted Iranian interference in Iraqi Shia affairs, briefly adopted the idea of *velayat-e-faqih* and declared himself the *wali faqih* of Iraq's Shias. Iran severed its ties with him. See "Iraq's Muqtada Al-Sadr: Spoiler or Stabiliser?" *Crisis Group Middle East Report* 55, no. 11 (July 2006).

5. Thomas Collelo, "Lebanon: A Country Study," in *Lebanon: Current Issues and Background,* ed. John C. Rolland (Hauppauge: Nova Science Publishers, 2003), 29–179.

6. Fouad Ajami, *The Vanished Imam: Musa al Sadr and the Shia of Lebanon* (Ithaca: Cornell University Press, 1987).

7. Helena Cobban, "Hizbullah's New Face: The Search for a Muslim Democracy," *Boston Review* April/May 2005. http://bostonreview.net/BR30.2/cobban.php.

8. Hamzeh, A. Nizar, *In the Path of Hizbullah* (Syracuse, NY: Syracuse University Press, 2004).

9. For detailed accounts of the groups' transformation from being a purely militant to a political one, see Richard Augustus Norton, *Hezbollah: A Short History* (Princeton: Princeton University Press, 2007); Judith Palmer Harik, *Hezbollah: The Changing face of Terrorism* (London: I.B. Tauris, 2005). Also see Sami G Hajjar, *Hizballah: Terrorism, National Liberation, or Menace?* (Carlisle: Strategic Studies Institute, U.S. Army War College, 2002).

10. Lara Deeb, "Hizbullah: A Primer," Washington, DC, *MERIP*, July 31, 2006. http://www.merip.org/mero/mero073106.

11. "Syria: Sowing Discord within Hezbollah?" January 4, 2010. Stratfor: Austin, TX. Available online via subscription at http://www.stratfor.com/analysis/israel-syria-direct-talks-and-hezbollahs-demise.

12. Kevin Simon, "Hezbollah: Terror in Context," 2012 AHS Capstone Projects. Paper 18. http://digitalcommons.olin.edu/ahs_capstone_2012/18.

13. Rodger Shanahan, "Shia Political Development in Iraq: The Case of the Islamic Dawa Party," *Third World Quarterly* 25, no. 5 (2004): 943–54.

14. Since its founding in 1982 until 2007, the group's name was the Supreme Council of the Islamic Revolution in Iraq (SCIRI). It then changed its name to the Islamic Supreme Council of Iraq (ISCI) in order to reflect its new position as an Iraqi group seeking to work within the democratic framework of post-Baathist state. See "Iraq: Transforming Iran's Shiite Proxy, Assisting the United States," May 11, 2007. Austin, TX: Stratfor. Available online via subscription at: http://www.stratfor.com/analysis/iraq-transforming-irans-shiite-proxy-assisting-united-states. In this work, we refer to the group by its new name. Likewise, after 2003 a large group of militiamen from the group's armed wing, the Badr Corps, were incorporated into the Interior Ministry's security forces while the entity itself was transformed into a political group, the Badr Organization, which eventually became independent from ISCI.

15. Marisa Cochrane, *The Fragmentation of the Sadrist Movement* (Washington, DC: Institute for the Study of War, January 2009), Iraq Report, 12.

16. Mahan Abedin, "The Sadrist Movement," *Middle East Intelligence Bulletin* 5, no. 7 (July 2003).

17. Leslie C. Longtin, *Restoring Medinat al-Salaam: The Rise of Muqtada al-Sadr's Jaysh al-Mahdi*. M.A. in Liberal Studies Thesis submitted in 2010 at Georgetown University, Washington, DC.

18. Patrick Cockburn, *Muqtada: Muqtada Al-Sadr, The Shia Revival, and The Struggle for Iraq* (New York: Scribner, 2008).

19. Robert C. Hunter, *Brothers or Rivals? Iran and the Shi'a of Iraq*. M.A. in National Security Affairs Thesis submitted in June 2006 at the Naval Postgraduate School, Monterrey, CA.

20. Soren Schmidt, "The Role of Religion in Politics: The Case of Shia Islamism in Iraq," *Nordic Journal of Religion and Society* 22, no. 2 (2009): 123–43.

21. "Iraq: Al-Sadr Navigates through a Shiite Division," August 25, 2005. Stratfor: Austin. TX. Available online via subscription at: http://www.stratfor.com/analysis/iraq-al-sadr-navigates-through-shiite-division.

22. "Iraq's Shifting Shiite Power Structure," June 7, 2004. Stratfor: Austin, TX. Available online via subscription at: http://www.stratfor.com/analysis/iraqs-shifting-shiite-power-structure.

23. In addition to being involved in the regime-change efforts and the post-Saddam transition, Dawah and ISCI gained a disproportionate amount of control over the Shia alliance because they operated through the two separate parties. Dawah's share of seats was divided between the main Dawah party and its breakaway faction, Hizb al-Dawah–Tandheem al-Iraq. Similarly, ISCI had its own allotment and separate seats for its former military wing, the Badr Organization.

24. The Sunni boycott of the polls led to the UIA and the Kurdish Alliance winning a disproportionate amount of seats. The Shia and the Kurdish blocs won 140 and 75 (out of a total of 275), respectively, while Allawi's Iraqi List won 40 seats.

25. The UIA was largely but not exclusively Arab Shia Islamist, for other ethnic and religious groups had token representation as well.

26. "Iraq: Signs of Sunni Unity and Shiite Disunity," October 27, 2005. Stratfor: Austin, TX. Available online via subscription at http://www.stratfor.com/analysis/iraq-signs-sunni-unity-and-shiite-disunity.

27. The compromise over the security posts ensured that no major Shia party got any of these three positions. SCIRI had to give up interior to an independent UIA member Jawad Bolani, who had been affiliated with several Shia Islamist groups (mostly small ones). National security remained in the hands of the splinter of Dawah, Hizb al-Dawah–Tandheem al-Iraq, with Shirwan al-Waeli assuming the post from Abdul Karim al-Anizi. Defense remained under Sunni control, but was given to an independent backed by the main Sunni parliamentary bloc, Abdul Qadir Obaidi, who had served under Saddam but fell out with him after the 1991 Gulf War.

28. The three-member Presidency Council was established by Transitional Administrative Law (TAL), signed in March 2004 by the Iraqi Governing Council. It took effect when the CPA transferred limited authority in June 2004 to the Allawi-led Interim government. Giving the presidency to the Kurds was part of the broader power-sharing agreement made in the lead-up to signing the TAL. It was an effort to give the ethnic minority, which was more interested in regional autonomy, a major stake in the federal

government. The two rival sects were given a stake in the Presidency Council by having a vice-president representing both the Shia and the Kurds. This formula was first operationalized after the transnational parliament elected in January 2005 PUK chief Jalal Talabani as president with ISCI No. 2 Adel Abdul Mahdi and major tribal chief Ghazi al-Yawer as the Shia and Sunni VPs, respectively.

29. "Iraq: Tehran's Shiite Housekeeping and U.S. Talks," April 16, 2007. Stratfor: Austin, TX. Available online via subscription at www.stratfor.com/analysis/iraq-tehrans-shiite-housekeeping-and-us-talks.

30. "Iraq: The Provincial Elections and Al-Maliki's New Prospects," February 5, 2009. http://www.stratfor.com/analysis/iraq-provincial-elections-and-al-malikis-new-prospects

31. Kurdish–Shia relations had deteriorated over the years, particularly since al-Maliki's rise because of the dispute over the KRG's demand for energy autonomy. Baghdad had opposed this since 2005, when the constitution was being drafted.

32. Lina Khatib, "Hizbullah's Political Strategy," *Survival: Global Politics and Strategy* 53, no. 2 (2011): 65.

33. Hizbullah, "Identity and Goals," 2004, reproduced in Joseph Al-Agha, "Shifts in Hizbullah's Ideology," doctoral dissertation, Free University of Amsterdam, 2006, 245 as quoted in Khatib, "Hizbullah's Political Strategy," 62–3.

34. Khatib, "Hizbullah's Political Strategy," 63.

35. Ibid., 61–76.

36. Nicholas Blandford, *Killing Mr. Lebanon: The Assassination of Rafik Hariri and Its Impact on the Middle East* (London: I.B. Tauris, 2009), 190, as mentioned in Khatib, "Hizbullah's Political Strategy," 61–76.

37. Naim Qassem, *Hizballah: Al-Manhaj, al-Tajribah, al-Mustaqbal* (Beirut: Dar al-Hadi, 2008), 290.

38. Hizbullah, "Manifesto," 23, as quoted in Khatib, "Hizbullah's Political Strategy," 62.

39. Robert G. Rabil, "Hezbollah, the Islamic Association, and Lebanon's Confessional System," *The Levantine Review* 1, no. 1 (Spring 2012), 49–67.

40. Amin Elias, "Qira'a fi Wathiqatayy Tayyar al-Mustaqbal wa Hizbillah: Al-Watan al-Ghamidh," *An-Nahar*, October 25, 2010, www.annahar.com; Hizbullah Manifesto, 2009, reproduced in Ziad Majed, *Hezbollah and the Shiite Community: From Political Confessionalization to Confessional Specialization* (Washington, DC: The Aspen Institute, 2010), 21–4.

## 10   Post-Islamism: The Case of Turkey's AKP

1. Ahmet T. Kuru, "Globalization and Diversification of Islamic Movements: Three Turkish Cases," *Political Science Quarterly* 120, no. 2 (2005): 253–74, 273. For an overview of how institutional constraints and democratic rewards helped the transformation, see R. Quinn Mecham, "From the Ashes of Virtue, A Promise of Light: The Transformation of Political Islam in Turkey," *Third World Quarterly* 25, no. 2 (2004): 339–58.

2. Ihsan Yilmaz, "AK Party between Post-Islamism and Non-Islamism: A Critical Analysis of the Turkish Islamism's Transformation," (February 27, 2011). Available at SSRN: http://ssrn.com/abstract=1771905

3. Ahmet T. Kuru "Changing Perspectives on Islamism and Secularism in Turkey: The Gülen Movement and the AK Party," in *Muslim World in Transition: Contributions of the Gülen Movement*, ed. Ihsan Yilmaz. (London: Leeds Metropolitan University Press, 2007), 140–51, 141.

4. Ahmet T. Kuru, "Muslim Politics without an 'Islamic' State: Can Turkey's Justice and Development Party Be a Model for Arab Islamists?" *Policy Briefing*, February 21 (Washington, DC: Brookings Doha Center, 2013).
5. Banu Eligur, *The Mobilization of Political Islam in Turkey* (New York: Cambridge University Press, 2010), 1.
6. Ibid., 277.
7. Mustafa Akyol, "The Turkish Model," *The Cairo Review of Global Affairs* (Cairo: The American University in Cairo).
8. Ruqen Cakir, *Ayet ve Slogan* (Verse and Ideology) (Istanbul: Meti, Yayinlari, 1990), 290, as mentioned in Metin Heper, "Islam and Democracy in Turkey: Towards a Reconciliation," *Middle East Journal* 51, no. 1 (Winter 1997): 43.
9. Yilmaz, "AK Party between Post-Islamism and Non-Islamism," 267.
10. Ibid., 259.
11. Jenny B. White, *Islamist Mobilization in Turkey: A Study in Vernacular Politics* (Washington, DC: University of Washington Press, 2002).
12. Banu Eligur, *Mobilization*, 1.
13. "Geopolitical Diary: The Power Struggle between Turkey's Military and the AK," March 2, 2007. Stratfor: Austin, TX. Available online via subscription at http://www.stratfor.com/geopolitical-diary/geopolitical-diary-power-struggle-between-turkeys-military-and-ak.
14. Eligur, *Mobilization*, 1.
15. "Geopolitical Diary: Envisioning Turkey under the AK Presidency," August 29, 2007. Stratfor: Austin, TX. Available via subscription at www.stratfor.com/geopolitical-diary/geopolitical-diary-envisioning-turkey-under-ak-presidency.
16. "Turkey: Taking the Army's Prerogative," August 5, 2010. Stratfor: Austin, TX. Available via subscription at http://www.stratfor.com/analysis/turkey-taking-armys-prerogative
17. Kuru, Ahmet. "Muslim Politics without an 'Islamic' State."
18. Eligur, *Mobilization*, 281.
19. Asef Bayat, "The Coming of a Post-Islamist Society," *Critical Middle East Studies* (Fall 1996): 43–52.
20. Gilles Kepel, "Islamism Reconsidered," *Harvard International Review* 22, no. 2 (Summer 2000): 22–7.
21. Olivier Roy, "Le post-islamisme," *Revue des Mondes Musulmans et de la Méditerranée* (1998): 85–6, 11–30. Also see Olivier Roy, "The Transformation of the Arab World," *Journal of Democracy* 23, no. 3 (July 2012): 5–18.
22. Henri Lauzire, "Post-Islamism and the Religious Discourse of Abd al-Salam Yasin," *International Journal of Middle East Studies* 37, no. 2 (2005): 241–61.
23. Amel Boubekeur, "Post-Islamist Culture: A New Form of Mobilization?" *History of Religions* 47, no. 1 (2007): 75–94.
24. Mojtaba Mahdavi, "Post-Islamist Trends in Postrevolutionary Iran," *Comparative Studies of South Asia, Africa, and the Middle East* 31, no. 1 (2011): 94.
25. Husnul Amin, *From Islamism to Post-Islamism: A Study of a New Intellectual Discourse on Islam and Modernity in Pakistan*, PhD dissertation, Erasmus University Rotterdam, 2010.
26. Bayat, "Post-Islamist Society," 44–6.
27. Asef Bayat, *Making Islam Democratic: Social Movements and the Post-Islamist Turn* (Stanford, CA: Stanford University Press, 2007), 95.
28. "Turkey's Historic Civilian-Military Power Shift," July 30, 2011. Stratfor: Austin, TX. http://www.stratfor.com/analysis/turkey%E2%80%99s-historic-civilian-military-power-shift
29. Heper, "Islam and Democracy in Turkey," 32–45.

## 11  Conclusion: Prospects for Muslim Democracies

1. Seyyed Vali Reza Nasr, "The Rise of 'Muslim Democracy,' " *Journal of Democracy* 16, no. 2 (April 2005), 13–27.
2. Carrie R. Wickham, *The Muslim Brotherhood: Evolution of an Islamist Movement* (Princeton: Princeton University Press, 2013).
3. *The World's Muslims: Religion, Politics, and Society* (Washington, DC: Pew Research Center, April 30, 2013).
4. Hisham Hellyer, "Rendering Unto the State: What Role do Egyptians Want for Religion?" (Royal United Services Institute London, UK), September 18, 2013.
5. Stephanie McCrummen, "In Egypt, a campaign to promote an 'Egyptian Islam'" *Washington Post*, October 10, 2013.
6. *The World's Muslims: Religion, Politics, and Society* (Washington, DC: Pew Research Center, April 30, 2013).
7. Asef Bayat (ed.) *Post-Islamism: The Many Faces of Political Islam* (Oxford: Oxford University Press, 2013).
8. Nathan J. Brown. "Egypt's Failed Transition". *Journal of Democracy* vol. 24; no 4 (Washington, DC: National Endowment for Democracy and The Johns Hopkins University Press, October 2013), pp.45–58.
9. Shmuel Eisenstadt (ed.). *Multiple Modernities* (Rutgers, NJ: Transaction Publishers, 2002).
10. Alfred Stepan, "The Multiple Secularisms of Modern Democracies and Autocracies," in *Rethinking Secularism,* ed. Craig Calhoun, Mark Juergensmeyer, and Jonathan VanAntwerpen (Oxford, New York: Oxford University Press, 2011)
11. Olivier Roy, *The Failure of Political Islam* (New York: Harvard University Press, originally published in 1994, reprinted in 2007).
12. Olivier Roy, "The Transformation of the Arab World," *Journal of Democracy* 23, no. 3 (July 2012), 5–18.
13. Olivier Roy "There Will Be No Islamist Revolution," *Journal of Democracy* 24, no. 1 (January 2013), 14–19.
14. Ibid.
15. Ahmet T. Kuru, "A Research Note on Islam, Democracy, Secularism," *Insight Turkey* 11, no. 4 (2009): 29–40.

# Bibliography

Abd al-Salam Faraj, Mohammed. "The Absent Duty," in *The Militant Prophet: The Revolutionaries,* ed. Rifaat Sayed Ahmed (London: Riad El-Rayyes Books, 1991), 2: 137–49. [in Arabic] *Abd al-Wahhab* (Riyadh: Jami'at al-Imam Muhammad bin Sa'ud al-Islamiyya, 1976), 1:153–81.

Abdullahi A. An-Na'im. *Islam and the Secular State: Negotiating the Future of Shari'a* (Cambridge: Harvard University Press, 2008).

Abedin, Mahan. "The Sadrist Movement," *Middle East Intelligence Bulletin* 5, no. 7 (July 2003).

Abed-Kotob, Sana. "The Accommodationists Speak: Goals and Strategies of the Muslim Brotherhood of Egypt," *International Journal of Middle East Studies* 27, no. 3 (1995): 331.

Abrahamian, Ervand. *A History of Modern Iran* (Cambridge, NY: Cambridge University Press, 2008). http://www.amazon.com/History-Modern-Iran-Ervand-Abrahamian /dp/0521528917/ref=sr_1_1?ie=UTF8&qid=1384224435& sr=8-1&keywords=A+ History+of+Modern+Iran#reader_0521528917

Abu-Amr, Ziad. *Islamic Fundamentalism in the West Bank & Gaza: Muslim Brotherhood & Islamic Jihad* (Bloomington and Indianapolis: Indiana University Press, 1994).

Ahmed, Irfan. *Islamism and Democracy in India: The Transformation of Jamaat-e-Islami* (Princeton: Princeton University Press, 2009).

Ajami, Fouad. *The Vanished Imam: Musa al Sadr and the Shia of Lebanon* (Ithaca, NY: Cornell University Press, 1987).

Akyol, Mustafa. "The Turkish Model," *The Cairo Review of Global Affairs* Issue 4 Winter 2012 (Cairo: The American University in Cairo).

al-Agha, Joseph. "Shifts in Hizbullah's Ideology," doctoral dissertation, Free University of Amsterdam, 2006, 245 as quoted in Khatib. "Hizbullah's Political Strategy," 62–3.

al-Ghannouchi, Rachid. *Al-Hurriyyat al-'Amma fi al-Dawla al-Islamiyya* (Beirut: 1993).

al-Matroudi, Abdul-Hakim. *The Hanbali School of Law and Ibn Taymiyyah: Conflict or Conciliation* (London and New York: Routledge, 2006).

al-Nafisi, 'Abd Allah Fahd. ed., *Al-Haraka al-Islamiyya: Ru'ya Mustaqbaliyya: Awraq fi al-Naqd al-Dhati* (Cairo: Maktaba Madbuli, 1989).

al-Zawahiri, Ayman. al-Qaeda's second in command, pointed out this difference in a 2005 communication to al-Qaeda's former leader in Iraq, Abu Musab al-Zarqawi, in an attempt to moderate the latter's uncompromising Salafi/Wahhabi views.

al-Zawahiri, Ayman. *Knights under the Prophet's Banner* [in Arabic] (serialized by *Asharq al-Awsat,* December 12, 2001).

Ali Riaz. *God Willing: The Politics of Islamism in Bangladesh* (Lanham, MD: Rowman and Littlefield, 2004).

Amin, Husnul. *From Islamism to Post-Islamism: A Study of a New Intellectual Discourse on Islam and Modernity in Pakistan,* PhD dissertation, Erasmus University in Rotterdam, The Netherlands, 2010.

Amir-Moezzi, Mohammad Ali. *The Divine Guide in Early Shi'ism: The Sources of Esotericism in Islam,* tr. David Streight (Albany: State University of New York, 1994).

Amir-Moezzi, Mohammad Ali. *The Spirituality of Shi'i Islam: Belief and Practices* (London: I.B. Tauris, 2011).

Amr, Ziad Abu. "Hamas: A Historical and Political Background," *Journal of Palestine Studies* 22, no. 4 (Summer 1993): 5–19.

Arjomand, Said. *Iran between Two Revolutions* (Princeton, NJ: Princeton University Press, 1982).

Arjomand, Said. ed., *Authority and Political Culture in Shi'ism* (Albany: State University of New York, 1988). This book traces the historical evolution of Shia political thought.

Arjomand, Said Amir. *After Khomeini: Iran under His Successors* (New York: Oxford University Press, 2009).

Arjomand, Said. *The Shadow of God and the Hidden Imam: Religion, Political Order, and Societal Change in Shi'ite Iran from the Beginning to 1890* (Chicago: The University of Chicago Press, 2010).

Asad, Talal. *Formations of the Secular: Christianity, Islam, Modernity* (Stanford: Stanford University Press, 2003).

Audi, Robert. *Religious Commitment and Secular Reason* (Cambridge, UK and New York: Cambridge University Press, 2000).

Audi, Robert. *Democratic Authority and the Separation of Church and State* (New York: Oxford University Press, 2011).

Ayoob, Mohammed. "Political Islam: Image and Reality," *World Policy Journal* XXI, no. 3, (Fall 2004): 1–14.

Ayoob, Mohammad. "The Future of Political Islam: The Importance of External Variables," *International Affairs* 81, no. 5 (2005): 951–60, 951–61.

Ayoob, Mohammed. *The Many Faces of Political Islam: Religion and Politics in the Muslim World* (Ann Arbor: University of Michigan Press, 2008).

Ayubi, Nazih. *Political Islam: Religion and Politics in the Arab World* (London: Routledge, 1991), 35–47.

Azza, Karam. "Democracy and Faith: The Continuum of Political Islam," in *The Struggle over Democracy in the Middle East: Regional Politics and External Politics,* ed. Nathan J. Brown and Bakhash, Shaul. *The Reign of the Ayatollahs: Iran and the Islamic Revolution* (New York: Basic Books, 1984).

Bale, Jeffrey. "Islamism and Totalitarianism," *Totalitarian Movements and Political Religions* 10, no. 2 (2009): 73–96.

Baran, Zeyno. "Fighting the War of Ideas," *Foreign Affairs* 84, no. 6, (November/December 2005): 68–78.

Bayat, Asef. "The Coming of a Post-Islamist Society," *Critique,* (fall 1996): 43–52.

Bayat, Asef. *Making Islam Democratic: Social Movements and the Post-Islamist Turn* (Stanford: Stanford University Press, 2007), 95.

Bayhom-Daou, Tamima. *Shaykh Mufid* (Oxford, UK: Oneworld, 2005).

Beinin, Joel, and Joe Stork. eds., *Political Islam: Essays from Middle East Report* (Berkeley: University of California Press, 1997).

Bellen, Eva. "Civil Society in Formation: Tunisia" *In* Augustus Richard Norton, ed *Civil Society in the Middle East.* pp. 120–47, vol. 1. Leiden: EJ Brill.

Black, Antony. *The History of Islamic Political Thought: From the Prophet to the Present,* 2nd ed. (Edinburgh: Edinburgh University Press, 2011).

Blandford, Nicholas. *Killing Mr. Lebanon: The Assassination of Rafik Hariri and Its Impact on the Middle East* (London: I.B. Tauris, 2009), 190, as mentioned in Khatib. "Hizbullah's Political Strategy," 61–76.

Blaydes, Lisa. *Elections and Distributive Politics in Mubarak's Egypt* (New York: Cambridge University Press, 2011), 162.

Blaydes, Lisa. *Elections and Distributive Politics in Mubarak's Egypt* (New York: Cambridge University Press, 2011), 151.

Bokhari, Kamran. "A Divided Epistemic Community and Political Islam: A Constructivist Approach to Understanding the Making of United States Foreign Policy," *The American Journal of Islamic Social Sciences* 19, no. 3 (Summer 2002): 11–30.

Bokhari, Kamran. "Salafism and Arab Democratization," October 2, 2012. Stratfor: Austin, TX. Available online at: http://www.stratfor.com/weekly/salafism-and-arab-democratization.

Bokhari, Kamran, and Farid Senzai. "Defining a Moderate," in *Debating Moderate Islam: The Geopolitics of Islam and the West,* ed. M. A. Muqtedar Khan (Salt Lake City: University of Utah Press, 2007).

Bonnefoy, Laurent. *Salafism in Yemen: Transnationalism and Religious Identity* (New York: Columbia University Press, 2012).

Boubekeur, Amel. "Post-Islamist Culture: A New Form of Mobilization?" *History of Religions* 47, no. 1 (2007): 75–94.

Boubekeur, Amel. *Salafism and Radical Politics in Postconflict Algeria* (Washington, DC: Carnegie Endowment for International Peace, 2008).

Brackman, Jarret M. *Global Jihadism: Theory and Practice* (New York: Routledge, 2009), 5.

Brahimi, Alia. "The Taliban's Evolving Ideology" *Working Paper* WP 02/2010 (London School of Economics: July 2010), 5.

Bratton, Michael, and Nicholas van de Walle. *Democratic Experiments in Africa: Regime Transitions in Comparative Perspective* (Cambridge, UK: Cambridge University Press, 1997).

Brown, Carl L. *Religion and State: The Muslim Approach to Politics* (New York: Columbia University Press, 2000).

Brooker, Paul. *Non-Democratic Regimes: Theory, Government and Politics* (New York, NY: St. Martin's Press, 2000).

Brown, Nathan J., Amr Hamzawy, and Marina Ottawa. *Islamist Movements and the Democratic Process in the Arab World: Exploring the Gray Zones* (Washington, DC: Carnegie Endowment for International Peace, 2006), 5–6.

Brown, Nathan J. *Jordan & Its Islamic Movement: Limits of Inclusion?* (Washington, DC: The Carnegie Endowment for International Peace, November 2006).

Brumberg, Daniel. "Islam, Elections and Reform in Algeria," *Journal of Democracy* 2, no. 1 (1991): 58–71.

Brumberg, Daniel. "The Trap of Liberalized Autocracy," *Journal of Democracy* 13, no. 4 (October 2002): 56–68.

Brynen, Rex, Bahgat Korany, and Paul Noble. *Political Liberalization and Democratization in the Arab World* (Boulder: Lynne Rienner, 1995).

Caeiro, Alexandre, and Mahmoud al-Saibl. "Qaradawi in Europe, Europe in Qaradawi? The Global Mufti's European Politics," in *Global Mufti: The Phenomenon of Yusuf al-Qaradawi,* ed. Bettina Graf and Jakob Skovgaard-Petersen (New York: Columbia University Press, 2009), 109–48.

Cakir, Ruqen. *Ayet ve Slogan* (Verse and Ideology) (Istanbul: Meti, Yayinlari, 1990), 290, as mentioned in Metin Heper. "Islam and Democracy in Turkey: Towards a Reconciliation," *Middle East Journal* 51, no. 1 (winter 1997): 43.

Calhoun, Craig, Mark Juergensmeyer, and Jonathan VanAntwerpen. eds., *Rethinking Secularism* (New York: Oxford University Press, 2011).

Calvert, John. *Sayyid Qutb and the Origins of Radical Islamism* (New York: Columbia University Press, 2010).

Carapico, Sheila. *Civil Society in Yemen* (Cambridge, UK: Cambridge University Press, 1998).

Carothers, Thomas. "The End of the Transition Paradigm," *Journal of Democracy* 13, no. 1 (January 2002): 5–21.

Caryl, Christian. "The Salafi Moment," *Foreign Policy* (September 12, 2012).

Chadwick, Owen. *The Secularization of the European Mind in the Nineteenth Century* (Cambridge, UK: Cambridge University Press, 1975).

Chatterjee, Kingshuk. *'Ali Shari'ati and the Shaping of Political Islam in Iran* (New York: Palgrave MacMillan, 2011).

Christina, Phelps Harris. *Nationalism and Revolution in Egypt: The Role of the Muslim Brotherhood* (The Hague: Mouton, 1964).

Christopher M. Blanchard. "The Islamic Tradition of Wahhabism and Salafiyya," *Congressional Research Service*, RS21695, (January 25, 2006).

Clark, Janine. A. *Islam, Charity, and Activism: Middle-Class Networks and Social Welfare in Egypt, Jordan, and Yemen* (Bloomington: Indiana University Press, 2004) as quoted in Zahid, *The Muslim Brotherhood and Egypt's Succession Crisis*, 19.

Cobban, Helena. "Hizbullah's New Face: The Search for a Muslim Democracy," *Boston Review* 30, no. 2 (April/May 2005): 36.

Cochrane, Marisa. *The Fragmentation of the Sadrist Movement* (Washington, DC: Institute for the Study of War, January 2009), Iraq Report, 12.

Cockburn, Patrick. *Muqtada: Muqtada Al-Sadr, The Shia Revival, and The Struggle for Iraq* (New York: Scribner, 2008).

Cohen, Yoram, and Matthew Levitt, with Becca Wasser. "Deterred but Determined Salafi-Jihadi Groups in the Palestinian Arena," *Policy Focus* 99 (Washington, DC: The Washington Institute for Near East Policy, January 2010).

Cole, Juan R. "The Ayatollahs and Democracy in Iraq," *ISIM Paper* 7 (Leiden: Amsterdam University Press, 2006).

Collelo, Thomas. "Lebanon: A Country Study," in *Lebanon: Current Issues and Background*, ed. John C. Rolland (Hauppauge: Nova Science Publishers, 2003), 29–179.

Collier, David and Steven Levitsky. "Democracy with Adjectives: Conceptual Innovation in Comparative Research," *World Politics* 49, no. 3 (April 1997): 430–51.

Commin, David. *The Wahhabi Mission*; Abdulaziz al-Fahad, "From Exclusivism to Accommodation: Doctrine and Legal Evolution of Wahhabism," *New York University Law Review* 79, (2004): 485–879.

Commin, David. *The Wahhabi Mission and Saudi Arabia* (London: I.B. Tauris, 2006).

Cook, Stephen. *Ruling but not Governing: The Military and Political Development in Egypt, Algeria, and Turkey* (Baltimore: the Johns Hopkins University Press, 2007).

Corwin, Smidt. "Religion and Civic Engagement: A Comparative Analysis," *Annals of the American Academy of Political and Social Science* 565 (September 1999): 176–92.

Council on Foreign Affairs. *The New Arab Revolt: What Happened, What It Means, and What Comes Next* (New York: Council on Foreign Affairs, 2011).

Dalacoura, Katerina. *Islamist Terrorism and Democracy in the Middle East* (New York: Cambridge University Press, 2011).

David, Cook. *Understanding Jihad* (Berkeley: University of California Press, 2005).

Deeb, Lara. "Hizbullah: A Primer," *MERIP* (Washington, DC, July 31, 2006).

Dekmejian, R. Hrair. *Islam in Revolution: Fundamentalism in the Arab World* (Syracuse: Syracuse University Press, 1985) provides a highly detailed account of Arab Islamist groups.

Dekmejian, R. Hrair "The Rise of Political Islamism in Saudi Arabia," *Middle East Journal* 48, no. 4 (autumn 1994): 629.

Delong-Bas, Natania J. *Wahhabi Islam: From Revival and Reform to Global Jihad* (London: I.B. Tauris, 2004).

Denoeux, Guilain, "The Forgotten Swamp: Navigating Political Islam," *Middle East Policy* 9, no. 2 (June 2002): 61.

Diamond, Larry. "The Globalization of Democracy," in *Global Transformation and the Third World,* ed. Robert Slater, Barry Schultz, and Steven Doerr (Boulder: Lynne Rienner, 1993), 32–8.

Diamond, Larry. and Marc F. Plattner. eds., *The Global Resurgence of Democracy* (Baltimore: The John Hopkins University Press, 1993).

Diamond, Larry, Juan J. Linz, and Seymour M. Lipset. eds., *Democracy in Developing Countries: Comparing Experiences with Democracy* (Boulder: Lynne Rienner, 1995).

Diamond, Larry. *Developing Democracy: Toward Consolidation* (Baltimore: The Johns Hopkins University Press, 1999), 7–15.

Diamond, Larry. "Thinking about Hybrid Regimes," *Journal of Democracy* 13, no. 2 (April 2002): 21–35.

Diamond, Larry, Marc F. Plattner, and Daniel Brumberg. eds., *Islam and Democracy in the Middle East* (Baltimore: Johns Hopkins University Press, 2003).

Diamond, Larry. and Marc F. Plattner. *Democratization in Africa: Progress and Retreat* (Baltimore: The Johns Hopkins University Press, 2010).

Donald, Eugene Smith. *Religion and Political Development* (Boston: Little, Brown, 1970).

Edward, Mortimer. *Faith and Power: The Politics of Islam* (New York: Faber and Faber, 1982).

Ehteshami, Anoushiravan. "Islam, Muslim Polities, and Democracy," *Democratization* 90 (2004): 90–110.

Eickelman, Dale, and James Piscatori. *Muslim Politics* (Princeton: Princeton University Press, 1996).

El-Affendi, Abdelwahab A. "The Elusive Reformation," in *Islam and Democracy in the Middle East,* ed. Larry Diamond, Marc F. Plattner, and Daniel Brumberg (Baltimore: The Johns Hopkins University Press, 2003), 252–7.

El-Affendi, Abdelwahab A. "On the State, Democracy, and Pluralism," in *Islamic Thought in the Twentieth Century,* ed. Suha Taji-Farouki and Basheer M. Nafi (London: I.B. Taurus, 2004), 172–94.

El-Affendi, Abdelwahab. *Who Needs an Islamic State?* (London, Malaysia Think Tank, 2008).

El-Affendi, Abdelwahab A. "The Islamism Debate Revisited: In Search of 'Islamist democrats'," in *Europe, the USA, and Political Islam: Strategies for Engagement,* ed. Michelle Pace (London: Palgrave, 2010), 125–38.

El-Affendi, Abdelwahab A. "The Modern Debate(s) on Islam and Democracy," in *Islam and Democracy in Malaysia: Findings from a National Dialogue,* ed. Ibrahim Zein (Kuala Lumpur: International Institute of Islamic Thought and Civilization, 2010), 3–68.

El-Affendi, Abdelwahab A., David Beetham, and Neil Walker. "Democracy and the Islamist Paradox," in *Understanding Democratic Politics: An Introduction,* ed. Ronald Axtmann (London: Sage, 2003), 311–20.

El Fadl, Khaled Abou. *Islam and The Challenge of Democracy.* (Princeton, NJ: Princeton University Press, 2004).

Elias, Amin. "Qira'a fi Wathiqatayy Tayyar al-Mustaqbal wa Hizbillah: Al-Watan al-Ghamidh," *An-Nahar* (October 25, 2010); Hizbullah Manifesto, 2009, reproduced in Ziad Majed, *Hezbollah and the Shiite Community: From Political Confessionalization to Confessional Specialization* (Washington, DC: The Aspen Institute, 2010), 21–24.

Eligur, Banu. *The Mobilization of Political Islam in Turkey* (New York: Cambridge University Press, 2010), 1.

Enayat, Hamid. *Modern Islamic Political Thought* (London: I.B. Tauris, 2005).

Epstein, David, Robert Bates, Jack Goldstone, Ida Kristensen and Sharyn O'Halloran. "Democratic Transitions," *American Journal of Political Science* 50, no. 3 (July 2006): 551–69.

Esposito, John L. ed., *The Iranian Revolution: Its Global Impact* (Miami: University Presses of Florida, 1990).

Esposito, John. ed., *The Iranian Revolution: Its Global Impact* (Gainesville: University of Florida Press, 1990).

Esposito, John L. ed., *Political Islam: Revolution, Radicalism, or Reform?* (Boulder: Lynne Rienner, 1997).

Esposito, John L. *Unholy War: Terror in the Name of Islam* (New York: Oxford University Press, 2002).

Esposito, John L. "Introduction: Islam and Secularism in the Twenty-first Century," in *Islam and Secularism in the Middle East*, ed. John L. Esposito and Azzam Tamimi (London: Hurst and Co., 2000), 1–12.

Esposito, John L. and Dalia Mogahed. *Who Speaks for Islam: What a Billion Muslims Really Think* (New York: Gallup Press, 2007).

Esposito, John L., and John Voll. *Islam and Democracy* (New York: Oxford University Press, 1996). For further reading on Ghannoushi's thoughts, see Tamimi, *Rachid Ghannouchi*.

Etzioni, Amitai. "Should We Support Illiberal Religious Democracies?" *The Political Quarterly* 82, no. 4 (October–December 2011): 567–73.

Euben, Roxanne L., and Muhammad Qasim Zaman. *Princeton Readings in Islamist Thought: Texts and Contexts from al-Banna to Bin Laden* (Princeton: Princeton University Press, 2009).

Fair, Christine C., Neil Malhotra, and Jacob N. Shapiro. "Democratic Values and Support for Militant Politics: Evidence from a National Survey of Pakistan," *Journal of Conflict Resolution* (March 21, 2013): 1–28.

Fandy, Mamoun. *Saudi Arabia and the Politics of Dissent* (New York: St. Martin's Press, 1999).

Fattah, Moatazz A. *Democratic Values in the Muslim World* (Boulder: Lynne Rienner, 2006).

Filali-Ansary, Abdou. "The Challenge of Secularization: Islam and Liberal Democracy." *Journal of Democracy* 7, no. 2 (1996): 76–80.

Filiu, Jean-Pierre. "The Origins of Hamas: Militant Legacy or Israeli Tool?" *Journal of Palestine Studies* 41, no. 3 (spring 2012): 54–70.

Fletcher, Holly. *Militant Extremists in the United States* (New York: Council on Foreign Relations, April 21, 2008).

Fournie, Michael. "Al-Wasat and the Destiny of Moderate Islamists in Egypt," *Civil Society* (September 2005).

Friedman, George. *America's Secret War* (New York: Doubleday, 2004).

Fukuyama, Francis. *End of History and the Last Man* (New York: Free Press, 2006).

Fuller, Graham. *The Future of Political Islam* (New York: Palgrave Macmillan, 2003).

Fuller, Graham. "Islamists and Democracy," in *Uncharted Journey: Promoting Democracy in the Middle East,* ed. Thomas Carothers and Marina Ottaway (Washington, DC: Carnegie Endowment for International Peace and Democracy, 2005).

Gallie, W. B. "Essentially Contested Concepts," *Proceedings of the Aristotelian Society* 56 (1956): 167–98.

Gasiorowski, Mark. "The Failure of Reform in Tunisia," *Journal of Democracy* 3, no. 4 (1992): 85–97.

Gellner, Ernest. *Muslim Society* (Cambridge, NY: Cambridge University Press, 1981).

Gellner, Ernest. "Islam and Marxism: Some Comparisons," *International Affairs* 67, no. 1 (1991): 1–6.

Gellner, Ernest. *Postmodernism, Reason and Religion* (London: Routledge, 1992).

Gellner, Ernest. *Conditions of Liberty: Civil Society and Its Rivals* (London: Hamish Hamilton, 1994).

Gerges, Fawaz. *Journey of the Jihadist: Inside Muslim Militancy* (Orlando: Harcourt, 2006).

Gerges, Fawaz. *The Far Enemy: Why Jihad Went Global* (New York: Cambridge University Press, 2009).

Gerges, Fawaz. *The Rise and Fall of Al-Qaeda* (New York: Oxford University Press, 2011).

Gill, Anthony. *Rendering unto Caesar: The Catholic Church and the State in Latin America* (Chicago: University of Chicago Press, 1998).

Greenwalt, Kent. *Religious Convictions and Political Choice* (New York: Oxford University Press, 1991).

Gunther, Richard. *Politics of Democratic Consolidation* (Baltimore: The Johns Hopkins University Press, 1995).

Hajjar, Sami G. *Hizballah: Terrorism, National Liberation, or Menace?* (Carlisle: Strategic Studies Institute, U.S. Army War College, 2002).

Hale, Henry E. "Hybrid Regimes: When Democracy and Autocracy Mix," in *The Dynamics of Democratization: Dictatorship, Development, and Diffusion*, ed. Nathan Brow (Baltimore: Johns Hopkins University Press, 2011), 23–45.

Hamzaway, Amr. "The Key to Arab Reform: Moderate Islamists," *Policy Brief 40* (Washington, DC: Carnegie Endowment for International Peace, August, 2005), 4.

Hamzawy, Amr. "Islamists in Electoral Politics: Politics and Strategies of the Egyptian Muslim Brotherhood," UCLA International Institute (April 20, 2006).

Hamzawy, Amr. *Party for Justice and Development in Morocco: Participation and Its Discontents* (Washington DC: The Carnegie Endowment for International Peace, July 2008). Report no. 93.

Hanson, Eric O. *Religion and Politics in the International System Today* (Cambridge, UK: Cambridge University Press, 2006).

Harik, Judith Palmer. *Hezbollah: The Changing face of Terrorism* (London: I.B. Tauris, 2005).

Harris, Frederick C. "Something Within: Religion as a Mobilizer of African-American Political Activism," *Journal of Politics* 56, no. 1 (February 1994): 42–68.

Hasan al-Banna. *Mudhakkirat al-Da'wa wa'l-Da'iyya* (Cairo: Dar al-Kitab al-Arabi, 1974).

Hashemi, Nader. *Islam, Secularism, and Liberal Democracy: Towards a Democratic Theory for Muslim Societies* (New York: Oxford University Press, 2009).

Hassan, Riaz. *Faithlines: Muslim Conceptions of Islam and Society* (Karachi: Oxford University Press, 2002).

Haykel, Bernard. "On the Nature of Salafi Thought and Action," in *Global Salafism: Islam's New Religious Movement*, ed. Roel Meijer (New York: Columbia University Press, 2009), 34.

Heern, Zachary M. *Usuli Shi'ism: The Emergence of and Islamic Reform Movement in Early Modern Iran and Iraq* (Ph.D. diss. Submitted to the University of Utah, Salt Lake City, UT, 2011).

Hefner, Robert W. ed., *Remaking Muslim Politics: Pluralism, Contestation, Democratization* (Princeton, NJ and Oxford, UK: Princeton University Press, 2005), 26.

Hefner, Robert W. ed., *Shari'a Politics: Islamic Law and Society in the Modern World* (Bloomington and Indianapolis: Indiana University Press, 2011), 4.

Hegghammer, Thomas. "Global Jihadism after the Iraq War," *Middle East Journal* 60, no. 1 (January 2006): 11–32.

Hegghammer, Thomas. *Jihad in Saudi Arabia: Violence and Pan-Islamism since 1979* (Cambridge, UK: Cambridge University Press, 2010)

Higley, and Gunther. "Elites and Democratic Consolidation" in *Issues in Democratic Consolidation*, ed. Mainwaring, O'Donnell, and Valenzuela.

Higley, John and Richard Gunther. *Elites and Democratic Consolidation in Latin America and Southern Europe* (Cambridge, NY: Cambridge University Press, 1992).

Hiro, Dilip. *Iran Under the Ayatollahs* (London: Routledge, 1985).

Hope, Bradley. "Postponement of Egypt's Elections may Deepen Turmoil," *The National* (March 28, 2013), Available online at http://www.thenational.ae/news/world/middle-east/postponement-of-egypts-elections-may-deepen-turmoil

Hourani, Albert. *Arabic Thought in the Liberal Age: 1798–1939* (Cambridge, NY: Cambridge University Press, 1983).

Hunter, Robert C. *Brothers or Rivals? Iran and the Shi'a of Iraq*. M.A. in National Security Affairs Thesis submitted in June 2006 at the Naval Postgraduate School, Monterrey, CA.

Huntington, Samuel P. "The Modest Meaning of Democracy," in *Democracy in the Americas: Stopping the Pendulum*, ed. Robert Pastor (New York: Holmes and Meier, 1989).

Huntington, Samuel P. *The Third Wave: Democratization in the Late Twentieth Century* (Norman: University of Oklahoma Press, 1991), 5–13.

Huntington, Samuel P. "The Clash of Civilizations?". *Foreign Affairs*. 72, no. 3 (1993): 22–49.

Hurd, Elizabeth Shakman. *The Politics of Secularism in International Relations* (Princeton: Princeton University Press, 2008).

Hwang, Julie Chernov. *Peaceful Islamist Mobilization in the Muslim World: What Went Right* (New York: Palgrave Macmillan, 2009), 3.

Ibn Muhsin ibn 'Ali Jabir, Husayn. *Al-Tariq ila Jama'at al-Muslimin*, 3rd ed. (al-Mansura, Egypt: Dar al-Wafa', 1989).

Inglehart, Ronald, and Christian Weizel, *Modernization, Cultural Change, and Democracy: The Human Development Sequence* (New York: Cambridge University Press, 2005).

Iqtidar, Humeira. *Secularizing Islamists? Jama'at-e-Islami and Jama'at-ud-Da'wa in Urban Pakistan* (Chicago: University of Chicago Press, 2011), 13.

Joseph, Richard. "Africa's Diehard Autocracies," *Africa Demos* 3 (July–August 1993): 1

Kalyvas, Stathis N. "Democracy and Religious Politics," *Comparative Political Studies* 31, no. 3 (June 1998): 292–320.

Karl, Terry, and Philippe Schmitter. "Democratization around the Globe: Its Opportunities and Risks," in *World Security: Trends and Challenges at Century's End*, ed. Michael T. Klare and Dan Thomas (New York: St. Martin's Press, 1993).

Karl, Terry. "Dilemmas of Democratization in Latin America," *Comparative Politics* 23 (1990): 1–21.

Karl, Terry Lynn. "The Hybrid Regimes of Central America," *Journal of Democracy* 6, no. 3 (July 1995): 72–87.

Keddie, Nikki R. *Roots of Revolution: An Interpretive History of Modern Iran* (New Haven: Yale University Press, 1981).

Keddie, Nikki. *An Islamic Response to Imperialism: Political and Religious Writings of Sayyid Jamal ad-Din "al-Afghani"* (Berkeley: University of California Press, 1983).

Keddie, Nikki R. *Religion and Politics in Iran: Shi'ism from Quietism to Revolution* (New Haven: Yale University Press, 1984).

Keddie, Nikki R. *Qajar Iran and the Rise of Reza Khan: 1796–1925* (Costa Mesa: Mazda Publishers, 1999).

Kedourie, Elie. *Democracy and Arab Political Culture* (Washington, DC: Washington Institute for Near Eastern Policy, 1994).Kelsay, J. and J. T. Johnson, eds., *Just War and Jihad: Historical and Theoretical Perspectives on War and Peace in Western and Islamic Traditions* (New York: Greenwood Press, 1991).

Kennedy, Hugh. *The Armies of the Caliphs: Military and Society in the Early Islamic State* (New York: Routledge, 2001).

Kepel, Gilles. *Allah in the West: Islamic Movements in America and Europe* (Palo Alto: Stanford University Press, 1997).

Kepel, Gilles. "Islamism Reconsidered," *Harvard International Review* 22, no. 2 (2000): 22–8.

Kepel, Gilles. *Jihad: The Trial of Political Islam* (Cambridge, MA: Harvard University Press, 2002).

Kepel, Gilles. *The War for Muslim Minds: Islam and the West* (Cambridge, MA: Harvard University Press, 2004).

Kerr, Malcolm H. *Islamic Reform: The Political and Legal Theories of Muhammad 'Abduh and Rashid Rida* (Berkeley: University of California Press, 1966).

Khalil, Magdi. "Egypt's Muslim Brotherhood and the Political Power: Would Democracy Survive?" *Middle East Review of International Affairs Journal* 10, no. 3 (March 2006): 44–52.

Khan, M. A. Muqtedar. ed., *Islamic Democratic Discourse: Theory, Debates, and Philosophical Perspectives* (Lanham: Lexington Books, 2006).

Khatib, Lina. "Hizbullah's Political Strategy," *Survival: Global Politics and Strategy* 53, no. 2 (2011): 65.

Khomeini, Ruhollah. *Islam and Revolution: Writings and Declarations of Imam Khomeini (1941–1980),* tr. Hamid Algar (New York: Mizan Press, 1981).

Kienle, Eberhard. "More Than a Response to Islamism: The Political Deliberalization of Egypt in the 1990s," *Middle East Journal* 52, no. 2 (spring 1998): 227.

Kitschelt. Herbert. "Linkages between Citizens and Politicians in Democratic Polities" *Comparative Political Studies*, 33, no. 6/7 (August/September 2000): 845–879.

Kramer, Martin. "Islam vs. Democracy," *Commentary* 95, no. 1 (January 1993): 35–42.

Kramer, Martin. "Coming to Terms: Fundamentalists or Islamists?" *Middle East Quarterly* X, no. 2 (spring 2003): 65–77.

Kuru, Ahmet T. "Changing Perspectives on Islamism and Secularism in Turkey: The Gülen Movement and the AK Party," in *Muslim World in Transition: Contributions of the Gülen Movement,* ed. Ihsan Yilmaz, conference proceedings from October 2007, London. Page Range is 140–150. Available online at: https://www.google.ca/url?sa=t&rct=j&q=&esrc =s&source=web&cd=1&ved=0CCkQFjAA&url=http%3A%2F%2Fwww.academia. edu%2F333441%2FMuslim_World_In_Transition_Contributions_of_the_Gulen_ Movement&ei=le1iUvqiDe6w4APqmYDYAQ&usg=AFQjCNFHnrgq8ELVoP0UwJlc sopcTdI2YA&bvm=bv.54934254,d.dmg&cad=rjt

Kuru, Ahmet T. "Globalization and Diversification of Islamic Movements: Three Turkish Cases," *Political Science Quarterly* 120, no. 2 (2005): 253–74, 273.

Kuru, Ahmet T. "Muslim Politics without an 'Islamic' State: Can Turkey's Justice and Development Party Be a Model for Arab Islamists?" *Policy Briefing 23*, February 21, 2013 (Doha, Qatar: Brookings Doha Center, 2013): 1–10.

Lacroix, Stephane. *Awakening Islam: The Politics of Religious Dissent in Contemporary Saudi Arabia* (Cambridge, MA: Harvard University Press, 2011), 10.

Lahoud, Nelly. "The Forgotten Recantation" at http://www.jihadica.com/the-forgotten-recantation/ Posted: January 8, 2010.

Laurence, Jonathan. *The Emancipation of Europe's Muslims: The State's Role in Minority Integration* (Princeton: Princeton University Press, 2012).

Lauzire, Henri. "Post-Islamism and the Religious Discourse of Abd al-Salam Yasin," *International Journal of Middle East Studies* 37, no. 2 (2005): 241–61.

Lawson, Fred. "Demands for Political Participation in the Arab Gulf States," *International Journal* 49, no. 2 (1994): 378–407.

Lee, Robert D. *Religion and Politics in the Middle East: Identity, Ideology, Institutions, and Attitudes* (Boulder: Westview Press, 2010), 267

Leiken, Robert S. and Steven Brooke, "The Moderate Muslim Brotherhood" *Foreign Affairs* 86, no. 2 (March–April 2007): 111.

Levitsky, Steven, and Lucan A. Way. "The Rise of Competitive Authoritarianism," *Journal of Democracy* 13, no. 2 (April 2002): 51–65.

Levitsky, Steven, and Lucan A. Way, *Competitive Authoritarianism: Hybrid Regimes after the Cold War* (Cambridge, NY: Cambridge University Press, 2010).

Lewis, Bernard. *The Political language of Islam* (Chicago, IL: University of Chicago Press, 1988).

Lewis, Bernard. "The Roots of Muslim Rage," *Atlantic* 266 (September 1990): 47–54, 56, 59, 60.

Lewis, Bernard. "Islam and Liberal Democracy," *Atlantic* 271, (February 1993): 89–94.

Lewis, Bernard. "A Historical View: Islam and Liberal Democracy," *Journal of Democracy* 7, no. 2 (1996): 52–63.

Lewis, Bernard. *What Went Wrong: The Clash Between Islam and Modernity* (New York, NY: Harper Perennial, 2002).

Lewis, Bernard. *The Crisis of Islam: Holy War and Unholy Terror* (London: Weidenfeld and Nicholson, 2003).

Lewis, Bernard. *What Went Wrong: The Clash Between Modernity and Islam in the Middle East* (New York: Harper Perennial, 2003).

Lia, Brynjar. *Architect of Global Jihad: The Life of Al-Qaida Strategist Abu Mus'ab Al-Suri* (New York: Columbia University Press, 2008), 134–6.

Linz, Juan J., and Alfred Stepan, eds., *The Breakdown of Democratic Regimes: Crisis, Breakdown, and Reequilibration* (Baltimore: The John Hopkins University Press, 1978).

Linz, Juan, and Alfred Stepan. *Problems of Democratic Transition and Consolidation: Southern Europe, South America, and Post-Communist Europe* (Baltimore: The Johns Hopkins University Press, 1996).

Lockman, Zachary. *Contending Visions of the Middle East: The History and Politics of Orientalism* (Cambridge, UK: Cambridge University Press, 2004)

Longtin, Leslie C. *Restoring Medinat al-Salaam: The Rise of Muqtada al-Sadr's Jaysh al-Mahdi.* MA in Liberal Studies Thesis submitted in 2010 at Georgetown University, Washington, DC.

Luciani, Giacomo. "Economic Foundations of Democracy and Authoritarianism: The Arab World in Comparative Perspective," *Arab Studies Quarterly* 10, no. 4 (1988): 457–75.

Luciani, Giacomo. "Allocation vs. Production States: A Theoretical Framework," in *The Arab State,* ed. Giacomo Luciani (Berkeley: University of California Press, 1990), 65–84.

Luciani, Giacomo. "The Oil Rent, the Fiscal Crisis of the State and Democratization," in *Democracy without Democrats? The Renewal of Politics in the Muslim World,* ed. Ghassan Salamé (London: I.B. Tauris, 1994), 130–55.

Lust-Okar, Ellen. "Elections under Authoritarianism: Preliminary Lessons from Jordan," *Democratization* 13, no. 3 (June 2006): 459.

Lust-Okar, Ellen, and Amaney A. Jamal. "Rulers and Rules: Reassessing the Influence of Regime Type on Electoral Law Formation," *Comparative Political Studies* 35, no. 3 (April 2002): 336–66.

Lynch, Marc. *The Arab Uprising: The Unfinished Revolutions of the New Middle East* (New York: Public Affairs, 2012).

Madawi, Rasheed. *Contesting the Saudi State: Islamic Voices from a New Generation* (Cambridge, NY: Cambridge University Press, 2007).

Mahdavi, Mojtaba. "Post-Islamist Trends in Postrevolutionary Iran," *Comparative Studies of South Asia, Africa, and the Middle East* 31, no. 1 (2011): 94.

Mahmood, Saba. "Is Liberalism Islam's Only Answer?" in *Islam and the Challenge of Democracy,* ed. Khaled Abou El Fadl (Princeton: Princeton University Press, 2004).

Mainwaring, Scott, Daniel Brinks, and Aníbal Pérez Liñan. "Classifying Political Regimes in Latin America, 1945–1999," *Studies in Comparative International Development* 36, no. 1 (spring 2001): 37–65.

Mainwaring, Scott, Guillermo O'Donnell, and J. Samuel Valenzuela, eds., *Issues in Democratic Consolidation: The New South American Democracies in Comparative Perspective* (South Bend: University of Notre Dame Press, 1992).

Malik, Iftikhar. *State and Civil Society in Pakistan* (London: MacMillan Press, 1997).

Mandaville, Peter. *Global Political Islam* (New York: Routledge Press, 2007), 241.

Marechal, Brigette. *The Muslim Brothers in Europe: Roots and Discourse* (Leiden and Boston: Brill, 2008).

Marshall, Monty G. and Keith Jaggers. *Polity IV Project: Political Regime Characteristics and Transactions, 1800–2002* (University of Maryland, 2002).

Mawdudi, Abul A'la A. *Jihad in Islam* (Pakistan: Islamic Publication, 1998).

McCants, William. "The Lesser of Two Evils: The Salafi Turn to Party Politics in Egypt," *Middle East Memo* (Washington, DC: The Brookings Institution, May 2012).

McGraw, Barbara A., and Jo Renee Formicola. eds., *Taking Religious Pluralism Seriously: Spiritual Politics on America's Sacred Ground* (Waco: Baylor University Press, 2005).

Mecham, R. Quinn. "From the Ashes of Virtue, A Promise of Light: the Transformation of Political Islam in Turkey," *Third World Quarterly* 25, no. 2 (2004): 339–58.

Meijer, Roel. ed., *Global Salafism: Islam's New Religious Movement* (New York: Columbia University Press, 2009). This book represents an attempt to capture the various manifestations of Salafism around the Islamic world.

Migdal, Joel S. *State in Society: Studying How States and Societies Transform and Constitute One Another* (New York: Cambridge University Press, 2001).

Mitchell, Richard. *The Society of the Muslim Brothers* (Oxford, NY: Oxford University Press, 1993).

Mneimneh, Hassan. "The Spring of a New Political Salafism?" *Current Trends in Islamist Ideology* 12 (Washington, DC: Hudson Institute, 2011): 21–36.

Momen, Moojan. *An Introduction to Shi'i Islam: The History and Doctrines of Twelver Shi'ism* (New Haven: Yale University, 1987).

Monroe, Steve L. "Salafis in Parliament: Democratic Attitudes and Party Politics in the Gulf," *Middle East Journal* 66, no. 3 (2012): 409–24.

Munck, Gerardo L. "Democratic Transitions in Comparative Perspective," *Comparative Politics* 26 (1994): 355–75.

Musharraf, Pervez. "A Plea for Enlightened Moderation," *Washington Post* (June 1, 2004): A23.

Muslih, Muhammad, and Augustus Richard Norton. "The Need for Arab Democracy," *Foreign Policy* 83 (Summer 1991): 3–19.

Nasr, Seyyed Hossein, Hamid Dabashi, and Seyyed Vali Reza Nasr. *Expectation of the Millennium: Shi'ism in History* (Albany: State University of New York, 1989).

Nasr, Vali R. "The Rise of Sunni Militancy in Pakistan: The Changing Role of Islamism and the Ulama in Society and Politics," *Modern Asian Studies* 34 (2000): 139–80.

Newman, Andrew J. *The Formative Period of Twelver Shi'ism: Hadith as Discourse between Qum and Baghdad* (Richmond, Surrey, UK: Curzon Press, 2010).

Nizar, Hamzeh, A. *In the Path of Hizbullah* (Syracuse: Syracuse University Press, 2004).

Norris, Pippa, and Ronald Inglehart. *Sacred and Secular: Religion and Politics Worldwide* (Cambridge, NY: Cambridge University Press).

Norton, Richard Augustus. *Hezbollah: A Short History* (Princeton: Princeton University Press, 2007).

Norton, Richard. ed., *Civil Society in the Middle East,* 2 vol. (New York: E. J. Brill, 1995).

O'Donnell, Guillermo. "Delegative Democracy." *Journal of Democracy* 5, no. 1 (January 1994): 55–69

O'Donnell, Guillermo. "The Perpetual Crises of Democracy," *Journal of Democracy* 18, no. 1 (January 2007): 8–9.

O'Donnell, Guillermo, Philippe Schmitter, and Laurence Whitehead. eds., *Transitions from Authoritarian Rule: Prospects for Democracy* (Baltimore: The Johns Hopkins University Press, 1986).

Ochenwald, William. "Saudi Arabia and Islamic Revival," *International Journal of Middle East Studies* 13, (1981): 271–26.

Ottaway, Marina. *Democracy Challenged: The Rise of Semi-Authoritarianism* (Washington, DC: Carnegie Endowment for International Peace, 2003).

Ottaway, Marina, and Thomas Carothers, *Greater Middle East Initiative: Off to a False Start* (Washington, DC: The Carnegie Endowment for International Peace, March 2004). Policy brief no. 29.

Piscatori, James P. "Ideological Politics in Saudi Arabia," in *Islam in the Political Process*, ed. James P. (Cambridge, NY: Cambridge University Press, 1983).

Poston, Larry. *Islamic Da'wah in the West* (New York: Oxford University Press, 1992).

Przeworski, Adam. *Democracy and the Market: Political and Economic Reforms in Eastern Europe and Latin America* (Cambridge, NY: Cambridge University Press, 1991).

Qassem, Naim. *Hizballah: Al-Manhaj, al-Tajribah, al-Mustaqbal* (Beirut: Dar al-Hadi, 2008), 290.

Quandt, William B. *Between Ballots & Bullets: Algeria's Transition from Authoritarianism* (Washington, DC: The Brookings Institution, 1998).

Qutb, Sayyid. *Social Justice in Islam* (Oneonta, NY: Islamic Publications International, 1953).

Qutb, Sayyid. *Ma'alim fi'l-Tariq* (Cairo: Kazi Publications, 1964).

Qutb, Sayyid. *Milestones* (Plainfield: American Trust Publications, 1990).

Qutb, Sayyid. *Ma'alim fi'l-Tariq* (Beirut: Dar al-Shuruq, 1991; originally published in 1964), 67–8, 82, as quoted in Roxanne L. Euben, and Muhammad Qasim Zaman. eds., *Princeton Readings in Islamist Thought: Texts and Contexts from al-Banna to Bin Laden* (Princeton: Princeton University Press, 2009), 41.

Rabil, Robert G. "Hezbollah, the Islamic Association, and Lebanon's Confessional System," *The Levantine Review* 1, no. 1 (Spring 2012): 49–67.

Rahnema, Ali. *An Islamic Utopian: A Political Biography of Ali Shariati* (London: I.B. Tauris, 2000).

Ramage, Doug. *Politics in Indonesia: Democracy, Islam, and the Ideology of Tolerance* (London: Routledge, 1997).

Rapoport, Yossef, and Shahab Ahmed. *Ibn Taymiyah and His Times* (New York: Oxford University Press, 2010).

Rashid, Ahmed. *Taliban: Militant Islam, Oil, and Fundamentalism in Central Asia* (New Haven: Yale University Press, 2001).

Robert, Leiken S., and Steven Brooke. "The Moderate Muslim Brotherhood," *Foreign Affairs* 86, no. 2 (March–April 2007): 110.

Ross, Michael L. "Does Oil Hinder Democracy?" *World Politics* 53, no. 3 (2001): 325–361.

Ross, Michael L. "Oil, Islam, and Women," *American Political Science Review* 102, no. 1 (2008): 107–123.

Roy, Olivier. *The Failure of Political Islam* (Cambridge, MA: Harvard University Press, 1996).

Roy, Olivier. "Le post-islamisme," *Revue des Mondes Musulmans et de la Méditerranée*, (1998): 85–86, 9–30.

Roy, Olivier. *Globalized Islam: The Search for the New Ummah* (New York: Columbia University Press, 2004).

Roy, Olivier. "The Transformation of the Arab World," *Journal of Democracy* 23, no. 3 (July 2012): 5–18.

Rubin, Barnett R. "Arab Islamists in Afghanistan," in *Political Islam: Revolution, Radicalism, or Reform?* ed. John Esposito (Boulder, CO: Lynne Rienner, 1997)

Rubin, Barry. ed., *The Muslim Brotherhood: The Organization and Policies of a Global Islamist Movement* (New York: Palgrave Macmillan, 2010).

Rueschemeyer, Dietrich, Evelyne Huber Stephens, and John D. Stephens. *Capitalist Development and Democracy* (Chicago: University of Chicago Press, 1992).

Rutherford, Bruce. *Egypt after Mubarak: Liberalism, Islam and Democracy in the Arab World* (Princeton: Princeton University Press, 2008), 177.

Sachedina, Abdulaziz. *Islamic Messianism: The Idea of the Mahdi in Twelver Shi'ism* (Albany: State University of New York, 1981).

Sachedina, Abdulaziz. *The Just Ruler in Shi'ite Islam: The Comprehensive Authority of the Jurist in Imamite Jurisprudence* (New York: Oxford University Press, 1998).

Sadiki, Larbi. "Popular Uprisings and Arab Democratization," *International Journal of Middle East Studies* 32, no. 1 (2000): 71.

Sadiki, Larbi. "Bin Ali's Tunisia: Democracy by Non-Democratic Means," *British Journal of Middle East Studies* 29, no. 1 (2002): 57–7.

Sadiki, Larbi. *Rethinking Arab Democratization: Elections without Democracy* (Oxford and New York, Oxford University Press, 2009)

Sadiki, Larbi. "Re-constituting Egypt," *Al-Jazeera* (November 29, 2012), Available at: http://www.aljazeera.com/indepth/opinion/2012/11/2012112881631548791.html.

Sadowski, Yahya. *Political Vegetables: Businessman and Bureaucrats in the Development of Egyptian Agriculture* (Washington, DC: Brookings Institution, 1991), 130.

Salame, Ghassan. *Democracy without Democrats?: The Renewal of Politics in the Muslim World* (London: I.B. Taurus, 1994).

Sankari, Farouk A. "Islam and Politics in Saudi Arabia," in *Islamic Resurgence in the Arab World*, ed. Ali E. Hillal Dessouki (New York: Praeger, 1982), 178–95.

Schedler, Andreas. "Elections Without Democracy: The Menu of Manipulation," *Journal of Democracy* 13, no. 2 (April 2002): 36–50.

Schedler, Andreas. "The Nested Game of Democratization by Elections," *International Political Science Review* 23, no. 1 (2002): 103–22.

Schedler, Andreas. *Electoral Authoritarianism: The Dynamics of Unfree Competition* (Boulder: Lynne Rienner, 2006), 3–7.

Schmidt, Soren. "The Role of Religion in Politics: The Case of Shia Islamism in Iraq," *Nordic Journal of Religion and Society* 22, no. 2 (2009): 123–43.

Schmitter, Philippe C. and Terry Lynn Karl. "What Democracy Is . . . and Is Not," *Journal of Democracy* 2, no. 3 (summer 1991): 75–89.

Schumpeter, Joseph. *Capitalism, Socialism, and Democracy* (New York: Harper, 1947).

Schwedler, Jillian. ed., *Towards Civil Society in the Middle East?* (Boulder: Lynne Reinner, 1995).

Schwedler, Jillian. *Faith in Moderation: Islamist Parties in Jordan and Yemen* (Cambridge, NY: Cambridge University Press, 2006), 166.

Shanahan, Rodger. "Shia Political Development in Iraq: The Case of the Islamic Dawa Party," *Third World Quarterly* 25, no. 5 (2004): 943–54.

Siddiqui, Kalim. *Stages of Islamic Revolution* (London: The Open Press, 1996).

Simon, Kevin. "Hezbollah: Terror in Context," 2012 *AHS Capstone Projects.* Paper 18.

Sivan, Emmanuel. *Radical Islam: Medieval Theology and Modern Politics* (New Haven: Yale University Press, 1985).

Smith, Peter H. *Democracy in Latin America: Political Change in Comparative Perspective* (Oxford: Oxford University Press, 2005)

Soroush, Abdolkarim. *Reason, Freedom, and Democracy in Islam* (New York: Oxford University Press, 2002).

Soroush, Abdolkarim. *Reason, Freedom, and Democracy in Islam: Essential Writings of Abdolkarim Soroush,* Abdolkarim. Mahmoudand Ahmad Sadri (New York: Oxford University Press, 2002).

Stepan, Alfred. *Rethinking Military Politics: Brazil and the Southern Cone* (Princeton: Princeton University Press, 1988).

Stepan, Alfred. "Religion, Democracy, and the 'Twin Tolerations,' " *Journal of Democracy* 11, (October 2000): 27–57.

Stepan, Alfred. "The Multiple Secularisms of Modern Democracies and Autocracies," in *Rethinking Secularism,* ed. Craig Calhoun, Mark Juergensmeyer, and Jonathan VanAntwerpen (Oxford, NY: Oxford University Press, 2011).

Strasser, Mark Philip. "Moral Philosophy of John Stuart Mill," Longwood Academic (Wakefield: New Hampshire, 1991).

Sullivan, Denis. *Private Voluntary Organizations in Egypt: Islamic Development, Private Initiative, and State Control* (Gainesville: Florida University Press, 1994).

Tabataba'i, Allamah Sayyid Muhammad Husayn. *Shiite Islam,* tr. Seyyed Hossein Nasr (Albany: State University of New York, 1979) offers a rather comprehensive account of the evolution of Shia thou.

Tamimi, Azzam. "The Origin of Arab Secularism" in John L. Esposito and Azzam Tamimi (eds) *Islam and Seculalrism in the Middle East* (London: Hurst, 2000).

Tamimi, Azzam. *Rachid al-Ghannouchi: A Democrat within Islamism* (New York: Oxford University Press, 2001).

Tamimi, Azzam. "Palestine Question and Islamic Movement: The Ikhwan (Muslim Brotherhood) Roots of Hamas," *Kyoto Bulletin of Islamic Area Studies* 1, no. 1 (2007): 30–51.

Tessler, Mark. "The Origins of Popular Support for Islamist Movements," in *Public Opinion in the Middle East: Survey Research and the Political Orientations of Ordinary Citizens,* ed. Mark Tessler (Bloomington: Indiana University Press, 2011).

Tibi, Bassam. *Islamism and Islam* (New Haven: Yale University Press, 2012).

Van de Walle, Nicolas. "Elections Without Democracy: Africa's Range of Regimes," *Journal of Democracy* 13, no. 2 (April 2002): 66–80.

Vidino, Lorenzo. *The New Muslim Brotherhood in the West* (New York: Columbia University Press, 2010).

Walbridge, Linda S. *The Most Learned of the Shi'a: The Institution of the Marja' Taqlid* (New York: Oxford University Press, 2001).

Weiner, Myron. "Political Change: Asia, Africa, and the Middle East," in *Understanding Political Development,* ed. Myron Weiner and Samuel Huntington (Boston: Little, Brown, 1987).

Welzel, Christian. "Theories of Democratization," in *Democratization,* ed. Christian W. Haerpfer, Patrick Bernhagen, Ronald F. Inglehart, and Christian Welzel (Oxford, UK: Oxford University Press, 2009), 80.

White, Jenny B. *Islamist Mobilization in Turkey: A Study in Vernacular Politics* (Washington, DC: University of Washington Press, 2002).

Whitehead, Laurence. *Democratization: Theory and Experience* (New York: Oxford University Press, 2009).

Wickham, Carrie Rosefsky. *Mobilizing Islam: Religion, Activism, and Political Change in Egypt* (New York: Columbia University Press, 2002).

Wickham, Carrie Roshefsky. "The Path to Moderation: Strategy & Learning of the Formation of Egypt's Wasat Party," *Comparative Politics* 36, no. 2 (January 2004): 205–28.

Wiktorowicz, Quintan. *The Mangement of Islamic Activism: Salafis, the Muslim Brotherhood, and State Power in Jordan* (New York: State University of New York Press, 2001).

Wiktorowicz, Quintan. "Anatomy of the Salafi Movement," *Studies in Conflict & Terrorism* 29, (2006): 207–39.

Willis, Michael. *The Islamist Challenge in Algeria: A Political History* (New York: New York University Press, 1996).

Wright, Lawrence. *The Looming Tower: Al Qaeda and the Road to 9/11* (New York: Knopf, 2006).

Yilmaz, Ihsan. "AK Party between Post-Islamism and Non-Islamism: A Critical Analysis of the Turkish Islamism's Transformation" (February 27, 2011), Available at SSRN: http://ssrn.com/abstract=1771905 or http://dx.doi.org/10.2139/ssrn.1771905.

Young, Dennis O. "Overcoming the Obstacles to Establishing a Democratic State in Afghanistan," *Report* (Carlisle: Strategic Studies Institute, 2007), 5–6, Available at: http://www.strategicstudiesinstitute.army.mil/pdffiles/pub818.pdf.

Zahid, Mohammed. *The Muslim Brotherhood and Egypt's Succession Crisis: The Politics of Liberalization and Reform in the Middle East* (New York: I.B. Tauris, 2010), 18, 20, 21.

Zakaria, Fareed. *The Future of Freedom: Illiberal Democracy at Home and Abroad* (New York: W.W. Norton & Co., 2003).

Zelin, Aaron Y. "Democracy, Salafi Style," *Foreign Policy* (July 20, 2012), Available at: http://www.foreignpolicy.com/articles/2012/07/19/democracy_salafi_style

Zollner, Barbara. *The Muslim Brotherhood: Hasan al-Hudaybi and Ideology* (London: Routledge, 2008).

# Index

Note: Page numbers in italics refer to figures, tables, and charts.

Printed in the United States of America